THE COMPLETE SMALL GARDEN

Graham Rice trained in horticulture at Kew and since then has created a series of small gardens of his own, the smallest being on a balcony only 6 foot square. He is now a full-time garden writer contributing to BBC *Gardeners' World* and to *Practical Gardening*, *The Gardener* and *Garden News* magazines. He has also written a number of books including *Plants for Problem Places* (Helm), *Perfect Plants* (Anaya) and, with Christopher Lloyd, *Garden Flowers from Seed* (Viking). He is now creating another garden in Northamptonshire.

THE COMPLETE SMALL GARDEN

The Big Book for Small Spaces

Graham Rice

PAPERMAC

First published 1991 by
PAPERMAC
A division of Pan Macmillan Publishers Limited
Cavaye Place London SW10 9PG
and Basingstoke

Associated companies in Auckland, Delhi, Dublin, Gaborone,
Hamburg, Harare, Hong Kong, Johannesburg, Kuala Lumpur,
Lagos, Manzini, Melbourne, Mexico City, Nairobi, New York,
Singapore and Tokyo

ISBN 0-333-48100-3

A CIP catalogue record for this book is
available from the British Library

Typeset by Wearside Tradespools, Boldon, Tyne and Wear
Printed in Hong Kong

Contents

List of Plates

Introduction:
What is a Small Garden?

In 1952 Brigadier C. E. Lucas Phillips first published *The Small Garden*, an invaluable book whose sound and cheerful advice helped many new gardeners learn about plants and gardening without it seeming a chore. In it he tells us what exactly he means by a small garden: 'I have borne in mind a limit of about an acre ...' Gardens have changed a lot since then and an acre would now be thought of as a huge garden; no wonder he felt restricted by the need to catch the 8.30 up to town every morning. His assumption that people with a garden half that size would have the help of a gardener adds an additional air of unreality.

To take another example: in the introduction to *Creating Small Gardens*, a most inspiring book with plenty of stylish design ideas, Roy Strong starts by telling us about his own small garden – half an acre plus a field of cows.

This book makes no such assumptions but opts for what you might call practical realism. I take to heart these words of Leonard Meager in *The New Art of Gardening*, published, I might say, in 1697: 'Let me caution all, not to undertake more than can be well looked after with hands enough for the well management of things in their proper season; for a small Plot of ground well ordered, turns to greater advantage than a large one neglected ...'

I will not be rigid and insist that a small garden must be less than a quarter of an acre, or 1,000 square yards, or 300 square yards (which is a large plot on some new estates). Apart from anything else, few novice gardeners can visualise a garden of 1,000 square yards. Rather, I will use measures which relate to the gardener rather than to the garden.

First of all there's time. A garden 30ft square may be too large if the gardener is on shift work, travels all over the world or simply hates gardening. Perhaps, like Leonard Meager, I could suggest that a small garden is one which can be managed comfortably by the gardener concerned – and for some a balcony will be too large. But I would expect a small garden to require at most no more than a day's care at the weekend plus the occasional summer evening. I do not expect paid help to be available.

Second, you can measure a garden according to the inclination and enthusiasm of the gardener. Any garden which frustrates the gardener by its restricted size could be described as small – or perhaps that should be phrased more carefully: a garden is small if the gardener must constantly consider how all the plants, features and activities he or she wishes to accommodate can actually be fitted in.

This book is intended to make your small garden seem bigger. Not just by nifty design and *trompes l'œuil*, but by helping you fit in more of everything than you thought possible without crowding, and by explaining how to maintain it all effectively without lavish expenditure.

Crucial to the enjoyment of a small garden is the realisation that it is effective planting which makes a garden satisfying. So the choice of plants – from trees to alpines, plums to peas – is designed to provide colour, interest and food all the year round. And that is possible in even the smallest of gardens.

The book is called *The Complete Small Garden* and books with the word 'complete' in the title always make me a little nervous: surely the book can't include absolutely everything? Well, at 448 pages it certainly covers plenty of subjects other books leave out and I'm confident that if something *is* omitted, then you can create a beautiful small garden without it!

PART ONE

The Garden

CHAPTER ONE

USING THE GARDEN

The activities which take place in a garden and the plantings and features which form it vary enormously – every gardener has his or her own priorities, which blend to create a unique combination. Garden owners keen enough to read this book may have one special idea on which they wish to concentrate, or there may be competing demands from other priorities or from other members of the family. Establishing priorities and then integrating them to form a cohesive whole can be the most difficult task of all, so to help assess these factors it seems wise to start by simply discussing them all.

Atmosphere

Creating an atmosphere in which you feel comfortable is easy for some people and more difficult for others. In a garden it depends on developing a structure in sympathy with the house and with your own tastes, adding features which are within your budget and within your capacity to build well, and planting in a way which holds everything together and provides colour, interest and subtlety when you want it – and preferably all the year round.

A crucial part of achieving these aims is to be ruthless. It is important not to tolerate anything which spoils the effect, for in a small garden eyesores like an ugly path, a tumbledown fence or a dying tree have so much more impact than they would in a wider space – they constantly offend. Fortunately, inexpensive materials are as valuable as costly ones, and plants and gravel can be used as effectively as York stone and statuary in creating a cohesive whole.

But my most earnest recommendation is to do *something* – don't just sit back and wait. You wouldn't do that with a new sitting-room; don't do it in your new garden either.

Entertaining

Entertaining outside demands atmosphere and facilities. If the garden gives you and your guests an uneasy feeling, no one will enjoy your parties. As well as fostering a congenial atmosphere you will need a flat, hard area for standing and for seats. Also, you may need somewhere for the barbecue. This can either be built in to a wall or be portable and free-standing – in which case you will need somewhere to store it. You don't necessarily need a lawn.

Your entertaining area (let's call it the patio) can consist of a small area near the house or can take up most of a town garden, with the planting around it. Don't feel that you have to be conventional; if you think that most of your enclosed garden should be paved, then go ahead and pave it.

Food

If you want to grow food crops you can usually find the space. A growing bag will hold three tomato plants; runner beans or gooseberries can be trained on the fence, grapes around the door; you can mark out a small plot for salads or perhaps even a larger one for cordon apples, blackcurrants, early potatoes and cabbages. Whether on a small scale or as a top priority, food plants can always find a productive home.

Play

Kids need somewhere to play, and in a small garden many other plans may need to be delayed until they create less wear and tear. A lawn may be an important requirement, or perhaps a soft-surface play area; the likelihood of ball games may suggest waiting before building a greenhouse. It may be wise not to use gravel, although a patio will be useful in autumn and winter. In general it pays to wait before creating carefully planned features and plantings until the children are of an age when their activities are less likely to damage them.

Plants

Some gardeners fill their plots with plants, retaining only a small area for sitting and a winding path through the vegetation. Others are less single-minded, but if plants are not seen as fundamental you might as well build an extension. The infinite variety of easy-to-grow plants available and the many ways they can be used give gardens their unique character and also allow a constant refreshing **state of change**, not only from season to season but from year to year.

Plants are given a dominant position in this book, and in most gardens they will dominate too; not in the sense of taking over, but because their character and the way in which they are used will be fundamental in creating the atmosphere, providing the colour and interest and setting the style.

Pets

Dogs are a pain in a small garden – even, or perhaps especially, the smallest varieties. They can be remarkably destructive, battering plants, scratching in borders, urinating and worse on the lawn. Think hard before starting to make your small garden special if you have a dog.

Practical and functional

Different families have different uses for the garden – hanging out washing, repairing motorbikes, golf practice, archery, sculpting, stripping paint off doors and so on. The atmosphere and the plants are secondary. If this is the case all you need is a large paved area and perhaps a lean-to glass roof – like a conservatory with no sides. And you need good access, an accessible drain and an outside tap and power point. This is the only place in the book where such activities will be considered. It is, after all, a book for gardeners, not motocross drivers.

Relaxing

Relaxation is perhaps the garden's most important use. It should be a haven from the bustle at work and in the kitchen, a place to recuperate, meditate and recharge. You need a patio with a table and chairs, a sun lounger or hammock, a bench, or just a small square to stand a chair. You'll soon realise that even in a small town yard you'll need more than one area. The sun will move round and you will want to move into it (or out of it). Some areas must be accessible in slippers, some must be screened from neighbours. For you to make the most of your garden it must be private, comfortable, quiet and easy to make use of at all times.

CHAPTER TWO

FIRST THOUGHTS

Perhaps your first thought of all should be whether to start on the front garden or the back. On some new estates this problem is solved for you, because the front gardens are run together to make a communal area and maintained by the local council or by contractors. Many Victorian terraced houses have no front garden, or only a tiny walled area. But if you have a front garden that needs attention, think first about a path. It doesn't matter what sort of path you have, as long as there is a dry walkway from the street to the front door. In new gardens my advice is to kill the weeds on the rest of the area, or cut the grass if the builders have grassed it for you, and then get on with the back garden. In an established garden don't be tempted to remove trees and wild bushes, although it's no bad thing for neighbourly relations to trim branches which overhang your boundaries. Ensure that the way to your door is clear and dry – you may need to do this to get the wardrobe up the path, so pack the pruners in the car, not in some inaccessible tea chest.

Don't worry if your front garden is not pretty enough for the neighbours to admire. Think of yourself and your family first, and set about creating somewhere attractive and private where you can relax – you'll need it after the trauma of moving house. Worry about the look of the front garden later.

The Brand New Garden

1. WHAT HAVE YOU GOT?

Gazing optimistically from the kitchen window on a sunny Sunday morning is not the best way to assess what you're stuck with in your new garden. You should go out, in your boots if necessary, and take a closer look.

Aspect

The first thing to do is work out where the sun rises. This is usually one of the primary things a keen gardener does when house-hunting, but in case you forgot, first work out where south is. That tells you which are the sunniest and the shadiest (north-facing) parts of the garden.

Builder's rubbish and spillage

Are there any obvious piles of builder's rubbish? This can vary from bags of rock-solid cement to hardcore, piles of scrap metal and wood, teapots, old newspapers and worse. If there's more than will go in two or three fertiliser sacks (*not* flimsy bin bags) – and if there's some on view there's bound to be more buried underneath – hire a skip; a mini-skip may be big enough.

Next you need to investigate what's underground. If there's any wire or metal peeping from the soil and waiting to trip you up, investigate. The worst are the long reinforcing rods that go under the fence and end up under next door's path. Dig them out as best you can, and get your neighbour's help if necessary. Occasionally you may find that reinforcing rods end in a large block of concrete. A club hammer and steel bolster should help break it up in the hole and the pieces can then be removed more easily.

Chain-link fencing is an especially infuriating problem, as it may be laid flat under the soil over a wide area. Even if you intend laying grass, remove it, as you'll only find it again in a year or two when you come to dig a pond or plant a tree. Find and expose one edge first, then proceed across the netting, moving the soil to behind you and rolling the netting as you go.

Concrete

Your new 'garden' may have been concreted over by an insensitive predecessor. If the concrete is in good condition, check the foundations by digging a hole alongside. If they are sufficiently solid to carry traffic (see page 93), the concrete will be a very useful base for paving, which can be laid on top. The areas of concrete where you want beds or lawn can then be broken up and removed, using a pneumatic drill. These can be hired but are no fun to use and it will be very hard work. Alternatively, areas for planting can simply be broken up to let water drain through and then raised beds constructed to take the plants.

If the concrete is in poor condition, uneven and cracked, it may have been laid straight on to the soil. Even if you intend to lay paving, cracked concrete will make a poor foundation and is best removed. The site can then be prepared properly and you will have a supply of hardcore to hand. It should be relatively easy to break up and remove to a skip.

Soil which has been buried under concrete will need thorough cultivation to reduce compaction and let in air before a lawn is laid or plants put in.

Soil

Having removed the rubbish, you're now in a position to examine the soil. There are two sad and almost inevitable consequences of building work. First, the soil tends to get moved about so that you're quite likely to end up with nasty, infertile subsoil on the top and all the rich topsoil 2ft (60cm) down. Secondly, machinery may have compacted the soil so much that it's difficult even to get a spade in without cursing. Water will also drain away very slowly.

The first way to assess your soil is simply by looking at it. If it's black that's a good sign. If it's very dark brown that's quite good too. If it's yellow, pale brown, grey, streaky or mottled that's less good. The blacker it is the more organic matter it contains, and the more organic matter there is the easier the soil will be to work, the better your plants will grow and the less you'll have to water them. Now pick some soil up and rub it between your fingers. If it feels smooth and a bit like plasticine and if it sticks together in a lump, that means it has a lot of clay in it. If you can see the stones it's (you've guessed it) stony and if it falls apart quickly it's sandy.

Soil with a lot of clay in it poses the most problems but can end up being especially fertile. Clay soils:

- are sticky;
- are badly drained;
- are difficult to dig or hoe when wet;
- stick to your shoes when wet;
- stick together in big clods;
- crack badly when dry;
- are potentially very fertile;

- hold water well;
- hold plant foods well.

There are two ways of improving clay soil – you can add organic matter such as peat or you can add gritty material such as sharp sand or fine gravel. Organic matter increases fertility and helps improve drainage; grit only improves drainage. The branded preparations advertised for curing the problems of clay soils are very expensive, and although they can work if applied regularly and in liberal quantities, this is a singularly uneconomic way of improving clay. Your money is better spent on a few bags of good manure.

Soil which is sandy or gravelly is easier to dig and hoe but needs more water and more feeding. Sandy soils:

- are well drained;
- are easy to work, even shortly after rain;
- need lots of watering;
- let plant foods wash out quickly so need more feeding.

Here again organic matter is the answer, as it holds water and plant foods in the soil without making it sticky.

Organic matter

Organic matter is one of the most important materials to the gardener – indeed, it's almost a universal panacea. It supplies plant foods, holds moisture, breaks up clay soils, binds together sandy soils, makes soil more workable and prevents weed growth when spread on the surface. It comes in many forms.

Manure

Well-rotted farmyard manure is the richest form of organic matter, but it is messy and not easy to come by unless you live in the country. Stable manure is sometimes advertised at the roadside, but always take it from the bottom of the stack where it will be well rotted. Never put raw, fresh manure on the garden. If nothing else is available, stack it for a year before you use it. Well-rotted manure in bags and an increasing range of other bulky organic products are becoming widely available in garden centres.

Garden compost

Weeds and vegetable refuse can be made into useful compost in the garden (see page 73). This will often contain weed seeds, so is best dug into the soil and not spread on the surface where the weeds will soon grow.

Lawn mowings

These are a poor source of organic matter. Never spread grass cuttings directly on your beds and borders, as they almost always contain grass seeds which will soon produce a forest of weeds. Compost them, using a compost activator like Garotta to help them rot down.

Leaves

Leaves are a good source of organic matter but they are best stacked on their own without weeds or other vegetable waste. They can take two years to rot down.

Peat

Peat is easily available in the garden centre, conveniently packed and easy to handle. It is low in nutrients but long-lasting, and is getting more expensive. The quality varies. Brown moss peat lasts longer than the finer black sedge peat and is usually more acid. If you buy it, get the biggest bales you can as they are more economical. Using peat is not now recommended, however, as the peat bogs from which much of it comes are rapidly being destroyed. Alternatives are available.

Peat alternatives

As gardeners become more worried about using peat, an increasing number of alternatives are appearing in garden centres. These may be made of wood waste, paper waste, bark, coconut fibre, fruit fibre, sewage sludge or manure, and are ideal soil improvers.

Bark

This comes in two forms – chipped and composted. Chips are used as a mulch on the surface to retain moisture, suppress weeds and produce a neat finish, while composted bark is used to improve the soil before planting.

Mushroom compost

Spent mushroom compost is special compost which has grown a crop of mushrooms and is then sold off for the garden. It's usually made up of a mixture of stable manure and peat, but lime is added, which is not ideal for all plants.

Whether your soil is heavy (with lots of clay) or light (sandy or gravelly), it has other qualities which are less obvious.

All soils contain lime, but amounts vary, and the amount of lime in the soil governs the plants you can grow easily. You can buy a simple test kit, such as the Rapitest pH Tester, to tell you roughly how limy your soil is. Lime levels are measured on what is known as the pH scale and your kit will give you a rough figure. pH7 is neutral, while higher figures indicate more lime and lower figures more acidity and less lime. Most soils vary between about 5.5 and 7.5, with 6.5 a rough average.

It is also possible to buy a test kit to tell you how rich your soil is in plant foods, and the information with the kit will tell you how much fertiliser to put on for the plants you intend to grow. These tests are generally less accurate than lime tests, and the recommendations sometimes involve you in buying a number of bags of specialised fertiliser which will clutter up the shed for years before they are used up. For most crops an annual application of general fertiliser is sufficient.

Walls

If your garden is a new one the only walls you'll have are likely to be the house walls, although you may be lucky enough to have boundary walls as well. There's nothing more useful around a garden than a 6ft (1.8m) wall, as it provides privacy, shelter, useful shade and a warm 'storage heater' for sun-loving and tender plants.

Don't be afraid to plant self-clinging climbers up new walls, for they will not be damaged. Allow for planting areas at the base. Lower walls are sometimes provided as boundaries, and these are usually best enhanced by fixing trellis mesh on top to bring them up to about 6ft (1.8m). The trellis also provides a ready-made support for plants.

Fences

You are much more likely to be faced with fences than with walls. These can range from two or three loose strands of wire, through chain-link wire fences, to square pattern trellis – the more elegant patterns are rarely used on new developments. Lapboard timber fencing is more solid, and feathered board fencing is the most solid timber fencing of all (see page 84).

Loose strands of wire must be regarded as strictly temporary, as they won't even keep the dog in – or out. Chain-link fencing at least keeps the dog from roaming and provides a good support for annual climbers. Trellis is excellent, as it provides an effective barrier, a good support for climbing plants, and lessens the sense of enclosure, creating a more relaxed atmosphere in a small space.

Lapboard or woven fencing is often provided for small gardens, and after it has weathered for a year it makes a good background for plants, allowing you to forget the boundaries for a few years. Woven fencing is less sturdy and less soundproof than lapboard, and is likely to be well warped, though still standing, after five years. The really heavy-duty, close-boarded style is rarely used except where the fence backs on to a busy path or roadway. You should be well pleased with it.

Manhole covers

Some architects have no idea about manholes. They site them where most sane people would put the patio, and you then have to cope with an infuriating obstacle. In fact you can deal with a manhole wherever it is, as long as you note its surfave level and appreciate that this dictates the level of the surrounding paving or soil. You must *not* bury it.

Manhole covers can be disguised in various ways. Recessed planting covers are available, which provide space to fill with compost before planting, and there are also recessed covers designed to be filled with the same paving material that surrounds the manhole. There are plenty of spreading plants that can be set alongside. The manhole can even be raised to a more convenient level. But remember, one day you may need to remove the lid.

Concrete house surrounds

New houses, especially bungalows, are often blessed with a concrete surround about 2ft (60cm) wide which runs like a path all the way round the foot of the wall. This pointless and unattractive border effectively stops you planting any climbers on the house wall and also neatly prevents the house ever seeming part of the garden. You can line pots up along it I suppose, but sooner or later, if you're serious about plants, it will have to go. Hire a pneumatic hammer – better still, hire the operator as well. The hardcore your demolition produces can be used as a base for new paths.

Paths and drives

Your new garden may not even have a path to the front door, but at least this enables you to lay your own exactly where you want it. Don't plan anything too fancy or indirect. You may be provided with a straight path up to the front door, which is fine. The path to the front door may be combined with the drive to the garage, and there's not much you can do about that without further recourse to the Kango hammer. Don't forget that if what marks the boundary to the street is relatively impermanent, you can move the entrance along a little, although you may need permission from the local authority.

Influences outside the garden

Now that much more attention is being paid to retaining mature trees on new housing developments, you may find one overhanging your new and empty garden. It may shade your window, its leaves may clog up your drains, its piddly little pears may litter your lawn.

You are entitled, if you wish, to remove any branches that project over your side of the boundary, but if you must let in a little more light, co-operate with your new neighbour and agree for a branch to be removed at the trunk. Do it sensitively. In practice, machinery may remove the lower branches, intentionally or otherwise, during building. Any tree that is the subject of a Tree Preservation Order must not be pruned, let alone removed, without permission. Note where the tree is in relation to the sun and where its shadow falls. The soil will be drier under its branches, and even a tall, upright conifer with no branches overhanging your side will have roots taking moisture from your soil.

You may also find that there is an unappealing view from your garden which would be better masked. This can be done with a fence or a tree, but in some circumstances you can distract attention from it by orientating the main outdoor activities in another direction.

Looking at neighbours' gardens

You can get some idea of how your garden is going to be by looking at your neighbours'. If their gardens are full of weeds, yours may be too. Not because the soil is full of weed roots and seeds, but because seed from nearby will blow into your plot. If your neighbours grow big nettles the soil is probably fertile. And if they grow good rhododendrons or blue hydrangeas you will know at once that the soil is acid – you too will be able to grow them, together with azaleas and pieris. If there are clovers and buddleias, then rhododendrons and azaleas are unlikely to thrive.

2. BASIC CONSIDERATIONS

When you start to plan what you're actually going to do with your brand new garden, it's easy to think, 'I'd really like a rose in that corner,' before any part of the garden is ready to receive plants. There are some considerations that you should keep in mind right from the start, to avoid wasting both time and money.

Time available

If you have a busy job, or if both you and your partner have demanding careers, then there's no point in planning a garden full of fiddly flower-beds that take lots of looking after – unless you are going to pay someone to do it for you. Think about it.

Primary uses of the garden

Outdoor room, playing field, botanic garden, dog's toilet – people have different requirements from their garden. If you like to use your garden as a summer room outside it must have a broad open space, be light and sheltered, with hard surfaces and perhaps a built-in barbecue. If the whole family is out all day, a west-facing sitting area for relaxing after work is imperative. If it's plants that matter, you will need to create different conditions for different plants and you may want little more than a meandering path through a garden packed with flowers and foliage.

Financial considerations

Your plans must, of course, match your budget. These days you can get a loan to have your garden designed, built and planted, for building societies now recognise that a beautiful garden adds value to your property. (This may be practical while interest rates are low, but not when they're high.)

Professional design is expensive but can be excellent value if you have specific requirements and apparently insoluble problems. Hard landscape (paving, gravel, walls, fences and the like) costs a lot more than soft landscape (lawns and plants). But don't be deceived. A garden with lawns and plants raised from seed or given by friends and family can look as good and be just as enjoyable as one designed and made by professionals with the finest stone and the choicest plants.

Children

If you have a small garden and young children, laying a lawn is probably a mistake. It's impossible to keep a small but well-used lawn looking good. Use stylish paving or, for a soft surface, bark chips.

Pets

Take the dog out regularly. A cat of your own will keep out neighbours' cats, though it might be cruel to birds to install a bird table.

Personal enthusiasms

If you insist on keeping koi carp, investigate the best situation for their pond before doing any work on it. If you want to play badminton, allow a very generous area for play – otherwise the flower-beds will be trampled on. If you want to grow a collection of special plants – woodland plants, for example – consider their requirements and don't put the shed in the only shady spot.

3. INITIAL PLANNING – WHERE TO PUT THE BASICS

Ensuring that you get the basic, immovable features in the right place will make life so much easier later that it's worth putting a little thought into it right at the start.

Bins

How far do you want to walk with your rubbish? How far do you want to cart the bin for the binman to pick up? Not far, in either case. Site your bin near the back door and near the exit to the street. It's best to put it in a corner, where plants can be set around it or an elegant piece of timber fencing or even walling can screen it unobtrusively. But don't just build a small piece of screening that doesn't merge with the rest of the garden – you might as well look at the bin.

Clothes line

Gone are the days of the long straight path alongside the long straight clothes line – thank goodness. I'm sure it only encouraged long straight borders with long straight edges. And growing a grape vine up the clothes pole was never a very good idea. The washing whirly which fits into a hole in the patio solves all the problems. It's only there when you need it, all the washing is just a short walk from the house so you can get there quickly when it rains, and you can go out to the line in your slippers if you feel like it. Build a little hideaway near the bins to store the beast when it's party time.

Patio

Whichever direction the back of your house faces, you need a sitting area there – you won't always want to walk to the far corner of the garden for a brief rest. The most important place for a patio, however, is facing west or south-west, so that for as much of the year as possible you can sit in the sun when you get home from work. And on those warm summer evenings, your alfresco parties will catch the very last of the sun.

Of course, in a very small garden where there's no grass and all the unplanted area is paved, you can sit anywhere that takes your fancy, sun or shade.

Paths

The garden with no grass will be all path in the same way as it is all patio, and this is surely the best solution for the smallest areas. If you have paths through or around lawns, don't plan them as stepping stones in the grass; not only do you have to set the height just right to avoid snagging the mower or stepping into a hole, but you have to clip the grass round each one.

A diagonal path will make the garden look bigger, as will one which narrows a little as it goes away from the house. A slightly curved path, or one of irregular width with dwarf, overhanging plants, looks better than a straight one with bare parallel sides.

Shed

In a small garden you cannot avoid looking at your shed, so there's no point in trying to hide it away, though it can be camouflaged with climbers, of course. The first question is: what are you going to keep in your shed? If the answer is bicycles – put it near the gate or the access to the street; garden tools – anywhere; workbench – anywhere; pram – near the street access and the house; armchair and bottle of Scotch – as far away from the commotion of the house as possible.

Looking at the problem from another angle: which is the worst patch of soil or the place most unsuited to plants? Put the shed there.

Conservatory

It's surprising how many people put the conservatory in a place where they have to go right out of the house to get into it! Ensure that you can walk straight in, through patio doors if possible, so that it really is an extra room. Also, try and pick a wall with a radiator on the inside – that way you can heat the conservatory by adding an extra radiator without too many yards of new pipework.

If your conservatory is north-facing it will be hardly warmer than outside in winter and probably cooler than outside in summer – good for growing ferns. East-facing, it will warm up well in the morning; outdoor east walls are not good spots for many plants. South-facing conservatories will become very, very hot in summer but lovely and warm on sunny winter days. Those that are west-facing are warm on autumn evenings, prolonging the summer as long as possible.

Greenhouse

If you choose an elegant design for your greenhouse and plant right up to it, you can be proud of how it looks. If you are running power and water to it, site it as near to the house as is reasonable to save expensive excavations and cable. This will also save you being drenched on winter mornings when you go to check if the seedlings have come through, or in summer thunderstorms when you nip out to pick a few tomatoes. You need a good path all the way to the door.

The greenhouse needs to be in a sunny spot, if possible, although shade for half the day would be quite acceptable. Align the axis north–south if you can, so that all sides get the sun, but this is not essential.

Barbecue

If you plan to use your garden for entertaining during the summer months, it makes sense to build a barbecue outside while building

BARBECUE
A barbecue can be built in sympathetic materials to harmonise with the patio and nearby brickwork and with integrated storage and work surfaces.

your patio and surrounding walling. It can be built of similar materials and can even have co-ordinated seating and storage so that the whole thing harmonises with its surroundings.

Compost heap

A compost heap is useful in even the smallest garden, so that no organic matter is wasted. Neither manufactured plastic bins nor home-made timber ones are especially elegant, so they are best sited in a discreet corner. But remember that they need moisture, either from rain or from a pipe.

Laying on power

Electricity, for the greenhouse, for a pool pump, for outdoor lighting and for a waterproof outdoor power point for a mower and other equipment, is best considered right at the start so that the main cables can go under paths where drainage is good and there's no chance of disturbance. Get a qualified electrician to do the job for you to ensure maximum safety, and install a circuit breaker for the outside supply if for no other.

Water

In a very small garden, one ouside tap should be sufficient. Ideally you should also run a pipe to the greenhouse. Install a tap in the conservatory if you plan a tiled rather than a carpeted floor and intend to grow specimen plants that demand a lot of water. Take the greenhouse and conservatory pipes straight underneath the floor to come up in a corner.

4.   HOW TO PLAN

Planning is always necessary, and a few weeks or months of thought and discussion is worth any amount of diving in and getting started, only to change everything later.

Planning on paper

Take a photograph of the garden from an upstairs window, using either a black and white or a colour film, and have it enlarged to about A4 size. Buy a few sheets of clear acetate film from the stationer's, and a wipe-off pen – perhaps two or three, in different colours.

Place a sheet of acetate film over the photo of your garden and mark in those existing features that are relevant – a manhole cover, an existing path you want to or must retain, perhaps the overhang of a mature tree. Then add your own ideas, drawn in very simply. Start with the patio, then the conservatory, greenhouse and shed, and then the paths. Adjust the shapes and areas by rubbing out with tissue paper and redrawing.

When you have all the basic features fixed, trace off a neat version in black, place it over the photograph, and lay another clean piece over the top so that you can experiment with your planning and planting ideas, drawn in another colour. First mark any areas of shade cast by trees inside or outside your garden, then choose an area for any special plants that you particularly like to grow wherever suits them best. If there are no trees around the boundaries, or even if there are, decide on good places to plant one or two new trees. Don't forget to mark where their shadows will fall.

When you have your final version, with patio and paths, shed and conservatory, planting areas and trees all marked in, photocopy your acetates and this will give you a permanent record of your plans. Don't forget that having photographed your garden from an angle, from an upstairs window, the perspective and scale will be distorted.

Planning on the ground

In a brand new garden which is all lawn or all bare soil, planning on the ground can be simple and successful. You can use a combination of posts, pegs, canes, boards, heavy-gauge twine and hosepipe to mark out your features on the ground exactly where they are to go.

A selection of 3ft (90cm) and 6ft (1.8m) canes can be used to mark straight-edged areas like patios and conservatories, and when these are decided upon, the canes can be replaced with pegs and string for permanence. Use 6ft (1.8m) canes or posts to mark sites for trees. Hosepipes are excellent for marking out curves (you may need to borrow extra from your neighbours). Laminated hose, being very flexible, is best for marking out the edges of beds, as it's easy to move slightly until it is positioned just where you want it. (It's also the best kind of hose to use for watering.) Choose a warm day if you can, as the hose will be more flexible.

When you have the design fixed, it's not a bad idea to transfer the whole scheme to paper for a permanent record. One day your neighbours will want their hosepipes back.

This method can also be used in a relatively established garden where you intend to make few changes. But unless you do it in winter when there is little foliage and top growth to get in the way, it will drive you potty.

Hiring a designer

This can be a chancy business, as there are some around whose brains are singularly devoid of ideas. There are also a lot of people with nothing better to do, who spend a few days on an expensive course and think they know it all.

Ask around among friends and see if you can find anyone who has had their garden designed. Go and look at it and have a chat about it. Gardening magazines run design or planting services of various types. You send in details of your garden, its size, location and soil, together with any strong likes and dislikes, and back comes a plan. This may be an outline plan or it may include planting plans as well, depending on the package you buy.

The better garden centre chains also offer garden design services – full garden plans or planting plans, sometimes with an additional construction service. It should not be difficult to get an idea of the reputation attached to your local centre. Their designs are likely to be safe and competent rather than adventurous.

Finally, you can go to the Society of Garden Designers. This is the professional society for designers of private domestic gardens, as distinct from larger-scale landscape design. They will recommend members in your area.

A few fundamental principles

- Don't put up with what you don't like – change it.
- Do things the way you like them, even if others try to persuade you otherwise. Your garden should be as personal as your house.
- Plan for changing needs. You may have a family, your young

family may soon be grown up, your children may soon leave
home – keep these points in mind.

- Provide adequate paths for regular access.
- Make paths and plant trees first. Leave the fiddly bits till later.
- Take account of what's outside as well as what's inside the
  garden.
- Match the materials you use outside to the materials used in
  the construction of the house.
- Remember that shade can be as pleasant to sit in as sunshine.

5.   REALISTIC OBJECTIVES

What you can achieve in a given period depends entirely on the
time, money and skill available.

Year one

Given a fair wind, and not too many problems with interest rates, it
should be quite possible to get the basic structure of your new
garden in place by the end of the first year. Of course this also
depends on the size of the garden.

In the smallest of new gardens, it should be possible for everything to be done in the first year and for you to end up with a
colourful garden. At the other extreme, it should be possible to get
paths and patio laid and grass established at the very least. Some
planting areas could be prepared and planted, but I'd never recommend putting a conservatory up yourself – that's a job for the
expert.

Year five

By year five, unless you're very unlucky and there have been big
problems, your dreams should have come true – especially if you
follow the advice of this book! Trees will be looking like trees,
shrubs will be maturing, climbers will be covering fences, borders
will be looking well established and may even need a certain amount
of thinning and replanting.

6. GETTING STARTED

We all have to start somewhere, but if you're new to gardening and indeed new to building, deciding where best to start can be difficult.

What to do first

I always advise laying paths first, as once you have good surfaces to walk on, everything else is so much easier. Even a simple gravel path which you might upgrade later makes a big difference. Your feet won't get muddy, the barrow will run smoothly, it's easy to move materials about – everything else takes half the time.

Next can come either the fences or the patio. It is very useful to have the patio at the start, especially as in these early stages of development it makes a good space to store materials off the wet ground. Remember, if you're planning to put a conservatory on part of the patio, the foundations must be strong enough to take the weight.

Once you have a patio where you can sit for your coffee break, you'll see the importance of privacy and want to get the fences up.

You can either put the barbecue and bin surround in place when you build the patio or stack the materials and wait until later. If you want the whole lot to match, it pays to buy the materials all at once. A later batch of what is supposed to be the same thing may turn out to be slightly different. Don't forget the socket for the washing spinner when you make the patio.

If you wish, you can put the whole of the rest of the garden down to lawn and just eat into it with each new development. But if you're planning a concrete base for your greenhouse or shed, I'd be inclined to get that over with at the same time as the patio. Then all that sort of work will be behind you, and you won't need to hire a cement mixer again.

While all this construction work is going on, there's one more thing that mustn't be forgotten – the weeds. They never stop growing, so they must be dealt with regularly either by using a non-persistent weedkiller or by regular hoeing. That way they will never become a problem.

What to leave till later

All the fine details can be left till later. There's no point in buying delicate alpines and preparing special soil for them when you are surrounded by wheelbarrows and concrete. Hanging baskets will probably get in the way and be knocked off their hooks, bulbs will get trodden on as they peep through, and an odd row of parsley for the kitchen is unlikely to survive the comings and goings of all those boots and may well be accidentally hoed off with the weeds.

Planting trees

The only plants to think about putting in at an early stage are trees, or, more probably in a small garden, a tree. Trees take a long time to mature and should be planted sooner rather than later. It's a good discipline to decide to plant your tree early, as it ensures that the rest of your plan is carefully considered at an early stage as well – trees having such an influence on the rest of the garden.

Plants from a previous garden

Most of us, when we move house, have favourite plants that we like to bring from our previous garden. And when moving into a first home, parents, relatives and friends are often generous with new plants and divisions from their own gardens. But what do you do with them when the garden is unprepared? The answer is probably to prepare a 'nursery bed', an area out of the way of all the comings and goings where new plants can be set in rows for a year or so before being planted in their permanent homes. Anything can be transplanted happily a year after planting, so do not be afraid to plant shrubs or border plants with the idea of moving them later.

You may also spot attractive plants in nurseries, garden centres or catalogues. Rather than put off buying these for a year, a few can go in your nursery bed too.

The Existing Garden

Taking over an existing garden may prove to be a great relief or it may prove singularly frustrating. It's good to have a mature tree without having to wait for years, but not if it fills the garden and casts so much dense shade that you can hardly see out of the back door. You may have been attracted to the garden by the delightful patio, but if it slopes back towards the house so that the rain soaks the brickwork you may not think yourself so lucky.

1.   KEEPING THINGS TICKING OVER

The first lesson is not to lose what you already have; if you let beds get weedy and let the grass grow it will eventually take far more time to get back into order than if you looked after it all properly in the first place.

Lawn-mowing

Keeping the lawn under control is vital for four reasons. First, if the lawn is cut you won't feel guilty every time you look outside. Second, it will give you somewhere to sit out even if there's nowhere else. Third, sooner or later it will have to be cut, so it may as well look reasonable right from the start. And last, it keeps the grass healthy if you cut it regularly. This is important even if eventually you intend to dig some of it up.

The lawn may be long and lanky when you arrive – departing house-owners are not well known for keeping their lawns neatly manicured. If you don't have a lawn-mower, borrow one – new neighbours will surely sympathise and may be willing to help with the loan of a machine. But if you intend to keep the grass, you'll need a machine of your own sooner or later.

Weeding

As in so many aspects of gardening, there is an old saying that applies here. This is the only one this book will repeat: 'One year's seeding is seven years' weeding.' The point being that once weeds have shed their seed you'll spend the next seven years pulling out the weeds that grow from that one batch.

You need to think about removing weeds almost as soon as you arrive. In fact, if you do nothing else in your first year but cut the grass and weed the borders you'll have had a very constructive year.

When taking over an established garden, 'weeding' can mean anything from a little light hoeing to slashing through brambles.

You can do it by hand, or you can use weed-killers and weed-preventers to help do the job less arduously. Don't go heavy-handedly through the borders with a spade, as you will probably dig up perennials and bulbs that you would rather keep, and don't forget weeds in the lawn – these are easy to control with a spring feed-and-weed treatment like M&B Supergreen Feed, Weed and Mosskiller.

Pruning

Pruning is something that you don't need to devote much time to. Only if branches from your own or neighbouring trees are hanging off dangerously will you need to pay them attention. The only other plants that need concern you are bush roses and buddleias, which will suffer if not pruned every spring. Cutting both back to about 9in (23cm) is an acceptable rough and ready rule for this first year.

2. TAKING STOCK

Perhaps the first, very elementary, thing that ought to concern you is this: are there many plants in the garden? It's remarkable how sparse some people's gardens are. If your new 'established' garden really is sparse, you may be able to treat it as a completely new one!

Soil and soil testing

Many of the comments made in the section on assessing the soil in new gardens (page 8) apply here, but in the case of an existing garden you have the extra complication of not knowing how well the previous owner has cultivated the soil. Some less thoughtful gardeners sow seeds, set plants and do nothing for them except perhaps give them a little peat when planting and an occasional scattering of fertiliser. Not only will their results have been poor, but soil that has been treated in such a way will need revitalising.

Others will have used both fertiliser and organic matter well, and in that case the soil should be in good heart. It will usually be clear from the overall appearance of the garden if it is in good shape, and if the previous owners express interest in the degree of your own horticultural enthusiasm you can be pretty sure they feel they are leaving behind something worth having (of course they might just be wrong). If they ask to take one or two special plants with them, so much the better.

There are other things you can look out for in assessing the soil of an older garden. If it is full of nettles, for example, then the soil is rich and fertile. If moss and green slime are growing on the lawn and in the borders the drainage must be poor. Are there shrubs cluttered with dead branches? (Check in spring when the first leaves are appearing.) If so, you can bet that the other plants are similarly neglected.

In an older garden the soil will probably vary, but you may not discover this until you start making changes. If you start to dig up the lawn or remove a tree or a large shrub, it's quite possible that the soil you reveal will be desperately in need of revitalising. Organic matter is usually the answer, and in an older garden you may have the opportunity to create your own fairly quickly. Fallen leaves can take a couple of years to make really good leafmould, but you may find yourself with a good supply.

Weeds too may be present in great abundance and these will also rot down to provide useful organic matter – and rather more quickly.

The most likely problem in an older garden is a general impoverishment of the soil, the result of years of neglect. Organic matter and moderate feeding will solve the problem.

Aspect

You will probably have considered the garden's aspect before buying the house, but if not, here are a couple of points.

a. Don't forget that fences and trees can increase or reduce the influence of the aspect and that these influences can either be removed (in some cases) or capitalised upon.
b. There are two sides to everything – a sunny patio at the back of the house where you can grow tubs of colourful summer plants means there must also be a shady place at the front where shade-loving plants should thrive

Aspect, however, also implies prevailing winds – in much of the UK wet winds come from the south-west and cold winds from the north-east. This should strongly influence your attitude to trees, which may have been planted specifically to provide shelter (see below).

Outside the garden

The chances are that if the garden you are taking over is not new (it may not be mature or established either, of course), the same will apply to the gardens around. So there may be mature trees, large shrubs or even climbers encroaching from next door, which you must take into consideration.

Trees may help shelter your garden from the wind, they may drop bullet-like pears into your pond, their leaves will undoubtedly collect in corners and the shade may or may not be welcome. Co-operate with your neighbour over any pruning – sometimes just removing one or two lower branches in their entirety can let in a lot more light without spoiling the overall appearance of the tree.

If the tree is near your boundary its roots will probably have grown into your garden and will be taking moisture and plant foods from your soil. This is more difficult to combat, but slates or corrugated iron sunk into the ground along the fence line should keep many roots out.

Large shrubs can have a similar effect, and again discussion over pruning is usually the answer. You may also find that shrubs planted some way from a fence on your neighbour's side have grown such stout branches that they are damaging the fence (see below). This will need urgent attention. Climbers, if left unpruned, can also weigh down a fence.

There is another side to all this. There may be eyesores outside the garden which you do not wish to see as you sit relaxing over a glass of wine. These can be masked by careful siting of trees, but in a small garden a tree large enough to blot out a power station may also cast black shade over virtually the whole plot. One useful thing to remember is that a small tree planted nearer to where you sit will block out as much from your view as a large tree further away. What's more, a tree at the edge of the patio will also provide valuable shade from the midday summer scorch.

There are views that you do *not* wish to obscure, of course. The prospect of an ugly house or a tumbledown workshop may be more likely than a glimpse of green fields, but if the fields are there, planting trees that will obscure them is plain foolish. That's not to say that you shouldn't plant trees at all, but rather to remind you that trees come in all shapes and sizes. A tall, narrow specimen tree can give you height and act as a focal point without blocking the view.

Fences and other timber

Although you may have inspected the various garden features when you viewed the house, they rarely get proper attention. Once you've moved in it will pay to check them over.

First of all, go and give the fences a good shake and lean on the posts; if bits come away in your hand then at least you'll know it's vulnerable and won't be shocked when it disappears in a storm. It may simply be that the panels are coming away from the posts, in which case new nails may be all that's required. You may find the gravel board running along the bottom is rotten and requires re-placing.

If the posts themselves are rotten you have two options. If the problem is below ground level, you can take them and the fence down, remove the rotten stumps, and re-erect the posts using steel post holders – the base of the post fits in at about ground level. Once the panels start coming away from the posts and rails, you are in rather more trouble, and although a certain amount of nailing and renewing battens can be worthwhile, there comes a point when replacement is the only option.

Pergolas and timber arches need much the same attention, but when it comes to trellis you may find repairs more difficult. Most trellis is fixed with staples at the crossing points, and once these corrode the whole thing starts to fall to pieces. Check the solidity of the fixings to the wall, and if the crossing points are weak, a small screw in a pre-drilled hole will make a solid job of securing them.

Paving and paths

It's usually obvious if paths are cracked or patios collect the rain in puddles. What is less obvious is what's underneath, and this is important if you are considering heavy traffic or building on existing hard surfaces. Short of actually digging them up to see, the only way to find out how substantial the footings of paths and paved areas are is to excavate in the border or lawn alongside, so that you can see a cross-section of the way the footings are built up.

You will be surprised how many slabs are just laid on the soil; these will take only the lightest traffic.

If the footings are solid and there are still cracks in the path or patio, these may simply be due to poor pointing and renewing it should be sufficient. Once the water gets into the cracks and freezes, it makes them wider.

Greenhouse, conservatory and other buildings

Floors and surrounds should be checked for cracks and subsidence in the same way as paths. After the hot summers of the late 1980s, subsidence has become increasingly common. Broken panes will be obvious – if they seem askew between the glazing bars, this may also be a clue to subsidence. Check the state of the timberwork and probe carefully if you find any rot. Has it been regularly painted or treated with preservatives?

Old aluminium greenhouses are often the most difficult to repair. Manufacturers come and go, and finding the right replacement parts can be a real headache; it is often simpler to take a ramshackle greenhouse down and start again from scratch. But don't do it straight away, as the limited protection that even a badly damaged greenhouse can provide for plants may prove valuable in the short term.

Finally, if you have any doubts about buildings, especially old outhouses that you may wish to use, consult a surveyor.

Assessing the basic layout

There may be features of the garden or aspects of its layout that offend you straight away; try to change these as quickly as possible, as they are bad for your peace of mind. Others you will only discover as you get used to the garden. You will also discover that the very fact that the paths, the shed and so on are in the positions that they are will itself wean you away from your first ideas for change. It's OK to go along with that to some extent, but don't persuade yourself that you can live with your predecessors' ideas just because it involves less work.

Trees

First of all, look at your trees in the winter. Deciduous trees reveal the state of their branches when bare of leaves. You will be able to see branches which are rubbing and causing wounds, cankerous patches, the red speckles of coral spot disease, splits in branches and bracket fungi. Early spring is a good time to remove branches of this sort.

Look again later in the spring when the leaves are starting to shoot. This is the time when it's easy to see if any branches are dead. It's at this stage that you may discover that your tree is not worth keeping. You'll have to weigh up the value of a substantial tree which may not be as elegant as you would like after all the dead wood is removed, against the possibility of growing a new tree which will eventually be a better shape. The position of the tree and the importance of having another one in a different spot may tip the balance one way or the other.

Shrubs

Shrubs can be assessed in much the same way as trees – look for disease and damage in the winter and dead shoots in the spring. Then decide later if you actually like that particular variety or not; if not, have it out, however healthy it is. And do it at once, before you get too used to it. If you leave it in place you may find that you cease to dislike it enough to remove it, but never like it enough to really appreciate it. Be tough.

Other plants

Plants such as perennials, bulbs and alpines are more tricky, as, to put it bluntly, you can't always see they're there. You really need to give things a season to show themselves and for you to decide whether or not you like them. If the garden is a little neglected some plants may put up a pretty poor show, but at least give them the chance to show themselves.

Some people have the urge to blast everything with weed-killer and start completely afresh, and I have to say I have a certain sympathy with that approach. But old gardens often shelter interesting plants, which will flourish if given a little care and attention.

The problems of shared access

Shared access can be a tricky problem, and in my experience it is one that can cause difficulties with neighbours unless approached sensitively by all concerned. Sharing a passage alongside or between terraced houses does not usually cause trouble – it's when there is a right of way behind your house for the neighbour further away from the passage that the problems start. The regularity of this traffic necessitates leaving an open way between house and garden, which can disrupt your ideas for design and also makes the garden less private than it might be.

You might solve the problem simply by delaying the start of the garden, as you might put it: pave the area immediately behind the house and begin the garden on the other side of the pathway. You could erect a low picket fence, or put up a 6ft (1.8m) fence with a gate into the private part of your garden so that when you sit there any number of neighbours can pass back and forth without knowing that you've slipped out of your cossie to make the most of the sun.

Imposing your own ideas

One of the themes of this section has been the very definite advice to make the garden your own – and to do it earlier rather than later. Make it reflect your own character and that of your family, rather than allow yourself to be forced to follow the scheme that suited the previous occupant. I would even go as far as to say that plants or features that you dislike should be removed as early as possible – even if you are not able to replace them at once. The resulting gap will inspire you to action.

Time, availability of funds, alternative priorities and enthusiasm will all govern how quickly you are able to make your new garden your own. The big things, those that offend you most, should be changed first and changed radically. Then the setting is ready for you to add the details.

3. MAKING CHANGES

There'll be a temptation to plant your favourite plants, sow seeds or fling up a conservatory the moment you move in to your new house, at the same time as wallpapering bedrooms and hanging curtains. Wait, and think first.

Priorities

Safety should always come first, but you must also deal with any plants that you have brought with you from your previous garden and make it possible to sit out in the garden without being faced with an infuriating view.

Safety first

There are some things which demand immediate attention. If you have any large trees, inspect them very carefully for damaged branches. It's not just storms and hurricanes that tear limbs from trees, and if there are branches partially torn off or caught in lower branches they can come down at any time and cause damage or serious injury. And if they overhang the pavement and injure someone when they fall, you'll be liable to pay compensation. If the branch is not accessible from a short, sturdy stepladder, get the professionals in to do it properly. Choose a tree surgeon who belongs to the Arboricultural Association (see page 428).

Checking the fences and paving, as I've just mentioned, will reveal any obvious safety problems, but you should also inspect ponds. This is vital if you have children, and perhaps even more so if you have friends with children who will be visiting you – statistics show not only that children can drown in just a few inches of water but that more children drown in ponds when visiting friends than in their own gardens. If it's at all likely that young children will be using the garden, drain the pond straight away. Covering it with netting or erecting a low fence around it are just not good enough, as kids have an alarming aptitude for getting where they want however difficult you make it.

Having removed any aquatic plants, fish, frogs and other wildlife to a neighbour's pond (if you can't find a home for it all, contact your local naturalists' trust), don't puncture the liner to allow the water to drain away but fill it with soil to make a bog garden. This can be planted with primulas and other bog plants and will make a lovely feature – unless it's in an inconvenient spot. The alternative is to fill it with large pebbles or small rocks with no sharp edges to just above the water level. It will be wet but safe, as the water will be below the level of the stones. Marginal plants will grow in it quite well. When the children are older the rocks can be removed. Either way, the look and atmosphere of the garden will be completely changed.

If you inherit a large, captivating mature pool that is an integral part of the garden design, you will have to consider making it secure by using a temporary high fence until the children are old enough to treat it responsibly.

Plants from your previous garden

Looking at your new garden, it may seem impossible to pick a place to plant the treasures that you've brought with you. Don't expect to be able to find them permanent homes right away, but choose a spot – anywhere – that is fairly free of other plants and fork the soil over to remove all (and I mean all) perennial weeds. Mix in plenty of organic matter for all the plants except those that require good drainage, as this will encourage a fibrous root system which will help them when you move them again.

Don't worry about how you arrange them. Planting in rows is the best course, as it makes weeding more straightforward.

Adapting a layout

The technique described on page 19 of photographing the garden from an upstairs window and then using acetate sheets and non-permanent pens to try out changes works well with an established garden too, but it needs to be adapted a little. Lay your first acetate over the enlarged photograph, then trace off those paths, paved areas, flower-beds or other features and any specimen trees or shrubs that you wish to retain and that are too big to move. Mark in the boundaries too. Then put your original photograph to one side and place a new acetate over the first tracing. Try out your ideas in a pen of another colour on the clean acetate. When you've made your decisions, photocopy the two acetates together as before.

Once you've decided which features and plants you wish to keep you will see that by looking at them alone it is possible to transform the garden into a layout and style that suits you. Removing all but necessary thoughts of what's there already by discarding your original picture makes it all so much simpler.

Fitting in a shed

Some small gardens are just too small for a shed – assuming you want to sit in the garden and hang out your washing as well. But if you have a family with bicycles or need a shed for DIY, potter's wheel or pigeons, space must be found somehow.

Small lean-to stores in timber or steel are now available which provide waterproof storage for a bicycle or a lawn-mower and a few tools. If you need more outdoor storage space, however, a shed is the answer.

Dare I say it: I'm sure it pays to buy a shed which is larger than you think you need. Then that little extra space will be there when you do need it – as you will. OK, we know about Parkinson's law, but the fact is that there will always be things that need outside storage and if the bicycles and tools take up every inch, you'll only end up regretting not buying something a little bigger.

When it comes to siting your shed, there are a number of factors to take into account. If it is to house the bikes, you don't want to have to wheel them right through the garden all the time, so site it as near the access as possible. Look for the shadiest, driest spot – the part of the garden least likely to appeal to plants – and consider this first. Under the overhanging branches of next door's sycamore is a superb position for a shed.

If the shed is for a hobby and you need electricity, a position nearer the house will save on cable-laying. Remember that you need a good path right to the door, so that you never get your feet muddy.

Don't worry if you have to site it very near the house – put it outside the back door if you like. It can be made to blend into the garden by covering it with climbers – in most gardens extra space for climbers will be most welcome.

Greenhouse or conservatory?

Which of these should you have? They are not really alternatives – each serves a different purpose. A conservatory is for living in, with perhaps more plants than you would have in a room indoors. A greenhouse is for raising plants and for growing tomatoes and plant collections. In a small garden a conservatory should come first – especially as there may not even be space for a greenhouse. The design will need careful consideration, as it should be big enough to be comfortable yet not so big that it dominates the garden. And you will have to take account of features and levels near the house that you wish to retain or that can't be altered. The smaller the garden, the less scope you have to make changes, especially in levels, and you may find that a little creative planning is required.

It may be impossible to fit a standard conservatory into the space available, but many companies design and build conservatories to fit particular situations. This may not be as expensive as you think, as they try to adapt relatively inexpensive standard aluminium or timber components to an original design which fits your individual circumstances. Choose a timber, natural or coloured aluminium structure to go with the style and materials of your house, and don't forget to think from the start about how it will relate not only to the house but also to the rest of the garden. Read too my thoughts on conservatories in new gardens (page 17).

When it comes to a greenhouse, your approach should perhaps be the opposite of the one used to find a site for a shed. In a garden which is established, there may not be too many places of sufficient size which are light and with reasonable access. So there may be only one spot for the greenhouse – put it there. Ideally it should run on a north–south axis, but again you may find that you just have to fit it in where it will go.

To some extent the nature of the ideal greenhouse site depends on what exactly you want to grow in it. If you intend to raise plants from seed, an open site which gets plenty of light in the late winter and spring is important. If you intend to grow alpines the same applies. Tomatoes benefit from a little shade in the summer, while if your aim is to have a place for house plants to recover from your central heating, shade for part of the day all the year round would be beneficial – an east–west orientation will give you a shady side.

You're unlikely to be given such choices, however, so put it in the lightest place possible and at the very least not shaded from the south.

Cold frame

A cold frame is a simple low-level structure which helps protect plants from the cold. It usually has short sides just a foot or two high made of glass, timber or blocks, and a glass or polythene cover.

Many people see cold frames as a poor alternative to the greenhouse, but they are valuable in their own right. If an important reason for having a garden is to grow plants then a cold frame can be very useful. Again, exactly where it is to be sited depends a lot on

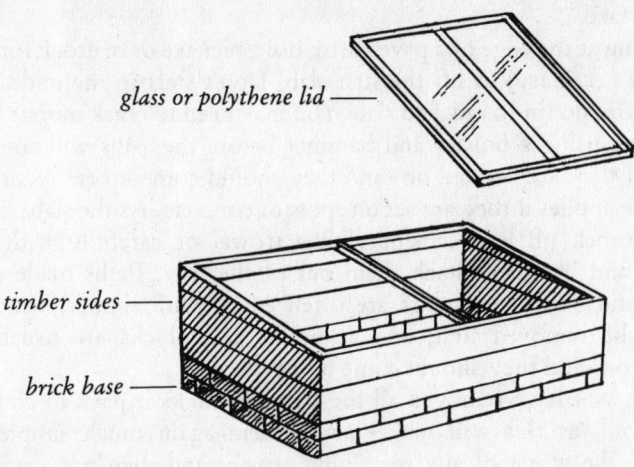

glass or polythene lid ——

timber sides ——

brick base ——

COLD FRAME
You can use old railway sleepers or concrete blocks to build the main
structure but the easiest is tongue-and-groove boarding treated with
preservative. Site it on a brick base to help prevent rotting.

what you want to use it for. Many seeds need to be left outside to be
chilled in a cold frame after sowing, and if this is your intention the
frame should go at the foot of a north-facing wall or fence. If you
intend to raise lots of half-hardy annuals from seed, then the frame
in which they will become acclimatised before being planted out is
probably best sited facing west.

In a small garden the most economical way of using the space is to
site your frame against a fence, and if you build your own frame
using old railway sleepers or concrete blocks you will be able to
ensure that it fits into exactly the space available. You will have to
make a lid too, from a timber frame and clear polythene held in
place with battens.

Lifting and re-using slabs and bricks

Once you have investigated existing paths and paving you may find
that although the materials used are appropriate, they would be
better used in a different way. Most materials can be re-used unless
laid on solid concrete, and this is sometimes a good option. Even

ugly concrete paths can be broken up and used as hardcore under a new surface.

Starting at the edge of a paved area, use a pickaxe or mattock (or a spade if necessary) to lift the first slab. Don't start in the middle, even if you do find a cracked slab. You may need to crack mortar in the joints using a bolster and hammer before the slabs will come away. If they are bedded on sand they should come up easily, and the same applies if they are set on spots of concrete. As the slabs are lifted, knock off any cement with a trowel or carefully with a bolster and hammer. Stack them out of the way. Paths made of bricks and concrete paviors are often edged with timber, which should be removed first, and as bricks and blocks are usually bedded on sand they should come up easily.

When you have removed all the slabs or bricks it pays to clean them well, as this will make laying them again much simpler. Remove the worst of any remaining cement and then use a wire brush to remove traces of other debris. Wear eye protection for this sort of work.

You may also need to deal with remaining sand and hardcore. The sand can go on a part of the garden with heavy soil and the hardcore can be set aside for the new work. Some slabs may have been laid on compacted soil which will have become very hard over the years. It will need a thorough forking over to loosen it and let in air. The soil under hardcore will also need forking over well.

You will probably find yourself left with a hole, which can be filled partly by improving the soil with organic matter and partly by filling with soil from the area where you intend to re-use the materials, where a certain amount of excavating will doubtless be necessary.

Moving trees and shrubs

You may find that you have inherited some specimen plants which you would like to retain but which are in the wrong place. What is possible and what is not are probably best summed up in a number of guidelines.

a. You can move surprisingly large plants as long as you prepare well, move them carefully and look after them afterwards.

b. Large conifers are not easy to move, and other evergreens are also difficult. Deciduous plants are more likely to survive.

c. Move conifers and other evergreens in September or April. Deciduous shrubs can be moved at any time when they are without leaves and when soil conditions are good; November and March are good months.
d. Always retain as much soil on the roots as possible.
e. If possible, prepare the plants by cutting around them with a spade in the spring before you intend to move them. For details of how exactly to go about moving established trees and shrubs, see page 65.

Think before you change

Taking over an established garden gives you one big advantage over moving to a brand new one – time, the time the plants have had to mature while your predecessor was in residence. So think twice before you throw that away, as it will take years for you to catch up. Large plants give a garden an air of maturity even if all around has been remade and replanted, so even if you decide that substantial plants have got to go, it may pay to leave some of them for a few years until your other plants have had time to reach a substantial size.

Be ruthless

Once you have decided to remove something, do so straight away, as the sight of anything you find ugly will be continually offensive. But wait to install features that capture your enthusiasm until you have the time and resources to ensure that you can do a good job.

The Big Splash

While all the hard work is going on and you're not only giving the garden the attention it needs but also putting work into the new house, it's very encouraging and gives you a heartening sense of achievement if you can arrange to have some attractive colour in the garden quickly.

Spring and summer bedding

Bedding plants are those temporary plants that flower for one season only and are then thrown away. They are among the most colourful (some would say garish) of all garden plants and can either be bought from the garden centre at the appropriate season or raised from seed. As we want to achieve a quick splash of colour while other jobs are pressing, it's off to the garden centre.

Spring bedding plants include polyanthus, wallflowers, pansies, forget-me-nots and double daisies. These are sold and planted in the autumn for flowering in the spring, although some polyanthus and pansies will flower in the winter too. Polyanthus and pansies are also sold in the spring.

Polyanthus and pansies are sold in trays and in pots, forget-me-nots and daisies usually only in strips or trays. Wallflowers are sold in strips and trays but more usually in bunches of plants dug from the open ground. Avoid buying wallflowers in trays as they are usually too small to make a good flowering plant by spring. In spring, buy only pot-grown pansies and polyanthus. After flowering they can all be discarded and replaced with plants that will flower in the summer, although if there are any polyanthus in colours you especially like, they can be lifted and planted elsewhere to flower again the following year.

Spring bedding plants can be used to fill a large empty bed or spaces between other plants. The occasional plant can be slotted in wherever there is a gap – though it has to be said that large groups look better. A large group of wallflowers fronted by forget-me-nots looks especially good.

Summer bedding plants include marigolds, petunias, busy lizzies (impatiens), begonias, geraniums, asters, lobelia and alyssum. These plants are bought in late spring and planted in the garden as soon as possible after the last frost in your area – usually at the end of May or in early June. Generally they flower until the first of the autumn frosts – sometimes beyond – although in poor soil and dry summers flowering may end prematurely.

These plants too are sold in small pots or in strips or trays. Plants in strips or trays are more economical, but are generally smaller and slower to grow away after planting. Petunias, geraniums and marigolds are especially successful in the hottest and sunniest spots, while busy lizzies and begonias are good in the shade.

Both spring and summer bedding plants require some preparation. Forking in a 2–3in (5–7.5cm) layer of organic matter and scattering a handful of general fertiliser to the square yard before planting will give them a good start.

Containers

It's quite possible that there won't be the time to do anything in the garden except keep it ticking over. In that case containers, and especially tubs, could be the answer; avoid hanging baskets and window-boxes at this stage, as they need too much looking after. Tubs can be sited where you most frequently pass – outside the front and back doors, by the shed – and within sight of the kitchen and living-room windows. And if you choose big ones, time spent caring for them will be limited.

You can splash out on beautiful tubs or urns that will fit well into your new garden, or you can buy much cheaper, more functional ones. Large glazed or terracotta pots make wonderful house-warming presents, so drop a few hints before you move.

If you'd rather buy something less expensive, there are various alternatives. The cheapest are compressed wood fibre, which will last two years but will become increasingly fragile, and plastic, which can be cheap and disposable but is hardly chic. Going up in price a stage we come to half-barrels – often the best bargains are at petrol stations or by the roadside. Purpose-made timber containers, earthenware and other ceramics are too expensive to be thought about only as short-term options.

There is another alternative which is ideal if funds are short but time is no object. Using reclaimed floorboards and scrap timber, treated generously with timber preservative, you can make good-sized planting boxes very economically. It's important that these should be big; to avoid depressingly frequent watering and feeding, I would recommend 15in (35cm) diameter for a tub – 12in (30cm) will do if absolutely necessary, but 18in (45cm) is better. Square planting boxes can be made to a minimum of 15in (35cm) across and the same in depth, while rectangular ones can be a minimum of 12in (30cm) deep and 15in (35cm) across and up to 6ft (1.8m) long – but don't fill them with compost until you have them in the right place. 24in (60cm) is a manageable length. (More details can be found on page 119.)

Fill your pots with spring and summer bedding plants changed twice a year, and also with bulbs. Plants sold in pots rather than trays may be more expensive, but as you will be buying only a few and they will be of better quality, always buy pot-grown plants for tubs if you can.

Bulbs

The great thing about bulbs is that they're absolutely guaranteed to bloom; you have to do something pretty odd to them to prevent them producing at least a small flower. This is because when you buy bulbs, most varieties already contain a miniature flower bud. They just need the right amount of moisture and warmth to flower beautifully. Without this warmth and moisture (if you leave the pack on the garage shelf, for example!) flowers will still appear at the right season but they won't be up to much.

Spring bulbs are ideal companions for spring bedding plants, and in particular I would suggest that you use them in containers. Tulips are good growing through wallflowers, grape hyacinths are lovely among polyanthus.

The term summer bulbs usually covers many plants, dahlias for example, which are not bulbs in the botanical sense but are treated as if they are. Indeed, dahlias give perhaps the best value of all summer bulbs, producing vast quantities of flowers well into the autumn on big, bushy plants. Gladioli are flamboyant too, and begonias are probably the best summer bulbs for tubs – the trailing varieties are ideal hanging over the edge with taller, bushier plants behind them.

Quick-growing plants

In a brand new garden, quick-growing plants can make the garden seem mature in just a year or two. There are plants that will grow to a good size very quickly – but what happens then? Some, like Leyland's cypress, just keep getting bigger and bigger, growing at 12–15in (30–35cm) a year or more until you don't know what to do with them. Others are relatively short-lived plants which conveniently die on you, leaving a space for replanting.

Here are a few suggestions for plants that grow quickly. More details can be found on page 261.

YARROW (*Achillea millefolium* Many varieties)   Feathery-leaved plant with flat heads of flowers in many different colours.

WORMWOOD (*Artemisia* 'Powis Castle')   Fine, silver foliage on a widely spreading bush.

BUTTERFLY BUSH (*Buddleia* Many varieties)   Purple, lilac, pink or white flowers on an upright shrub.

CALIFORNIAN LILAC (*Ceanothus* 'Autumnal Blue')   Clouds of small blue flowers on an evergreen shrub.

SPOTTED DEAD NETTLE (*Lamium maculatum* Many varieties)   Creeping plant with foliage in combinations of green, silver and yellow plus red, pink or white flowers.

TREE MALLOW (*Lavatera olbia*)   Pink flowers on a spreading plant with upright stems.

LUPIN (*Lupinus* Many varieties)   Flamboyant spikes, easy to raise from seed in large quantities.

TREE LUPIN (*Lupinus arboreus*)   Yellow lupin spikes on a rounded bush.

GARDENER'S GARTERS (*Phalaris arundinacea* 'Picta')   Creeping plant with narrow, white and green striped leaves.

PERIWINKLE (*Vinca major* 'Variegata')   Low creeping stems with yellow-splashed leaves.

Making the Most of Small Spaces

The one thing that the small size of a garden should never restrict is the imagination. I grant that there will be no room for vast lakes, tennis courts or avenues of lime trees, nor should you attempt to replicate such schemes in miniature. But in the same way as there is a challenge in planting a park effectively, there is as much of a challenge in deciding how to plant that pocket handkerchief outside your back door.

At its best a small garden functions as an extra, outdoor room. There may be cupboards (shed) and cooking facilities (barbecue) but there will also be the 'floor', in plants, lawn or paving, and décor, in plants. The crucial difference between an indoor and an outdoor room is not, strangely, the fact that one is inside and the other out. The crucial factor is change: because a garden is furnished with living organisms that respond to the seasons it is constantly changing. And it is change that gives it that special appeal. It should be planted to reflect the constantly changing year, and planned so that it is possible to enjoy as much of this annual change as possible.

We have to live in this outdoor room, however, and in a small space, where there is little leeway for error, the functional elements have to function efficiently. Access to storage, to activity areas of various sorts and for maintenance must give as little concern as a good carpet in the house – and need rather less regular attention.

You would never put the drinks cabinet or the kitchen equipment you use most in the least accessible place, so don't put the bin where it's furthest from the back door and from access to the street. And when it comes to décor, you don't put up with the horrid wallpaper left by your predecessor or forget to match your new scheme to the style of the house and its situation. With plants as the paints, wall-coverings, ornaments and works of art, there is a vast, ever-increasing and sometimes bewildering choice available. Never assume that you can get it right first time without a little guidance – either from this book or from friends, magazines and the TV.

It's plants that provide the opportunities, and although up to now plants have featured but meagrely in this book, that's because up to now we've been considering the setting in which the plants can give their best. If chosen carefully, plants can enhance those changes which the seasons inexorably bring. One plant can provide four or five visual changes over a year, and one square yard of garden can be constantly captivating. Plants provide this versatility but we must prepare for them.

Don't be afraid to stick to what you feel is right even if it's unconventional. A garden should be furnished and decorated in a way that reflects your character just as your living-room does. It won't be possible to do everything all at once, especially as plants take time to mature, but contentment in the room outside is an achievable goal.

CHAPTER THREE

TOOLS AND PRACTICALITIES

Choosing Tools

Choosing the right tools can be as difficult as it is important. Everything is made easier if we have the right equipment to hand, yet most of us find ourselves with a collection of tools made up of cast-offs or presents from relatives, plus oddments we found in the shed when we moved into our new home. This is then augmented with what we buy, with a greater or lesser degree of inspiration, from the garden centre. Sometimes this makes up an adequate collection, sometimes not.

1. WHAT YOU NEED AND HOW TO CHOOSE

If the worst comes to the worst it's possible to get by with just a border fork and a bread knife – possible, but not very convenient. I would suggest that the basics are: spade, border fork, hoe, rake, secateurs, trowel, sprinkler and hosepipe. If you have a lawn you will also need a lawn-mower and edging shears.

Spade

A stainless steel spade will make preparing the soil in a new garden a great deal easier but will also be expensive. The fact that soil doesn't stick to a stainless steel blade makes digging less arduous, ordinary steel blades need cleaning much more often, especially in heavy soil. Choose a spade with a tread at the top of the blade to prevent the narrow top edge cutting into your boots. One model from Bulldog also has the top corners rounded off so that if your foot slips, there is no sharp corner to cut into your leg.

Shafts may be in timber or steel. My preference is for timber (ash), as it's very slightly flexible, yet very strong and also warm to the touch. Most spades have D-shaped grips, and whether you choose one in timber, steel or plastic-coated steel is a matter of personal preference. I find wooden handles warmer, and in time they wear slightly to fit your own grip.

Compare different brands and models in the garden centre, as blade size and handle length vary – as does the price. The cheapest will usually be the least reliable; mid-priced own-branded tools are sometimes excellent value.

Shovel

This is necessary only if you're doing a lot of building work, such as laying paving or building walls for raised beds. It's also useful if you're making a lot of your own potting compost – or shifting snow. Otherwise don't bother.

Digging fork

This is very useful if you are preparing heavy soil in a new garden or if you are keen to do a very thorough job when preparing soil generally. Otherwise you will rarely use it, except perhaps for turning garden compost and spreading organic matter. The same points regarding handles and grips as apply to spades are valid for digging forks.

Border fork

One of the most useful of all tools, the border fork (even now sometimes called a lady's fork!) is a smaller version of a digging fork. It's useful for a wide variety of tasks, including loosening the soil surface and working in organic matter, preparing for planting, handling organic matter, collecting debris. Because the tines are relatively close together it can double as a rake and spade.

Buy the very best quality, as you will probably find you use your border fork a lot. My comments on grips and handles for spades apply here too, but you will also often find border forks with T-shaped handles. Whether or not you find these comfortable is purely a matter of personal taste – I find them difficult but many people like them.

Hoe

There are many types of hoe. The most widely used is the Dutch hoe, with the handle attached to both sides of the blade, but I find this awkward if I'm working close to plants. A Paxton hoe has the blade attached to the shaft with a single central stay, and I find that this allows the ends of the blade to slip under foliage without damaging it.

There are various other designs, and again there is the option of stainless steel, which is worth investing in if you intend to grow a lot of vegetables – it's here that the hoe will be most useful. The rest of the garden should soon be so well covered with plants that few weeds will appear, and your hoe should spend most of its time in the shed.

Hoes with plastic-coated alloy handles are now widely available, and their light weight makes them very easy to use.

Garden rake

A rake is essential for seed-sowing and for helping to prepare the soil in a new garden for making a lawn, sowing seed or simply producing a neat finish. It can also be used for collecting leaves from the lawn. Rakes come in two types: those which seem to be made of a row of nails set in a flat bar are less satisfactory than those pressed out of a single piece of flat steel. An alloy handle again takes the hard work out of raking.

Secateurs

A good pair of secateurs, well looked after, is a vital piece of equipment. They can be used not only for pruning but for cutting flowers for the house and even for taking cuttings. It's not always easy to handle them in the shop, but try to choose a pair that fits your hand – if you have small hands, don't buy a large pair of secateurs. Remember, though, that a small pair will not be able to cut thick branches. If you over-strain them they will cut badly – use long-handled loppers for heavier branches.

Avoid those secateurs with swivelling handles, which are good for professionals with hundreds of roses to prune every spring but are difficult to get used to.

Keep them well oiled, wipe them clean after use, and store them in a dry place.

Long-handled loppers

If you have fruit trees or vigorous shrubs like buddleias that need pruning every spring, my advice is to invest in a pair of long-handled pruners and take the strain off both you and your secateurs. For branches that are larger than your secateurs can cope with, long-handled loppers are vital. And although it's unlikely that you will use them every week, they make light work of even those heavier jobs that you can just about manage with secateurs.

Hedging shears

These are obviously required only if you have a hedge. In most circumstances I would suggest hiring or borrowing an electric hedge-trimmer, as cutting hedges by hand is hard work. Hedges like laurel, with large leaves, are best cut with secateurs.

Trowel

A stainless steel trowel is going to get plenty of use, not only in a new garden where there will be regular planting to do but also in any garden where improvements are being made. Look for one with the thinnest possible blade – it will be easier to use and still adequately strong. Avoid those with plastic handles, which will give you blisters after a few minutes' use, and don't be afraid to use sandpaper on the end of a wooden handle to make it smoother and more comfortable.

Some gardeners paint the handles of their trowels, hand forks and secateurs with a luminous orange paint so that they are less likely to be overlooked and thrown out with the rubbish. I don't find this necessary but you may think it worth considering.

Hand fork

A hand fork, or weeding fork, matches the trowel in size; it's not essential, but is certainly very useful and if you're thinking of asking for a trowel for a Christmas present you might as well ask for a trowel and hand fork set. A hand fork is invaluable for tidying and weeding between small plants, and can even be used for planting if your trowel goes missing. The remarks about trowel handles also apply to hand forks.

Planting spade

You could say that a planting spade is really a spade from a jumble sale – a spade so worn down by use over the years that the blade is only half the length it was originally. This may seem pretty useless, but I've found such a spade very useful for planting anything that needs more than a trowel. Nowadays I use what's known as a boy's spade!

Bucket

A black plastic 2-gallon bucket, if not two or three of them, will be invaluable for collecting weeds, carrying compost and many, many other jobs. These buckets are also cheap, resilient and clank less than galvanised ones.

Carry-all

Not all gardens generate so much material that a barrow is necessary, but a carry-all will always be very useful. This is simply a very heavy-duty plastic sheet, often woven, with two or four handles to help you carry it about. Some are flat, others more or less bag-shaped. Your rubbish or other material is simply heaped in and you can carry it away.

Sprayer

This is an essential item, not because I'm recommending that you cover your plants in noxious chemicals – far from it. But even organic products have to be applied somehow, and a 4-pint or 5-litre sprayer is the way to do it.

  If you use a lot of weed-killer, it pays to keep a sprayer specially for that use to avoid catastrophic confusion. But in a small garden it's unlikely that you will use much weed-killer except perhaps in the early stages. So my advice is to use the sprayer for weed-killer at first, when there is ground to clear. When there is no more weed-killing to be done, wash it out very thoroughly with water and washing-up liquid – then do it again to make sure there's not a trace of weed-killer left. Then never use it for weed-killer again.

Sprinkler

A sprinkler is essential for any garden in these times of unpredictable summers, but especially so when many new plants are going in or when mature specimens are being moved. Don't forget that you need a licence from your local water authority to use it.

Many types of sprinkler are available, but the kind that combines the most even water distribution with adjustability and the ability to function well on low pressure is not the common rotating type – choose instead the type with a slowly oscillating curved bar punctured with holes to create a fan-shaped spray. The extra advantage of these, sometimes known as lawn sprinklers though they work well on beds and borders too, is that they water a more or less square or rectangular area, which is often more convenient than a circular spray pattern.

You will find that if set among tall plants the spray will be blocked by foliage, so the sprinkler must be raised up by setting it on an upturned bucket.

Hosepipe

It's no good having a sprinkler if you have no hosepipe to connect it to the tap. Simple advice – buy a laminated hosepipe reinforced with braided nylon and buy a length which is long enough to reach every corner of the garden with some to spare. At the same time buy a hose reel to keep it all stored neatly, and quick-locking hose fittings with automatic water stops which cut off the water when you disconnect the sprinkler.

Bulb planter

If you anticipate planting a lot of bulbs, especially in an area of rough grass, then a specially designed bulb planter that takes out a core of soil to the required depth is very useful. But a trowel will do if you are planting only a few.

Lawn-mower

There has been quite a controversy over the best type of small lawn-mower to buy. For a small garden I would always recommend a mains electric machine.

My experience is that hover mowers, even those with grass-bags, scatter the grass where it's not wanted – such as over gravel paths where it's difficult to gather up. I would suggest one of two options. Go for a conventional cylinder mower with a roller at the back to give you stripes and a rear-mounted, rather than front-mounted, grass-box which allows you to get close to walls, fences and plants. Or choose a rotary mower with four wheels at the corners, or with two at the front and a roller for stripes at the back. The grass-box or bag will be rear-mounted.

You will need a dry place to store the mower and a circuit breaker to protect you in case of accidents with the cable.

Lawn-edger

I've known people cut the edges to a small lawn with the kitchen scissors, but I can hardly recommend that. A pair of edging shears with vertically set blades is what you need – as distinct from grass shears with horizontally set blades for cutting the grass round trees and along fences. You'll have little use for these. My only tip is that before buying you should clip the handles together vigorously and if your knuckles touch even slightly, choose another pair.

Lawn-edging machines are also available, hand or electrically powered, but are unnecessary in a small garden.

2.   WHAT YOU CAN BORROW OR HIRE

There are some tools that you will need occasionally but not often enough to be worth buying. Some you can hire, others you can share with a friend or neighbour.

Wheelbarrow

Whether you buy or borrow really depends on exactly how small your garden is. For tiny town courtyards a barrow will never be necessary, but many small gardens generate enough waste and demand so much carrying about that a wheelbarrow is most helpful.

Borrow one if you can, but if you decide to buy one don't buy a flimsy little galvanised garden barrow. Buy a large Ballbarrow with a spherical front wheel, which is easy to push and is not made of steel so won't rust. Alternatively choose a builders' barrow, which is tough and should have pneumatic tyres.

Wire rake

A wire rake is useful for removing thatch from the smallest lawns but is very hard work on a larger scale; an electric lawn-raker is far more satisfactory. A wire rake can also be used for collecting leaves and other debris but is not usually an essential item. Borrow one when you need it. Only if you have areas of gravel is a wire rake a necessity.

Hay rake

In the garden a large wooden hay rake is used for raking leaves, but in a new garden it is also especially useful for levelling soil. However, once you are past this phase you will have little use for it. Borrow one or do without.

Lawn-raker

An electric lawn-raker is an incredible machine for removing moss and dead stems from the lawn and generally revitalising it. But as you are likely to use it only once a year, hire one when you need it.

Heavy-duty brushcutter

If you take over a garden which is overgrown with weeds and brambles, a brushcutter will make quick work of cutting it all down – in a fraction of the time it would take with a scythe or shears. The heavier, more powerful and therefore more effective brushcutters are usually petrol-powered, with an operating head at ground level which consists of a rotating nylon cutting line (these models are sometimes known as strimmers) or, for heavier work, a steel blade.

These machines can be obtained from most hire shops. They can be very dangerous and you should always wear protective goggles and stout leather boots when using them.

Chain-saw

If you have trees to remove, hire a chain-saw, but it you have the slightest qualms about removing a tree, or for anything taller than about 15ft (4.5m), call in an expert to do it for you. In a small garden it's so easy to smash a fence, a greenhouse, a window or even yourself when a branch or the whole tree falls the wrong way or topples you off your ladder.

And remember you can probably buy a large bow-saw for the cost of hiring a chain-saw for a day, and a bow-saw can be used again and is much safer.

Hedge-trimmer

Although you can buy hedge-trimming attachments for electric drills, a purpose-made mains electric hedge-trimmer is lighter and more reliable. Models with cutting edges on both sides of the bar are easier and quicker to use.

Even if your hedge is a short one it's still worth hiring a trimmer, and don't forget hedges need trimming only once or twice a year.

Pruning saw

Obviously this item will be redundant in a new garden in which there are no trees or shrubs to use it on, as a pruning saw is used mainly for those larger pruning jobs that secateurs or long-handled pruners can't cope with. In an established garden there will probably be a need for a pruning saw, although your long-handled pruners will do some of the tougher jobs.

3. WHAT YOU CAN MAKE

Some things you don't need to borrow and don't need to buy – you can make them.

Garden line

A garden line is what it says it is – a piece of string that you use for guidance whenever you need a straight line. You simply take some stout sisal string or polypropylene twine, tie one end securely to an 18in (45cm) piece of scrap timber, wind on more than you think you'll need, and tie the other end to another piece of timber. End of story.

Do not use baler twine as it twists badly and is difficult to handle.

Measuring stick

This is one of the most useful of all tools, and simplicity itself to make. Take a 2m piece of 2 × 1in (50 × 25mm) timber and make a saw cut across one side every 6in and across the other every 200mm. Add extra cuts every inch and every 25mm for the first 12in and 200mm, to give smaller measurements over a short length. Then give the whole thing two coats of green outdoor timber preservative. When it's dry mark every major division (12in and 200mm) with two red-headed drawing-pins, and every 6in and 100mm with one pin so that you can see the marks at a glance.

Use your measuring stick when planting out, sowing seeds, as a guide when drawing drills. The only danger is that you'll tread on it and snap it in two!

4. WHAT YOU DON'T NEED AT ALL

You don't need a sieve, a daisy grubber, any hand-operated tool with a rotating head, any trowel divided into prongs, or anything described in advertisements as revolutionary.

5. TOOL STORAGE AND MAINTENANCE

There's no point in buying good tools if you don't look after them.

Storage

Tools need storing in a dry place and the shed is the obvious spot, but there are alternatives (see page 35). Inside you can either fit a purpose-made tool-rack or simply use nails. I use 6in (15cm) nails, knocked in pre-drilled holes to avoid splitting the timber, with a pair for each D-handle; the rake and hoe go in the roof space, laid on the cross-supports. Nails can also be placed to take shears and so on. Trowel and hand fork usually live in an empty bucket, while secateurs are better kept in the house, where it is warm and dry and rust is less likely to attack the cutting edge.

Hosepipe should be kept out of the weather when not in use, and not left lying on the ground filled with water in frosty weather.

It's vital that electrical equipment, for example lawn-mowers, be stored in the dry, so check existing garden sheds to ensure that they really are waterproof.

Maintenance

All tools should be wiped clean of loose dirt after use – that, at least, most of us can manage. The next stage is attended to less frequently. Every so often spades and forks are best washed down, dried and sprayed with an oil aerosol. Cutting tools need the same treatment.

Secateurs which have become encrusted with plant sap can be cleaned by soaking them overnight in a solution of vinegar or biological washing powder, and this is even more successful if they are dismantled first. Never leave tools outside when you've finished using them.

Mowers should be cleaned after each use. In particular, grass which has collected under the hood and on or around the blades should be scraped off. Dry grass sometimes collects around the motor, so ensure that this is removed or it could result in overheating. Inspect the cable every few weeks for damage. Do not attempt to repair cuts and abrasions with tape; either shorten the cable by removing the section from the point of damage to the nearest end, or replace the cable entirely.

6. CHOOSING SUNDRIES

Garden centres are full of all sorts of useful and useless items that you may be tempted to buy. Some are vital, others are a waste of money.

Dry fertilisers

Fertilisers are essential in one form or another. Although they do little lasting good to the soil, they are of great benefit to plants in the short term. Many different types are available, often specially formulated to suit particular plants – tomatoes, roses, vegetables, etc.

My advice is to buy the biggest bag you can afford of just one general fertiliser – Growmore or, if you prefer an organic material, fish, blood and bone. To make it last it must be stored in a dry place with the bag re-tied. Apply it at around 2oz (about a full handful) per square yard (60g per square metre) every spring to all cultivated areas and rake it in. It can also be used in a planting mix made up of one bucketful of compost to two handfuls of fertiliser, which is forked into the planting holes before you set the plants in place.

Special fertilisers for specific plants can wait until the garden is established, or you can use liquid supplements. Always wear rubber or disposable polythene gloves when handling fertilisers.

Liquid feeds

Liquid feeds are absorbed by the plant more quickly than dry fertilisers, so are very useful for giving plants a tonic, reviving a sickly specimen or providing a special balance of plant foods suitable to one particular crop. If you grow tomatoes, for instance, either in the greenhouse or outside, using a special tomato feed will greatly increase your crop. Liquid feeds are available for tomatoes and cucumbers, roses, flowering pot plants, foliage pot plants, orchids, African violets and so on. There is also a general liquid feed suitable for a wide variety of crops.

Spraying a liquid feed on to the foliage usually has little effect; it's much more useful watered on the soil around the plant or into the pot. Some liquid feeds boast of their 'trace element' content. Trace elements are minor plant foods which are sometimes in short supply in the soil or in the compost in a pot. This shortage leads to poor and sometimes discoloured growth.

Lawn treatments

There are both liquid and dry lawn treatments. Dry materials are easier to apply, as their bright colour, which soon disappears, makes it easy to see which areas have been treated. But they need to be washed into the soil by heavy rain before the lawn can be used, so if you have pets or young children I would suggest using a liquid material. Once this has dried on the grass, pets and children can use the lawn. Some treatments are intended for spring, others for autumn use, and it's important to follow the instructions on the pack and not use them at the wrong time of year.

At its simplest a lawn treatment simply feeds the lawn, and this in itself can quickly transform an old, patchy, yellowing lawn into a lush green carpet. You'll be astonished at the change one feed can make. Some treatments also include a moss-killer, which is very useful if moss is a problem; others include a weed-killer.

Neglected lawns are rarely without weeds, and you may be surprised at how much clover and trefoil is preventing the grass growing well. By including weed-killer with the lawn feed, the spaces left by the dead weeds are soon filled by the newly stimulated grass.

Lime

Only on the vegetable plot is liming likely to be necessary. Cabbages and similar crops like a limy soil. Your soil test kit (see page 8) will tell you the pH (alkalinity/acidity) of your soil and advise you how much lime to apply. Always wear protective gloves when handling lime.

Organic matter

Organic matter improves almost any soil and is especially useful in new and neglected gardens. It helps improve the workability of the soil and provides a reservoir of water for plants, while at the same time allowing surplus to drain away. As it rots away it releases plant foods, which are taken up by the plants. It needs to be constantly replaced.

Fork it in before planting; spread it on the surface after planting (see page 9).

Soil improvers

You will find products on sale described as soil improvers, clay breakers, clay cures. These can work quite well, but it often takes a number of years for them to improve the soil and you may need quite substantial quantities. They are not cheap. I would always advise that you spend the money on mushroom compost or some other bulky organic material which will do the same job, probably better, while also improving the soil in other ways.

String

Polypropylene twine lasts the longest but tends to come in unpleasant colours. Tarred string lasts a long time but is smelly and the tar comes off on your fingers. Green twine lasts well enough, and indeed for tying up climbers it helps if the string rots after a couple of years as this prevents it cutting into the swelling stems.

Labels and markers

Among gardeners who build up collections of specific types of plants (alpines, roses, etc.), labelling is a matter of regular discussion. Which labels last the longest? But even for less fanatical gardeners labelling is useful, as it is satisfying to be able to tell a visitor the name of a plant that is particularly admired.

Plants usually come with labels when you buy them but these vary from long-lasting but obtrusive plastic tags, perhaps with a picture, to lolly sticks with the name written on in pencil. Anodised aluminium labels on which you write the plant name in pencil are unobtrusive and last for years, but are expensive. I use the cheaper 4in (10cm) white plastic labels, writing the plant name with a fine-tipped, black, oil-based, waterproof marker. This lasts for three or four years – more if sprayed with aerosol varnish after writing.

Canes and stakes

Bamboo canes are becoming more and more expensive but are still the most suitable for many jobs. If you think you will need long ones for beans and sweet peas and also shorter ones for perennials buy a stock of 8ft (2.4m) canes and cut them in half to give 4ft (1.2m) canes for perennials. One 8ft cane is generally cheaper than two 4ft canes. For large and weighty plants like dahlias, 1×1in (25×25mm) stakes are necessary. Treat them with preservative if they are not already treated, and repeat the treatment when you pull them out and clean them in the autumn.

Netting

There are many types of plastic netting and it has many uses. Wide mesh netting, about 6×4in (15×10cm), is used to keep pigeons off vegetables and fruit and also as a support for peas, beans, sweet peas and other annual climbing plants. Small mesh netting, about 1×1in (2.5×2.5cm), is used to keep small birds like sparrows and bull-finches off fruit and vegetables and to keep birds out of the greenhouse.

Heavy-duty netting with a 2×2in (5×5cm) mesh is fixed to walls and fences to support perennial climbers like clematis and is also used to form compost and leaf heaps.

Heavy, but very fine-meshed netting is used as greenhouse shading, and there are also special grades for use as windbreaks.

Cloches

If you like to grow salads, a cloche or two can be very useful in bringing on early crops and protecting late crops from frost. Complicated wire structures for supporting sheets of glass and flimsy polythene tunnel cloches are best left alone. Instead, try the pre-formed polythene, tent-shaped Melbourne cloches, with their rigid frames which not only have ventilation but also let rain through while still giving the crops protection.

Pesticides

Some gardeners are happy to use pesticides when necessary, taking the appropriate safety precautions. Others prefer only organic preparations, while some refuse to use any at all. I would say only that especially in a small garden, which is likely to be densely planted, you will be very lucky to get away with using none at all and still have healthy plants.

Specific recommendations are given on pages 380–405 but there are a few general points worth emphasising.

- Check the capacity of your sprayer before buying pesticides.
- Remember that pesticides can be dangerous, so treat them with respect from the moment you look at them in the garden centre.
- Look out for unbreakable bottles and child-resistant caps and read the information on the pack before you buy, to ensure that the product will do what you want it to do and that it is suitable for the plants you wish to treat.
- Many pesticides now come with a measure (or the cap may double as a measure), but if your sprayer holds 4 pints and the minimum amount of spray you can make up using the measure provided is one gallon, you obviously have a problem.
- Do not plan to mix different products together to treat two different problems; look instead for the products with a wide range of applications or which deal with all the common problems of a specific plant, such as ICI Roseclear for mildew and greenfly on roses.

Practicalities

Even the absolute and rank beginner can succeed in growing healthy plants, partly because the basic gardening skills are not all that difficult to pick up, but also because plants are amazingly tough.

They have an unfailing urge to grow, and you have to treat most of them extremely badly to prevent them doing so.

My only proviso would be that collectors' plants, plants that are recognised as needing special care, should not be attempted until you've mastered the basic skills. But it will not take long to develop the skills necessary to grow the plants you'll find on sale in the garden centre.

1. ESSENTIAL SKILLS

There are some things you just have to learn in order to make a garden and maintain the plants.

Digging

There are two types of digging – single digging and double digging. They differ in the depth to which the soil is dug.

Before you even start, fork over part of the plot and look for the roots of nasty perennial weeds. These can usually be recognised, as they may be narrow and carrot-like or white and wiry. At this stage you may well want to destroy them before you start digging. It will certainly save you time and effort.

Single digging involves turning over and breaking up the top spit, about 10in (25cm), of soil. More accurately, a spit of soil is the same depth as the length of the blade on the spade you are using. The purpose is to loosen the soil and make it more suitable for planting, and to improve the soil by adding organic matter.

The area to be dug should be cleared of debris, and any plants you wish to keep should be removed before you start. Next, divide the plot in half, using your garden line to create two rectangles. Start at the narrow end of one rectangle. Mark out an area 18in (45cm) long, using your measuring stick, and if the plot is weedy slice off the top inch of soil together with the weeds and stack it on a sheet of polythene alongside the end of the other rectangle, at the same end of the plot.

Now, using your digging spade, dig out all the soil from the measured area to the depth of your spade and stack this on a sheet of polythene too. If you have not used a weed-killer and you have perennial weeds, their roots will now be seen and should be removed and kept separate from other weeds for burning later. This is the point at which the organic matter is added. Simply spread it in the bottom of the trench to a depth of 2–3in (5–7.5cm).

At this point the difference between single and double digging becomes apparent. In double digging, you now fork over the bottom of your trench to the depth of your digging fork, mixing in the organic matter; this is often easier if you make the trench a little wider, say 2ft (60cm) rather than 18in (45cm). In single digging, you leave the bottom of the trench as it is.

The next step is to slice off any annual weeds from the next 18in (45cm) of soil and lay them in the trench on top of the organic matter. Now work backwards down the plot, excavating the next 18in (45cm) of soil and using it to fill the trench in front of you, covering the organic matter and weeds. You should then be left with 18in (45cm) of soil rather higher than the rest of the plot, followed by a new trench. The organic matter goes in the new trench, is forked in if you're being extra thorough and double digging, and so on down the plot until you get to the end.

The hardest thing when you're learning to dig a plot is to leave a level surface, and this is especially difficult if the plot is of uneven width. Don't be afraid to use the garden rake or hay rake to level out.

Before long you will get to the end of the plot and have an empty 18in (45cm) trench with nowhere to go next – except back down the other side of the plot in the opposite direction. So the weeds and soil from the strip alongside your empty trench are turned in, and you then work in exactly the same way back up the other side of the plot to where you started. When you get to the other end you will find a pile of soil and weeds from the very first trench. These are used to fill the last trench. You can then go and have a shower and a glass of wine and swear never to lift a spade again.

A few further hints:

- Eliminate all perennial weeds, either by weed-killing before you start or carefully removing the roots as you go.
- Heavy clay soil is best dug in the autumn and early winter, as the frost helps break down the clods. Lighter, sandy soil can be left until early spring.
- If you are not used to digging, do just a little at a time. It's far better to do half an hour every evening after work and two

DOUBLE DIGGING

The most thorough and
effective soil preparation
unfortunately requires the
most work . . .

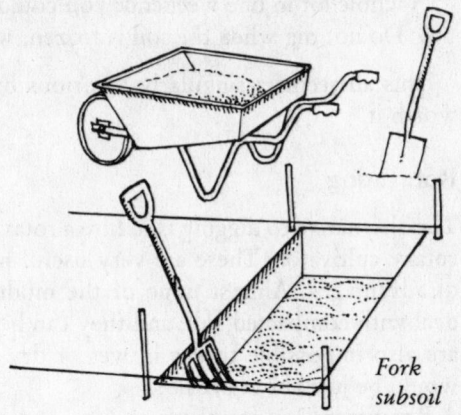

Dig out to the depth of a
spade and load on to a
barrow. Wheel away to
top end of plot . . .

Fork
subsoil

and return with organic
matter.

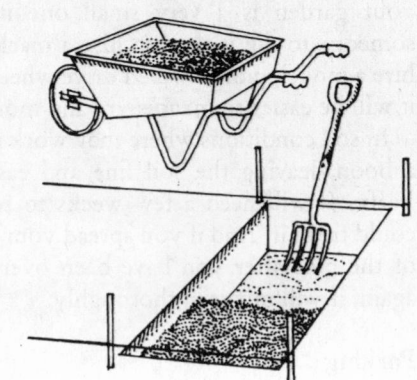

Fork in organic matter to
bottom of trench.

Dig out a new trench but
throw the soil forward.

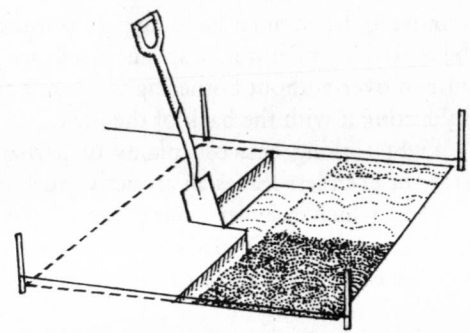

half-hours each day at the weekend than attempt to do the whole lot in one weekend; you could well injure your back.
- Do not dig when the soil is frozen, waterlogged or bone dry.

This all seems a singularly laborious business, and it is; but it's worth it.

Rotavating

The alternative to digging is to hire a rotavator – or more correctly a rotary cultivator. These are very useful machines but have certain disadvantages. Almost none of the models available for hire will deal with compacted soil, and they can be difficult to handle. They are also impossible to use in wet or dry conditions when digging would be just about possible.

Rotavators are not cheap to hire, and you may even find that if your garden is a very small one it's more economical to pay someone to dig it than to hire a machine for a day. Always try to hire a model with powered drive wheels as well as powered tines, as it will be easier to manoeuvre and more likely to do a good job.

In soil conditions where they work well, rotary cultivators can be a boon, leaving the soil fine and easily worked – although very fluffy. It will need a few weeks to settle before planting, or you could tread it. And if you spread your organic matter on the surface of the plot after you have been over it once and then go over it again, it will mix it in thoroughly.

Forking

Areas which are in reasonably good heart benefit from being forked over with the border fork between plantings. For example, after removing the summer bedding plants in the autumn, the soil should be forked over before the spring plants are put in. The soil is simply turned over without bothering to make a trench, and broken down by hitting it with the back of the fork.

Light forking between plants to perhaps half the depth of the tines or even less leaves an attractive surface finish.

Soils which are very heavy and have been neglected can be difficult to dig with a spade. In that case digging using a digging fork may be easier – the same routine applies.

Treading

It may seem strange, having conscientiously loosened the soil by digging, to firm it again, but if left loose not only will it sink after you've planted your plants or sown seeds, but the water will drain through too quickly; the increased amount of air in the soil will also encourage it to dry out.

Soil should be trodden in an organised way, it's no good just wandering about. Start in one corner and shuffle along the edge leaving a row of heelprints in a side-by-side pattern. Then move across and make another row alongside the first until the plot is covered. This is an exhausting business, so do it in two or three stages rather than in one session if you need to.

Raking

After digging, levelling roughly and treading, you will need to rake the soil level to leave a good finish before planting or sowing seeds. The secret of effective raking is to move the rake in long flowing strides and not in short stabs. You may find it easier to bend over to achieve this, as there's a tendency to work in short stabs when standing upright. Try not to remove too many stones or you will find the whole business never-ending.

For beds and borders the level does not have to be perfect, especially as it will be altered by the soil you remove when digging out planting holes. For a lawn it's more important, and it pays to rake level as best you can after treading and then leave it until after a heavy downpour. Then, when the soil has dried out a little, rake again. If you're adding fertiliser, do so after the final raking and then rake again lightly.

Planting and aftercare

Different plants require different planting techniques.

Container-grown trees

Both ornamental and fruit trees are now most commonly sold growing in containers, which are usually large black polythene bags, sometimes semi-rigid black pots. They can be planted at any time when the ground is not bone dry, waterlogged or frozen, but spring and autumn are the best times.

Having decided on where your tree is to be planted, dig out a hole twice as wide as the pot and the same depth as the blade of your spade. Pile the soil around the hole, Fork over the bottom of the hole, then fork in a bucketful of organic matter – garden compost is ideal, or alternatively use a peat substitute product like J. Arthur Bowers Mulch and Mix. Firm it with the toe of your boot. Then mix some more compost into some of the soil from the hole.

Now stand the plant in the hole. Lay a bamboo cane across the hole and add or remove soil until the top of the compost in the container is 1in (2.5cm) below the cane. Make sure that the best side of the tree is facing in the direction you require. Remove the pot or take a sharp knife and slit the polythene from top to bottom, then slide it off, disturbing the compost as little as possible. Refill the hole around the roots with soil and compost mix until it is just above the surface of the compost; firm with your toes as you go. A slight depression should be left to collect water, and the area should then be mulched with compost.

The tree will need staking, use two 3ft (90cm) stakes knocked in on either side of the root ball, a cross-piece nailed between them and a tree tie fixed to the tree about 12in (30cm) above the ground. Finally, water in well and keep watered until well established.

Evergreens in exposed positions will benefit from a windbreak. This can consist simply of plastic windbreak netting nailed to three stakes in a V, pointing into the wind.

Bare-root trees

Some trees are still lifted from the nursery and sold with their roots bare. November is the best time to plant bare-root trees, although any time before they start to grow in spring is acceptable.

The hole for bare-root trees is prepared in the same way as that for container-grown trees. The size of the hole should be such as to leave a 9in (23cm) space around the roots. However, the guide for the final level will not be the surface of the compost in the container but the old planting level, usually the top of the wet stained portion at the base of the stem.

The tree should be orientated so that a gap in the roots through which a stake can pass is on the windward side. The tree can then be removed and a 3ft (90cm) stake can be knocked in, leaving 12in (30cm) above the final soil level. The tree can then be replaced and the hole refilled. When refilling the hole, jiggle the roots slightly to ensure that soil filters around them and that no air spaces are left. Finally, use a tree tie to secure the tree to its stake.

Container-grown shrubs

These are planted in much the same way as container-grown trees, although it's often easier to firm the soil around the root ball with the fingers rather than the toes. Small specimens may not need such thorough preparation – twice the depth of the pot is usually sufficient. Most shrubs do not need staking.

Container-grown shrubs are often planted in summer while in flower, but will then need regular watering.

Bare-root shrubs

These are rarely sold these days, but are planted in the same way as bare-root trees; they will need smaller holes and no staking.

Small plants

Small plants such as hardy perennials, rock plants, bedding plants and vegetables do not usually have individual holes prepared for them, except when they are being planted into established beds. For new beds, thorough preparation of the whole bed is sufficient.

Plants are put in with a trowel, taking out a hole just a little wider than the root ball and sufficiently deep to leave the crown of the plant at soil level. Soil is worked around the roots with the trowel or with the fingers and firmed with the fingers.

Bulbs

Bulbs are planted in beds and borders with a trowel. Plant them in clumps or irregular drifts and not in rows, except for temporary bedding schemes. Ensure that they are planted at the recommended depth; err on the deep side if in doubt. Ensure that the base of the hole is flat and that there is no gap under the bulb where water can collect. On heavy soils a handful of grit under the bulb helps prevent rotting; make the initial hole slightly deeper.

When planting bulbs in grass, a bulb planter is very useful. This tool removes a core of soil, the bulb is dropped in the hole and the core is replaced. Again, plant in drifts or clumps rather than in rows.

Hoeing

Dealing with weeds using a hoe is not something I would recommend for mature and established borders. Hoeing is ideal for crops grown in rows, like vegetables, and for new planting where there is plenty of space, but in established borders there should be little space for the hoe in the growing season, as the ground should be more or less covered in vegetation.

The first thing to check is that your hoe is sharp. Use a file if necessary to ensure that you have a good cutting edge. A good hoeing action consists of keeping the blade horizontal and moving it back and forth just under the soil surface. Do not dig it into the ground at an angle. Some weeds will be cut off, others will be pushed out of the soil. They will not need collecting up afterwards unless they are large and about to drop their seeds or have their roots still attached.

The best time for hoeing is when the soil surface is dry and the weather is sunny; weeds will then soon shrivel and die. You will also find it much less time-consuming in the long run to hoe every couple of weeks even if there seem to be very few weeds. That way, weeds never get a hold and there are only very small weeds present which can be hoed off easily.

Hand-weeding

There are a number of situations where weeds may be growing close to other plants – among seedlings, in rows of vegetables, among groups of bulbs and in the middle of clumps of perennial plants, for example. They cannot be safely hoed off, so need to be removed by hand; they can often simply be pulled out.

On rock gardens and raised beds, where there are a number of small plants and bulbs growing close together, it is impossible to use a hoe, and pulling by hand is simpler. A hand fork is a most useful tool for loosening roots prior to pulling weeds out.

Finally, in mature borders, your plants may shed seeds which come up around them; the hoe does not discriminate between these and the weeds. Hand-weeding enables you to remove the weeds and leave the special seedlings.

Spraying

The first thing to remember when it comes to spraying is that whatever material you are spraying you need to take precautions. Even organic materials can be irritating or even poisonous if treated carelessly.

So first some safety advice.

- Always, and I mean always, read the instructions on the pack before even filling the sprayer.
- Follow those instructions carefully – don't think that you know better than the manufacturer.
- Never skimp on any safety precautions recommended, and never use more concentrated chemical than is laid down – you may end up harming both yourself and your plants without curing the original problem.
- Use granular materials whenever possible, rather than liquid concentrates.
- Spray in calm conditions, preferably in the evening but not in hot sunshine. Never spray in the greenhouse in hot sun.
- Do not spray plants in the conservatory if you can possibly avoid it. Take the plants outside and then bring them back when the material has dried on the leaves.
- Never mix different chemicals together unless it is specifically suggested that this is safe.
- Wear gloves when handling liquid concentrates, and leave the top off the bottle as little as possible.
- Do not inhale vapours when spraying. A surgical mask is useful protection.
- Ensure that as much skin as possible is covered when spraying – don't wear shorts, roll down your sleeves, wear gloves.
- Keep pets and children away while spraying and until the spray has dried.
- Clean out the nozzle before filling the sprayer and adjust it to give a fine spray.
- Ensure that the whole plant is covered in spray, including as much of the underside of the foliage as possible. Do not overdo it; once the liquid has started to drip off the leaves, move on.
- Wash out the sprayer thoroughly after use.
- Store chemicals out of reach of children and where accidents cannot happen, preferably in a locked cupboard.

Watering

As our climate gets drier, watering becomes more important for both food and ornamental plants. Enriching the soil with organic matter helps it retain moisture, but there will always be times when you need to water.

It's a big mistake to worry too much about watering and to start as soon as there is a week or two without rain. For vegetables and fruit the situation is more critical, as so much of their bulk is made up of water. The problem arises if you apply a fairly modest amount of water when there are still reserves deeper in the soil. For instead of questing deeper for moisture, roots will come to the surface, attracted by the small amount you have applied, which will not have sunk in very far. And as the surface is the quickest area to dry out, the plants will then be more likely to suffer than if you had put no water on at all.

So when you water, leave the sprinkler on for an hour and a half so that it sinks in well. And don't forget that you need a licence to use a sprinkler, or indeed any hose attachment, so get one from your local water authority.

Pruning

Pruning is not the mystery it sometimes seems. There are straight-forward rules to follow which will de-mystify the whole business.

Firstly, how to make the cuts. All pruning cuts are best made just above a healthy shoot, leaf joint, leaf or bud. They should be made at a slight angle, so that any water running down the cut is not guided on to the bud or leaf joint. Try to make your cut leaving about 1/8–1/4in (3–6mm) of stem above the bud or joint; leave too much and the stem will rot, cut too close and the bud may be damaged.

Use a sharp and clean pair of secateurs. Never, ever, use a pruning knife – they can be very dangerous. For shoots thicker than about 1/2in (12mm), use long-handled pruners rather than secateurs.

Now we come to which plants to cut and when. It's mainly shrubs and climbers that need regular pruning, though some trees may need to be pruned at times. It pays to look at your shrubs and climbers every spring when they are growing well and cut out any dead shoots, any especially feeble and spindly-looking ones, any that are damaged or split, any that are rubbing and creating wounds.

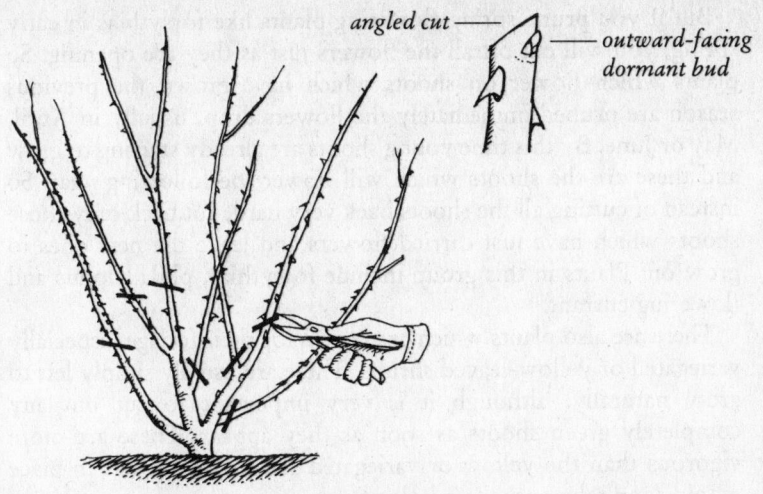

PRUNING SUMMER-FLOWERING SHRUBS
Roses and other summer-flowering shrubs such as buddleias should be
pruned by cutting back hard in spring. Cuts should be made at an angle
above an outward-facing bud.

This can be a little difficult on plants like clematis and philadelphus
with masses of twiggy growth, but I'm sure you get the idea.

The idea of pruning is not only to create a generally healthy plant
but to encourage it to give generously of the attractive features for
which you planted it. So now you need to stop and think before
pruning them more thoroughly. Most shrubs and climbers are
grown for their flowers, but different plants produce flowers on
different sorts of growth. Some roses and buddleias, for example,
flower in summer at the ends of shoots which have been growing
since spring. Others, like forsythia, flower along shoots which have
grown during the previous season.

The idea is to encourage growth which will produce flowers, and
as pruning generally encourages growth, plants like buddleias are
pruned hard in the spring, at any time from February to April, as
they start to grow. This encourages plenty of new shoots which will
grow during the spring and flower prolifically in the summer and
autumn. All the shoots that have flowered the previous year are cut
back hard, to within a few inches of the really old wood.

But if you prune spring-flowering plants like forsythias in early spring, you will cut off all the flowers just as they are opening. So plants which flower on shoots which have grown the previous season are pruned immediately the flowers drop, usually in April, May or June. By this time young shoots are already starting to grow and these are the shoots which will flower the following year. So instead of cutting all the shoots back very hard, cut back only those shoots which have just carried flowers and leave the new ones to grow on. Plants in this group include forsythias, philadelphus and flowering currant.

There are also plants which are grown for their foliage, especially variegated or yellow-leaved shrubs. These are usually simply left to grow naturally, although it is very important to cut out any completely green shoots as soon as they appear. These are more vigorous than the yellow or variegated shoots, and if left in place would soon take over the whole plant.

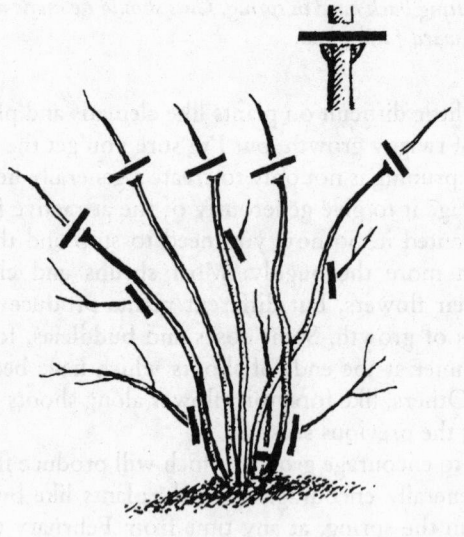

PRUNING SPRING-FLOWERING SHRUBS
Philadelphus, forsythias and other spring-flowering shrubs should have the shoots which have flowered removed when the petals fall and new shoots left for next year.

A few plants, dogwoods for example, are grown for their brightly coloured stems, which are especially attractive in winter. The aim here is to encourage as many long stems as possible, so these too are cut back hard in spring every year.

That covers 90 per cent of shrubs and climbers. Some, like clematis, are more particular, and advice on these and others with particular requirements is given in the plants section on page 165.

Compost-making

Organic matter, as you will have gathered if you've read this far, is one of the most crucial elements in successful gardening and it has to come from somewhere. The most sensible place for it to come from is the garden itself, via the compost heap.

Garden compost is simply well-rotted organic matter and is made up of almost every sort of vegetable waste from both garden and kitchen: annual weeds and the top growth of perennial weeds will make up a substantial part of the mixture, together with outer leaves and peelings from vegetables. Fallen leaves are best stacked separately to make leafmould, and although some grass mowings can go on the compost heap, they should not make up more than 25 per cent of the whole.

You can buy plastic compost bins to keep the heap together, and in a very small garden which yields little waste this would be quite adequate. However, in all but the smallest gardens a home-made timber bin constructed of reclaimed floorboards will be most useful. Timber (or brick) has useful insulation properties and can be used to make a bin of exactly the size that space allows. A bin 3 × 3ft (90 × 90cm) square and the same high is a basic minimum, 4ft (1.2m) each way is better. The size helps the heap to heat up well and this heat helps kill weed seeds and pests.

In a small garden, the flow of suitable vegetable waste for the compost heap will be slow and unpredictable. My advice is simply to fling the waste into the bin as it accumulates and then, as it nears full capacity, empty the whole thing out and re-build in the traditional way.

Start by setting a few bricks in the base to support 6in (15cm) of dry twiggy material; this will let valuable air into the heap. Then fork in 9in (23cm) of compost material and top it with a scattering of proprietary compost activator or farmyard manure. Next, add another layer of compost material, then more activator. The instructions on the pack of activator may vary slightly from this: follow them. When the bin is full, cover it with a piece of old carpet to keep excess rain out and the heat in. The compost should be ready in just a couple of months in summer. Heaps made in autumn will be ready in spring.

Feeding

Plants derive their nutrients from the soil and are fed in two ways. The soil itself can be improved so that there is a natural reservoir of plant foods constantly available. This is done by the regular application of organic material. Alternatively, neat plant foods (fertilisers) can be applied which feed the plants directly but which are gradually dissipated.

Most gardeners use a combination of the two methods. They add organic matter when preparing the soil and when planting, and apply extra every year or two by mulching (see page 79). In addition, dry fertilisers are applied annually, usually in spring.

Greedy plants like roses and many vegetables and fruits are also sometimes fed with a quick-acting dry or liquid fertiliser during the growing season to promote maximum flower production or maximum yields. Products designed for specific crops and groups of plants are available at the garden centre. (See also page 56.)

Dry fertiliser should be applied evenly and the granular formulations make this easy. Follow the recommendations – putting on extra can be harmful or wasteful. To help apply the fertiliser evenly, the area to be fed can be marked out in yard- or metre-square sections using canes and a garden line. The required amount per square yard or square metre can then be sprinkled on each square.

Propagation

Plants can be propagated in the following ways: removing rooted shoots, dividing the clumps, sowing seeds and taking cuttings. This is covered in more detail on pages 266–280.

Lawn-mowing

It sounds simple: you push the mower backwards and forwards over the lawn until it's all cut, then you put the machine away. End of story. But like most things in life, it can be done well or badly.

Safety should be the first consideration. If you have an electric mower, make sure your cable is easily long enough to reach the farthest corner of the area to be cut.

Cylinder mower

Start by cutting to one mower width all the way round the edge. Then, if your mower is electric, leave the cable coiled on the newly mown strip at the edge nearest the power source. Mow in parallel stripes from there until you get to the other side.

Wheeled rotary mower

Check to see if the mower cowling has a slight overhang to one side. If so, mow a strip all the way round the lawn with this overhang cutting the very edge of the grass. Then mow in parallel stripes.

Hover mower

One way is to mow the edges and then in rows as above. Alternatively, if you have a petrol-powered machine you can make use of the air cushion. Mow round the edge as before but then start on one side and, moving slowly backwards, swing the machine from side to side in a series of arcs until you reach the other side and the lawn is cut. This method can be less tiring, but is not suitable for electrically powered machines as there is a danger of the mower running over the cable, which is difficult to keep clear.

To look their best, lawns should be cut every week when they are growing strongly, less often in dry spells and early and late in the year. They may even need cutting in December or January in mild winters. Set the height of cut so that the lawn is not scalped, leaving bare soil. The next to lowest setting is usually right for fine lawns; leave it longer on rougher, bumpier surfaces.

Lawn-edging

Whenever you cut the grass, cut the edges too; it makes such a difference to the look of the garden. Do not use a half-moon edging tool which shaves off a sliver of soil at every cut, as by the end of the season your lawn will have shrunk dramatically. Using a pair of edging shears, stand upright with your feet side by side at right angles to the edge. The lower blade should be nearest to the lawn.

Then simply shuffle along, cutting the grass sticking out towards the border with a scissors motion, leaving the clippings where they fall. When you get back to where you started, gather the clippings together in a series of small heaps, using the hand fork as a rake, and then collect them up.

It is much easier to clip the edges if the soil edges to the lawn are vertical and cleanly cut, the soil then sloping up to the bed. You can use a spade or a half-moon edging tool to create a clean edge each spring. A board or a tight string will help you cut in a straight line.

2.   SECONDARY SKILLS

It's the details that count – the finer points and the special skills which will really make your garden a success.

Staking

Many plants – trees, perennials and annuals – need support to protect them from wind, rain, snow and their own weight.

Trees need support from a stake in their early years before their roots have grown sufficiently to do the job. Research has shown that a short but solid stake is actually far more effective in the long run than a tall one. A 3ft (90cm) stake, knocked in about half-way, with a stout tie a few inches below the top, is ideal. Choose a purpose-made tree tie which can be loosened as the trunk expands.

Perennials and annuals can be supported with a number of different materials. Brushwood and canes are the traditional choices. Brushwood (especially the traditional hazel twigs) is now difficult to buy, not easy to store and is short-lived, but it is still the most effective method and the least visible when in use. Brushwood is sometimes available through local naturalists' trusts and other local conservation groups which manage woodland.

Bamboo canes are altogether easier to use. One cane for two or three single stems of a border perennial, three around the outside for a stout plant, five or seven around a group. Although it may be easier to push in the narrow end of the canes, they will be more secure if the fat end goes in first. Where just one cane is used, single ties at different levels can be used to support up to three stems. For a group, run string round the outside and cross it and loop it between the canes to support both the outside and the insides of the group.

Steel and plastic-covered frames are now available for supporting border plants; they make a ring around the outside, and the more sophisticated versions have a mesh of crossing wires through which the stems can grow. These are very effective. A home-made version can be constructed by nailing a piece of rigid 2in (5cm) plastic mesh to the tops of four 1 × 1in (2.5 × 2.5cm) posts.

Climbing plants like runner beans and sweet peas need tall supports. The simplest system is a wigwam-like structure made of a ring of 8ft (2.4m) canes, pushed into the ground by about 2ft (60cm) with the tops tied together with twine.

If you're growing more than just a few plants, a pair of stout stakes with a wire tensed between them at top and bottom to support wide-mesh plastic netting is ideal.

Dead-heading

Almost all flowering plants will be more productive if the dying flowers are picked off as they fade. This kids the plant into thinking that it still needs to flower in order to reproduce. Very small-flowered plants like alyssum and lobelia are of course difficult to dead-head, although they can be clipped over with hand shears as long as this is not followed by a dry spell. Shrubs that produce large numbers of small flowers are impracticable to dead-head.

Larger flowers are easy to dead-head and are managed in different ways.

- Geranium flowers can be snapped off where they join the stem.
- Roses must be cut just a few leaves below the flower.
- Dahlias should be cut above the next flowering shoot lower down.
- Dwarf rhododendrons should have the flower snapped off on its short stalk.
- The dying flowers of most other plants are simply cut off above the next bud down.

Training shrubs

Most shrubs need little training. They are often pruned back by about one-third after planting to encourage bushy growth from low down on the plant, but otherwise, apart from any necessary regular pruning, they are simply left to get on with it.

Shrubs trained on walls and fences need more care. Both walls and fences should be wired to assist training (see page 88), which at its simplest will consist of choosing a number of major shoots and training them evenly into a fan shape to cover the space. A number of bamboo canes arranged against the fence in a fan shape and fixed to the wires provide support for the main branches selected to make the fan. One should be more or less upright, the others roughly in pairs on either side.

When planting, the shrub should be orientated against the fence so that the maximum number of shoots are close to the wall for tying in. After planting the shrub, the canes can be slid into position and tied in and the shoots can be tied to them. Smaller side shoots not tied to canes should be tied to wires. Any vigorous shoots growing out into the border should be cut back by half.

Training climbers

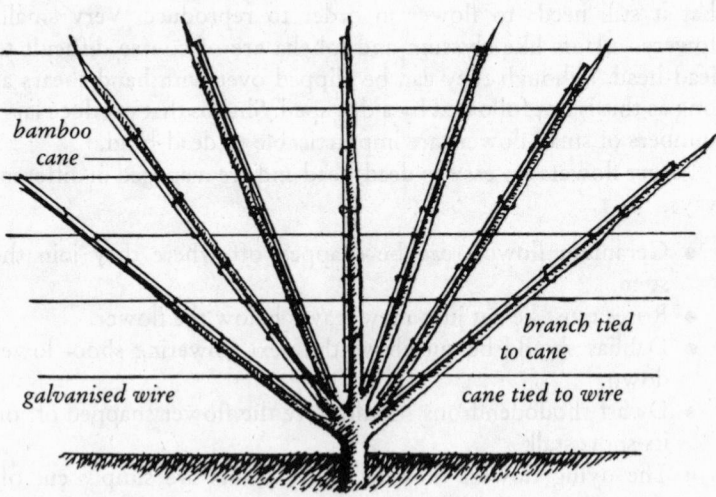

bamboo cane

branch tied to cane

galvanised wire

cane tied to wire

TRAINING WALL SHRUBS
The most convenient way to train wall shrubs is to wire the wall, tie canes to the wires and then tie branches to the canes.

Much the same procedure outlined for shrubs applies for climbers, although their shoots are often more unruly and difficult to organise. You may find it easier to fix trellis to your fence or wall. Galvanised steel pig netting is also recommended and is very effective, as this gives you far more secure points at which ties can be made.

Mulching

Mulching is a method of applying organic matter to borders by simply spreading it over the surface of the soil between the plants. The mulch helps to conserve moisture in the soil, suppresses weeds, improves the soil and provides plant foods. It is essential that weed-free materials be used, such as spent mushroom compost, composted bark or bark chips, well-rotted manure, good-quality garden compost or one of the various peat substitutes. A depth of about 2–3in (5–7.5cm) is usually about right.

The best times to apply organic mulches are in spring, when the soil is moist, or (preferably) in autumn after tidying the borders and weeding thoroughly. Try to ensure that clods of mulch do not smother young shoots.

Raised beds or rock gardens where plants requiring good drainage are grown are usually mulched with grit or fine gravel at about 1in (5cm) deep.

Removing branches

Occasionally a large branch needs to be removed from a mature shrub or tree, and there is a right way of going about it. First of all, do not attempt to remove branches from large trees yourself, as it can be very dangerous to you and your house. Call in an expert.

If possible, branches should never be cut off leaving a stump. Try to cut back to another healthy branch.

Branches which are easily accessible and over about 2in (5cm) across should be removed using the following technique.

1 Remove much of the lighter growth using loppers or secateurs to leave a more or less bare branch.
2 About 12in along the branch from where your final cut is to be made, use your saw to make a cut upwards into the branch from underneath. This cut should go about one third of the way into the branch.

3 Just a little further out along the branch, make a cut from above
to remove the branch. The aim is for the branch to break as the
second cut approaches alongside the first; the presence of the first
undercut prevents the bark tearing back towards and down the
trunk when the branch breaks, which would create a wound.

4 You will be left with a short stump which can be removed with a
cut from above and is light enough for you or a helper to hold,
preventing the bark being torn.

5 The final cut should be just a little proud from the branch to
which it is attached.

6 Paint the wound with a wound-sealing paint such as pbi Arbrex.

Preventing Problems

The sad fact is that at some time in their lives your plants are going
to be attacked by various unwelcome organisms. These may be
pests, usually insects or their relatives, although sometimes they
might be larger creatures; they may be diseases, some of which are
so microscopic that you can't even see them; or they may be weeds,
which can be invasive wild plants or even garden plants growing too
enthusiastically.

1. PREVENTIVE MEASURES

As usual, prevention is better than cure, but that's not always as
easy as we'd like. However, there are some sensible measures we
can take which can prevent a range of problems.

- Check new plants for pest and disease problems and for weeds
  in the pots before buying them. Check well-intentioned
  presents from friends, too.
- Ensure that your plants are grown in situations they like, so
  that they are not constantly weakened by their fight against an
  inhospitable site.
- Keep plants watered when they need it and do not overwater
  when they require drying off.
- Feed plants according to their requirements. Over-feeding and
  starvation can weaken them and lay them open to attack.

- Remove dead flowers, leaves and fruits which might be infected with disease or harbour pests.
- Prune correctly and at the right time of year, cutting out dead and weak wood if nothing else.

Pests

There are also some specific points to bear in mind which help prevent pest attack.

- Inspect any plants that you are buying, and more especially those you are given, to make sure that they are not harbouring pests. It's good practice to spray all new plants as soon as you acquire them, just in case.
- Encourage a wide variety of insects, like hoverflies, lacewings and ladybirds, and other garden wildlife that will help keep the pests in balance.
- Grow plants in conditions as near to ideal as possible. Vigorous healthy plants have in-built resistance.
- Choose pest-resistant varieties whenever you can.

Diseases

There are specific measures you can take to prevent infection.

- Check that plants you buy are not infected with disease. It's a wise precaution to spray them anyway.
- Deal with natural reservoirs of infection by clearing rubbish in the garden and keeping weeds down.
- Grow your plants in conditions as near as possible to those that suit them best, so that they are able to withstand attack.
- Choose disease-resistant varieties whenever possible.

Weeds

Weeds are always with us, but a great deal of weed growth can still be prevented.

- Never let weeds produce seed.
- Always clear the ground of all weeds, especially perennial types, before planting.
- Apply a weed-suppressing mulch to borders in spring and/or autumn.

2. GARDEN CHEMICALS

A well-stocked garden centre will carry a wide range of garden chemicals. Most of them you will never have to use – you may even choose to use none of them and get along very well. But especially for the busy gardener, there are products which can be helpful yet not dangerous. I dislike using chemicals, but I do use a few (ICI Rapid and pbi Supercarb, for example), as I simply do not have the time for more labour-intensive methods.

The first thing to remember, and I do not hesitate to mention this again, is to read the instructions on the pack carefully and follow them. Follow the safety advice on page 69 too. The companies that make garden chemicals have become increasingly aware of the needs of gardeners as against their own convenience, and are now packing their products in shatterproof bottles with child-resistant caps. They also give much more comprehensive instructions, and the foolproof measuring systems built into some bottles make diluting the concentrate very straightforward.

My advice is to use as few chemicals as possible, but when you do need to use them, choose the right product and do the job thoroughly.

3. ORGANIC GARDENING

When I first became interested in organic gardening I was regarded as a crank; now gardening without chemicals is eminently respectable. In short, it involves not using artificial fertilisers or other garden chemicals. Instead, the soil is fed with bulky organic matter, and the plants with organic fertilisers derived from plants and animals. Natural predators and parasites are encouraged to help deal with pest problems, along with carefully considered cultural methods and natural insecticides when such treatments are necessary. A great deal of the success of organic gardening, though, is due to encouraging a balance of nature so that pests never get out of control, and growing the plants well so that they ride out any attacks from which they may suffer.

This book emphasises the organic approach, even though much of this section has dealt with chemical solutions for those that prefer to use them.

CHAPTER FOUR

CREATING
ESSENTIAL FEATURES

The Essentials

In the end, it's the quality of the plants and the way they are arranged and grown which determines the success or failure of a garden. But before you get as far as actually planting anything, there is a lot to be organised. For however impressive the planting, if the basic structure is not right then the plants will never be seen quite at their best.

The boundaries are crucial – they define our own personal space, instantly set the style and highlight the opportunities. The patio and paths form an almost unchangeable framework and so must be considered very carefully, while in a very small garden I would urge you think about whether you really need a lawn.

1. BOUNDARIES

Fences, walls or hedges?

This is simpler than it sounds. Building a boundary wall is usually prohibitively expensive, and in most cases is ruled out for that reason. A wall is, however, the very best boundary you can have – it's permanent, it needs little maintenance, it's attractive, it shows off plants well and it gives you a real feeling of privacy and security.

A hedge is the least suitable choice, except in what you might call the larger small garden. The hedge itself will take up at least 2ft (60cm) of valuable garden space, and if you plant in front of it you will need to allow an absolute minimum of another 2ft (60cm) for access. Then there are the roots, questing for moisture and plant foods and depriving the plants in your borders. Hedges also take a few years before they reach a size sufficient to do their job.

This leaves us with fences, of which there are many types, in many materials and at many prices. They are less expensive and less solid than walls. A fence needs more maintenance and does not last as long as a hedge, but it also takes up less space than a hedge and of course you can train shrubs on it.

Choosing fence materials

Concrete

Fences constructed of concrete panels are occasionally available, but they are generally ugly and expensive, though more or less maintenance-free.

Wire

Chain-link wire fences are often provided on new estates, but are usually only 2–3ft (60–90cm) high and are intended simply to mark the boundaries. Ignore them when planning your new boundaries. Taller, 6ft (1.8m) high, chain-link fences at least keep the neighbours' dogs out (or yours in) and you can train climbers up them. But in the end they will sag and droop under the weight of growth – and they never make the solid, comforting barrier that you need in a small garden when you may be sitting just a few feet from your neighbours.

Plastic

Fences made of plastic are ugly and deteriorate surprisingly quickly. Blissfully uncommon.

Timber

The only practical choice for most people, timber fences come in a variety of styles and usually in panels in a number of standard sizes. The timber used in fences should be pressure-treated with preservative by the manufacturer to give long-lasting protection against rot, but it will still fade over the years, especially on the sunny side.

Close-boarded fencing This is made of overlapping, straight-edged vertical boards fixed to horizontal rails. It is usually the toughest type and provides the most solid barrier; it also cuts out the most noise but is the most expensive. It does not come in panels so is the most laborious to put up. Not everyone likes the vertical alignment of the boards.

Lapboard fencing This has horizontal, wavy-edged, overlapping boards in standard sized panels. It is generally solid and fairly soundproof, though the boards may eventually warp.

Woven fencing   This comes in standard panels made of even thinner boards, and rather than overlapping, these boards are woven around a number of vertical struts. This is less substantial, much less soundproof, and has small gaps through which children like to peer.

Trellis   Trellis is an open arrangement of narrow timbers making a square or diamond lattice structure, the timbers usually being about 6–9in (15–23cm) apart. This obviously provides no barrier to sight or sound but lets light through. Trellis can be usefully used in combination with other panels, especially to let light through above a solid fence. Interesting and stylish designs are now available which are especially suited to town gardens.

Fences can be made of a variety of other timbers in various forms. Bamboo fences can be very attractive in a suitable setting, the canes set closely together vertically to create the barrier. Wattle hurdles make appropriate temporary fences in rural situations, while flexible chestnut paling is the urban equivalent. Very occasionally I've even seen old railway sleepers set on end to make a fence.

Erecting timber fences

Timber fences are hung on stout posts, usually 6ft (1.8m) apart. These posts are either sunk into the ground or set in special steel post-holders. About 2ft (60cm) of the length of the post should be sunk in the ground, so if the fence is to be 6ft (1.8m) high you need 8ft (2.4m) posts. For a 6ft (1.8m) fence the post should be 4in (10cm) in diameter, for a 4ft (1.2m) fence 3in (7.5cm) posts will do.

The simplest method of burying posts is to use a post-hole borer which digs out a hole just a little wider than the post itself. The narrow space left after the post is inserted is then packed with soil. To ensure that most of the water is kept away from the post and so increase protection against rotting, it's better to dig out a hole larger and deeper than is required. Put some gravel or crushed hardcore in the bottom, set the post in at the correct height, then fill up to the top with more gravel, ramming as hard as possible as you go. (Keep this gravel weed-free.) Alternatively, after the hardcore is rammed in, fill the hole with a runny concrete mix.

Post-holders are a useful alternative. A post-holder consists of a long, steel flanged spike, with a socket at the top to take the foot of the post. This socket may be adjustable to enable you to get the post vertical. The post-holder is simply knocked into the ground with a heavy hammer, then the post is fitted in the top, adjusted until vertical and tightened well. Post-holders are impractical in rocky soil as the spike tends to be forced out of alignment as it is knocked in.

To erect a fence, first secure the help of a friend or neighbour. Next, use your garden line to mark the line of the fence. Erect the first post, checking that it is vertical by using a spirit level. Nail the first panel to the first post, making sure that it is level and getting your helper to support the other end.

You can now mark the position of the next post, swinging the panel slightly to one side to give yourself enough room to set it. The panel can then be swung back into position and nailed in place.

Continue in this way to the end of the run. If you find that the length of your boundary is not an exact multiple of the width of your panels, it's possible to dismantle the framework at the end of the last panel, saw the boarding to the appropriate length, rebuild the framework and nail it in place.

Finish by nailing weather caps on to the tops of the posts to prevent water soaking into the endgrain.

Staining fences

Most off-the-peg panels come in a pale red or orange-brown shade which becomes even paler as it weathers. But a range of coloured preservatives is now available which will colour outdoor timber to exactly the shade you prefer. This is especially effective in a tiny garden or small yard. Brightly-coloured stains are also available and can look very stylish.

Choosing walling materials

When choosing materials for garden walls you should always consider the walls of the house and any outbuildings – the walls don't necessarily have to be exactly the same but they must be sympathetic in colour and style. Stone walls with a stone house, brick walls with a brick house – these are the ideals, but it's not always possible to match materials in this way. Matching the age (old brick walls with an old stone house) is a reasonable compromise; walls made of sparkling new bricks butting up to an old stone house are less successful.

If it's not possible, or if you doubt your capacity, to build a wall of the appropriate materials to the full height you require, a valid compromise is to build it to 3 or 4ft (0.9–1.2m) only and top it with a simple square pattern trellis.

When building a wall, always set in eye bolts for taking wires as you build (see below).

Building walls

Do not attempt to build anything more than a low dividing or retaining wall unless you have plenty of experience and have developed your skill; there's nothing worse than spending all your spare weekends for months building a wall that turns out uneven, ugly and in constant danger of falling down.

Footings

For low walls up to 3ft (90cm) in height, your footings need to be 4in (10cm) wider than the wall on each side and 4in (10cm) deep. Use a mixture of 4 parts aggregate, 2 parts sharp sand and 1 part cement.

Mark out the line of your wall using your garden line, allowing for the width of the footings. Do not attempt any fancy curves. Dig out a trench of the exact size to accommodate the footings, aiming for a flat bottom and vertical sides so that it forms a mould for the concrete. Ram the soil firm, using a 14lb hammer. Tip the concrete mix in to the right depth and smooth off level using a piece of wood; check the level with a spirit level. Cover with polythene and leave for a week to set.

Building the wall

As this book is about gardening rather than building, I suggest you consult one which describes the process in more detail (for example, *Outdoor Projects* by Mike Trier, published by David & Charles). Here I will only outline the process. And again, don't be too ambitious.

Decide on your bonding pattern, using at least a one quarter brick overlap. Then lay out a row of unmortared bricks with ⅜in (10mm) gaps to check how the bricks fit into the required length. Now lay a few bricks at each end of the site; mortar joints should be ⅜in (10mm) thick. The mortar is made of 3 parts soft sand to 1 part cement. Use these first bricks as anchors for a line to provide a level for the rest of the row. Finish the first row, removing any excess mortar from the facing in case it stains the finish. Build up the remaining courses, moving the line as you go and checking that the wall is absolutely vertical.

When you've reached the final height of the brickwork, lay a coping of bricks on edge, tiles, slates or purpose-made coping stones to keep out the water.

If you're building a pair of walls to give a planting space in between, leave the mortar out of every other vertical joint in the second course of bricks; this allows water to drain away.

Wiring fences and walls

If you intend to grow climbers and wall shrubs on walls and fences – and I insist you should – they will need support. With trellis, it's easy, and you simply tie your plants to the struts. But other fences and walls need to be provided with a means of securing the plants.

For walls, one of the simplest methods is to cover the wall with pig netting. This is a stout, large-mesh wire netting which can be fixed to cover the entire wall surface. Drill holes in the wall every 12in (30cm) along the top line of the netting, insert plugs, and screw in some stout hooks or eyes to which the mesh can be fixed. Do the same at the sides, along the middle and at the bottom. It's a tedious business but worth it.

For fences and walls, a simpler method is to use wires.

Fences

3in (7.5cm) steel eye screws are screwed into the end posts at 12in (30cm) intervals, starting at 12in (30cm) above ground. Smaller rings are screwed into the other posts and the central strut of each panel. Straining bolts are then inserted into the rings in the end posts with the eyes facing along the fence. Galvanised wire is twisted thoroughly on to one eye, threaded through the rings at the end of the fence, then tied to the last bolt. The nuts are then tightened at both ends to tension the wire.

Walls

In new walls, eye bolts can be set in the wall during building at the same heights as for fences and every 3ft (90cm) along the length. In existing walls, holes must be drilled and plugged before fitting rings and wire as above.

Once the wires are in place, canes can be tied to them for fan training shrubs in a carefully controlled way, or shoots can simply be tied to the wires as necessary. For training techniques, see pages 78 and 343.

Choosing hedging plants

Even if your garden is large enough to cope with hedges it still pays to choose your hedging plants carefully. The last thing you want is to be forced into cutting a hedge all the time when you have more important things to do.

Some selections of hedges for different purposes can be found on page 250. Leyland's cypress is a foolish choice for a small garden unless you love hedge trimming and never fall ill, for it grows very quickly and needs a lot of attention to keep it from getting out of hand. It can grow up to 3ft (90cm) in a year, so be warned! Privet is also a mistake, for although if looked after it makes a neat hedge, its roots are shallow, widely spreading, greedy and thirsty and plants growing nearby suffer greatly. If in doubt go for yew, unless you plan to move in a year or two.

Planting hedges

The technique for planting a hedge is just the same as for planting a single shrub (see page 67), except that the whole process is linear. It's important to remember that your hedge will be in place for many years and you will be constantly stimulating its growth by pruning, so the site needs good preparation.

You are going to dig a trench 12in (30cm) wide, so mark the edge on the neighbour's side with your garden line. Dig out the trench as deep as your spade and pile the soil along your side. Spread organic matter in the bottom of the trench 2–3in (5–7.5cm) deep and fork it in. Mix as much again with the soil you have excavated, then put the whole lot back and tread it well. Leave the surface of your trench 1–2in (2.5–5cm) below the level of the adjoining border; spread the surplus soil on the border.

Take up the line and stretch it along the middle of the prepared area. Using your measuring rod, set out your hedging plants at the spacing specified on page 196. Plant them with a spade or a trowel according to their size. The depression along the length of the trench allows you to water them in easily.

Initial hedge training and care

Most hedging plants are best cut back by half immediately after planting, to encourage them to bush out and make a dense hedge. The following year they should be cut back by a third, and again every year until their final height is reached. Make sure they are well watered, especially in their first summer.

Maintaining hedges

Hedges are best cut so as to leave their profile narrower at the top than at the base. A flat top is easier to cut evenly than a rounded one. Cut them regularly as recommended; if they are left uncut for too long they become thin, sparse and ineffective.

For descriptions of hedging plants, see page 196.

2. PATHS AND DRIVEWAYS

After the boundaries, getting the patio and the paths right should be your next priority. The ability to keep your feet dry and mud-free from early on is a great incentive to use the garden, even in winter, and makes the addition of winter plants all the more valid. Paths do not necessarily have to be permanent. You can use temporary materials for temporary paths and after a year or two you can make adjustments.

Siting paths and drives

You are unlikely to have a choice about the route of the drive to a garage or parking area. But you can make a drive seem less obtrusive in a relatively small front garden by making the whole area a gravel garden. Set solid foundations under the area which the car is to use – perhaps with some large stones inset along the edge for guidance – and when the car is not there, the drive will simply look like an open area in the gravel garden.

Paths need to be both functional and decorative. The overall layout will dictate the line of the paths, but even in the smallest garden it pays to avoid dead-end paths – if you can walk round in a loop rather than just down the path and then back again, it makes even going to the dustbin interesting.

In a very small garden or yard, a single loop of path with borders at the sides and grass, gravel or more planting in the centre is simple and effective. The bins, washing whirly, barbecue and shed can all be set just off the path so that the same path gives access to them all. The central area could even be paved for the patio, so that in effect the path runs round the margin of, and merges with the patio. The path could be picked out in a different but complementary material.

Straight paths are awkward, unless you wish to use them to distort the perspective. A straight path which narrows slightly towards the far end will make a small garden look longer, but a long straight path parallel to a boundary can look dull unless the whole design of the garden is intentionally formal. Edged with low box hedging, a straight path can make a stylish feature, but don't bisect a small garden with a central path – run it closer to one side. Individual stones set in grass look old-fashioned and are fiddly to maintain.

Choosing materials

Choosing the right material for paths and patios is probably more important than choosing sympathetic walling or fencing, for paths will not eventually be covered with plants. Your choice will be governed not only by the material used in your walls but also by the size of garden, price, ease of laying and the importance of permanence.

Brick

In the smallest of gardens, brick is one of the best choices. The scale is right, and bricks weather to give such an attractive finish. Bricks can be mystifying in their variety, but whatever type you choose they must be frost-resistant, otherwise the surface will break up after a frosty winter. Second-hand stocks give an instantly mature look, and brick pavers come in variety of muted colours.

Concrete paving blocks

Similar in scale to bricks but, as well as the usual rectangles, they come in a variety of more angular shapes. The colour range is less wide and the individual shades and colours are more uniform. Concrete pavers are ideal in association with new houses.

Stone slabs

These are mellow and very elegant, but are also very expensive, and come in large sizes which can be heavy and difficult to handle. But they are perfect for larger areas and alongside stone houses.

Reconstituted stone slabs

These can be surprisingly effective, especially as some actually contain a large proportion of ground stone. The finish of many resembles riven stone, and as they come in more manageable sizes and at a more manageable price they are deservedly popular. (If you consider laying a chequerboard of old-fashioned pink and yellow slabs this book will jump up and bite you.)

Setts

Small square setts are very attractive but expensive and fiddly to lay. Prefabricated slabs made up of a series of 'setts' are now available in various patterns and are laid just like slabs, to give a sett-like finish which is only an inch deep.

Cobbles

Cobbles (or dogs' testicles as they are known in the landscape trade) are useful as edging or as a boundary between a path or patio and an area where you wish to discourage people from walking. They are very uncomfortable to walk on.

Concrete

Straightforward concrete laid on site to form a pad is inelegant as a final surface and should be avoided, but such pads are often necessary under buildings or under drives which will be taking heavy loads.

Gravel

This is a very useful and inexpensive surfacing. It is not suitable for patios but is ideal for informal paths and for small gardens, where paths can merge into beds which can also be gravelled to keep down weeds.

Bark chips

You can use bark chips in a similar way to gravel, and they are especially good as paths in shady areas.

Timber

This is becoming more popular as a surfacing material – but more among landscape designers than among gardeners, I suspect. Rounds cut from trunks make interesting paths where the load is only light and occasional, and can also be used for surfacing wider areas that take little load. Fill in between with gravel or bark. Decking made from timber planking looks good but can be slippery when wet and needs careful construction. It looks especially good in small areas and helps create harmony in a garden with timber fences.

Grass

Finally there's grass, which makes a very attractive but relatively high-maintenance path. While good for sunbathing, it is too soft to support chairs without their legs sinking in and tipping out their occupants.

By mixing materials thoughtfully you can create some very interesting effects, and also deal imaginatively with the transition from one area to another. Stone and brick, stone and gravel, brick and gravel, two different coloured bricks, timber and bark – all look good together if the colours are chosen well.

Preparing sites

The way in which a site is prepared before the surfacing is laid depends partly on the eventual surface but rather more on the sort of traffic it's going to carry – obviously an occasionally used path in the back of a border needs less in the way of foundations than a drive which will be taking the weight of a car.

Occasional path

An occasionally used path made of brick or concrete pavers or of rough stone can be laid on well-compacted soil, but the addition of 1in (2.5cm) of sand will help bedding in.

Normal footpaths

Footpaths in brick, concrete pavers or small slabs can be laid on compacted soil plus 1in (2.5cm) of sand, but paths taking regular heavy loads, full wheelbarrows for example, are best laid on a sub-base of 3in (7.5cm) of compacted hardcore topped with 2in (5cm) of sharp sand.

Patios

3in (7.5cm) of hardcore on compacted soil plus 2in (5cm) of sharp sand will give a solid base to support regular use.

Drives

The extra stress caused by the regular use and extra weight of the family car calls for an even more solid construction. Start with 6in (15cm) of compacted hardcore on a firm soil base; ensure that all crevices are filled with dry sand. Next lay 2in (5cm) of sharp sand and then your brick or slab surface.

It always pays to err on the side of extra stability, and for drives, 4in (10cm) of hardcore then 2in (5cm) of concrete topped with slabs is probably more reliable, although if bricks or pavers are laid well and vibrated into place thoroughly they will certainly be strong enough.

Laying paths and drives in various materials

Brick

For paths which don't have to take the weight of a car, make sure the site is level and excavated to a depth of 5in (12.5cm), plus the thickness of the bricks, after ramming firm. Edges which don't abut walls or another solid vertical surface need edging to keep the bricks in place. Use 1in (2.5cm) thick softwood planks held in place from the outside by 2 × 2in (5 × 5cm) posts knocked in well below the eventual finished level.

Start by putting in 3in (7.5cm) of hardcore, roughly levelled and well rammed down. Fill any crevices with sand, then spread 2in (5cm) of dry sharp sand and level it off neatly with a plank. Decide on the basic pattern, then start to lay the bricks, working from a board – never stand on the sand. Don't worry about filling odd angles as you go along – finish laying the whole bricks and then fill the odd spaces with pieces of brick, cut using a bolster and hammer. The bricks should end up about ⅜in (10mm) above the final level. When you've finished, use a hired plate vibrator to work the bricks down firm, then spread some sharp sand over the surface and brush it in. Go over it all with the vibrator to settle the sand in the cracks.

For drives which will carry the car, use 6in (15cm) of hardcore and 2in (5cm) of sharp sand. For extra stability brush in a dry mortar mix of 3 parts sand to 1 part of cement.

Concrete blocks

Concrete pavers come not only in the usual rectangular format but also in a variety of more angular shapes. The range of colours is more limited. They are laid in just the same way as bricks.

Stone and concrete slabs

These too are laid in just the same way as bricks, but for extra support they can be set on five spots of mortar rather than simply laid on sand. Use a fist-sized dollop of mortar (1 part cement to 4 parts sand) in each corner and one in the middle. For drives which will have to take the weight of a car – or heavier – lay a 2in (5cm) thickness of concrete over the whole area.

Setts

These are bedded in sand in the same way as bricks, but make sure you allow for the extra depth when calculating the depth of your excavations.

Cobbles

These can be laid loose but are better laid in a mortar mix. Start with 3in of compacted hardcore, then add 2in (5cm) of dry concrete mix. Set the cobbles packed closely together in the dry mix with about half the cobble buried. Finally, lightly sprinkle the whole area with a spray of water to harden the concrete and wash the concrete off the pebbles.

Gravel

A good base is needed to prevent the cars churning up the gravel every time they use the drive. Start with 4in (10cm) of rammed hardcore, then 2in (5cm) of coarse gravel mixed with sand. Roll this flat, then top with ¾in (2cm) of pea gravel raked level and rolled in. It's essential to provide an edging of brick or boards where there is no existing solid boundary, otherwise the gravel will creep. For paths taking much lighter loads, a 1in (2.5cm) layer of gravel on compacted soil retained by a firm edging is enough.

Bark

Bark can be laid in the same way as gravel, although a greater depth, say 2in (5cm), is usually advisable.

Wood

Logs should be cut into rounds about 6in (15cm) deep to give good stability. Treat them all thoroughly with a timber preservative and excavate the area to a depth of 8in (20cm). Put 2in (5cm) of aggregate in the base and firm it well. Place the logs in position, screwing them firmly into the aggregate, then fill up the gaps with more aggregate, topping with a couple of inches of gravel or bark if you prefer. Alternatively, simply fill the spaces with bark chips.

Timber decking

Treated hardwood planks make an attractive, long-lasting and natural surface, although laying them involves a great deal more than simply nailing planks to battens. Brick piers are required to support a framework of joists, and the planks are then nailed to the joists in a diagonal or right-angle pattern.

Decking is a convenient way of creating a level sitting area on a sloping or very uneven site. It looks good with water, requires only occasional maintenance and is a soft and natural way of linking house and garden. But it must be solidly built and can become slippery, especially after rain and in shady situations. It pays to consult a joiner while still at the planning stage.

Squares of treated timber decking can be bought at some garden centres and DIY stores. These are fitted together like paving stones and are useful on small areas. Consult the manufacturer's literature for details of the necessary preparation and support.

With any decking it is wise to ensure that all weeds are killed in the soil before you start work or they will surely appear through even the smallest cracks.

Grass

See 'The Lawn' (page 99).

Mixing materials

The big problem with mixing materials, especially when mixing different slabs and bricks, is the variation in thickness. The best approach is to prepare your base for the thickest materials and then add extra, firmed sand to support the thinner ones.

3. PATIOS

The patio is a place to sit and relax, to eat and to have parties. In a small garden there is not always a great deal of choice as to its siting, but perhaps the time when you will use it most and the uses to which you will put it should dictate its position. If you like to relax outside after work, then a west-facing site will give you the best light and warmth at that time of day. Bear this in mind when planting to the west of the patio site.

If you use the patio mainly at weekends for lunching, maybe with friends, then it is important that it should be south-facing. If the back of the house faces south or west, then this is the obvious place for it. If you need to site it farther down the garden, try to choose an area as near the house as possible, or build in one or two spots where you can fit a chair or two so that if you have ten minutes with the paper you can just nip out of the door.

Materials

Like all 'hard' materials they should harmonise with the house, the garden and other surfaces. Gravel and bark are not suitable, as they are simply not firm enough to take chairs and tables. Bricks, concrete pavers, stone or the more stylish concrete slabs are ideal.

Preparing the site and laying the patio

This is no different from those techniques discussed under laying paths (see pages 93–7).

4.   CONCRETE

Wide stretches of concrete in the garden look so ghastly that I'm almost inclined to refuse to explain how to lay them. However, you will need the skill in order to build a base for your greenhouse or conservatory, or maybe for a base for a drive – *not* to build a path or patio, though.

First decide exactly the area where your concrete is to be laid. If you are building a base for a greenhouse or conservatory this is usually a simple rectangle. Mark out the area with four individual lines pegged 12in (30cm) outside the rectangle, the string crossing to mark the corners. Check that the rectangle is 'square' by measuring the diagonals – they should be equal.

Remove the lines (leave the pegs in place) and excavate the area, adding an extra 6in (15cm) on all sides. For a greenhouse base you will be laying 3in of hardcore and 3in (7.5cm) of concrete, so you will need to excavate to a depth of about 6in (15cm) below your eventual finished height. Level the bottom of your excavation using a board, and ram it or use a heavy roller to firm it well.

Your concrete will need support from timber shuttering while it's drying, so you need to erect a framework of timber within your excavation. Replace the lines and use 1in (2.5cm) softwood planks set on edge (old floorboards are just right) and held in place by 2 × 2in (5 × 5cm) stakes, using one to every 3ft (90cm) of board. The top edge of the board and the top of the stakes must correspond exactly to your final desired level, so spend a little time getting the level right.

This is the time when you have to think about the fall – the slight slope on the concrete to allow water to run off. A fall of about 1in (2.5cm) in 6ft (1.8m) is suitable for patios and greenhouse bases, but make sure your fall runs away from other buildings, and think at this stage about which way your guttering will run and where your drain or rain-barrel will be placed.

When the boards are in place, tip in about 3in (7.5cm) of hardcore and ram it down well so that it is compacted at 3in (7.5cm). Remove any especially large lumps and also any soft plaster and the like.

If conditions are frosty, leave the actual concreting until the weather warms up. Your concrete is best mixed in a hired mixer – electric models are very useful. Tip it into a barrow and push it along planks to your prepared site. Ensure that the plank is well supported as it passes over your shuttering, otherwise the weight of the barrow on the edge of the shuttering will lower its level and ruin your careful planning.

Start to fill with concrete in one corner and work across the site, eventually raking level and leaving the concrete about ¾in (2cm) above the shuttering. Now take a long plank, 2in (5cm) thick and longer than the width of your site, and, resting it on edge, tamp down the concrete to the level of the shuttering sides. Fill in any hollows and re-tamp. Then borrow a neighbour, and using a sawing action and with the plank resting on the shuttering, work across the site sawing off surplus concrete.

Cover your work with a sheet of polythene, weighted down at the edges with bricks, and leave it for a week before removing the shuttering and starting to erect your building.

5. THE LAWN

Why have a lawn in a small garden? If you like the look of a sheet of grass to offset plants that's fine, but remember this – the lawn is likely to get a lot of wear and so be difficult to keep looking good. In a small garden, where the lawn is before your eyes all the time, it really does need to look impressive. Mowing a small area is fiddly and you need a decent lawn-mower to do a good job – plus somewhere to keep it, and probably a power point.

So in general I'm very much against making a lawn in a very small garden, even if it's not going to get a great deal of wear. And perhaps the main reason is that if you take up a substantial area with grass there will be much less room for interesting plants.

In some situations, however, a lawn can be very effective in providing a setting for plants. It can provide space for restrained games and for relaxing, and it will certainly create a generally verdant atmosphere.

Turf or seed?

There are two ways of establishing a lawn – you can sow seed or you can buy grass 'ready grown' as turf.

Turf   is more expensive;
         gives a green finish straight away;
         can be walked on soon after laying;
         gives a guaranteed even finish if laid well.

Seed   is cheaper;
         needs more care to create an even finish;
         is available in a wider variety of types for different situations;
         cannot be walked on for many months;
         needs careful looking after in the early stages.

In a small garden, where of course you won't need all that much, my advice is always to go for turf if you can afford it. But don't just buy turf on spec from an advertisement in the local paper. Buy specially grown, cultivated turf such as Rolawn, which is raised specifically for gardens from selected seed and should be weed-free. It will be absolutely even in thickness, so if you have prepared a level surface, your lawn will end up level. Turf bought through your local paper may well be stripped from fields, full of coarse grasses and weeds, and may not be evenly cut.

If you grow your lawn from seed, you need the time to prepare well and look after the lawn carefully in its early stages.

Preparation

The preparation for your lawn is much the same whether you are going to use turf or seed. Fork over the area to the depth of a digging fork, then spread 2–3in (5–7.5cm) of organic matter over the surface and fork it in. If the soil is heavy and sticky, 1–2in (2.5–5cm) of grit forked in would also be helpful. It's best to do this preparation before planting borders, as any spare soil can be spread there.

After forking, the whole area needs treading. If it's not firmed well it will only sink after the lawn is down and, what's more, will probably sink unevenly. Now rake level carefully, removing any stones or lumps of organic matter. If you find that the level is rather uneven, rake soil from the heights to the hollows but then tread the refilled hollows before raking level again.

The next job is to spread a pre-sowing fertiliser as recommended on the pack and to rake it in evenly. This will stimulate root growth and give seed or turf a good start.

Ideally it pays to prepare the soil and rake level some weeks before you apply the fertiliser and sow the seed. Any weeds then have a chance to germinate and can be hoed off or weed-killed and so cause much less trouble later.

Sowing seed

Grass seed can be sown in spring or autumn. In the autumn you have fallen leaves to contend with, and these can smother young seedlings. In spring you have the risk of a dry spell when the grass seedlings are still young, and that means you must water them. I favour September, if only because there are so many other things to do in the spring. If you find that you have to sow when the soil is dry, water well, using a sprinkler, after preparation and about a week before you intend to sow.

Grass seed comes in mixtures, each for a different use and each blend being specially formulated from a variety of grasses for an individual situation or purpose. So you will find hard-wearing mixtures, mixtures for shade, fine-leaved mixtures for the most elegant lawns, and so on. Choose the mixture that suits your purpose.

When you come to sow your grass seed, you will need a number of 4ft (1.2m) or 6ft (1.8m) canes, as well as your measuring rod, a paper cup, a felt-tip pen and the kitchen scales. The pack will tell you the amount of seed to put on each square yard of soil. Weigh this amount out on the scales and tip it into your paper cup. Shake it so that the surface of the seed is level, then mark the level it reaches on the inside of the cup with the felt-tip pen.

Next, lay long canes end to end down one side of the area to be sown, and lay another row parallel, a yard away. (You can use your garden line for this if you don't have enough canes.) Finally, use 4ft canes to mark off your yard-wide strip into square yards.

To sow the correct amount of seed, simply use one cup filled up to your marked level for each square yard. Simple. (Of course you can do the whole thing in metric if you prefer.) To help ensure an even coverage of each square, sprinkle about half the seed over the square, working from side to side, then go over the same area again, working from top to bottom. When the whole plot is done, remove the string and canes and rake gently to mix the seed into the surface of the soil.

Birds can be a big problem on newly sown lawns – they not only eat the seed but also take dust baths in the fine soil. This is best prevented by covering the area with fine-mesh plastic netting, simply laid on the soil and secured with a few stones around the edge.

If the soil dries out after sowing you may need to water – use a fine sprinkler and give it a good soak.

Caring for newly sown lawns

In a couple of weeks a green haze will start to appear and will get greener and greener; weeds will probably start to appear too. Remove the plastic netting when the grass is about 1in (2.5cm) high, and when it's about 2in (5cm) high it can be cut for the first time. Use a cylinder or a wheeled rotary mower if you can (borrow one if necessary), and collect the mowings in the grass-box. Cut to about 1in (2.5cm) in height.

For autumn-sown lawns this may be the last cut of the year, but spring-sown lawns should then be cut every week or ten days, lowering the height of the cut to about ½in (12mm) by July.

It's important to deal with weeds as early as possible, but if weed-killers are used when the grass is still young they may damage it. Annual weeds will be killed by mowing, isolated perennial weeds can be carefully dug out by hand while still small. But you may need to use a weed-killer such as ICI Verdone 2 if your weed problem is a bad one. You can use this treatment from six months onwards. In the meantime, use the Spot Weeder aerosol formulation.

Try to keep off the lawn for at least three months, except when mowing, and preferably for longer.

Laying turf

Turf can be laid at any time of year when the soil is not parched, frozen or waterlogged. It follows that spring and autumn are the best times.

Like grass seed, specially grown turf comes in a number of grades for different purposes, though there is probably less variety than is available as seed. Your turf will be delivered in rectangular pieces, which are usually rolled up for easier carrying. Turf from meadows is usually 3 × 1ft (90 × 30cm); specially grown turf usually comes in larger pieces. Stack it in a shady place and spray it over with water if you are not able to lay it at once.

When you come to lay turf you will need a stout plank, a rake, an old kitchen knife and some used but not lumpy sowing or potting compost. Start by unrolling turves end to end around the edge of the area to be turfed. Use an old kitchen knife to cut the ends to fit and when you go round corners. Tap them into place using the flat of the rake.

Now place your board along the edging row of turf and work from it without treading on either the newly laid turves or the prepared soil. The board helps spread your weight. Starting in one corner, unroll more turves across the plot from one side to the other in a straight line. Cut the ends of the turves to fit accurately, but do not attempt to bend them to match any curves in the parallel edge – just leave some narrow gaps for the time being.

When the first row is done, move the board across, cut a turf in half and lay that at the start of the next row and then continue with full-sized turves as before. The purpose of starting with a half-turf is to ensure that the joins between turves do not coincide. Continue in this way across the plot. You will probably be left with a long, fairly narrow gap at each end, some spare turves and quite a few offcuts. Use these to fill the gaps, but don't make a patchwork of small bits, try to use the largest possible pieces, as large pieces are less likely to move about.

Clear away any mess, then sprinkle the old compost lightly over the whole area – not more than half a bucketful to the square yard. Using the back of the rake, work it into the grass, paying special attention to the joins between the turves. Finally water well, using a lawn sprinkler.

Caring for newly laid turf

Your newly turfed lawn will probably need mowing in a couple of weeks. Again, use a cylinder or wheeled rotary mower with a grass-box, and cut it to about 1in (2.5cm). If the turf has been laid in

spring it may need watering regularly until the roots have pene-
trated well. You will be able to use the lawn in a couple of months.

Long-term care routine

Once established, lawns still need regular attention – and not just
from the lawn-mower. It's very disheartening to put all that work
into creating a well-prepared, level and weed-free site if the lawn
deteriorates once it's in use.

Mowing

Regular mowing is essential if you want a neat, traditional lawn
with fine grass and stripes to set off you borders. Ideally I would
suggest mowing once a week when the lawn is growing. This may
seem arduous, but you will find that the less there is to cut off, the
less time it takes. To get the stripes you will need a cylinder mower
or a wheeled rotary mower with a rear roller. (For more on
mowing, see pages 74–5.)

Edging

Every time you cut the lawn you should cut the edges with a pair of
edging shears to give a really neat finish. Tatty edges let a garden
down badly. (See pages 75–6.)

Feeding

Not many people think about feeding their lawn – the last thing that
they want to do is to make it grow. But it's not that simple. If you
feed your lawn in spring using a feed specially formulated for that
time of year, the transformation will amaze you. You'll suddenly
realise that it wasn't green at all but a curious yellowish shade. The
different brands vary in their staying power: some last all season,
some just a few weeks, so you may need to treat the lawn more than
once.

It's important not to use the spring feed too late in the season.
Change to an autumn feed which stimulates root growth and sets
the lawn up for the winter.

Lawn feeds are available in liquid formulations to be applied
using a watering can, or as dry powders to be applied by hand or
using a specially designed spreader.

The liquid is more difficult to apply evenly – and if you miss a bit you'll have a yellow patch among the lush green. But liquids are preferable if you have pets; they dry quickly and there will be no chance of pets licking up the fertiliser or getting it on their paws. Not that lawn feeds are actually harmful, but it's best to play safe.

Weeds and moss

Weeds in a small lawn are especially disfiguring but are also particularly easy to deal with. There are a number of products like Fisons Evergreen Extra which combine a spring and summer lawn feed with a weed-killer, and treatments of this type are especially effective. The feed stimulates the grass to grow into the gaps left by the dead weeds.

Lawn weed-killers are available in liquid or dry formulations but must be kept off plants in the beds and borders, as they will kill these too. If you decide to use a liquid one, buy an extra watering can, label it, and keep it just for weed-killers. After all, you don't want to risk watering weed-killer onto any prize plants.

On a small lawn, however, these weed-killing treatments are not always necessary. Rosette weeds like daisies and dandelions can often be removed simply by cutting the roots with an old knife. And there are aerosols like ICI Verdone 2 Spot Weeder (ozone friendly, of course), which can be used to squirt a dab of foam containing a lawn weed-killer on to isolated weeds.

Moss can be more of a problem. It's not difficult to kill moss, but unless you deal with the reasons for its presence it will keep coming back. Many lawn weed-killers also contain a moss-killer, and specific moss-killers are also available. These are very effective and kill moss quickly. Murphy Tumblemoss also prevents moss growth for the rest of the season.

Moss is usually caused by shade or poor drainage, or both – these conditions are not only good for moss but bad for grass. In small gardens which are unavoidably shaded, the answer is usually to dig up the lawn and lay a hard surface. You can prepare for new lawns on badly drained sites by forking in grit. But it's more difficult to deal with moss in an established lawn that you wish to keep and which is unavoidably shaded. Improving the drainage is usually the only answer.

Drainage and aeration

It's a straightforward but arduous business to improve lawn drainage once the lawn is down; it's just as well we're limiting the discussion to small gardens. In autumn or spring, using a digging fork, make holes to about half the depth of the prongs all over the lawn; each set of holes should be about 6in (15cm) apart. Then spread some sharp sand over the surface and work it into the holes, using a stiff broom or the back of a garden rake. Keep this up until the holes are full of sand. These drainage holes will help take the water away from the soil surface quickly.

Another important task which will help discourage moss and also keep the grass growing vigorously is to rake out all the dead stems (thatch). In old lawns you will often find that the green shoots are actually growing on top of a 1in (2.5cm) layer of thatch. You can use a wire rake but it's very hard work, so I recommend hiring a mains electric Black & Decker Lawn Raker, which will do a wonderful job. The only problem will be how to get rid of all the debris – and there will probably be a lot. The compost heap is the answer.

Repairs

No matter how well you look after your lawn, you may sometimes need to do repairs. A patch may sink, the barbecue may fall over and cover it in hot charcoal or, which is most likely, a plant in the border will spill out and smother the grass at the edge.

Whatever the problem, you start repairing all patches within the main lawn area in the same way. Make an H-shaped cut about 2in (5cm) deep in the lawn, using the spade. The cross-piece of the H should run across the middle of the problem area. Slide the tip of the spade under the grass, starting at the central bar of the H. Working along between the parallel sides of the H, cut under the grass leaving about 1in (2.5cm) of soil and roots attached. When you have undercut to the ends of the H, the grass can be rolled back. Do the same at the other end.

If the patch was too high, scrape away some soil and simply roll the grass back again, firming it gently. If the patch was too low, build the soil up to the right height with some old potting compost. If the grass in this area is so badly damaged that it needs replacing, use the spade to cut across between the ends of the arms of the H and simply remove the old grass. Then top up with soil and sow a little grass seed.

Worn, bare or wavy edges can also be repaired. Using the spade, cut out a rectangular shape taking in the damaged edge and any other damaged area plus 2–3in (5–7.5cm) of good lawn. Undercut it from the edge and lift it out on to a hard surface. If it is too big to lift out in one go, cut it into two or three pieces. Cut off the bare and worn pieces and trim to a straight line. Replace this good piece at the edge of the lawn and line it up with the existing edge. You will then be left with a space behind, which you can fill with old potting compost and sow with grass seed.

6. BEDS AND BORDERS

This is what gardens are all about. It's very nice to have patios for barbecues and lawns to relax on, but it's the plants that really count.

First of all, perhaps we ought to decide the difference between a bed and a border. Any planting area entirely surrounded by grass, paving or path is a bed. Any long, wide planting area backed by a wall, fence, hedge or path is a border. But a small area tucked in backing on to a wall and surrounded by paving may well be called a bed, and a long narrow area alongside a straight path may be called a border. Hmmm.

Siting

The positioning of beds and borders is fundamental to the design of the garden, and while I am not going to show you a range of garden designs with borders used in different ways, here are a few pointers:

- Be more cautious about making planting areas too small than too large.
- Try to ensure that all walls and fences have planting areas in front of them.
- Avoid long straight borders parallel to boundaries unless you can raise them (see page 113) or they are part of a consciously formal plan.
- Beds and borders in a mixture of formal and informal shapes can jar. Think carefully before mixing them.
- Don't make them all the same shape and size.

Guidelines

It's a good idea to think about what is going to be planted in your beds as you decide where to site them and how big they are to be. If you like grey and silver foliage plants, think about making a big planting area, or two smaller ones, in the site they prefer – facing south. If you want one area for temporary bedding and like the formal approach, you should consider a formal bed – rectangular or circular. Do you prefer mixed borders with shrubs, climbers, perennials, bulbs and annuals, or do you take a more traditional approach and like to keep hardy herbaceous perennials all together?

Here is my general advice.

- Make much, but not all, of the planting mixed, but make provision for at least one area devoted to a narrower group.
- Give most beds and borders themes. This not only gives them character but helps you plan what you're going to plant. Examples of broad themes might be: spring flowers, winter colour, foliage plants, seasonal bedding, cottage garden plants, alpines. Examples of narrower themes might be: grey foliage, white flowers, primroses and snowdrops, old-fashioned roses.
- Don't be restricted by your soil. In a small garden, making raised beds for different planting mixtures is not difficult.
- Always make provision for temporary plantings of annuals and spring bedding either in containers, in gaps in mixed borders or in beds of their own.
- All guidelines are there to be adapted to suit your own wishes.

Planting design

Giving advice on planting is a risky business, because although many gardeners find the task of planning a planting difficult and daunting, whatever recommendations an author makes there will be plenty of people to disagree.

In the most general terms there is some advice I can give with which it must be almost impossible to disagree.

- After two years there should be no bare soil visible.
- Foliage is just as important as flowers.
- Don't be afraid to try something new but if it isn't a success, abandon it.
- If something doesn't work, change it.

The first point perhaps needs amplification. Dense planting implies a well-filled, mature-looking garden with lots to see and little space for the weeds to get through. Obviously it would be unrealistic to expect all your shrubs to reach maturity almost instantly, but the gaps between them can be filled with annuals and easily propagated ground-cover plants whose allocation of space can be reduced as the more important plants spread. In fact it's important not to let annuals shade out the lower branches of young shrubs, because their shape may be ruined.

It hardly needs saying that tall plants should go at the back and shorter ones at the front. But it *is* worth saying that you should not stick rigidly to this rule; if you do, the result is likely to be regimented and boring.

In mixed borders you need shrubs to create a permanent framework to your planting. In many cases these can be trained against walls and fences so that they don't take up too much space. It may be tempting to choose only evergreens, but this can be dull. Mix them with deciduous types for more variety.

Don't be afraid to mix things – there's more advice on this subject later, starting on page 263. For example, if you plant daffodils and hostas together, the hosta foliage not only follows the daffodil flowers but also hides their dying foliage. And you can plant climbers like clematis under shrubs to scramble up through them.

Preparation

Once you have marked out the area of your bed or border, it should be dug over and plenty of organic matter worked in (see page 61). This is the time to prepare soil for different types of plants. So if you want to grow woodland plants on a gravelly soil, fork in even more organic matter than you would normally and if necessary raise the level of the beds a little using rocks, old bricks, timber or half-poles (known as logroll). If you plan a Mediterranean bed and your soil is heavy, this is the time to add grit to improve the drainage in winter.

It's vital that the roots of perennial weeds are removed at this stage, and there is a good argument for growing mostly annuals and other bedding plants in the first year. If a mass of bindweed comes up among the petunias, it's not serious if you have to dig them out to get at the bindweed roots – they would only last a season anyway; moving your newly planted magnolia is another matter.

Planting

Although the books all say 'plant the shrubs first', the fact is that we all buy plants just because we like them and they must then be found a home. Don't worry about it – just put them into a suitable space and give them room to grow. Putting the shrubs in early is good advice, however, for not only do they take longer to mature, but it's easier to fit the smaller, more moveable plants in around them rather than to find room to fit the shrubs in among the perennials.

Don't take any notice of the old rules about only planting in the autumn, or the more modern inclination to plant only in the spring. Now that most plants are available in containers, except sometimes those from specialist mail-order nurseries, they can be planted at any time of year when the ground is suitable; that is, usually, between March and November.

There is, though, the important proviso that if you plant in summer you must keep your plants well watered. This is especially important now that so many plants are sold in peat-only or peat-based composts. For if these dry out after planting, it's very difficult to re-wet them again.

It's often convenient to accumulate the plants for a bed while it is being prepared and then to put in all the permanent plants in one go. This is a very helpful approach if your planting is to have a particular theme. Planting in one burst also gives a great sense of achievement, and if the gaps are filled with annuals, the bed will be full in its first year.

Use a planting mix of organic matter and fertiliser to give the plants a good start, and water them in with a liquid feed.

Short-term maintenance

Mulching

Whenever you plant anything that is not temporary, and especially if you plant up a whole bed at once, it pays to mulch straight afterwards. It makes an attractive finish, helps retain moisture, prevents weed growth and sets off the plants well.

What you use depends on the bed and the plants growing in it. Alpine and Mediterranean beds are best covered in gravel or stone chips. Make sure that the colour of the gravel or chips fits in with the other materials in the garden. Woodland plants and beds in shady planting are best mulched with compost, bark chips or a peat substitute. But for any beds except those requiring quick drainage and those containing acid-loving plants, spent mushroom compost is probably the best material easily available in bulk, unless you are an expert garden compost maker.

Watering

Watering will be important in the first season – more new plants die from lack of water than from anything else. Any weeds that appear must be removed at once, but if you have mulched thoroughly then hoeing will not be necessary.

Check-ups

All the routine jobs like staking, looking out for pests and diseases and dead-heading are important, of course, but you should always be on the look-out for individual plants which are not thriving as they should. This may be due to drought, or you may have planted something in soil it hates – this may need checking elsewhere in this book or in a comprehensive reference book. The plant may have been damaged while planting, or it may have suffered from a cat, a dog, a bird, the heel of a boot or some other outside agent.

Perhaps the most important point, apart from watering, is to ensure that annuals planted as fillers are kept from smothering more important plants, which may be small and will take some time to get well established.

Long-term maintenance

The pruning of shrubs needs attending to at the correct time, which is indicated on page 168. Some plants, choice primroses and choice border campanulas, for example, need dividing regularly, and this must be a high priority (see page 278).

Tying in

Shrubs and climbers will also need tying up regularly. Pruning time is as good a time as any to attend to this, but it also pays to check all ties in the late summer or early autumn, as autumn is becoming increasingly stormy. Even in a well-sheltered small garden, storms, not to mention snow, can cause havoc to badly supported plants.

Trees may need to have their ties loosened or renewed, and stout wall shrubs may need their sisal ties replaced with stronger material as they grow larger and heavier.

Clear out

Borders need a grand clear-out every spring or autumn. Autumn always used to be the favourite time for this, but more and more people are realising how valuable winter stems and dead heads can be, so the job gets left until spring. In spring, however, there are so many other things to do that everything is rather rushed. Dead stems are removed, crowded perennials are lifted, divided and replanted, debris of all sorts is removed, weeds are dug out, and in spring shrub pruning is done.

Feeding and mulching

After the grand clear-out it's time for more planting, and then everything will need feeding. A handful of Growmore to every square yard of the border in spring will do for most plants. Mulches on borders should be checked. Those beds which have been mulched with compost should be forked over before feeding, then the mulch can be replaced. Other more permanent coverings can simply be renewed where necessary.

The Finishing Touches

Every garden needs its special features, and these are particularly important when the garden is a small one where there will be no expansive views or specimen trees to captivate the gaze – just our own little plot. The fine details, the finishing touches, must be carefully planned, well executed and regularly maintained if they are not to let the garden down. For although a special feature can add new dimensions to a small garden, if it fails there's no running away from it.

1. RAISED BEDS

Raised beds are always valuable in small gardens. They bring the plants closer to your eye, which is useful when there will naturally be a tendency to grow small plants. The variation in level adds variety and a change of style without taking up any extra space. The extra height gives you the opportunity to grow plants in good soil if the soil at normal levels is, for example, soaked with oil or full of hardcore. And raised beds enable you to grow plants that would not otherwise grow in your soil.

This last point is especially worth remembering, for if you look on a raised bed as a giant container which can be filled with whatever special compost you like, you will appreciate what a variety of plants you could grow. You can build a raised bed in the sun and fill it with gritty soil for alpines, or you can build one in shade and fill it with a peaty mixture for woodland plants. Alternatively, in any spot where the basic soil is inhospitable, it can be filled with good soil for growing anything.

Siting

A raised bed can go anywhere, but it's important that the siting, the soil mixture with which you fill it and the plants you intend to grow are all compatible. In a very small garden most beds are likely to be set at the sides, against boundaries, and the aspect will have a great influence.

A north-facing bed can be filled with a well-drained but peaty mixture to grow woodland plants. An east-facing bed can have a less well-drained mixture for the same plants, but the plants will have to be tougher, or some will suffer from the early morning sun thawing frosted shoots too quickly. A south-facing bed is ideal for Mediterranean plants, and a well-drained soil mixture with a grit mulch is ideal. A west-facing bed, also with a well-drained soil mix, will suit alpines.

Beds not backed by walls or fences but sited out in the open can be provided with a deep, well-drained soil for alpines or a richer soil for smaller border plants.

Materials

Like the materials for paving and paths, those used for raised beds should suit the surroundings. If you have a stone house, use stone for the raised bed walls. Old bricks (frost-resistant of course) are also good.

Timber is an increasingly popular material and blends well in many situations. Railway sleepers are excellent for rectangular beds and they age well. Short pressure-treated poles are available which can be knocked in vertically to retain the soil, and these are especially useful if you have to cope with variable levels. Half-poles, sometimes known as logroll, are also available stapled to a wire support, making a timber roll which can be bent to fit curves. These half-poles are also available in rigid straight runs. Wherever you use poles it pays to line them with heavy-duty black polythene to prevent soil filtering through any cracks. Tree trunks about 6–8in (15–20cm) thick are also sometimes used to retain raised beds, but as they are difficult to treat with preservative they have a relatively short life.

Site preparation

If you are making your retaining walls from mortared stone or brick, footings are important to create stability (see page 87). For dry stone walls compacted hardcore will be sufficient, plus a row of especially large flat stones for the first layer.

For sleepers no special preparation is required save compaction of the soil. For individual poles no preparation is required, while for logroll it's advisable to dig out a trench just a couple of inches deep along the line of the logroll and fill it with gravel, so that the cut ends of the timber rest on a well-drained medium to help prevent rotting.

All retaining walls and timber should be erected before the soil is prepared. You should aim for a depth of at least 12in (30cm) of soil mixture even if your raised bed is a low one of only 9in (23cm). It's important that drainage be good, and for rock plants or Mediterranean plants allow for at least 3in (7.5cm) of hardcore plus 2in (5cm) of coarse gravel. On top of this lay a sheet of Plantex (an open matting) to prevent soil blocking the drainage. Your soil mixture can go on the top.

For beds where good drainage is less necessary, simply removing any soil to leave enough room for the correct depth of soil mixture and then forking over the existing soil to allow for free natural drainage will be sufficient.

Construction

Brick retaining walls for raised beds should be 9in (23cm) thick unless they are less than four courses of bricks high. With taller walls it's advisable to incorporate seep holes in the bottom course of bricks by simply leaving the mortar out every third vertical joint. Dry stone walls should be laid so that they slope downwards slightly on the bed side for extra stability and so that water is guided back into the bed.

Railway sleepers can be laid on edge to make a bed about 9in (23cm) high. Two can even be laid on edge on top of each other, but more than that are likely to be unstable. If you wish to use sleepers for a higher bed, lay them on their sides rather than their edges. Sleepers laid on edge can be retained in position by rustic poles knocked in on the open side. Alternatively you can knock in some 4 × 4in (10 × 10cm) posts on the inside to a level about 3in (7.5cm) below the surface of the topmost sleeper, drill through post and sleeper, and bolt the two together. Sleepers laid flat are best secured

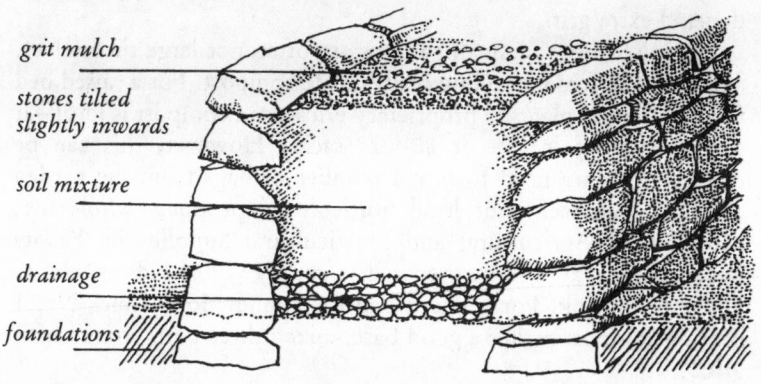

grit mulch

stones tilted slightly inwards

soil mixture

drainage

foundations

RAISED BED IN ROUGH STONE
A raised bed built with dry stone walls makes an elegant feature and is ideal for sun-loving alpines. A grit mulch will help the plants and show them off well.

by drilling vertically through them all at the point where the ends overlap and knocking in a steel rod so that about 15–18in (38–45cm) penetrates the soil beneath.

Rustic poles are simply knocked in to a depth of half their length, protecting the top of each pole with a piece of scrap timber. Logroll is secured in place every 2–3ft (60–90cm) by knocking in vertical 3×3in (7.5 × 7.5cm) posts and screwing them to the logroll.

Soil mixtures

Sometimes you will have spare soil in the garden to form the basis of a mixture for your raised bed – if you're digging a pond, for example. But this is not always the case and if, for example, your soil is limy and you want to build a bed for lime-hating plants your present soil will be useless.

If you are able to utilise some of your own soil, what you add to it will depend on the type of soil you have and it's very difficult to be precise about quantities. You will need grit for drainage, and composted bark, a peat substitute or other organic matter to retain moisture. For example, I made a raised bed for alpines using two parts of my rich, neutral but well-drained soil, one part of grit and one of peat substitute (all by volume). For another raised bed for heathers I used equal parts of soil and peat. Heavier soils would demand extra grit.

But raised beds in small gardens are often not large themselves, and it can be feasible to buy ready-made compost. For a raised bed for lime-hating plants, a proprietary ericaceous compost is ideal – it can be bought in 70- or 80-litre sacks. However, this can be expensive if you need to buy a number of bags from the garden centre, so contact your local horticultural products wholesaler, listed under Agricultural and Horticultural Supplies in *Yellow Pages*. They may well be prepared to supply your needs as long as you buy in bulk. For a raised bed for alpines, John Innes No. 1 potting compost makes a good base, mixed three parts to one with grit.

Fill your raised bed, treading well as you go and taking special care with dry stone walls to ensure that the mixture fills all cracks and crevices. Fill to the top, but do not plant up your new bed straight away. If possible leave it for a couple of months to allow the mix to settle, topping up with mixture if there is any sinkage.

Planting

Try to get your plants together in good time so that you can plant up most of the bed in one go. Set the plants out on the surface where you intend to plant them, and move them about until you have them in the right positions. After planting, water in well. With alpines or Mediterranean plants especially, check throughout their first summer that the plants do not dry out. For recommended plants, see page 249.

After planting and watering in, mulching is sensible. For subjects requiring a well-drained compost, a mulch of grit is the thing; for lime-hating plants use a proprietary mulch such as J. Arthur Bowers Mulch and Mix or bark chips; for less demanding plants, bark chips or spent mushroom compost are ideal. All mulches will help prevent weed growth and conserve moisture. Grit also takes moisture away from the crowns of susceptible plants and prevents low-growing flowers being splashed.

Possible planting themes

Rock plants   Full sun or west-facing, well-drained soil.
Woodland plants   North-facing with well-drained but water-retentive soil, or east-facing with slightly less drainage, but preferably under deciduous trees.
Lime-hating plants   Partial shade with lime-free compost.
Mediterranean plants   Full sun or south-facing, well-drained soil.
Herbs   Full sun or west-facing, well-drained soil.
Grey foliage plants   South- or west-facing, well-drained soil.
Heathers and conifers   Full sun, east- or west-facing or an open position, lime-free compost.
Bulbs   Full sun, well-drained soil.
Dwarf shrubs and dwarf perennials   Full sun, partial shade, east- or west-facing, improved garden soil.

Short-term maintenance

Watering will be the priority in the first six months. If you use bought, bagged compost, weeding will not be a problem whether or not you use a mulch. Compost based on your garden soil might produce lots of weeds, especially if you haven't removed all the roots of perennial weeds; perennials will get through any mulch.

But you must get weeds out at the start, otherwise you'll never be rid of them.

Long-term maintenance

Keeping an eye out for weeds is never-ending. Drainage in raised beds is always better than in the rest of the garden, so you'll always have to be prepared for watering in hot spells. The mulch should be renewed every spring or autumn when the soil is moist. Otherwise, the plants will need to be looked after according to their normal requirements.

2. TUBS

All gardens should have a few tubs, urns or other types of large planters for either permanent or temporary plantings. If you plant them with temporary summer or spring plants, you can have a regularly changing display that will always be different from the planting in the rest of the garden. As permanent plants you can use those which demand a soil type different from that in the garden itself, or those which are a little tender and need winter protection, in which case they can be moved in the autumn.

These tubs can be set in places where they will enliven their situation in times when the plants around them are not at their most colourful or interesting. But it's not just the planting of the tubs that justifies their appearance in small gardens. Their very shape and form is so different from most others in the garden that they can justify their presence on that score alone. Indeed, some gardens feature large but empty urns for this very reason.

Choosing tubs and urns

Things you can use:

- Glazed or unglazed earthenware pots and pans (flat or half-depth pots), plain or decorated.
- Reconstituted stone urns in classical styles.
- Glazed urns in various elegant shapes – oriental styles are especially popular.
- Half barrels – in natural colour or painted.

- Concrete planters – cylindrical, dish-shaped, globular or square.
- Timber boxes and troughs – you can make your own.
- Various found objects – leaky watering cans, wheelbarrows, toilets, old boots, shopping trolleys, chimney pots . . .

There can be problems with large earthenware pots. Many are imported from southern Europe or north Africa, and the clay may not be sufficiently pure for the pots to survive the rigours of a British winter. Pots which curve in at the top are especially susceptible to damage. Always inquire about this point before choosing, or buy pots with a guarantee.

This is not to say that you shouldn't buy pots which are not guaranteed frost-resistant, but you will need to ensure that they are protected in winter. The obvious thing is to plant susceptible pots with susceptible plants, so that moving them into a porch or cold greenhouse in autumn will protect both.

Siting pots

Large elegant urns make features in themselves and can be sited at the end of a short vista, in an alcove framed by evergreens or as the focal point of a small formal area. Their size is such that they will have to be left in place permanently.

Pots of a more manageable size can be sited in small groups, though not so close that the individuality of the pots is lost; above a manhole cover is always a good spot! Groups of three pots in a similar style but in a variety of sizes look good together in a corner, and a pair could mark the start of a path. A collection of pots of different styles and sizes, though perhaps in similar materials, makes an interesting display around the back or front door or the door to the summerhouse.

In your first year or two in your new home, when funds might be stretched, large plastic flower-pots can be used. But they will need to be set a little closer together than normal so they don't show, and some will need to be planted with trailing plants to hide them.

Building timber tubs

Home-made timber tubs are among the most useful of containers, for they can be made to exactly the size and shape you require. They can be made in a triangular shape to fit into corners, and square and

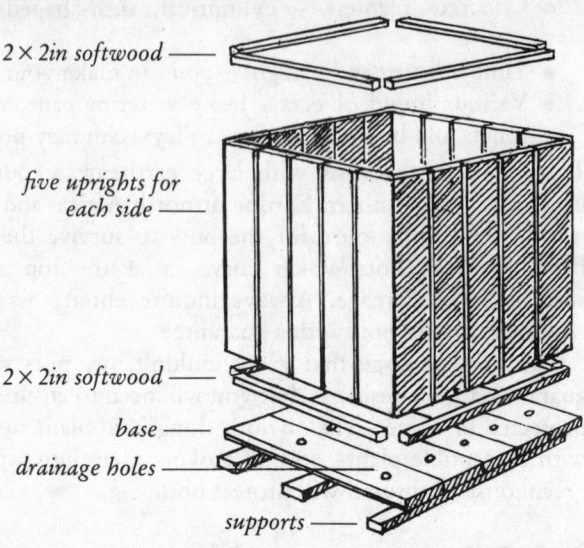

2 × 2in softwood ———

five uprights for
each side ———

2 × 2in softwood ———

base ———

drainage holes ———

supports ———

TIMBER TUB
Timber tubs and planting boxes can be made with tongue-and-groove
boarding and softwood. Advanced DIY skills are not required.

rectangular planters can be built to specific sizes to fit particular spaces.

Materials

Tongue-and-groove boarding is perhaps the simplest material for the less than expert DIY practitioner. Ordinary softwood boards can also be used, as can reclaimed floorboards, as long as you plane them to a good finish first.

Construction

Tubs and planting boxes are best made in five sections (four sides and a base) which are then screwed together to make the box. A box which is much longer than it is high is best made with the boards running vertically to lessen the apparent length, and a short wide box is probably better made with the boards running horizontally. Decide for yourself – vertical boards accentuate the height, horizontal boards emphasise the length. The following instructions refer to a long rectangular box.

To make the sides, your tongue-and-groove boards will be slotted together vertically. From your original bought lengths of approximately 2m (6ft 6in), boards must be cut to the depth you require plus the thickness of the boards. A total depth of 16in (40cm) will give you five uprights from each 2m (6ft 6in) length.

Cut enough for the length of one side and lay them out flat on the ground, slotting them together. Next take a piece of 2 × 2in (5 × 5cm) softwood, lay it along the length of the panelling 4in (10cm) from what will be the top, and cut it to size, leaving a 2in (5cm) gap at each end; draw along the length of each side with a pencil. Then cut another piece of 2 × 2in (5 × 5cm) timber the same length and lay it along what will be the bottom, but closer to the ends of the boards leaving a gap equal only to the thickness of an individual board, about ½in (12mm). Lay this piece in place and draw along each side with a soft pencil.

Now mark a point on each board half-way between the two lines and in the middle of each board. These points mark the screw holes; do this top and bottom. Take the boarding apart and drill right through each board at each marked point, finishing off with a countersink bit on what will be the outside.

Repeat the process for all four sides, then screw them together using 2½in (6cm) brass screws. The base is constructed in the same way except that the 2 × 2in (5 × 5cm) supports are sited 4in (10cm) from each end of the boards. Screw the base together.

Next cut four corner posts of 2 × 2in (5 × 5cm) timber; their length should be the same as that from the bottom side of the lower strut to the top side of the upper one. Screw them to the ends of the two longest sides, drilling first, then fit the ends in the same way.

To fit the base, lay it in place, drill through each board into the strut which is already fixed to the sides and ends, then screw into place. Next cut lengths of 2 × 2in (5 × 5cm) timber to screw on under the base for the planter to stand on. They should be sited 6in (15cm) from each end and every 18in (45cm) in between, and should be 2in (5cm) shorter than the front and back of the box.

Finally, drill drainage holes 1in (2.5cm) across in a staggered row along the base (missing the supports), with one hole in each board. Sand down any rough edges and your DIY planter will be complete – and you must then take it to pieces. All the timber must be thoroughly treated with timber preservative, but there's no point in doing it until all the cutting and drilling has been done, otherwise untreated cut surfaces will be left exposed to wet soil. And if you paint on preservative after the planter is built, unexposed surfaces will not get treated but water will still seep towards them.

Find an old wooden box or bath and line it with polythene. Pile in all the cut timber and then fill it to just above the surface of the cut timber with preservative. Do not use creosote, which can damage plants. Leave to soak for a couple of days, topping up when necessary, then remove the timber and let it drain and dry before screwing it together again.

Finish

Now that effective timber preservatives are available in a range of attractive colours, you may well find that your planter needs no further treatment after soaking if you choose a shade of preservative you like. Alternatively, your planter can be painted with primer, undercoat and gloss to suit your taste.

This is a simple, plain planter which should fit into a number of garden styles, but remember that the finish should match the house, paving and other features in your garden.

Siting

Purpose-made timber planters are ideal for providing planting space where there is paving or another hard surface which cannot reasonably be removed – in a side passage, in corners near doors and so on. They are especially useful in small yards with no access except through the house. In these situations, digging up old concrete paving and removing it then improving the soil with compost is often beyond the patience of even the less houseproud, as it will not only create great inconvenience but will be very messy.

But the materials for large planters can be carried through the house easily, the planters can be built in the yard, and proprietary bagged compost can also be carried through without mess.

These large planters can go in any situation, and like raised beds, the compost and plants must match the situation.

Maintenance

If built carefully and thoroughly treated with preservative, the planter itself will need little maintenance. Just make sure debris doesn't collect underneath to encourage rotting.

Planters used for seasonal plantings can be brushed out every year and washed out and treated again with preservative every other year. When changing permanent plantings, empty the planter completely, wash down thoroughly and allow to dry, then give a couple more coats of preservative.

Compost

The compost you use depends on the plants you intend to grow. In larger containers with a generous capacity, small shrubs and perennial plants will thrive. In that case, John Innes Potting Compost No. 3 is usually ideal, perhaps with extra grit at about four parts compost to one part grit. If you intend to grow lime-hating plants – dwarf rhododendrons, for example – a lime-free compost such as J. Arthur Bowers Ericaceous Compost is essential.

Before filling with compost you will need some drainage material. I suggest 1–2in (2.5–5cm) of coarse washed gravel first, levelled out and topped with a rectangle of green plastic greenhouse shading material or Plantex to help prevent the compost washing into the gravel and clogging it up, and to keep out worms.

Permanent or temporary plantings

I suggest that when building your own planters you give them a sufficiently generous capacity to allow you to grow shrubs, perennials and bulbs, rather than using them only for temporary seasonal displays which will be happy in containers with less root room. Dwarf evergreen or variegated shrubs, slow-growing conifers, perennials, bulbs and alpines, with perhaps an occasional appropriate seasonal bedding plant, are best choices and ideal for larger containers, be they home-made or bought.

Some large pots also make good homes for temporary seasonal plantings; the opulence and the exotic air you can create with tender summer plants is unmatched by shrubs, and they will look their best in an urn. Smaller pots can be used for just one type of plant rather than a mixture, whether it's lilies, a scented-leaved geranium or some special daffodils. These can be brought into prominence as they approach their best, and then removed.

Maintenance

The plants themselves will need maintenance. They will need watering regularly, but a mulch of grit, coarse gravel or bark as appropriate will help retain moisture.

Feeding will be necessary too. Regular liquid feeding is ideal for temporary seasonal plantings. Permanent plants, especially after the first year, will benefit from a general fertiliser like Growmore, a handful to the square yard, each spring; additional liquid feeds in summer might also be useful.

3. WINDOW-BOXES

Many gardeners feel romantic about window-boxes, but the number of miserable plants you see languishing in them just shows that looking after them is not as easy as people like to think.

Choosing window-boxes

If you've a mind to, you can buy one of those little plastic boxes and sit it in your windowsill. You can plant it up with busy lizzies or petunias and all will be well. Then you can go away for a week's holiday or for a long weekend, and when you come back they'll all be frazzled. Almost all window-boxes in garden centres are too small for the job they are trying to do – unless you or a neighbour are around every day to water and feed the plants.

There are earthenware and reconstituted stone window-boxes which are of a more suitable size, but the only way you can be sure of having one big enough is (surprise, surprise) to make it yourself.

Building window-boxes

Making your own window-box is a little more straightforward than building a large planter. Simply use 9in (23cm) planks of planed softwood cut to the length you require for the sides, ends and base and screw together with brass screws, drilling first. A staggered row of 1in (2.5cm) drill holes will do for drainage. Assemble the box and sand off the corners, then dismantle and soak as before. If the sill slopes, you may need to cut slightly wedge-shaped feet to keep the box level.

Siting and fixing window-boxes

Window-boxes are supposed to be sited in front of windows. Originally they sat on the wide sills in front of sash windows; the

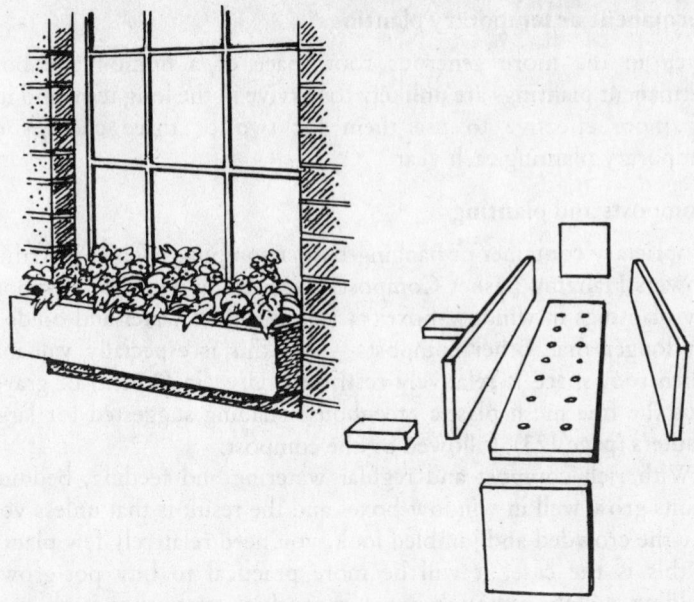

WINDOW-BOX
It's far easier to build a window-box to fit your own windowsills than try and find a ready-made box in exactly the right size.

sill was wide enough to support the box and as the window opened vertically the plants could be close to the glass. In this situation window-boxes can be very effective. Casement windows provide something of a problem, as their sills are often too narrow to support boxes and as they open outwards plants get in the way. Boxes can be set on brackets fixed to the wall below the casement, so that the window opens over the top of the flowers, or the brackets can be set higher in front of windows which don't open. But to be frank boxes displayed in this way can look rather silly.

My feeling is that in a small garden details matter a lot, and that window-boxes in slightly unlikely positions look odd and are irritating. So if you have sash windows and wide sills, window-boxes can be very effective in bringing fresh groups of plants and a variety of style to the garden. Without these conditions I'm inclined to feel that colour should be introduced around windows by other means, such as hanging baskets at the sides, planting in the soil beneath or the use of large planters set on paving beneath windows.

Permanent or temporary plantings

Even in the more generous root space of a home-made box, permanent plantings are unlikely to survive in the long term and it's far more effective to use them for two or three changes of temporary planting each year.

Composts and planting

Proprietary container or hanging-basket compost, such as J. Arthur Bowers Hanging Basket Compost, is especially useful for temporary plantings in window-boxes as it holds more water and holds it for longer than other composts – and this is especially valuable when root space is relatively restricted. Use 1in (2.5cm) of gravel plus the fine mesh plastic greenhouse shading suggested for large planters (page 123), followed by the compost.

With rich compost and regular watering and feeding, bedding plants grow well in window-boxes and the result is that unless you like the crowded and jumbled look, you need relatively few plants. If this is the case, it will be more practical to buy pot-grown bedding which, although more expensive, establishes itself very quickly and may well be in flower when you buy it.

Maintenance

Regular watering is vital, so it's important to make arrangements with friends or neighbours for watering to be continued if you go away. Feeding will also be necessary – one dose when watering in your new plants and then from about six weeks after planting. Use Liquid Growmore or any general purpose liquid feed.

Regular dead-heading is important, and a little judicious trimming is also very helpful in maintaining the look of your plants.

Judging the time to replant for the next season is not always easy. The warmth from the wall helps the plants flower for longer in the autumn, and it can be hard to persuade yourself to rip them out to make way for spring plants. You can delay a little, as the warmth will also help spring-flowering plants establish themselves quickly.

4. HANGING BASKETS

In recent years hanging baskets have become increasingly popular. The result has been that not only are there more pretty displays round windows and front doors but there are also more shrivelled sticks poking out of rusty wire. For without careful and constant attention, hanging baskets are difficult to keep looking attractive. My advice is that if you intend to be away from home a lot or are by nature forgetful, don't bother with them. But if you have the time and the temperament, hanging baskets can bring variety, new shapes and styles and new plants to your garden, and that's always welcome in a small space.

Choosing hanging baskets and liners

The traditional hanging basket is a dish- or bowl-shaped wire lattice construction lined with sphagnum moss to prevent the compost falling out and then filled with compost. There are now other alternatives.

The traditional wire basket is still seen, though these are tending to become shallower, so holding less compost, which is unfortunate. Look for a deep basket which will hold more.

Sphagnum moss is available in bags at garden centres but can be of poor quality – it should be a bright green shade. Some gardeners collect moss if it is growing near their home, but with the increasing pressure on wild plants of all types this is not to be recommended in most areas. Moss is still preferred by most gardeners – it looks good and can be easily parted so that plants can be set in the sides of the basket.

Rigid plastic liners are available, but these rarely fit the basket exactly, often have no drainage holes, and plants cannot be put through the sides unless you cut holes.

The same applies to pressed wood pulp liners which, although not intended to be, are watertight. Some people simply use black polythene sheeting and cut drainage holes in the bottom and planting holes in the sides with scissors. These look fine when the plants have bushed out to hide the polythene.

If good-quality moss is hard to obtain there are two sensible possibilities. Green or black plastic shade netting is not stiff; being full of holes it is well drained, and it can also be cut easily for planting through the sides. In black or dull green, the colours are not obtrusive and it can be made to fit any shape of basket. There are also foam liners in a mixture of sensibly dowdy shades, with slits in the sides so that they can be expanded to fit any shape and through which you can plant.

Plastic baskets are also available in various sizes and shapes, some with so-called water reservoirs and with drip trays. Almost all are less than elegant, and many are too shallow to be of any practical use, even if they do hold a little water in the base. Only the relatively narrow and deep types, more like large flower-pots, have space for sufficient compost, and some even have holes in the sides.

Ceramic baskets, attractively decorated, are also worth looking at, though they are rarely large. They are ideal for a single specimen plant, however.

Siting baskets and fixing brackets

You see baskets in some funny places, but what looks right in one style of garden will look odd in another. Putting them on either side of the front door is a high risk strategy, for if they are not 100 per cent successful they show you up constantly. But they really can look marvellous in such a spot. They can go on either side of windows, in the space between windows, on fence posts near the patio, although you need the right setting to put one on every fence post all down the garden.

Sometimes baskets are seen swaying on windy corners where they may not only knock into the wall but some of the plants are unlikely to thrive. A little shelter is always helpful. Baskets need to be above the head height of your tallest resident or regular visitor when hanging in place, and preferably a little higher than that to allow for trailing foliage.

Brackets must be securely fixed – a basket full of plants and wet soil is very heavy and must not come crashing down in the height of summer, or at any other time for that matter. Use long screws and tight-fitting plugs, and please use all the screw holes on the brackets.

Compost

In recent years the uncertainty has been taken out of choosing compost for summer baskets by the arrival of some compost specially formulated for containers, such as J. Arthur Bowers Hanging Basket Compost. These contain special water-retention agents to help prevent the baskets from drying out and they also contain a different, longer-lasting fertiliser formulation. Being

peat-based, they are not as heavy as John Innes soil-based composts, and they also incorporate a wetting agent so that if the
compost does get dry, re-wetting it is not a problem.

Container composts can be less successful for spring baskets
which are planted in the autumn, as they can hold too much water
and encourage the roots to rot in winter. A standard peat-based
compost, perhaps with 20 per cent extra grit or the lighter perlite, is
more appropriate. You can keep your basket under cover where
watering can be controlled, or you can buy your plants in the spring
and plant up then.

Permanent and temporary plantings

I think that unless you have a large deep basket, permanent
plantings are a waste of time. Even then they take some careful
looking after, because container compost can lie too wet in winter
and run short of nutrients in the second season. If you intend to use
permanent plantings, choose something simple like variegated ivy
and leave it at that. This can be very effective in a shady sheltered
spot.

Temporary plantings come in two seasons: the spring display is
planted in autumn or late winter, the summer display is planted in
late spring.

For a spring show choose spring bedding plants, the tougher
spring rock plants and dwarf bulbs. For summer choose from the
wide range of dwarf and trailing summer bedding plants.

Planting

The planting style of your basket should match its setting. In some
carefully planned and controlled gardens, baskets planted with a
riotous mixture of varieties look out of place and plants of just one
variety would be more appropriate. In a more cottagey garden a
cool one-colour, one-plant basket may look contrived, where a
mixture of varieties would look just right.

It is difficult to give specific advice about planting, as so much
depends on what varieties you choose and the size of your basket.
Generally the idea should be to have one plant, or even as many as
three, in the centre of the basket, a ring around the edge and another
ring, staggered with the first, half-way down the side. This will
ensure complete coverage. How you mix them is up to you.

Watering

Watering and feeding are vital. However, watering a basket hanging on a bracket 8ft (2.4m) from the ground with a watering can is a little tricky. On the old private estates the baskets were removed from the brackets and dunked in baths of water to soak up as much as they needed; this is hard work.

There are special pulley systems available for lowering baskets, but these are not cheap. There are also pump action containers with a long spout to reach up to the basket, but they hold only a little and are hard work.

Much better are the lances for attachment to hosepipes, which have a hooked top to direct water downwards into the basket. These too have a very slow flow, but by unscrewing the handle the governor can be removed to improve this. An effective home-made version can be made simply by tying a 4ft (1.2m) bamboo cane along a length of hosepipe with about 12in (30cm) spare at the end. This allows you to hold the hosepipe vertically and the hose at the end will droop to one side for watering.

Feeding

Feeding is also important. The simplest system is to use fertiliser pellets, which can be put in the compost and break down over the season, releasing plant foods gradually. But most people opt for regular liquid feeding, which after about the first six weeks is probably best done every week. You can get special feeds for containers which are excellent, or you can use an old favourite like Maxicrop.

Other maintenance

Dead-heading is important, as is checking for pests and diseases, but aside from those, perhaps the important thing to do is to turn the basket regularly. If left in the same position all the time, the side next to the wall will become bare and brown. But if the basket is turned every week you will end up with much more uniform growth.

5.   TROUGHS

You may be wondering how exactly a trough differs from a planter, as some people refer to timber window-boxes as troughs. For the sake of argument, let's agree that by a trough I mean a free-standing, relatively shallow stone or concrete container most commonly used for alpines and other dwarf plants.

Choosing troughs

In this section I include stone sinks, stone drinking troughs, white enamelled sinks, pre-cast reconstituted stone sinks and troughs and home-cast concrete troughs of various sorts.

Stone sinks

The shallow stone sinks once found in sculleries everywhere are now much in demand for alpines. They are often cleanly and evenly cut but very shallow, sometimes as little as 4in (10cm), so are suited to a very restricted range of plants. The soil depth can be increased a little in places by judicious use of suitable small rocks. There will of course be a drainage hole.

Stone drinking troughs

Deeper than sinks and much more variable in size and shape, troughs can sometimes be almost cube-shaped and may be quite large. There is often no drainage hole.

White enamelled sinks

These successors to stone sinks are larger, much deeper, and a ghastly glaring white shade. They can be covered with hypertufa (see page 132) to create a replica of a stone trough. There's always a drainage hole.

Reconstituted stone sinks

Sinks and troughs in various shapes and sizes are now cast in reconstituted stone and are very effective, as they have a good depth, an attractive finish and of course good drainage.

Home-cast troughs

It's relatively straightforward to cast your own troughs using hypertufa – a mixture of sand, cement and peat. You can make them in any size you like, and a little weathering soon makes them look very natural.

Making hypertufa troughs

You can cast your own small hypertufa troughs using the following method. You will need two stout cardboard boxes, one about 3in (7.5cm) larger than the other all round. You will also need some bricks, polystyrene packaging blocks, chicken or reinforcing wire, a sheet of heavy polythene, an old broom handle, sharp sand, cement and finally moist, medium-grade, sphagnum moss peat.

Lay out the sheet of polythene on a hard, flat surface and stand the larger of the two boxes in the middle; stand a row of bricks around the outside, tight up against the box. Cut a piece of chicken

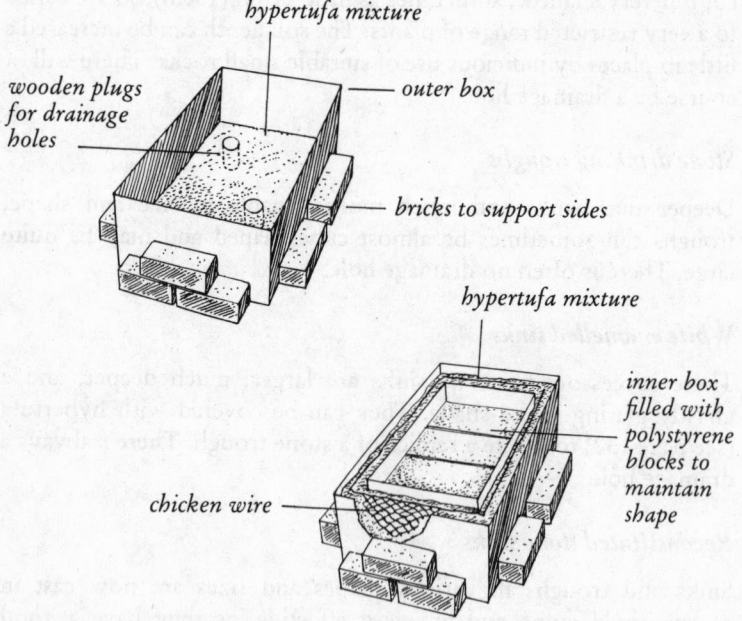

hypertufa mixture

wooden plugs
for drainage
holes

outer box

bricks to support sides

hypertufa mixture

inner box
filled with
polystyrene
blocks to
maintain
shape

chicken wire

IMITATION STONE TROUGH
You can make a replica stone trough by casting with a special concrete mix (hypertufa) using cardboard boxes to form a mould.

wire that will fit down one side of the box, across the bottom and up the opposite side, stopping 2–3in (5–7.5cm) from the top. Cut another piece for the other two sides. When you've checked that the pieces of wire will fit, remove them from the box and keep them till they are needed. Cut a number of 3in (7.5cm) lengths of broom handle, one for each of the drainage holes – which should be 6in (15cm) apart.

Mix up your hypertufa in the ratio of one part cement, one part sharp sand and two parts peat by volume. Add enough water to give it a creamy consistency and add a PVA bonding agent like Unibond, as recommended on the pack for preventing the flaking of concrete floors.

Pour 1in (2.5cm) of the mix into the bottom of the box, then push in the pieces of broom handle to make the drainage holes. Next put the reinforcing chicken wire in place, bending it around the broom handle pieces if necessary. Top up with hypertufa to the top of the broom handles, making sure the wire is well covered. Now place the second box in position, sitting it on the pieces of handle and with the wire folded into the gap between the boxes.

Pack the smaller box with polystyrene blocks to keep the sides rigid, then fill the gap between the two boxes with hypertufa, stirring it with a stick as you go. Keep the wire roughly in the middle of the gap.

After a couple of days the sides of the outer box and the top couple of inches of the inner box can be removed and the finish of the exposed surfaces inspected. If you feel it needs a little treatment to make it look more natural, you can use a stiff brush and an old file to improve it.

Leave it for another week before removing the rest of the cardboard and knocking out the pieces of broom handle. Move your new trough to its site and treat it to encourage algal growth before filling. This can be done by painting it with an organic liquid: various substances can be used such as rice water, urine, sour milk, undiluted Maxicrop and manure water.

Re-covering old enamelled sinks

Old white enamelled sinks can be transformed by using the same material. Spread out a sheet of polythene on a hard surface, remove any unnecessary pipes and so on from the sink and stand it on a couple of bricks.

The outer surface, the top edge and the top 4in (10cm) of the inside will need roughening to help the hypertufa to cling. This can be done using a very stiff wire brush or a wire brush attachment to an electric drill. Next mix up some PVA adhesive to the strength recommended for bonding mortar to tiles, and paint it all over the prepared area.

While this is drying, mix up the hypertufa as before but adding much less water. It needs to be the consistency of stiff porridge so that it clings to the vertical surfaces. The addition of a PVA adhesive will again be very helpful.

Don a pair of rubber gloves and apply the hypertufa to the surface of the sink about ½–1in (12–25mm) thick, leaving the surface slightly uneven. Make sure the top edge and the corners are well covered. Leave to dry for a couple of days, then adjust the finish as before. After another week give the sink the same ageing treatment as above.

Siting troughs

There are two approaches to the siting of troughs and sinks. You can place them where they will look good and then plant them to suit that situation. Alternatively you can decide what you wish to grow in them and then site them accordingly.

For the alpines that most people grow in troughs, a site in full sun or one that gets sun for most of the day is necessary. Do not place a trough under overhanging trees. It's possible to grow some of the smaller woodland plants in troughs too, and for these a north-facing or partially shaded site is ideal.

The stone or stone-like finish of these troughs fits well into most gardens, although it does not perhaps go with certain kinds of brick. Troughs should be sited where the small plants grown in them can be seen easily. They can be raised up on bricks or concrete blocks; sinks with a drainage hole at one end should be tilted in that direction very slightly.

Compost and drainage

Drainage holes should first be covered with a piece of greenhouse shade netting or perforated zinc and then the whole base covered with drainage material. In a deep sink or trough you can allow 2–3in (5–7.5cm) of drainage material, in a sink only 3–4in (7.5–10cm) deep just a single layer. Washed coarse gravel is ideal, and this too should be covered with Plantex or greenhouse shade netting to let water through but hold back compost which will clog up the drainage.

For easy rock plants John Innes Potting Compost No. 1 is fine; for more exacting plants use No. 2 and mix it with one-third of its volume of grit. For lime-hating plants make sure you use a lime-free mixture. For woodland plants, use one-third extra peat or peat substitute instead.

Choosing plants

Small troughs can be planted with just one variety. A small shallow sink is just right for a sempervivum, and a trough full of gentians is an astonishing sight. A trough of any size could hold a collection of varieties of one plant – sempervivums, saxifrages, primulas – but in a very large trough they can look strange with no companions and the appearance can be dull when your chosen collection is not at its best.

Alpines like sempervivums and saxifrages are especially useful, as not only are they happy in shallow soil but their rosettes are attractive all the year round. In many troughs, mixtures of smaller alpines are the most effective choice. These should include dwarf shrubs and even very small conifers as well as conventional rock plants. Gentians, dwarf primulas, saxifrages, dwarf campanulas, tiny bulbs – all will thrive. For shadier sites there is a more select band of plants, such as different gentians, primulas, calceolarias and of course dwarf ferns.

Planting

The best approach is to locate your trough in its final spot then fill it with compost, firming well as you go. Fill to about 1in (2.5cm) from the top, then plant your plants with the top of their compost about ½in (12mm) below the rim. Firm the compost around them, level it off, then top with grit or washed pea gravel level with the rim.

Maintenance

Little maintenance is necessary, although watering in dry weather is important. Most alpines prefer being too dry to being too wet, but watering will still usually be necessary during the summer, when a thorough drenching using a slow hosepipe rather than a spray with a watering can is the way to go about it.

General tidying up is important, as is a little feeding. A general fertiliser at half the normal rate every spring is fine. Sometimes a plant will die or get too big and it can be removed, the space filled with identical compost and a new plant set in its place.

6. BALCONIES

For flat-dwellers the balcony is the ultimate small garden, perhaps smaller than a single bed. But although the opportunities may be very limited, it doesn't mean you should just give up.

Assessing the situation

First of all, is your balcony sunny or shady? This will affect your choice of plants and how often they need watering. Is it high and windy or are you low down? Maybe there are other buildings around? Are there railings to let light through or just a solid wall? Is there room to sit out? Is the access good or is it simply an opening window? If there is access and the space is large enough for two people to sit out, you can safely assume that the balcony is strong enough for pots of plants. If it's smaller and access is only through a window, be careful, as it may not be strong enough to support heavy pots.

Everything will, of course, have to be grown in pots and all materials carried through the room behind.

Options

A sunny, sheltered balcony large enough to sit out on is a real opportunity. You could create a Mediterranean atmosphere with large succulents in pots, morning glories and oleanders. Alternatively, bedding plants will create a most colourful show that people will admire from the street. Both will need plenty of watering. Plastic, fibreglass, glazed earthenware and stoneware and wooden containers will dry out less than terracotta.

Shadier balconies can be planted partly with evergreen shrubs, and these can be combined with appropriate seasonal bedding plants

– pansies and bulbs for spring and impatiens for summer. Climbers like clematis and sweet peas will also be very useful.

Windy and exposed balconies are the most difficult to deal with. Plants dry out exceptionally quickly and are scorched and battered by winds. Evergreen shrubs, especially those recommended for seaside gardens, have the best chance of withstanding the blast, and these should be planted in large heavy pots filled with a soil-based rather than a peat-based compost. Plants may still need tying to railings.

7. ROOF GARDENS

Plants, soil, pots and water, not to mention people, are heavy. Unless your roof has been constructed with a roof garden in mind, there may be the chance of you and your plants crashing through to the room below.

Caution

Obviously most flat roofs are strong enough to support the weight of a workman and a box of tools, but if you anticipate having parties, growing trees in tubs or building pools, get a surveyor to advise on what the roof will support. If the advice is 'not much', you could still add some plants by putting up baskets on the house wall. Often flat roofs have a low wall around the edge and you could stand timber planting boxes on these. But if the vegetation grows too tall the wind may catch them and topple them into the street. Setting planting boxes on the roof just inside the wall will give them the most support. Again, get advice on what is possible from the surveyor.

On a flat roof you will need to be most careful not to puncture the roofing surface; this is easily done if you take a patio chair and table up there – those legs can do a lot of damage. A piece of vinyl in one corner might be enough, or a square of slabs, but take the advice that relates to your particular roof.

You may have a problem with water. First of all, watering the beds or containers may involve carrying cans through the house. You could rig up a hosepipe attached to the bathroom taps (tap fittings are widely available), but it's a fiddly business. And where's the water going to go? This shouldn't be a problem actually, because the roof will be designed for the rain to drain away. But if you build beds the drainage could be disrupted, so get some advice.

Roof garden

If your roof turns out to be built to take a lot of weight then you can simply treat it like a patio – although a pool may still be out of the question. Large planting boxes or raised beds can be used for shrubs and perennials, trellis can hold off the wind and you can lay brick, slabs or gravel as a hard surface. But my advice, when so very much depends on you getting it right, is to go to an expert from the Society of Garden Designers (see page 429).

8.   WATER GARDENS

Water is an invaluable asset, bringing to the garden atmosphere, sound, wildlife and a different range of plants. Even on the smallest scale a water garden, pool or fountain is worth considering. And now that small pumps and interesting fountain designs are available, you can make a simple water garden in even the smallest space. I like to site water with seating areas and near to the house, so that it provides as much enjoyment as possible.

Safety

In a small garden, and especially where there are young children, safety is a crucial consideration. But there are ways of incorporating water into the garden without creating a hazard. One is to have no open water at all, and the other is to cover the water with sturdy netting. On the smallest possible scale, a water garden can be created in a container as small as a half barrel. Miniature water lilies are now available that will thrive in such a small container – you can simply stand it on the patio.

Perhaps the safest type of water feature is a pebble fountain where there is no open water. A small fountain, perhaps a low bubble fountain, spills its water on to a tank which is filled with large smooth pebbles through which the water drains to be re-circulated by the pump. The great advantage of this system is that you can have the sound, the cool atmosphere and even some of the plants associated with water, but without danger to children. The only other relatively safe water feature would be a small stream powered by an electric pump, with no open water. This could be built into rock work or run in a rill across or alongside a patio, with a tank completely hidden below ground.

Until your children are older I would not suggest any other type of water feature unless the surface is completely covered with wire. Pools up to about 3ft (90cm) across can be made safe by covering them with stout wire mesh. If this is painted with black paint it is relatively unobtrusive. But of course the mesh must be heavy-duty grade and securely fixed to the surrounding brickwork.

Types of water garden

Pools can be formal or informal in shape. In a very small garden a formal rectangular pool is the simplest to build, and preformed fibreglass liners are available in various sizes and depths. Round fibreglass liners are also available, and if you want a circular pool this is the best option – fitting a sheet of butyl lining to a round shape will drive you crackers. Preformed fibreglass liners are also available in various other informal shapes, and these are often best fitted into a paved surround.

In informal areas pools in a variety of shapes and sizes can be constructed, using butyl liners which can be arranged to fit any pattern. These can be integrated with a small bog garden to enable you to grow marginal plants.

Siting a small pool

Pools can be sited anywhere away from overhanging trees, and although those with a large volume of water are usually best sited in an open sunny position, very small pools and barrels will heat up too much in summer if they get sunshine all day. Small water features are best sheltered from the sun for at least half the day. Bubble fountains and other features with no standing water can be sited anywhere.

Liners

As I mentioned earlier, liners come in two types – rigid fibreglass and flexible butyl. Polythene sheeting liners are also available, but although much cheaper than butyl, they have a limited lifespan and

I would not recommend them. Rigid fibreglass liners are ideal for smaller pools, especially for a formal pool on a patio, and they are now available in grey and dark brown in addition to the rather garish blue which many people now dislike.

There's a simple way of working out the size of the liner you need to order. Simply take the maximum length of your proposed pool and add twice the maximum depth; then take the maximum width and add twice the maximum depth. This will give you the correct dimension. There is no need to allow for any overlap at the edge, as the natural stretch of the material plus the recommended sloping sides to the pool will give you enough.

Preparation and construction – rigid liners

If you're going to lay a preformed liner you can simply lay it on the ground and mark around it to give you the size of hole you need to excavate.

Excavate the hole for a rigid liner about 6in (15cm) bigger all round, firm the base well, and lay 1in (2.5cm) of soft sand to provide a cushion for the liner. Make sure the liner is completely supported on the sand base and check that it's level, using a spirit level. Put a little water in the pool then start to fill the gap between pool and soil with sand, making sure it is worked under any shelves. Fill the pool with water in stages, packing the gap with sand as you go.

Preparation and construction – butyl liners

To mark the site for a butyl liner, choose a warm day and lay a hosepipe on the ground to mark out the area you wish your pool to cover. (Hosepipes are more flexible in warm weather.)

The correct minimum depth at the deepest part of the pool can be determined by the following guide:

under 25sq ft (2¼sq m) – depth 15in (38cm)
25–100sq ft (2¼ – 9sq m) – depth 18in (45cm)

The sides of a pool should slope at an angle of approximately 20°, that is 3in (7.5cm) inwards towards the centre of the pool for every 9in (23cm) of depth. A shelf for marginal plants should be constructed at a depth of 9in (23cm) and should be about 9in (23cm) wide.

It seems an obvious thing to say, but it's vital to ensure that the top of the pool is level otherwise the water will run out. Check with a spirit level then check again.

After careful excavation to the size and slope you require, the bottom and sides should be covered with a ½in (12mm) layer of soft sand to make a smooth surface and protect the liner from stones. If your soil is very stony, an inner lining of polyester matting, old carpet or old capillary matting is advisable.

Lay the liner loosely in the hole with an even overlap on all sides, and put a few bricks or pieces of clean timber around the edge to keep it in place. Start to fill the pool slowly with water, stretching and overlapping the liner where necessary to fit snugly into place. Do not hurry this part of the operation – you don't want to have to empty the pond and start again if it goes wrong.

When the pool is full, trim off any surplus liner leaving a 6in (15cm) flap. You are then ready to build a surround.

Guidelines on plants

The simplest way to plant a pool is to use plastic mesh planting baskets. These can be positioned on the shelf or on the bottom of the pool according to the plants they contain. Different plants require different depths of water over the top of their roots. The correct depth can be provided by utilising the different depths on the bottom of the pond and on the shelf, and by supporting planting baskets on bricks of an appropriate size (don't use concrete blocks, which leach lime into the water).

As a rough guide, a pool can cope with one water lily for every 25sq ft (2¼sq m) of water, although lilies now come in such a variety of sizes that there are far more options than there once were. They are unhappy growing in pools which also feature a splashy fountain. Marginal plants require anything from constantly wet soil but no covering of water, up to a depth of 18in (45cm), depending on the type. Oxygenating plants, which are vital to keep the pool well supplied with oxygen, will grow in anything from 1ft to 4ft (0.3–1.2m) of water and you need one bunch for every 2sq ft (0.2sq m) of water surface.

Guidelines on fish

A rough and ready guide as to how many fish a pond will comfortably take is 2in (5cm) of fish for every 1sq ft (0.1sq m) of water. It follows that in very small pools and barrels it's impractical to keep fish at all. If you have moré fish than the water can take, their waste products will tend to sour the water and in summer, when oxygen levels in the water are low, there may be insufficient oxygen to provide for so many.

Pools should be left for two or three weeks to settle down after planting before fish are introduced. The fish should be floated in the pool in a tied plastic bag full of water to accustom them to the water temperature before being released. Use of a water conditioner in the pool water will help the fish acclimatise themselves. The easiest fish to look after in a small pool are goldfish, shubunkins and golden rudd. Golden orfe tend to be very shy if you have only one or two. As well as fish, ramshorn snails are valuable for clearing up debris and swan mussels are useful to filter algae. Neither are likely to thrive in the smallest pools.

Fountains and electricity

Fountains and waterfalls should not be supplied by constant mains water which simply runs away into a drain. Instead a submersible pump should be used to constantly recirculate the same water.

Low voltage pumps which run on 24 rather than 240 volts are the safest. The pump sits in the bottom of the pool, a twin core cable runs out of the pool to a transformer in a nearby garage or shed, and this is connected to the mains. In most small pools the smallest, lowest-capacity pump is sufficient to provide an adequate supply.

The only maintenance the pump will need is regular cleaning of the filter. The pump is usually removed from the pool and stored for the winter, and this is the time for a ten-minute, do-it-yourself maintenance check. Spare parts are available for most models.

A wide range of fountain heads is available, including aerator heads which oxygenate the water and bell fountain heads as well as more conventional types. These are simply fitted to the pump of your choice to give the effect you prefer.

9. PEAT GARDENS

Many of the most delightful spring flowering plants grow naturally in the dappled shade and leafy soil of deciduous woodland. In the garden, leafmould is often difficult to come by in large quantities, and moss peat is usually used instead. As gardeners become more concerned about using peat in the garden, various peat substitutes are being tried out. At the time of writing, however, it is too early to say how successful they will be or whether growing techniques will need to be modified.

Siting

A peat garden should be sited either on the north, shady side of a wall or fence or under deciduous trees – as long as their shade is not too dense. If sited on the north side of a fence, the peat bed could still get too much sunshine at that time of midsummer when the sun is at its fiercest, so you may not be able to grow the more delicate varieties.

If peat gardens are made in the shade of a tree, conifers must be avoided. Certain deciduous trees such as beech and horse chestnut also cast a very deep shade. Only if the trees are tall and their lowest branches some distance above the ground should peat beds be made in such a situation, and if you *are* blessed with such conditions they are ideal, as the canopy keeps off the sun when it's at its hottest but the slanting rays of the morning and evening sun can still penetrate.

If you build a peat garden around a tree trunk, soil should not be banked up against the trunk to a height of more than 1ft (30cm). Instead you will need to build a back to the bed – any rough but stout timber or old bricks can be used, as they will not be visible. Corner sites are often the most successful, as they allow you to build a smaller high tier for pendulous plants and you can incorporate a few steps to allow access.

Most small gardens contain a shady area and have the necessary shelter for a peat garden, so it is a good feature to consider making.

Preparation and materials

A peat garden is usually made up of one or a series of raised beds filled with peaty soil. The place where the peat beds are to go should be marked out and then dug over to allow good drainage. For although one reason for using peat is to keep the soil moist, it should not be waterlogged. Little other preparation is needed before you start work.

Peat beds are usually made in tiers, perhaps with a narrow path to the top one to allow close inspection of the smaller, more delicate plants. Various materials can be used to retain the soil and build up the levels. Stone, brick or other materials suggested for raised beds can be used, but timber fits in better. Railway sleepers are often suggested, but I find they tend to exude sticky black tar in hot weather. Stout boards such as scaffolding boards can also be used, but the most popular materials are peat blocks and logs. Logroll (split logs stapled to a wire backing) can also be used and can look good in modern situations.

Peat blocks have understandably been the usual building materials and are bonded together like bricks, using a peat and water slurry as 'mortar'. The blocks must first be soaked in a barrel of water overnight before use. They are then bonded as if they were bricks in a wall, though it helps to set the occasional block end on so that it stretches back into the bed; this will help keep the wall secure. Peat blocks, however, are difficult to build into a rigid wall, will take no weight at all so can't be stepped on, and their use is yet another cause of peat bog destruction.

Natural logs are the easiest material to deal with and look the most fitting. In towns they are often available from tree surgery companies. The white bark of birch logs is most attractive but soon rots, so harder woods should be used if possible. Logs can also be used to build the risers of the steps, and the treading area can be filled with bark chips.

Building

Start by laying an edging of logs to mark the main outline. For stability, the logs can be sunk into the soil to about a quarter of their thickness or supported by stout pegs. They look best in single layers, partially buried, and if you can find logs 8–9in (20–23cm) across these are ideal. Use a bow saw to cut them all to the right shape and treat generously with clear or brown wood preserver (not creosote, which is dangerous to plants). Having laid your first line of edging and secured it in place, fill the whole area with compost and firm it down. The next layer of logs can then go into place making a second tier, and a small third tier can be built at the back.

Even if a path is incorporated into the design, it's often impossible to reach all the plants to look after them. Stepping stones made with rounds of treated timber cut from logs 12–15in (30–38cm) across can be set in appropriate spots before planting.

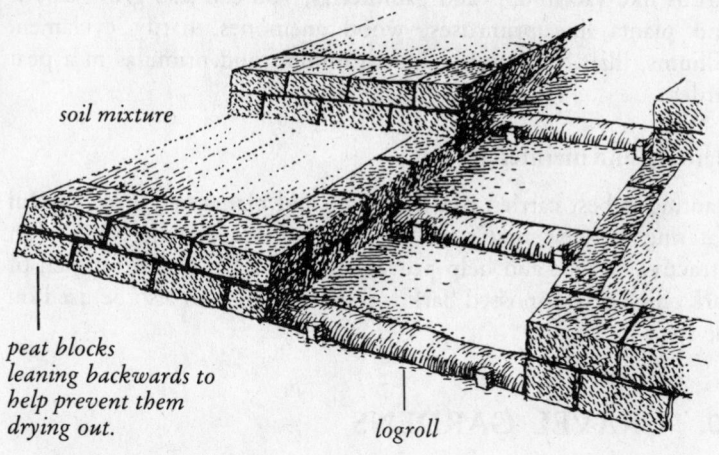

soil mixture

*peat blocks
leaning backwards to
help prevent them
drying out.*

logroll

MAKING A PEAT GARDEN
*A peat garden is the ideal place to grow shade- and moisture-loving
spring flowers.*

Compost

Although this is described as a peat garden, the compost used
should not be pure peat. Use a mixture of one part by volume of
medium grade moss peat, one part leafmould, one part acid-free grit
and one part good garden soil. Recent experience has shown that
replacing the peat with more leafmould gives a compost which is
suitable for many plants but which may not be acid. This reduces
the need to use large quantities of peat – something we must all bear
in mind. Leafmould is not easy to obtain in towns and new gardens,
however, and for gardeners who do not wish to use large quantities
of peat, experiments are continuing with the many peat substitutes
that are becoming available.

Guidelines on plants

If the compost is acid, then rhododendrons, azaleas and other
lime-hating plants can be grown, although if the underlying soil is
limy this will eventually seep into your new compost and the
lime-hating plants will begin to suffer. Apart from the dwarfer

rhododendrons and azaleas, together with related acid-loving shrubs like vacciniums and gaultherias, you can also grow woodland plants like primroses, wood anemones, hardy cyclamen, trilliums, lilies, meconopsis, erythroniums and primulas in a peat garden.

Planting and maintenance

Planting is best carried out in spring, and plants may need careful watering in their first year. To top off the planting, create an attractive surface and help prevent weeds, a 1in (2.5cm) mulch of bark chips or composted bark is ideal and this can also be used on the steps.

10. GRAVEL GARDENS

Many plants grow well in gravel, and gardeners find that if they have a gravel path or drive, plants will self-sow. In fact pea gravel makes a wonderful background for low shrubs, creeping perennials, bulbs, and indeed many sun-loving plants.

In gardens where there is little enthusiasm for a lawn but plenty for growing plants, a gravel garden can be a very attractive and labour-saving feature. Many slightly tender plants which would otherwise not survive the winter will survive under the protection of the gravel mulch. And in hot summers the gravel helps to reduce evaporation from the soil substantially.

Siting

Gravel gardens are best in an open, sunny situation, perhaps with shelter from east winds. That's all.

Preparation

Remove all perennial weeds either by digging them out or by using a weed-killer. If the soil fertility is poor, well-rotted compost or other organic matter can be forked in. If the soil is heavy and poorly drained, 1in (2.5cm) of gravel can be spread over the surface and forked into the top few inches of soil. The area should then be firmed by treading, and a light dressing of fertiliser – 1oz of Growmore per square yard (30g per sq m) – raked in.

Construction

On a slope, pieces of natural stone can be used to retain soil and the gravel can sweep around the ends. Stone can also be used on a flatter surface to break it up. Otherwise, all you need to do is spread 1in (2.5cm) of gravel over the whole area. Gravel is now measured metrically, and a good guide is that one tonne, laid 25mm deep, will cover about 34sq m.

Guidelines on plants

Mediterranean plants are ideal for gravel gardens, especially shrubs like cistus, lavender and rosemary. Dwarf bulbs such as iris and crocus do well in gravel, as do helianthemums, osteospermums, dianthus and perennial wallflowers. Hardy annuals, such as Californian poppies, annual lupins and love-in-a-mist, will usually self-sow generously.

Planting

Planting is best done in spring, except for spring-flowering bulbs, which should be planted in the autumn. Do as much of the planting as possible after the soil has been prepared and before the gravel mulch is applied. When plants need to go in later, just scrape the gravel away, put the plant in place with a little extra gravel mixed in for good drainage, and smooth it all over afterwards. Thorough watering is vital.

Maintenance

Weeds must be hand pulled or given a spot treatment of weed-killer as soon as they appear. Have a clear up in the autumn, when old flowering shoots and any blown leaves which have accumulated around the plants should be removed. Leave most of the cutting down until spring, as the foliage helps to protect tender roots from severe frosts. Rake the gravel to leave it looking neat and to make a good background for early spring bulbs.

11. SPECIAL PLANT COLLECTIONS

Sooner or later most gardeners develop enthusiasms for particular groups of plants. I like Mediterranean plants, my partner likes plants which attract insects, while for twenty years my father grew fuchsias and almost nothing else and then suddenly took an allotment and now grows only vegetables. But beds and borders have never interested him.

There is a lot of satisfaction to be had from taking a special interest in a limited group of plants. Collect different varieties, discover their requirements, look into their origins and, in a small garden, work out how a collection can be integrated into the rest of the garden.

Alpines

Alpines are perhaps the ideal enthusiasm for the owner of a small garden, as they are small themselves and a large collection can be grown in a small space. Most alpines need an open sunny situation and well-drained conditions. This is not always the easiest site to find in a small plot, so woodland plants which are often grown by alpine enthusiasts may be more appropriate.

The simplest way to grow alpines is in raised beds, while old stone troughs, or their newly manufactured equivalent, are ideal for the smallest species. Few gardeners now build rock gardens, and if your garden is a small one you may have no access to it except through the house; transporting large chunks of rock through the sitting-room is not everyone's idea of practical gardening. A few small terraced beds as described for peat gardens can look very attractive, and a ground-level scree bed is easy to make without too much heavy work.

Most alpines flower in the spring, but the season can be extended by seeking out those that flower later in the year and also by growing dwarf bulbs, many of which flower in the autumn. Dwarf shrubs and the occasional very dwarf conifer can add structure and colour in the bleakest months.

Some of the more choice alpines are less tolerant and require protection from wet weather in winter; these can be grown in a well-ventilated cold frame or, more conveniently, in a cold green-house. Ventilation in the greenhouse is paramount, for alpine plants need protection only from the damp air and rain which rots their foliage, not from the cold.

There is a thriving community of alpine growers. The Alpine Garden Society has local groups all over the country, and there is plenty of literature to help both the newcomer and the expert. All in all, alpines are perhaps the perfect enthusiasm for the small gardener.

Foliage plants

In a sense, all plants are foliage plants, for all plants have foliage. But in recent years there has been an increasing recognition that plants with patterned or colourful foliage can make a valuable contribution to the total effect of a garden. This is especially true in a small garden, where it is important that every square yard adds something to the overall impression for as much of the year as possible. By choosing plants which have attractive flowers as well as colourful foliage for much of the rest of the year, you can ensure that they still contribute something even when not actually in flower. Good examples are *Weigela florida* 'Variegata', *Buddleia* 'Harlequin', *Hosta* 'Honeybells', *Ajuga reptans* 'Variegata' and hardy cyclamen.

Variegated plants come to mind first, for there is a huge range of plants with leaves which are striped, blotched, edged or speckled in white, cream, yellow, pink or gold. It has to be said that they excite strong opinions on both sides, as there are gardeners who detest them. But if you add those plants that have yellow, gold, blue, grey, purple, bronze or coppery foliage, plus those with especially bold, lacy or sword-like foliage or leaves in other striking shapes, you have an enormous collection of possibilities for a gardener to select from.

Some gardeners specialise in grey and silver foliage plants, most of which like the same sunny, well-drained conditions, or in variegated plants, which are often more adaptable. But any small garden will benefit from the use of colourful and patterned foliage.

Hardy geraniums

As I write, hardy geraniums, or cranesbills, are among the most popular of hardy plants for many reasons. Almost all are easy to grow and very adaptable. They come in great variety to suit a range of different conditions. They are easy to propagate, they are relatively small in stature, many flower for a long period, they grow well with a wide variety of other plants, especially shrubs, and occasional seedlings appear which are different from the parents.

They are not flamboyant, like delphiniums or Michaelmas daisies, which were more popular thirty years ago when few people grew geraniums. But they fit in with other plants much better.

Roses

A rose collection takes up a lot of space, for roses are not small plants. However, some owners of small gardens eschew almost all other shrubs for the sake of growing as many roses as possible. And in addition to bush roses, climbers can be grown up walls and fences and through shrubs and small trees to add to the range. Beds of hybrid teas are probably not suitable – shrub roses usually fit best into crowded beds and borders. Miniature and dwarf roses are now becoming more popular, with an increasing number of varieties appearing, and it's possible to build a collection of these in a relatively small space – but they are not particularly elegant plants.

Dahlias

Dahlias represent an old enthusiasm and are difficult to deal with in any quantity in a small space. To be grown well they need generous soil preparation, plenty of space and a certain amount of careful attention plus a cool, frost-free place to store the tubers over the winter months. In a small space, the most appropriate way of growing them may be to have a few plants of different varieties set aside for cutting.

Fuchsias

For many years no one took much notice of hardy fuchsias, but as they fit in so well with other border plants more people are beginning to take them seriously. It is true that they are less exotic and flamboyant than the tender types, but for many gardeners without a greenhouse it's possible to grow only the hardier types. And they do look good in mixed borders.

If you wish to grow a collection of tender fuchsias you need a greenhouse or conservatory where the minimum winter temperature can be kept to 40°F (5°C), and you must be prepared to spray against whitefly, which is an almost inevitable pest.

Concentrating on fuchsias for outdoor containers is a sensible compromise, as rooted cuttings taken in late summer can be overwintered in a relatively small area and yet when planted in tubs and baskets in spring quickly make an impressive display.

Cacti

Cacti are not as popular as they used to be, but if you have a frost-free greenhouse they make an interesting subject for a collection and you can keep many varieties even in a small space. Some people are fascinated by the spines, some can't abide them. Contrary to popular opinion, they do not just flower once every seven years. In fact many can be easily raised from seed and some will flower in their second year.

Cacti don't need a great deal of looking after. They need dry, frost-free conditions in winter and more water and clean glass in summer. Many are small and spend most of their lives in small pots, and they have the most exquisite flowers.

Carnivorous plants

In spite of the fact that Venus's fly-trap plants are to be seen in chain stores all over the country, these and other carnivorous plants are not as easy to grow as you might think. They need either a cold or a frost-free greenhouse depending on the variety. Most need constantly moist conditions, with lime-free water and a compost with little in the way of nutrients. They require plenty of light in winter and humid, shady conditions in summer.

They are even more difficult to grow in the greenhouse with other plants than cacti, as the conditions they need are so specific.

Dried flowers

People don't exactly make collections of dried flowers, but they are a specialisation or enthusiasm which can be fitted very well into a small garden. It's surprising how many familiar garden flowers can be successfully dried and pressed (see page 258). Many annuals, such as larkspurs, statice and strawflowers, can be sown in gaps in borders. A few stems can then be cut for drying and the rest left to provide summer colour. Perennials like eryngiums and achilleas are good garden plants in their own right and won't miss a few stems cut in early summer. If you prefer, both annuals and perennials can be sown in short rows specifically for cutting and drying.

Fruit

As modern developments have led to smaller fruit bushes and trees, it has become increasingly possible to grow fruit successfully in a small garden. Some fruit trees and bushes can be integrated into borders, some grown in pots, and if a small area is set aside for a fruit garden it's possible to pick a heavier harvest of a greater variety of crops. (See page 317.)

Vegetables

Vegetables have always been grown in small gardens, ranging from a wigwam of beans at the back of the border to a whole vegetable garden producing a range of crops all the year round. But the development of the deep bed system of growing vegetables and recent research into the spacing of vegetable plants have enabled gardeners to produce heavier crops with less work and without giving over more of the garden to vegetable-growing. Any garden should be able to produce a few salads at least, and most gardens should be able to produce a lot more.

Herbs

Herbs are the easiest of the food crops to accommodate in a small garden, and it's possible to grow quite a range even if you have only a balcony. In fact, if a sunny balcony is all you have, a collection of herbs is the ideal choice to occupy such limited space.

Growing herbs in a small garden is made that much easier by the fact that many herbs are available in varieties which have some extra ornamental feature – coloured foliage, for example. And if they are worth their place as ornamental plants they can go into beds and borders with flowers if you prefer. Alternatively they can be used to make a herb garden which is unusually attractive and colourful – just the thing when every inch of space has to give its best.

Other collections and specialities

Gardeners make collections of all sorts of plants. Orchids are suitable if you have a heated greenhouse, sweet peas if you have a long stretch of 6ft (1.8m) wire fence to clothe. A collection of African violets can be grown indoors, but in a small garden one of the most suitable groups is dwarf bulbs. Many of these can be grown in the garden; the fussier ones can be kept in pots in a cold frame.

Other good plants for the small greenhouse would be miniature and dwarf pelargoniums, pleiones (dwarf orchids) and wild cyclamen. Scented-leaved pelargoniums make good collector's plants for pots and other containers, if you have somewhere to store them in the winter. Other collector's plants suitable for the open garden include double or other old-fashioned primroses, pinks and ferns.

Garden Themes

1. THE FRAGRANT GARDEN

So often scent creates an emotional response in us, and we are happy to grow unexceptional-looking plants if they have a scent to which we respond. Night-scented stock is a prime example – its flowers are not even open during the day. That's not to say that a scented garden or scented border need look dowdy, far from it. But it's true that some plants which are powerfully scented are endowed with this exceptional quality to make up for the fact that, when it comes to attracting pollinating insects, their flowers are small or their colours unattractive.

Scent is a very personal thing. Some people are 'blind' to certain fragrances, and opinions vary as to the acceptability of some smells. Smells are also difficult to describe, and most people describe one smell in terms of another.

It's important to remember that plants develop scents in two forms – their flowers may exude scent to attract pollinators, but their foliage may also contain essential oil which is given off when the leaves are rubbed or which vaporises on very hot days.

Scented plants in the garden

A garden full of fragrant plants would be a mistake. All those scents would simply mingle and you would end up with no distinctive pleasures. But there are some guidelines worth remembering to ensure that your scented plants give their best:

- Try to separate plants which are fragrant at the same time of year.
- Place scented plants where you can appreciate them fully – by doors and gates, behind seats, along paths, climbing over arches.
- In still air scent lingers, so scented plants are less effective set in exposed, windy places.

A fragrant corner

A corner of the patio is a fine spot to set a few fragrant plants. But of course few of us spend much time relaxing on the patio in winter, so winter plants such as witch hazel, Christmas box and winter honeysuckle are best set near the path. They can be hosts for summer climbers to give colour later in the year.

The rest of the plants should reflect the fact that you'll probably use the patio most in the period from late spring to early autumn. Whether you use it more in the evenings than during the day will depend on your own circumstances, but if you do use it in the evening, remember that there are some plants whose scent is at its best at this time.

Among the shrubs which are well worth planting are herbs with aromatic foliage, which can be flung with a flourish on to the barbecue if you are giving a party – rosemary and sage come to mind. One of the classic scented old-fashioned roses would be enough on its own for June and for late evenings. When it's warm enough to sit out well into the night, tobacco plants and jasmine are unsurpassable.

Contrasting aromas highlight their potency, and as well as the ever-popular sweet-smelling plants, plants with a more pungent fragrance such as rue, cotton lavender and curry plant are worthwhile additions and effectively emphasise the sweeter scents by contrast.

2. THE ALL-THE-YEAR-ROUND GARDEN AND THE SEASONAL GARDEN

The all-the-year-round garden is a much discussed ideal but is rarely achieved with any great success – at least, not in the way in which most people envisage it. A garden in which all the plantings look good all the year round is almost an impossible dream. The usual result is that the whole garden always looks well furnished, but never looks spectacular.

But there is a way in which you can have a colourful garden all the year round, and that is by assigning borders to specific seasons. For example, by gathering many of your winter-flowering and winter-colouring plants together in a sunny, sheltered spot where you can easily see them from the path or the kitchen window, you will get the best value from them. Similarly, autumn, spring and summer plants can be grouped separately to make striking displays in separate beds or borders, the interest moving around in the garden as the months go by. Of course, an autumn border need not be completely uninteresting in spring, for a simple carpet of dwarf bulbs will end up giving you a two-season border.

General planting ideas

Winter

A winter border could be based on winter-flowering shrubs, willows and dogwoods for their colourful winter twigs, a few variegated evergreen shrubs and ivies, smaller conifers, snowdrops, bergenias for their winter foliage and winter-flowering hellebores.

Spring

In an open situation, spring displays can be treated as bedding with wallflowers, pansies, forget-me-nots and double daisies planted with bulbs such as tulips and grape hyacinths. The display can be changed each year and can give way to a temporary summer bedding display in June. Alternatively, a partially shaded site such as under fruit trees or next door's oak tree can be given over to spring-flowering woodland plants, for example pulmonarias, late-flowering hellebores, bergenias, erythroniums, daffodils and other bulbs.

Summer

There is a huge range of plants that can be used for a temporary summer display to follow the spring bedding, from familiar seed-raised bedding plants such as marigolds, petunias, lobelia and salvias to the classier cuttings-raised tender perennials – argyranthemums, verbenas, gazanias and so on.

Autumn

Autumn flowers go with autumn foliage, for as the leaves of shrubs turn to orange and yellow so the blue salvias and ceratostigma, the fiery crocosmias and the garden chrysanthemums are at their best. The more lurid Michaelmas daisies need careful placing.

More specific periods

Some gardeners are tempted to plan their garden, or perhaps just one area of it, to be at its best at a more specific time – to tie in with an anniversary, perhaps, or with a regular summer visit to a holiday cottage. This sounds like a fine idea, but with the seasons becoming increasingly unpredictable, such planning can backfire badly. You may always have a big family party in the first week of July, for example, and like to plan for the area round the patio to be at its best at that time. But an unusually warm spring may bring flowering forward by as much as a month, or even more, ruining your plans. It's usually far more practical to be less specific and aim for a longer period of colour so that you can be sure that whether the season be early or late there will be plenty of colour and interest.

3.   THE COTTAGE GARDEN

Most of us have a vague idea of what constitutes a cottage garden. A straight path from gate to front door, lined with pinks or mossy saxifrages and with a tumble of plants behind – roses, hollyhocks, lupins, foxgloves, sweet peas. There may be a little topiary and a few fruit trees, there'll be plenty of vegetables, and any containers from buckets to Wellington boots will accommodate a geranium or a houseleek.

Cottage gardens have changed a lot from medieval times, when animals, especially chickens and the pig, were far more important than vegetables. Vegetables became more common in Queen Elizabeth's reign, and flowers and herbs were grown more, especially hollyhocks, columbines, carnations, sweet williams, peonies and love-in-a-mist. The nineteenth century was probably the heyday of the cottage garden; one wealthy coal-owner actually gave cottagers cabbage plants and fruit bushes from his own nursery, cleared their gardens for them, and even awarded prizes for the best-kept plots.

Well-meaning Victorian ladies with nothing better to do set about improving the lot of the cottager for their own satisfaction. In particular they promoted gardening as an alternative to going to the pub and similar 'immoral' activities.

By the end of the nineteenth century, however, agricultural depression and the drift from country to town had left many cottage gardens abandoned. And the influx of exotic new plants slowly changed those that remained.

The key to cottage gardening is that plants are treated as individuals, and unless they are prolific self-sowers or run rapidly they remain as individuals. It's true that there might be a row of pinks or London's pride along a path, but otherwise it's only in the vegetable garden that you'll find more than one or two of the same plant together. Perennials that could be chopped up with a spade and replanted, annuals that self-sowed and roses that could be grown from twigs simply stuck in the ground were the staple plants, and although many of the varieties that were grown in the nineteenth century are no longer with us and so many newer plants have since been introduced, by keeping in mind the basic ideas it's perfectly possible to create a modern cottage garden.

Siting

You can create a cottage-style garden in sun or shade, in a border or in a bed set in grass, but the most appropriate setting is probably the front garden, where the path can wind through to the front door.

Planning

Over-careful planning is perhaps the antithesis of the cottage garden ideal; allowing the plants to behave naturally is part of the art. And when it comes to which plants to put alongside each other, it's important to be guided by your own tastes and not to follow the recommendations in this or any other book too closely. The cottage garden approach really does involve letting you and the plants do your own thing without too much interference.

Maintenance

Maintenance can be time-consuming – although cottage gardens look fine without the pristine care devoted to showpiece herbaceous borders, they do need weeding, staking and dead-heading and it can be difficult to work among the tumble of plants. Weeds like groundsel and bitter cress can multiply unseen among the tangle of stems, and the roots of bindweed can take a hold before you notice them. Regular weeding is important, and a few stones set between the plants can help you work among them without too much damage.

Dead-heading is, as usual, important to help prolong the display, and although to some extent the plants will support themselves, discreet staking with pea sticks is often useful. A general feed of fertiliser in the spring is advisable, though cottage gardens always used to rely on little more than an annual mulch of well-rotted manure.

General thoughts on planting

Having suggested that you ignore planting recommendations from the likes of me, I shall now proceed to give you a few guidelines – although I hope they still give you plenty of leeway.

I suggest you avoid the most highly developed and highly bred plants, for example F1 hybrid bedding plants, modern hybrid tea and floribunda roses and miniature fruit trees. These may be fine in other situations, but their style is not quite right in a cottage garden. An edging and perhaps a row of espalier fruit trees might be the only concessions to formality, and these will simply mark the back and front of a border. Delphiniums, foxgloves, mulleins, holly-hocks, wigwams of sweet peas and roses on pillars provide height. Annuals and biennials like cornflowers and love-in-a-mist, pansies and sweet william can be allowed to self-sow. Tough perennials like phlox, golden rod, scabious and betony can be left to their own devices for some years, while special campanulas and double primroses need regular division.

4. THE WILDLIFE GARDEN

A 'wildlife oasis' has been the phrase used to describe the city back garden, and it's true that in the sixties and seventies gardens provided just about the only refuge for birds, butterflies and small mammals in some very un-green city areas. Things have changed a little, with local authorities incorporating more city parks and verdant verges in their plans, but gardens are still the prime wildlife habitat in many areas.

Providing for wildlife in a small garden usually ends up as a series of compromises. After all, a number of butterfly caterpillars feed on nettles, but how big a clump of nettles can a small garden cope with? (In fact, you don't really need to grow nettles in the garden, because if there's one plant that is likely to colonise any odd city corners it's the nettle, and you're quite likely to find a clump behind the phone box or in the yard behind the chip shop. I've dragged in a bit of a red herring here!)

How many thistles, then, can you leave to go to seed for the finches? How many damp corners can you leave for insects? How much grass can you leave to grow long for wild flowers and butterflies? How many rotting logs can you leave for beetles? How big a pond can you have and how broad can its shallows be?

Overall approach

You can encourage many different types of wildlife – wild flowers, birds, small mammals, fish and amphibians, butterflies, moths and other insects.

Wild flowers can be grown as specimen plants in borders or in mini-meadows and mini-woods, alongside ponds and even in pots; they usually look a little less tidy than most garden plants.

Birds need nest sites, and the requirements of the various species are different – dense twiggy bushes, tall open shrubs, high trees, holes in trees or logs, secluded ground sites. They need water all the year round and they need food, which can be fruits and berries, seeds, insects of all sorts including pests like aphids, and bird table food. They also need protection from cats.

Small mammals need cover for nesting and feeding. They need seeds, shoots and other vegetable matter or insects to feed on, and their presence is, shall we say, not always compatible with high horticultural standards. They too need protection from cats. Fish, frogs, toads and newts need water, of course, but they also need protection from herons, even in cities.

Butterflies need food plants for their caterpillars and these vary from one species to another. They need nectar for the adults and some need sheltered spots which are cool and dry for hibernation. The variety of conditions which other insects need can usually be provided by not being too rigorous in clearing away garden debris and so leaving both wet and dry corners undisturbed. Native shrubs usually encourage insects more than introduced garden shrubs.

You only need to skim through these requirements to see how many of them conflict with normal garden practice.

Essential constituents

The most important features for encouraging a variety of wildlife are nest sites for birds, nectar plants for butterflies, water and of course a bird table.

Shrubs on north walls and fences provide good nest sites – a pyracantha is an ideal site for thrushes and blackbirds, and there are also the berries later in the year. Nectar plants like buddleias and sedums will attract butterflies, but don't forget spring-flowering plants like aubrietas and honesty.

Ponds should have a deep area, preferably at least 18in (45cm), with shallower shelves and very shallow areas at the edges. They need floating plants like lilies to provide shade and marginal plants for cover, but they should be protected from the accumulation of falling leaves in autumn. If you have young children it's safer to do without the pond. A child can drown in just a few inches of water – and very quickly.

The bird table should be placed where you can see it from the house; keep it away from fences, and from shrubs or other cover where cats might lurk. You can even attach one to a windowsill – the birds will soon get used to coming right up to the house.

PART TWO

The Plants

A Note on the Plants

The plants I have chosen are those which I consider especially suitable for small gardens. Long-flowering varieties, varieties with more than one season of interest, those which are not too fussy and which require little attention have been given priority. Most varieties are available at good garden centres or from the larger seed companies, while the others are available from mail order nurseries (see page 418). The omission of some good plants does not necessarily imply my disapproval, but I have, of course, had to make a choice.

The plants in each section are divided into *First Choices*, those plants which I consider to be the most important and useful small garden plants, and *Special Selection*, a second range of almost equally good plants.

A Note on Names

There's no getting away from it, there are quite a few botanical names coming up. The trouble is that many plants don't have common names and even when they do, using common names can cause confusion. If I write about bluebells you might think you knew exactly what I'm talking about. In the south the bluebell is a prolific bulb that carpets the woods. Its Latin name is *Hyacinthoides non-scriptus*. But in Scotland the bluebell is quite a different plant, *Campanula rotundifolia*, which in the south is called the harebell.

There are plenty of other cases where confusion can arise, so using the botanical name is the only way we can be sure that we're all talking about the same plant.

Plant names are simply shorthand. So when we refer to a plant we don't have to say 'that blue, spring-flowering bulb which carpets deciduous woods in Britain'. We could say bluebell, but of course if we say bluebell there's danger of confusion, so we can learn to call it *Hyacinthoides non-scriptus*.

The name bluebell tells us something about the plant. *Hyacinthoides* does too: it means 'like a hyacinth', which is fair enough, and the name *Campanula* is actually the Latin for 'little bell' – it couldn't be more appropriate.

In this case the Latin name is actually more helpful than 'harebell', for not only does it tell you something about the plant but in some parts of the country harebell is used as a common name for the blue-flowered bulb!

Sometimes, Latin names are adopted as common names and there are plenty of such cases – rhododendron, dahlia and chrysanthemum are obvious examples. Names like buddleia, pyracantha and hosta are well on the way to achieving the same common usage. Many gardeners move from the stage of sticking to common names and cursing Latin to letting names like *Chamaecyparis* and *Arctostaphylos* roll off the tongue.

At first sight Latin names are pretty mysterious, but they needn't be bewildering. Like cars, the names of plants are made up of two main parts: the name *Anemone blanda* is the equivalent of Ford Escort and *Anemone blanda* is slightly different from *Anemone nemerosa*, as the Ford Escort is slightly different from the Ford Orion.

Like cars, plants often have an extra name to denote a special form or colour, so in the same way that there's a Ford Escort Estate and an XRi and you can get them in red or white, there's *Anemone blanda* 'Radar' and there's 'White Splendour'. As with cars, these extra names for plants sometimes describe a special feature, sometimes not. They are always given inverted commas.

In the entries that follow I've given the common names of plants where they have one and they come first, followed by the botanical name for the group (or genus). All dimensions give the height first.

CHAPTER FIVE

ORNAMENTAL PLANTS

The Plants

1. TREES FOR SMALL GARDENS

There are some wonderful trees which are small enough for our purposes, many featuring more than one attraction, be it bark, flowers, fruit or autumn colour. The most serious mistake to make when planting trees is to plant varieties that grow too large too quickly and then hesitate about removing them. Heights given are the average after ten years in the garden.

First choices

MAPLE (ACER) Choose the smaller species. The snakebark maple, *A. griseum*, has mahogany-coloured, peeling bark and fiery autumn colour, while the more upright-growing snakebark maple, *A. grosseri* var. *hersii*, has green and white streaked bark and autumn colour turning from yellow to crimson. Avoid sycamore, *A. pseudoplatanus*, which grows far too large and has very hungry roots.
Growing conditions: Most soils, except very limy ones.
Height: 15ft (4.5m).

BIRCH (BETULA) Attractive trees with white bark and yellow autumn colour, growing quickly though not too large. Silver birch, *B. pendula*, is very reliable and it has a delightful, elegant weeping form, 'Tristis'. For a very tight space there's 'Youngii', which is smaller and more weeping but less elegant. 'Jermyns' is a little larger but has lovely white bark and long catkins.
Growing conditions: Any reasonable soil that is not waterlogged.
Height: 25ft (7.5m), but casts only light shade ('Youngii' is a little smaller).

MOUNTAIN ASH (SORBUS) Smallish trees with white flowers followed by red, orange, yellow or white berries and good autumn colour. The rounded *S. vilmorinii* has red and purple autumn colour and dark pink berries fading to white. 'Sheerwater Seedling' is more upright, with red berries. Avoid the once popular 'Joseph Rock', which is prone to fireblight disease, and plant 'Xanthocarpa' instead.

Growing conditions: Best in a good soil and full sun, but very tolerant.

Height: 15ft (4.5m).

Special selection

ALDER (ALNUS)   For damp soils the cut-leaved alder, *A. glutinosa* 'Imperialis', is ideal, although it may eventually become too large.

Growing conditions: Any soils except dry ones.

Height: 30ft (9m).

CERCIDIPHYLLUM   *C. japonicum* is an elegant small tree grown mainly for its foliage, which emerges with a reddish tint, opens sea-green and then turns rich red and yellow in autumn.

Growing conditions: Good soil, dislikes strongly limy soil.

Height: 20ft (6m).

DOGWOOD (CORNUS)   A very small, tree-like shrub, *C. kousa* var. *chinensis* is upright in growth with large creamy white flowers, turning pink, in late spring and summer.

Growing conditions: Hates limy soil.

Height: 8ft (2.4m).

LEYLAND'S CYPRESS (× CUPRESSOCYPARIS)   This is a completely unsuitable tree for small gardens, as it grows to such a vast size. Tolerable as a hedge, but there are others as good with less tendency to romp.

EUCALYPTUS   Silver foliage on a tall and very quick-growing tree. *E. gunnii* is useful for providing a substantial feature very quickly and is easily removed later – which it should be. Grow from seed and plant when small.

Growing conditions: Prefers light and well-drained soil, but tolerant.

Height: 30ft (9m).

MAGNOLIA KOBUS   A small, spreading tree with large leaves and pure white flowers. Takes some years before it flowers well.
Growing conditions: Any reasonable soil.
Height: 20ft (6m).

CRAB APPLES (MALUS)   These are excluded from the 'First choice' section by their spreading habit and bushy growth, casting dense shade, plus their worrying eventual size. Nevertheless, they combine attractive flowers with a heavy crop of ornamental fruits later. 'Golden Hornet' is upright in growth with white flowers and yellow crabs; 'John Downie' is also fairly upright with white flowers and orange fruits which are the best for jelly; 'Royalty' is another upright grower with deep purple foliage, pink flowers and claret red fruits.
Growing conditions: Any reasonable soil, hates waterlogging.
Height: 20ft (6m).

FALSE ACACIA (ROBINIA)   Worthy of the 'First choice' section but demoted due to its recent overplanting – it's very striking but you can already see it in almost every street. *R. pseudacacia* 'Frisia' is a quick-growing, upright tree thriving on poor soils with bright yellow leaves all season. Thorny.
Growing conditions: Any reasonable soil.
Height: 20ft (6m).

WILLOW (SALIX)   Avoid the large weeping willows at all costs – they are far too large and the roots will undermine the foundations of your house. But the tiny Kilmarnock willow, *S. caprea* 'Pendula', is ideal, with silvery catkins on vertically hanging, purplish stems. There's also the rather bushy *S. exigua*, with long narrow silver foliage, and the taller, weeping *S. purpurea* 'Pendula' with purple stems and blueish leaves. Although it may eventually become too large, the corkscrew willow, *S. matsudana* 'Tortuosa', with spiral-ling twigs, is intriguing. All these willows cast only a light shade.
Growing conditions: Any soils, including wet ones.
Height: *S. caprea* 'Pendula' 10ft (3m); *S. purpurea* 'Pendula' and *S. matsudana* 'Tortuosa' rather taller.

WHITEBEAM (SORBUS)   White-flowered tree of upright growth with silvery undersides to the leaves and red berries in autumn. They can cast rather too much shade; *S.* × *hostii* has the neatest

growth and pink flowers followed by red berries.
Growing conditions: Any reasonable soil, good on chalk.
Height: 10ft (3m).

2. EVERGREEN SHRUBS

Evergreen shrubs provide the solid planting in many gardens and
it's important that they should not be too dour. The choice here
includes plenty of varieties with coloured foliage and generous
fruits and berries. Use them as support for lightweight climbers to
add colour at other times of year.

First choices

WORMWOOD (ARTEMISIA) An attractively spreading shrub,
'Powis Castle' has lacy, silver foliage though no flowers. Trim in
spring; roots easily from summer cuttings.
Growing conditions: Sunny, well-drained site.
Pruning: Cut back hard in spring to rejuvenate.
Height: 2 × 3ft (60 × 90cm).

CAMELLIA Upright or spreading, early spring-flowering shrubs
of modest size for moisture-retentive soils. 'Donation' is a double
pink, 'Adolphe Audusson' is blood red and 'Alba Plena' is a double
white. Do not plant where they catch the morning sun. Prune only
to keep in shape, make more by layering.
Growing conditions: Acid soil, light shade, must not dry out.
Pruning: Only occasional shaping after flowering usually required.
Height: 6ft (1.8m).

CALIFORNIAN LILAC (CAENOTHUS) Two types. 'Autumnal
Blue' is a vigorous shrub which can be grown free-standing in a
sunny bed and hard-pruned annually. It has dark leaves and clouds
of blue flowers through summer and autumn. It can also be trained
flat against a south-facing wall or fence, projecting shoots being cut
back each spring. Its quick covering power is most useful. 6 × 6ft
(1.8 × 1.8m). *C. thyrsiflorus* var. *repens* carries darker flowers,

earlier in the year, but more importantly has a useful creeping habit, trailing attractively down from a raised bed or over a rock. It's best left unpruned but can be shaped after flowering. 3 × 4ft (0.9 × 1.2m).
Growing conditions: Sun and well-drained soil.

PERENNIAL WALLFLOWER (CHEIRANTHUS)   One of the longest-flowering of all shrubs, 'Bowles' Mauve' all but flowers itself to death. It makes a rounded bush of narrow blue-green foliage covered with spikes of purple flowers in almost every month of the year, but especially in spring. 'Bredon' is similar but bright yellow. After two or three years they usually die, but they root easily from cuttings.
Growing conditions: Best in full sun.
Pruning: None.
Height: 1½ × 1½ft (45 × 45cm).

CONVOLVULUS CNEORUM   Silky silver foliage on a low, rather lax shrub with a continuous show of white bindweed-like trumpets for months in summer. Roots from summer cuttings.
Growing conditions: Full sun and good drainage.
Pruning: Occasional shaping only.
Height: 1½ × 2½ft (45 × 75cm).

ELEAGNUS PUNGENS 'MACULATA'   The sunniest of variegated shrubs, with an irregular, butter-yellow splash in the middle of each dark green leaf. This vigorous shrub can be grown free-standing or trained flat on a north-facing wall or fence. Roots from summer cuttings.
Growing conditions: Any reasonable soil, sun or light shade.
Pruning: Usually left unpruned but can be thinned and thoughtfully reduced in spring. Cut out any plain green shoots.
Height: 8 × 8ft (2.4 × 2.4m).

WINTER HEATHER (ERICA)   Neat spreading plants for winter flowering, *E. carnea* varieties grow in full sun in either acid or limy soil. 'Springwood White' is outstanding, as is the dark-leaved, dark pink-flowered 'Vivellii', but there are many more, some with coloured foliage. Never allow them to dry out. Rooted pieces can often be found where the shoots touch the soil.

Growing conditions: Full sun or very light shade; lime-tolerant but prefers acid conditions.
Pruning: Clip over after flowering.
Height: 1½ × 2½ft (45 × 75cm), but depends on severity of pruning.

BELL HEATHER (ERICA) With its pretty bell-shaped flowers, *E. cinerea* makes a loose mound of twiggy shoots tipped with flowers in summer and early autumn. Must not dry out. 'C. D. Eason' is pink, 'Alba Minor' is white.
Growing conditions: Acid soil, full sun or light shade.
Pruning: Clip over after flowering.
Height: 1 × 1½ft (30 × 45cm), but depends on severity of pruning.

CREEPING EUONYMUS (EUONYMUS) Small, attractive plants of spreading habit, coming in a wide variety of variegations. Thriving in sun or shade, 'Emerald 'n' Gold' has gold-margined leaves and turns pinkish in freezing weather. The less vigorous 'Silver Queen' has almost a white margin to the leaf. Low shoots will root into the soil.
Growing conditions: Very tolerant of soils; all thrive in full shade, though gold varieties are best in full sun.
Pruning: Prune to keep shapely if necessary.
Height: About 2 × 3ft (60 × 90cm), depending on variety and where planted.

SHRUBBY VERONICA (HEBE) Two types. The low silver-leaved carpeter with small clusters of white flowers in spring is 'Pagei', and it will root occasionally where the shoots touch the ground. 9in × 2ft (23 × 60cm). The more upright, dark-leaved 'La Seduisante', with its spikes of deep crimson flowers, is an especially long-flowering plant which needs hard pruning in spring. Roots from summer cuttings. 4 × 4ft (120 × 120cm). There are many other varieties in different colours.
Pruning: Trim and shape up in spring; can be cut back very hard for rejuvenation.
Growing conditions: Both types need good drainage and full sun.

PENCIL JUNIPER (JUNIPERUS) One of the smallest conifers for a trough or raised bed, *J. communis* 'Compressa' grows very slowly

and makes a small, pointed pillar of greeny-grey foliage. Difficult to root from cuttings.
Growing conditions: Demands good drainage and sunshine.
Pruning: None.
Height: 18 × 6in (45 × 15cm).

LAVENDER (LAVANDULA) 'Hidcote' is the neatest and most compact lavender, with stout spikes of violet flowers topping the aromatic grey-green foliage. Roots from summer cuttings.
Growing conditions: Sun and good drainage.
Pruning: Trim in spring and remove dead flowers.
Height: 18 × 18in (45 × 45cm), depending on severity of pruning.

GOLDEN PRIVET (LIGUSTRUM) Often grown as a hedge, the semi-evergreen golden privet, *L. ovalifolium* 'Aureum', is far better as a foliage plant in the border. The yellow leaves have green centres, though plain green shoots may appear and should be cut out. Very useful for cutting for flower arrangements. Roots from summer cuttings.
Growing conditions: Happy in most soils except very limy ones, and in full sun to full shade.
Pruning: Prune back by at least half in spring.
Height: 6 × 6ft (1.8 × 1.8m), smaller if pruned hard and regularly.

TREE LUPIN (LUPINUS) Quick to make a sizeable bush, but conveniently short-lived so it can be replaced with something more choice. The tree lupin, *L. arboreus*, can be very easily raised from seed and quickly makes a rounded bush with small, fingered lupin-like leaves and spikes of yellow or white flowers. Knock off snow, which may break the branches. Prone to attack from its exclusive big grey aphid.
Growing conditions: Best in full sun and any reasonable soil.
Pruning: Tidy up growth in spring.
Height: 4 × 4ft (1.2 × 1.2m).

FIRETHORN (PYRACANTHA) Spiny plants with white flowers in spring and red, orange or yellow fruits in autumn. Good on north walls. 'Mojave' has orange berries and is very prolific, 'Shawnee' is paler, while the best red-fruited form is probably *P. × watereri*.

Growing conditions: Tolerant of most soils and situations except chalk.
Pruning: None usually required, but can be reduced in late winter if necessary.
Height: 10 × 6ft (3 × 1.8m) unpruned.

DWARF RHODODENDRON (RHODODENDRON)   Dwarf rhododendrons are ideal for acid soils or raised beds, especially the *yakushimanum* hybrids ('yaks'). Varieties in this group, some named after the seven dwarfs, make tight, rounded bushes of attractive foliage covered in flowers in spring. Increase by layering.
Growing conditions: Acid soil, light shade.
Pruning: None usually required, though dead-heading useful.
Height: About 2 × 2ft (60 × 60cm), depending on variety.

MISS JESSUP'S ROSEMARY (ROSMARINUS)   A rosemary with upward-sweeping branches carrying the typical dusky-green leaves. The blue flowers appear on and off all year but especially in late spring. *R. officinalis* 'Miss Jessup's Upright' also makes a good informal hedge and won't resent losing sprigs to the kitchen. Knock off snow to prevent branches breaking. Summer cuttings root easily.
Growing conditions: Best in hot sun and well-drained soil.
Pruning: Tidy up in spring and cut out one or two older shoots entirely.
Height: 4 × 3ft (1.2 × 0.9m).

PURPLE-LEAVED SAGE (SALVIA)   Not only a useful culinary plant but very attractive, the purple-leaved sage, *S. officinalis* 'Purpurascens', makes a low, spreading mound of dusky-purple leaves with spikes of blue flowers in summer. There's also a very attractive yellow and green variegated variety ('Icterina'), a slow-growing and more temperamental purple, pink and white-leaved variety ('Tricolor'), and a plain yellow-leaved one ('Kew Gold'). Low shoots root into the soil.
Growing conditions: Sunny and well drained.
Pruning: Cut back latest growth by half in spring.
Height: 2 × 3ft (60 × 90cm).

CHRISTMAS BOX (SARCOCOCCA) For winter scent in a small garden, the Christmas box, *S. confusa*, is unrivalled. Dark green, pointed foliage on upright, slowly suckering shoots hides small white flowers with a powerful sweet scent in winter. Black berries sometimes follow. Slow-growing in early years, quickening later. Ideal by the front door or front gate. Detach rooted suckers from mature plants.
Growing conditions: Any reasonable soil in sun or shade.
Pruning: No pruning required.
Height: 2 × 2ft (60 × 60cm).

SHRUBBY RAGWORT (SENECIO) A rather lax shrub, 'Sunshine' has silvery foliage and clusters of bright yellow, ragwort-like flowers starting in early summer and continuing for many months. Low shoots can be layered.
Growing conditions: A sunny site which is not waterlogged.
Pruning: Tidy up in spring; cut old specimens hard back occasionally to rejuvenate them.
Height: 2½ × 2½ft (75 × 75cm).

RHEINGOLD (THUYA) A neat, conical conifer with fine gold (not yellow) foliage in summer turning coppery in winter. Knock snow off in winter. Rooting cuttings is difficult.
Growing conditions: Any reasonable soil that is not waterlogged, in full sun.
Pruning: Trimming rarely necessary.
Height: 2 × 2ft (60 × 60cm).

YUCCA A very distinct and architectural plant, *Y. filamentosa* produces a large rosette of long, grey, sharp-pointed foliage with curly threads along their edges, on a short trunk. Although slow to start, 6ft (1.8m) flower spikes carrying hundreds of white bells eventually appear in late summer. Rooted offsets can occasionally be detached.
Growing conditions: Can be grown in tubs, although this restricts the size, or in a sunny, well-drained bed.
Pruning: Cut out the flower spike when the flowers drop, or leave through winter and remove in spring; cut off ragged leaves too.
Height: 3 × 3ft (90 × 90cm).

Special selection

BOULEVARD (CHAMAECYPARIS)   C. pisifera 'Boulevard' is an unusual conifer with slightly curled sprays of sharp silvery blue foliage, especially colourful in summer.
Growing conditions: Partial shade and lime-free soil.
Pruning: Has a tendency for the foliage to brown; snip this out.
Height: 2 × 2ft (60 × 60cm).

CREEPING COTONEASTER (COTONEASTER)   A widely spreading but slow-growing creeping plant with small dark leaves, C. microphyllus has white flowers in spring followed by scarlet berries. Grows very flat.
Growing conditions: Any reasonable soil in sun or shade.
Pruning: Occasional shaping only.
Height: 1 × 3ft (30 × 90cm).

TALL COTONEASTER (COTONEASTER)   'Cornubia' is a tall, upright and vigorous shrub with long green leaves, clusters of white flowers in spring and masses of red berries. Good for a specimen or screen, it can even be trained into a small tree.
Growing conditions: Thrives in poor soil.
Pruning: None usually required, though can be reduced in late winter.
Height: 8 × 8ft (2.4 × 2.4m).

FATSIA   A fine sculptural evergreen for shade, F. japonica has large, dark, fingered foliage and open clusters of rounded cream flowerheads in spring. The less vigorous 'Variegata', with creamy margins to the leaves, needs shelter.
Growing conditions: Best in good soil and shade.
Pruning: None usually required but can be cut back hard in spring if necessary.
Height: 5 × 5ft (1.5 × 1.5m).

HOLLY (ILEX)   Most are too big for small gardens, but I. aquifolium 'Pyramidalis' makes a narrow upright pillar of foliage with red berries in autumn. It's also self-fertile, so needs no male plant. 6 × 1½ft (1.8m × 45cm). For a variegated holly, try the slow-growing but extra spiny 'Ferox Argentea', 2 × 2ft (60 × 60cm). All

are sometimes disfigured by leaf-mining caterpillars.
Growing conditions: Any soil, any conditions except deep shade.
Pruning: None usually required, but can be reduced in spring if necessary.

SPANISH JUNIPER (JUNIPERUS) An absolutely flat-growing juniper with horizontal branches, *J. sabina* 'Tamariscifolia' has dense bright green leaves, greyer at first. Good for covering manholes.
Growing conditions: Any reasonable soil in full sun.
Pruning: Can be shaped and reduced in spring if necessary.
Height: 1 × 3ft (30 × 90cm).

BAY (LAURUS) Bay, *L. nobilis*, can be grown in the open but is ideal in a large tub, where it can be trained into a pyramid or a round-headed standard.
Growing conditions: Sunny and well drained.
Pruning: Can be left unpruned or trimmed to shape.
Height: Depends on training.

WINTER HONEYSUCKLE (LONICERA FRAGRANTISSIMA) A twiggy, semi-evergreen bush for the back of the border or for training on a north-facing, but not overhung fence. The creamy flowers of *L. fragrantissima* are small but powerfully scented.
Growing conditions: Any reasonable soil, in sun or light shade.
Pruning: Prune after flowering, only to reduce size.
Height: 4 × 6ft (1.2 × 1.8m), more on a fence.

BOXLEAF HONEYSUCKLE (LONICERA NITIDA) An unlikely honeysuckle with almost invisible flowers, *L. nitida* 'Baggesen's Gold' has tiny golden leaves which in autumn colour especially well in sun.
Growing conditions: Dislikes very dry or very wet soil.
Pruning: Remove one-third of the wood each spring.
Height: 2 × 3ft (60 × 90cm).

OREGON GRAPE (MAHONIA) *M. aquifolium* is a slightly floppy, suckering shrub with dark leaves and clusters of yellow flowers in spring.

Growing conditions: Tolerates a wide variety of conditions, including dry shade.
Pruning: Cut out the oldest wood every three years.
Height: 3 × 3ft (90 × 90cm).

MAHONIA   A splendidly architectural plant, 'Charity' produces a few stout, upright branches carrying long leaves divided into pairs of holly-like leaflets. These are topped by 10in (25cm) upright spikes of yellow flowers in early winter; these can be damaged by birds, however.
Growing conditions: Best in soil with plenty of organic matter, in full sun.
Pruning: Cut out tops of shoots immediately after flowering for the first few years.
Height: 5 × 3ft (1.5 × 0.9m).

OSMANTHUS   A small and dark-leaved shrub with very sweetly scented small white flowers which line the branches in early spring. Can be fence-trained.
Growing conditions: Most soils, in light shade.
Pruning: None usually required.
Height: 4 × 4ft (1.2 × 1.2m).

PERNETTYA   Fruiting shrub with an irregular branch structure. The spring flowers of *P. mucronata* are small and white; the berries can be white, pink, red or purple and last for months.
Growing conditions: Acid soil; full sun or partial shade.
Pruning: When mature, cut out old straggly shoots occasionally.
Height: 1½ × 2½ft (45 × 75cm).

PIERIS   Lime-hating shrubs with bright red young foliage and strings of white, lily-of-the-valley flowers in spring. 'Wakehurst' has the brightest young shoots and is not too vigorous, 'Debutante' is neater with the most flowers, 'Variegata' is smaller still with creamy-white leaf edges but almost no flowers.
Growing conditions: Acid soil, light shade.
Pruning: None usually required.
Height: 5 × 3ft (1.5 × 0.9m) down to 2 × 2ft (60 × 60cm), depending on variety.

DWARF RHODODENDRON (RHODODENDRON) In addition to those mentioned on page 172 in the 'First choice' section, there are a large number of other dwarf rhodos with a wide variety of colours and flowering times. These include the bright yellow, upright-growing 'Yellow Hammer', the pure white 'Bric à Brac', the scarlet 'Elizabeth' and the late winter-flowering but deciduous pink 'Praecox'.
Growing conditions: Acid soil, light shade.
Pruning: Little usually required, though dead-heading is useful.
Height: About 2 × 2ft (60 × 60cm), depending on variety.

BUTCHER'S BROOM (RUSCUS) In dry shade and other very difficult spots, butcher's broom, *R. aculeatus*, does well. Upright growth, dark holly-like leaves and possibly red berries.
Growing conditions: All soils, all situations but full sun.
Pruning: None.
Height: 3 × 3ft (90 × 90cm).

RUE (RUTA) The blue leaves on their upright stems have a pungent smell, though it's not apparent unless you rub the leaves. The leaf colour of *R. graveolens* 'Jackman's Blue' is unique, and there are spikes of yellow flowers too. Can cause a rash.
Growing conditions: Like sun and good drainage.
Pruning: Trim lightly in early spring.
Height: 2½ × 3ft (75 × 90cm).

SKIMMIA Tough, bushy evergreens with white flowers in late spring and bright berries later. Berrying females need a male for pollination. *S. japonica* 'Foremanii' is the best fruiting variety, and 'Rubella', with purple-tinted leaves and pink buds, and the large-flowered 'Kew Green' the best males.
Growing conditions: Lime-free soil, in sun or light shade.
Pruning: None usually required.
Height: 1½ × 1½ft (45 × 45cm).

3. DECIDUOUS SHRUBS

First choices

CUT-LEAVED MAPLE (ACER)   Slow-growing but long-lived, the cut-leaved maple, *A. palmatum* 'Dissectum', makes a dome-shaped shrub with finely-cut green foliage turning to orange in autumn. There is also a purple-leaved variety, 'Dissectum Atropurpureum'. Makes a good tub plant as long as the tub is large.
Growing conditions: Avoid limy soil; best shaded from midday sun and sheltered from east winds.
Pruning: None usually required.
Height: 2½ × 3ft (75 × 90cm).

BARBERRY (BERBERIS)   A number of tolerant varieties, all spiny, with varying leaf colours and growing habits. The yellow leaved *B. thunbergii* 'Aurea', 3 × 4ft (0.9 × 1.2m), deepens from pale yellow in spring to deep yellow by late summer then in autumn reddens from the edge of the leaf inwards; best shaded from the midday sun. 'Atropurpurea' is a similar purple-leaved plant, but there are some interesting compact dark-leaved forms, like the narrow and upright 'Helmund Pillar', 2½ × 1ft (75 × 30cm), the foot-high bun of 'Bagatelle', and the exceptionally dark 'Dart's Red Lady', 1½ × 3ft (45 × 90cm). The spinier *B. wilsonae*, 3 × 4ft (0.9 × 1.2m), is grown for its pink and orange berries, which appear at the same time as the salmony autumn colour. All root from summer cuttings.
Growing conditions: Any reasonable soil and situation; dark-leaved varieties are best in sun.
Pruning: Remove the oldest shoots every year or two.

BUTTERFLY BUSH (BUDDLEIA) Strong-growing, fragrant shrubs, rapidly making large specimens but easy to keep in hand by drastic pruning each spring. All have long spikes of white, lilac, purple, reddish or almost black flowers which attract butterflies. The well-known *B. davidii* hybrids have the best colour range and also a white variegated form, 'Harlequin', while the lilac-flowered *B. fallowiana* boasts greyish leaves.
Growing conditions: Any reasonable soil, best in full sun.

Pruning: In spring, cut back to about 3in (7.5cm) from the base of previous year's growth.
Height: 7 × 5ft (2.1 × 1.5m), larger if not pruned.

SHRUBBY PLUMBAGO (CERATOSTIGMA)   One of the best of all autumn plants, *C. willmottianum* combines many weeks of sparkling blue flowers with red and yellow autumn colour. Growth is spreading and rather floppy. Divide carefully.
Growing conditions: Best in good soil and full sun.
Pruning: Trim back to ground level in spring.
Height: 3 × 3ft (90 × 90cm).

DOGWOOD (CORNUS)   The best of the dogwoods combine two very useful characteristics – coloured stems in winter and variegated foliage. *C. alba* 'Elegantissima' has bright red stems and white-margined leaves, white-mottled in the centre; 'Aurea' has yellow leaves; 'Gouchaltii' has yellow leaf margins. There's also 'Kesselringii', with almost black stems and very dark leaves. Easily rooted from hardwood cuttings or layers.
Growing conditions: Best in dampish soils and sun or light shade.
Pruning: Should be cut almost to ground level each spring to encourage the coloured stems.
Height: 3 × 3ft (90 × 90cm), much larger if unpruned.

DAPHNE   All daphnes are scented, but *D. × burkwoodii* 'Somerset' is one of the best. Neat in habit, with moderate growth, it's an ideal small garden plant. The clusters of pale pink flowers, darker in bud, appear in late spring and early summer and the scent will pervade the whole garden. Difficult to propagate. The more upright *D. mezereum*, with its purplish flowers lining the vertical shoots in late winter, is also powerfully scented and prefers rich limy soil. Self-sown seedlings may appear following red fruits.
Growing conditions: Best in rich limy soil and sun or partial shade.
Pruning: None usually necessary.
Height: 2 × 1½ft (60 × 45cm).

VARIEGATED FUCHSIA (FUCHSIA)   There's one genuinely hardy fuchsia that should be in all gardens. *F. magellanica* 'Versicolor' produces pink shoots early in the year, and the leaves unfold to grey-green margined with pink ánd cream. The dainty flowers, purple skirts with a red twirl, hang down from the arching branches for months. The one plant you must have. Summer cuttings root easily.

Growing conditions: Any reasonable soil, in full sun.
Pruning: Cut back almost to ground level in spring.
Height: 3 × 3ft (90 × 90cm).

MAGNOLIA   Many magnolias eventually become too big for the small garden, but *M. stellata* is an exception. A dense, rounded, twiggy shrub, white starry flowers cover it in early spring before the leaves appear. Plant it where the early morning sun will not damage frosted flowers. Make more by layering low branches.

Growing conditions: Any soil except a very limy one, and from full sun to light shade.
Pruning: No pruning needed.
Height: 5 × 6ft (1.5 × 1.8m).

MOCK ORANGE (PHILADELPHUS)   Sweetly scented, white-flowered shrubs for spring. Those with single flowers can be fleeting and also make very large bushes. 'Manteau d'Hermine' solves both these problems, as it's dwarf and its double flowers last much longer. 2½ × 2½ft (75 × 75cm). *P. coronarius* 'Aureus' has single flowers but the foliage is bright yellow for most of the season. The foliage is at its best in dappled shade. 4 × 2ft (120 × 60cm).

Growing conditions: Any soil and any site not fully shaded.
Pruning: Cut out about a third of the older shoots after blooming.
Problems: Blackfly.

SHRUBBY CINQUEFOIL (POTENTILLA)   Rounded twiggy bushes with a burst of flowers in late spring, followed by a constant spattering until well into the autumn. The flowers of *P. fruticosa* come in red, pink, orange, yellow and white depending on variety; the reds and pinks tend to fade in full sun. Layers well.

Growing conditions: Any reasonable soil, in full sun or a little shade.
Pruning: Only a little shaping in spring is needed usually, plus occasional removal of old shoots.
Height: About 2½ × 2½ft (75 × 75cm) depending on variety.

ROSES (ROSA) There are so many different roses available that it's possible to find at least one for almost every conceivable situation. Here among the premier shrubs I'll choose representatives from three types; the rest are in the 'Special selection'.

Old-fashioned roses The charm of old roses is again becoming universally appreciated. Most are rather large for a small garden, but two that combine modest size and sweet scent are the dainty 'Old Blush China', and 'Cecile Brunner'. 'Old Blush China' (also known as the 'Monthly Rose' for the consistency of its flowering) has pale pink flowers which darken with age, and grows to 4 × 3ft (1.2 × 0.9m). 'Cecile Brunner' has miniature blush pink, HT type flowers at 2 × 2ft (60 × 60cm). More modern but in the old style is 'Pretty Jessica', with perfectly formed, rich pink flowers, at 2½ × 2ft (75 × 60cm).
Pruning: Thin out by removing the oldest wood in spring.

Small floribundas Of the smaller floribundas I would pick out 'Margaret Merill' for its neat growth, dark bronzed foliage, pure white flowers and strong scent, at 2½ × 2½ft (75 × 75cm).
Pruning: Cut back to about 12in (30cm) in spring.

Miniature and patio roses Many of these have no scent but reach a maximum height of about 2ft (60cm). I would recommend the soft pink 'Gentle Touch' which *is* scented, the peachy 'Sweet Dream', the scarlet 'Born Free' and 'Cinderella' in blushed white.
Pruning: Cut back by about half in spring.
Growing conditions: Full sun and any reasonable soil.
Problems: Aphids, blackspot and powdery mildew are as troublesome as on most roses.

SPIRAEA Spiraeas come in many forms, but it's those with attractive foliage which concern us here, especially 'Golden Princess'. This is a neat bushy shrub whose young shoots emerge in a reddish bronze and change to gold as they mature. They retain this colour all season and carry flat heads of bright pink flowers in midsummer. These can be removed if the colour clash offends you. Roots from summer cuttings.
Growing conditions: Grow slightly shaded from the midday sun to avoid scorch.
Pruning: Prune hard in spring for the best foliage.
Height: 1½ × 1½ft (45 × 45cm).

WEIGELA   These tough shrubs come in many varieties, but the coloured foliage types are the most useful. W. *florida* 'Foliis Purpureis' is a dwarf variety with purple-coloured young shoots which become duskier as the summer progresses, also pink flowers from late spring, 2 × 2ft (60 × 60cm). W. *florida* 'Aureovariegata' makes a fine picture with its creamy-yellow edged leaves and soft pink flowers in generous bunches, 3 × 3ft (90 × 90cm). Roots from summer cuttings.

Growing conditions: Any reasonable soil, in full sun or part shade.
Pruning: Cut out about a third of older wood each year after flowering.

Special selection

ABELIA   A long-flowering shrub for summer and autumn, A. × *grandiflora* makes a rounded bush carrying dark, lustrous leaves and pink-budded, white, scented flowers. 'Francis Mason' is a yellow-variegated form.

Growing conditions: Any reasonable soil in full sun.
Pruning: Thin out shoots in spring.
Height: 4 × 3ft (1.2 × 0.9m).

CARYOPTERIS   A valuable grey-leaved, late-flowering shrub of modest size, C. × *clandonensis* 'Heavenly Blue' produces clusters of blue flowers towards the tips of the shoots in late summer and autumn.

Growing conditions: Any reasonable soil in sun.
Pruning: Prune hard in spring.
Height: 2 × 2½ft (60 × 75cm).

HERRING-BONE PLANT (COTONEASTER)   The distinctive fan-like, fish-bone structure of C. *horizontalis* carries white flowers in spring and red berries later with the orange autumn colour. Good as an angular shrub, especially against a north wall.

Growing conditions: Any reasonable soil in sun or partial shade.
Pruning: None usually needed, but can be reduced in spring.
Height: 1½ × 3ft (45 × 90cm).

BROOM (CYTISUS)   A popular plant, but of limited value owing to its fleeting spring flowering season, maybe as little as a couple of

weeks. *C. × kewensis* is a very small trailing variety with cream flowers, *C. × beanii* is similar but bright yellow. Both 9 × 24in (23 × 60cm). The many taller varieties come in a range of colours: 'Allgold' is yellow, 'Hollandia' purplish-red. 3 × 3ft (90 × 90cm).
Growing conditions: Full sun, and any reasonable soil that is not too limy.
Pruning: Newest growth can be cut by half after flowering, but best left unpruned.

WINGED EUONYMUS (EUONYMUS)   A slow-growing shrub with unusual winged stems, *E. alatus* is grown for its spectacular scarlet autumn colour. Tolerant of most soils and situations save deep shade.
Growing conditions: Full sun and any reasonable soil.
Pruning: None usually needed.
Height: 5 × 5ft (1.5 × 1.5m).

FORSYTHIA   An old favourite. 'Lynwood' is the best of the forsythias, with bright, butter-yellow flowers in early spring. 'Mini-Gold' is a little less vigorous and a little shorter. Good for cutting. Very tolerant.
Growing conditions: Any reasonable soil, and an open position.
Pruning: Cut out about a third of the oldest growth each spring.
Height: 5 × 3ft (1.5 × 0.9m).

FOTHERGILLA   A slightly fussy shrub, *F. major* is nevertheless generous with its fragrant white winter flowers and fiery autumn colours when happy.
Growing conditions: Acid soil and light shade.
Pruning: None usually needed.
Height: 3 × 3ft (90 × 90cm).

WITCH HAZEL (HAMAMELIS)   The scent from the yellow, spidery flowers of *H. mollis* 'Pallida' in winter is captivating. Eventually it becomes rather large, but it can be planted in a carefully chosen spot with this in mind. The yellow autumn colour is good too.
Growing conditions: Any soil that is not limy, in full sun or light shade.
Pruning: None required.
Height: 7 × 6ft (2.1 × 1.8m).

SEA BUCKTHORN (HIPPOPHAE)   A grey-leaved, orange-berried shrub for a screen or hedge, *H. rhamnoides* retains its berries well into the winter. Male and female plants needed for fruit set. Rather vigorous but open in habit, casting little shade.
Growing conditions: Light soil, in sun or partial shade.
Pruning: Cut hard in spring; hedges can be trimmed regularly.
Height: 6 × 6ft (1.8 × 1.8m) unpruned.

MOP HEADED HYDRANGEA (HYDRANGEA)   Large rounded heads of flowers, usually pink on limy soils, blue on acid ones. Attractive brown, dried heads last well into winter. Prone to capsid attack. *H. paniculata* is also good, with white conical flower spikes.
Growing conditions: Best in light shade on acid soil.
Pruning: Thin out the oldest shoots in early spring.
Height: 5 × 5ft (1.5 × 1.5m).

HYPERICUM   'Hidcote' is one of the best summer-flowering shrubs, with glossy leaves and huge yellow buttercup-like flowers from early summer to late autumn.
Growing conditions: Any reasonable soil, in full sun or light shade.
Pruning: Thin out established plants by about a third in spring.
Height: 3 × 3ft (90 × 90cm).

BEAUTY BUSH (KOLKWITZIA)   Although eventually becoming a little large, *K. amabilis*, with its pale pink, yellow-throated flowers, is a real gem and a good host for a light climber.
Growing conditions: Easy in any soil in full sun.
Pruning: Cut out about a third of the oldest growth each spring.
Height: 7 × 7ft (2.1 × 2.1m).

TREE MALLOW (LAVATERA)   A quick-growing, long-flowering plant with almost white, pink-centred flowers in huge quantities in summer and autumn. Often late to start into growth in spring. *L. thuringiaca* 'Barnsley' is an ideal new garden plant, as it's tough and grows quickly; 'Rosea' is pure pink.
Growing conditions: Good in any dry soil and full sun.
Pruning: Cut back hard every spring.
Height: 6 × 5ft (1.8 × 1.5m).

CAPE FIGWORT (PHYGELIUS)   With tubular flowers topping neat bushes, the modern phygelius hybrids are fine long-flowering plants. Look out for 'Devils' Tears' (orange-red), 'Moonraker' (creamy yellow), 'Pink Elf' (dwarf pink), and 'Salmon Leap' (orange with yellow throat).
Growing conditions: Any reasonable soil, in full sun.
Pruning: Cut back to ground level each spring.
Height: About 5 × 5ft (1.5 × 1.5m).

PHYSOCARPUS   *P. opulifolius* 'Dart's Gold' is a relatively new yellow-leaved shrub which tolerates wet soil better than most.
Growing conditions: Best in dappled shade for best colour and least leaf scorch.
Pruning: Cut out about a third of the oldest growth each spring.
Height: 5 × 5ft (1.5 × 1.5m).

ROSES – BUSH TYPES   There are many HT and floribunda roses worth choosing; the old-fashioned types are discussed on page 181 under 'First choices'. The following are chosen mainly for their scent. 'Canary Bird' is an unusual rose with arching growth. It's very early flowering, with large, single, butter-yellow flowers. 'Fragrant Cloud' is a coral-red HT consistently voted the best of all roses for scent. 'Royal William' is a new, deep crimson, powerfully scented HT.
Growing conditions: Any reasonable soil, in full sun.
Pruning: Cut back to about 9in (23cm) in spring, except 'Canary Bird', which should be left unpruned.

ROSES – FOLIAGE   Just one rose is grown specifically for its foliage – *R. glauca* (previously known as *R. rubrifolia*). Almost without thorns, the foliage is silvery mauve and sets off the small pink single flowers well. There are red hips to follow.
Growing conditions: Any reasonable soil, in full sun.
Pruning: Can be left unpruned, or cut back in spring as necessary.
Height: 5 × 5ft (1.5 × 1.5m).

ROSES – FRUITS   Many roses are grown for their hips, but *R. moyesii* 'Geranium' is perhaps the best and is reasonably compact. Large, deep red, single flowers precede orange-red, flask-shaped hips.

Growing conditions: Any reasonable soil in full sun.
Pruning: Best left unpruned, or can be shaped in spring.
Height: 8 × 6ft (2.4 × 1.8m).

ROSES – GROUND COVER   More and more roses of low spreading habit are being introduced, and these are good for trailing on to paving from the corners of beds. They flower continuously but have little scent. Many are named after counties, and 'Surrey' in soft pink is especially pretty. They vary in vigour. Look out too for the dainty white 'Snow Carpet'.
Growing conditions: Any reasonable soil, in full sun.
Pruning: Little usually needed, but can be shaped or reduced in spring.
Height: 2 × 4ft (60 × 1.2m), but varies with the variety.

ROSES – TOUGHIES   The varieties of *R. rugosa* are perhaps the most tolerant of poor conditions and the most disease-resistant, though they are very prickly. They also have good hips. 'Roseraie de L'Haÿ' is a crimson double, while 'Blanc Double de Coubert' is a semi-double white. There are other good ones.
Growing conditions: Almost any soil, in full sun or partial shade.
Pruning: Can be left unpruned, or cut back in spring.
Height: 3 × 3ft (90 × 90cm).

STEM WILLOW (SALIX)   Like some of the dogwoods, some forms of *S. alba* can be cut down each spring to encourage strong growth of coloured shoots. 'Chermesina' has orange twigs, the twigs of 'Vitellina' are bright yellow.
Growing conditions: Full sun and any reasonable soil, including soggy ones.
Pruning: Cut back very hard each spring.
Height: 2 × 2ft (60 × 60cm) if pruned.

BUSHY WILLOW (SALIX)   Several attractive willows are small enough for the small garden. *S. hastata* 'Wehrhanii' has silver catkins on neat, upright, deep red stems. *S. melanostachys* has deep burnished orange twigs lined with black and red catkins.
Growing conditions: Good in any soils, including wet ones and full sun.
Pruning: Little usually needed.
Height: 4 × 5ft (1.2 × 1.5m).

ELDER (SAMBUCUS)   Quick-growing shrubs with white flowers and, usually, black berries. Elders make good short-term shrubs for giving a quick air of maturity. *S. nigra* 'Albovariegata' has grey-green leaves with cream edges and should be cut back hard each spring. 'Guincho Purple' is purple when young, eventually greening and setting off the creamy flowers well. *S. racemosa* 'Plumosa Aurea' has brilliant yellow leaves and red berries. All stand pruning, so can be kept to size if necessary or discarded when too big.
Growing conditions: Tolerant of many soils, and of any site but deep shade.
Pruning: Cut out about a third of the oldest wood each spring.
Height: 10 × 8ft (3 × 2.4m).
Problems: Aphids.

LILAC (SYRINGA)   The familiar tall lilacs are not included, for they flower for only a couple of weeks, are boring for the rest of the year and grow far too tall. *S. velutina* is a rather upright dwarf lilac with pale lilac, fragrant flowers in spring and early summer. 2 × 2ft (60 × 60cm). *S. microphylla* 'Superba', with pink flowers, is a little larger.
Growing conditions: Any reasonable soil, in sun or light shade.
Pruning: Little necessary.

VIBURNUM   There are many sweetly scented spring-flowering viburnums, some of which also have good autumn colour. I choose *V. carlesii* 'Aurora', for its greyish leaves, pink buds and almost overpoweringly scented white flowers and red autumn colour, at 5 × 5ft (1.5 × 1.5m). For fruits I pick *V. opulus* 'Compactum', a dwarf form of our native guelder rose with white lacecap flowers followed by succulent red fruits on neat plants at 3 × 4ft (0.9 × 1.2m).
Growing conditions: Any soil, in full sun.
Pruning: Little usually needed.

4.   CLIMBERS AND WALL SHRUBS

Clothing fences and walls with climbers and wall shrubs helps bring variety to a small garden, adding planting in another dimension as well as making a good background against which to set other plants.

It's tempting to use plenty of evergreens but this can be claustrophobic, and a few deciduous plants plus a few places where the background fence or wall shows through helps the atmosphere.

First choices

CALIFORNIAN LILAC (CEANOTHUS) Vigorous spring- or summer-flowering evergreen shrubs ideal for new gardens. All have dense but branching heads of small flowers in various shades of blue. 'Autumnal Blue' belies its name by flowering from June into the winter; *C. impressus* 'Puget's Blue' has neat, dark, deeply veined leaves and deep blue flowers in spring.
Growing conditions: A sunny south- or west-facing wall or fence, with fertile but well-drained soil.
Pruning: 'Autumnal Blue' – spring, cut back near to base of previous season's growth. *C. impressus* – as lightly as is practicable, after flowering.
Height: 12ft (3.6m), but can be kept much smaller by pruning.

JAPONICA (CHAENOMELES) Tough, early-flowering deciduous shrubs with apple-like blossom sometimes followed by large yellow quinces. As well as being valuable spring shrubs, they are good hosts for delicate later-flowering climbers. 'Nivalis' has pure white flowers, 'Rowallane' is crimson.
Growing conditions: Any reasonable soil; good on any wall or fence and especially useful in open, north-facing situations.
Pruning: Cut back to within two or three buds of the new shoots after flowering.
Height: 6–8ft (1.8–2.4m).

MEXICAN ORANGE BLOSSOM (CHOISYA) A rounded, well-clothed, evergreen shrub with heads of pure white, fragrant flowers in June. In a sunny, sheltered spot *C. ternata* can flower almost all the year round. It may be damaged by late frosts. 'Sundance' has yellow foliage but is less vigorous and less hardy.
Growing conditions: Fertile soil, on any aspect that is sheltered from cold winds. Best facing west or south, tolerates northerly exposure given shelter.
Pruning: None usually needed, save occasional shaping.
Height: 6ft (1.8m).

CLEMATIS   Climbers clinging by their leaf stems, clematis come in a very wide range of types.

Winter flowering clematis   Two valuable evergreen types flower in winter. *Clematis cirrhosa* var. *balearica* has ferny foliage (bronzed in winter) and scented, creamy bells, speckled with maroon within, which appear in late winter and early spring; 'Freckles' is particularly richly spotted. *C. armandii* has larger, leathery leaves and larger pure white flowers, generally a little later. 'Apple Blossom' has larger, pink-flushed flowers.
Growing conditions: Warm, sheltered, west- or south-facing wall in good soil.
Pruning: After flowering if necessary.
Height: *C. cirrhosa* var. *balearica* 8ft (2.4m); *C. armandii* 20ft (6m), but often much less.

Small-flowered spring clematis   Vigorous, floriferous, spring-flowering deciduous plants which are ideal for new gardens but which may need stern attention in later years. *C. montana* is the most familiar, in various pinks and white. *C. montana* var. *rubens* has rosy flowers and purplish foliage; *C. macropetala* is soft blue, while the delightful *C. alpina* is similar but with a white centre, is less vigorous and is the best of the three for the smaller garden.
Growing conditions: Most reasonable soils and situations.
Pruning: After flowering, *C. montana* in particular may need drastic treatment.
Height: *C. montana* 20ft (6m)+; *C. macropetala* 12ft (3.6m); *C. alpina* 6ft (1.8m).

Small-flowered summer clematis   For smaller gardens, the daintier summer-flowering species are often more suitable than the more flamboyant types. The smaller *C. viticella*, such as 'Royal Velours' in velvety purple, 'Venosa Violacea' in white with purple edging and 'Purpurea Plena Elegans' with elegant deep, purple double flowers, are ideal and almost herbaceous, dying back in winter. These varieties are ideal for training through shrubs.
Growing conditions: Any reasonably fertile soil. Plant away from shrub roots to avoid too much competition.
Pruning: Cut back hard, almost to ground level in early spring.
Height: 6–8ft (1.8–2.4m).

Clematis 'Bill McKenzie' is much more vigorous and woody, with a long succession of yellow-orange, orange-peel flowers in summer followed by silky seed-heads.

Growing conditions: Any reasonable soil and a site facing west or south. This variety is usually too heavy to train up a shrub.

Pruning: Cut back to a branch framework in spring.

Height: 12ft (3.6m).

Large early-flowering clematis This group of large-flowered hybrids carries its flowers on short shoots from the previous year's growth. 'Vyvyan Pennell' has violet, red-tinted double flowers in late spring, followed by a flush of single flowers in early autumn; the well-known 'Nelly Moser' is pinkish-white striped red.

Growing conditions: Fertile, reasonably well-drained soil with the roots shaded from the hot sun. East and west walls are best, north is too cold, south encourages bleaching of colours.

Pruning: Train to fill the space required in early spring, removing crowded shoots. After flowering, cut back previous year's shoots to healthy buds.

Height: 10ft (3m).

Large later-flowering clematis Vigorous later-flowering varieties, usually starting to flower in early summer and often carrying on all season. 'Jackmanii' is purple, 'Niobe' is rich deep red, 'Hagley Hybrid' is soft pink.

Growing conditions: Fertile, reasonably well-drained soil with the roots shaded from the hot sun. East and west walls are best, north is too cold, south encourages bleaching of colours.

Pruning: Cut back hard in late winter, removing almost all the previous season's shoots.

Height: 'Jackmanii' 15ft (4.5m); 'Niobe' 10ft (3m); 'Hagley Hybrid' 6ft (1.8m).

Problems: Wilt, aphids.

CORONILLA   Eventually a dense, bushy, evergreen shrub which can sprawl at first, *C. glauca* has heads of bright yellow pea-flowers, which are at their most prolific in late spring and early summer but in sunny, sheltered spots may appear almost all the year round. 'Citrina' is a paler, sharper shade. Both are among the best of all small garden shrubs for a sunny place.

Growing conditions: Sun, shelter and well-drained soil give the bushiest habit and the longest flowering season.

Pruning: None usually necessary.
Height: 4ft (1.2m).
Problems: Aphids.

IVY (HEDERA)   Valuable, shade-loving, self-clinging evergreens for walls, fences and tree trunks. *H. helix* 'Glacier' has small grey-green and white leaves, 'Gold Heart' has small deep green leaves, splashed with gold. There are many others.
Growing conditions: Any reasonable soil, in full or partial shade. Do not train up walls with poor, loose mortar.
Pruning: None usually required, except perhaps to keep them to the required area.
Height: 10ft (3m).

CLIMBING HYDRANGEA (HYDRANGEA)   A self-clinging deciduous climber, *H. petiolaris* has large, lace-cap hydrangea flowers in summer. Slow-growing, and shy-flowering at first.
Growing conditions: Any reasonable soil and aspect; unhappy on south walls, good facing north.
Pruning: Little usually required, except when growth hangs too far away from the wall.
Height: 15ft (4.5m).

FIRETHORN (PYRACANTHA)   Tough, dark-leaved, thorny evergreen with white flowers in early summer and red, yellow or orange berries in autumn. Popular with nesting birds. 'Mojave' has orange-red berries and is disease-resistant, *P. rogersiana* 'Flava' has yellow berries.
Growing conditions: Any reasonable soil, good on north walls.
Pruning: Trim back projecting shoots in summer.
Height: 12ft (3.6m).
Problems: Fireblight.

CLIMBING ROSES (ROSA)   Invaluable roses for small gardens, many flower all summer with a good scent and can be kept to a reasonable size fairly easily. 'Madame Alfred Carrière' is scented, with white flowers opening from pale pink buds, and is also good on north walls; 'Gloire de Dijon' is scented, with pinky apricot flowers and is particularly long-flowering; 'Guinée' is deep red and well scented. Can be trained on pillars if necessary.

Growing conditions: Any fertile soil, preferably facing west or east; on south walls, flowers fade quickly and mildew is encouraged.

Pruning: Cut back shoots that have flowered to two or three buds in spring, and train shoots over area to be covered. Remove one or two older shoots near the base of older plants to encourage new growth.

Height: 6–8ft (1.8–2.4m), depending on pruning.

RAMBLING ROSES (ROSA)   Vigorous plants, less easy than climbers to keep a reasonable size. Often only flowering once, but spectacular for a few weeks. 'Albertine' is creamy and scented; 'New Dawn' is shell-pink and long-flowering.

Growing conditions: Any fertile soil facing west or east; mildew often devastating in a hot, dry site such as a south wall.

Pruning: Remove shoots that have flowered either after flowering or in winter, and tie in new shoots from low down. Cut back any short side shoots to two or three buds.

Height: 10–20ft (3–6m), depending on pruning.

Problems: Aphids, powdery mildew.

WHITE POTATO VINE (SOLANUM)   An exquisite, slightly tender twining climber, *S. jasminoides* 'Album' has open heads of pure white flowers all summer. Take a few cuttings in late summer just in case.

Growing conditions: Well-drained but rich soil, in a sheltered spot facing south or west.

Pruning: Cut back all dead growth to healthy buds in spring.

Height: 12ft (3.6m).

CANARY CREEPER (TROPAEOLUM)   An invaluable, delicate, annual climber, like a refined nasturtium with small, fingered foliage and pretty buttery flowers all summer. *T. peregrinum* is ideal for training through early-flowering shrubs to give colour later. Often self-sows.

Growing conditions: Good soil, in sunny or partially shaded conditions.

Height: 6ft (1.8m).

Special selection

AZARA Evergreen shrubs. *A. microphylla* has small, sweetly scented yellow flowers in early spring. Rather tender.
Growing conditions: Good soil, south or west wall.
Pruning: None usually required, except to tidy up after frost damage.
Height: 8ft (2.4m).

CAMELLIA Glossy-leaved evergreens thriving in wall protection. Varieties in reds, pinks, white and bicolours (see page 168).
Growing conditions: Lime-free soil that does not dry out, on a north, west or south-west wall or fence.
Pruning: Little usually required.
Height: 6–8ft (1.8–2.4m).

HERRING BONE PLANT (COTONEASTER) Deciduous shrub. *C. horizontalis* has a distinctive fishbone branch structure, small, white flowers in spring, red berries in autumn and good autumn colour. 'Variegata', with white-edged leaves, is prettier.
Growing conditions: Any reasonable soil and site.
Pruning: Little usually required.
Height: 5ft (1.5m).

ERCILLA Uncommon self-clinging evergreen. *E. volubilis* has dense spikes of mauve-white flowers in spring.
Growing conditions: Good on a north, or indeed any wall; clings less well to fences. Any good soil.
Pruning: Needs only to be kept in order after flowering.
Height: 10ft (3m).

FORSYTHIA 'Lynwood' is a cheerful and reliable shrub, with bright yellow flowers in late winter.
Growing conditions: Any reasonable soil, useful on a north or east wall.
Pruning: Cut out shoots that have flowered as the flowers drop, and reduce in size if necessary.
Height: 8ft (2.4m), depending on pruning.

ITEA   A glossy-leaved evergreen, *I. ilicifolia* has long, greenish-white catkins in summer.
Growing conditions: Any reasonable soil in a west- or south-facing situation.
Pruning: None usually required.
Height: 6ft (1.8m).

WINTER JASMINE (JASMINUM)   *J. nudiflorum* has yellow flowers in winter on untidy, trailing, almost leafless green shoots.
Growing conditions: Any reasonable soil in a north, east or west site.
Pruning: Remove a few old shoots and cut back flowered shoots hard after flowering.
Height: 6ft (1.8m), but needs regular tying in.

SUMMER JASMINE (JASMINUM)   *J. officinale* is a scented, twining climber with white flowers intermittently all summer.
Growing conditions: Any reasonable soil on a south- or west-facing wall. Needs support.
Pruning: Best left unpruned to get the best flowers; cut out large pieces low down if necessary.
Height: 15ft (4.5m)+, depending on pruning and training.

PERENNIAL SWEET PEA (LATHYRUS)   *L. latifolius* is a pretty, perennial but unscented version of the sweet pea. The variety names 'White Pearl', 'Pink Pearl' and 'Blushing Bride' are self-explanatory.
Growing conditions: Any reasonable soil in sun.
Pruning: None; allow to scramble over stout shrubs.
Height: 6–8ft (1.8–2.4m).

HONEYSUCKLE (LONICERA)   Popular, powerfully scented twiners. *L. periclymenum* flowers from early summer onwards; 'Belgica' flowers early in purplish-red fading to pale yellow; 'Serotina' continues until autumn in a deeper shade.
Growing conditions: Ideally it should have its roots in the shade and its flowers in the sun, so allowing it to roam through a large shrub is best. Rich soil preferred.
Pruning: Remove the occasional older shoot, low down, and any shoots that have flowered after flowering as necessary.
Height: 10ft (3m); can be restricted by pruning.
Problems: Aphids.

OSMANTHUS   *O. Delavayi* is a dark-leaved evergreen shrub with pure white, sweetly scented flowers in early spring.
Growing conditions: Good soil, any aspect, even north, though it must be sheltered from icy winds.
Pruning: None usually required. Don't be tempted to cut too much for the house.
Height: 4ft (1.2m).

RUSSIAN VINE (POLYGONUM)   Also known as the mile-a-minute vine, *P. baldschuanicum* is included only as a warning. This is a rampageous plant cheerfully scaling telegraph poles, and is highly unsuitable for the small garden.
Growing conditions: Any soil, almost any site.
Pruning: Usually ineffective at restraining it.
Height: 30ft (9m)+.

FLAME FLOWER (TROPAEOLUM)   A self-supporting herbaceous climber, *T. speciosum* has small, bright red flowers in summer.
Growing conditions: Leafy soil and partial shade; good growing up evergreen hedges but unpredictably difficult to establish.
Pruning: Cut away dead top growth in autumn or spring.
Height: 6ft (1.8m).

VINE (VITIS)   The ornamental vine, *V. vinifera* 'Purpurea', has claret-coloured leaves all season, turning purple in autumn, and deep purple, unpleasant-tasting grapes.
Growing conditions: Rich but well-drained soil, south- or west-facing.
Pruning: Cut back laterals to three buds in midwinter; also shorten main growths and remove whole shoots low down if necessary.
Height: 10ft (3m).

WISTERIA (WISTERIA)   *W. floribunda* has twining shoots with long strings of blue pea flowers in late spring. This species is the least vigorous.
Growing conditions: Any good, well-drained soil; may take some years to settle down before flowering.
Pruning: Cut back new growth to 6in (15cm) after flowering, then shorten side shoots to 3in (7.5m) in winter.
Height: 15ft (4.5m).

5. HEDGING PLANTS

BARBERRY (BERBERIS)   Spiny hedging plants, which should be used only occasionally in a small garden. *B. gagnepanii* is the most vicious, with one-inch thorns, and is mentioned mainly so that you can avoid it. *B. × stenophylla* is dense, twiggy and spiny, with dark leaves and long sprigs of orange flowers in spring.
Plant: 18in (45cm) apart, single row.
Clip: At once after flowering.
Maximum height at maturity: 5–6ft (1.5–1.8m).

BOX (BUXUS)   An easily managed formal hedge, ideal for topiary. For low border edging in formal situations, choose the slow-growing *B. sempervirens* 'Suffruticosa'.
Plant: 5in (12.5cm) apart, single row.
Clip: Two or three times during season, depending on growth and neatness.
Maximum height at maturity: 12in (30cm).
For taller hedges choose *B. sempervirens* 'Handsworthensis' which is more vigorous.
Plant: 18in (45cm) apart.
Clip: Midsummer.
Maximum height at maturity: 5ft (1.5m).
Problems: Box sucker.

HORNBEAM (CARPINUS)   A fine formal hedge and windbreak for wetter soils, very much like beech, *C. betulus* also retains its brown leaves in winter.
Plant: 18in (45cm) apart.
Clip: Late summer.
Maximum height at maturity: 8ft (2.4m).

LAWSON'S CYPRESS (CUPRESSUS)   One of the best formal ever-green hedges if the right variety is chosen. *C. lawsoniana* 'Green Hedger' has bright green foliage which sets off other plants well.
Plant: 18in (45cm) apart.
Clip: Late summer.
Maximum height at maturity: 8ft (2.4m).

ESCALLONIA   A fine informal flowering hedge, flourishing especially well by the sea. 'Donard Radiance' has shining foliage and large pink flowers in early summer.

Plant: 2ft (60cm) apart.
Clip: After flowering, and lightly in early spring.
Maximum height at maturity: 5ft (1.5m).

BEECH (FAGUS) A classic formal hedging plant and windbreak, *F. sylvatica* retains its brown foliage in winter. Good on all but wet soils, where hornbeam is better. Avoid purple beech which can be oppressive, though one or two in a predominantly green hedge are attractive.

Plant: 18in (45cm) apart.
Clip: Late summer.
Maximum height at maturity: 6–8ft (1.5–1.8m).

HOLLY (ILEX) Another spiny hedge. The crisp and sharp fallen leaves can be very irritating when weeding, though the variety *I. aquifolium* 'J. C. van Thol' has no spines.

Plant: 18in (45cm) apart.
Clip: Late summer.
Maximum height at maturity: 5–6ft (1.5–1.8m).
Problems: Leaf miner.

PRIVET (LIGUSTRUM) A dull-looking, vigorous and hungry hedge, suitable only for the poorest soils. Generally it pays to improve the soil and use a different hedging plant. The yellow-leaved form, *L. ovalifolium* 'Aureum', is less vigorous and more attractive.

Plant: 12in (30cm) apart.
Clip: Monthly, from spring to late summer.
Maximum height at maturity: 5–6ft (1.5–1.8m).

FIRETHORN (PYRACANTHA) A lovely dark-leaved evergreen hedge, though spiny, *P. rogersiana* has white flowers and red berries in spite of the clipping.

Plant: 18in (45cm) apart.
Clip: Early summer, plus late summer if necessary.
Maximum height at maturity: 5–6ft (1.5–1.8m).
Problems: Fireblight.

ROSE (ROSA)   Many roses make good informal flowering hedges, from the strong-growing upright 'Queen Elizabeth' with pink flowers, and the bushier white-flowered 'Iceberg', to the *R. rugosa* hybrids. Some climbers, like the thornless 'Zéphirine Drouhin', and large shrub roses make wide informal hedges, but these are probably too big for most small gardens.

Rosa rugosa   varieties
Plant: 3ft (90cm) apart.
Clip: Lightly in spring.
Maximum height at maturity: 5ft (1.5m).

Rose 'Iceberg'
Plant: 2ft (60cm) apart.
Clip: Lightly in spring.
Maximum height at maturity: 3–4ft (0.9–1.2m).

Rose 'Queen Elizabeth'
Plant: 2–3ft (60–90cm) apart.
Clip: Fairly hard in spring.
Maximum height at maturity: 5ft (1.5m).

Rose 'Zéphirine Drouhin'
Plant: 3ft (90cm) apart.
Clip: Spring, as necessary to keep to the space allowed.
Maximum height at maturity: 5–6ft (1.5–1.8m).

Problems: Aphids, powdery mildew and black spot.

ROSEMARY (ROSMARINUS)   A pretty, aromatic and flowering informal hedge for well-drained soils. 'Miss Jessup's Upright' has the necessary upright growth and blue flowers in early summer.
Plant: 2ft (60cm) apart.
Clip: Trim in spring.
Maximum height at maturity: 4ft (1.2m).

SNOWBERRY (SYMPHORICARPUS)   The profusion of white berries on 'White Hedge' plus its compact growth make it a good small garden hedge, especially for less fertile soils.
Plant: 18in (45cm) apart.
Clip: Trim in early spring.
Maximum height at maturity: 4–5ft (1.2–1.5m).

YEW (TAXUS) The classic evergreen garden hedge, with dense growth and a deep green colour to show off other plants well. Not as slow-growing as is often thought, but poor on soggy soil.
Plant: 18in (45cm) apart.
Clip: Late summer.
Maximum height at maturity: 8–10ft (2.4–3m).

WESTERN RED CEDAR (THUYA) As quick-growing a hedge as you will need, *T. plicata* 'Atrovirens' is a far better choice than Leyland's cypress. Dense growth and good green foliage.
Plant: 2ft (60cm) apart.
Clip: Late summer, preferably with secateurs. Two clips may be necessary.
Maximum height at maturity: 8–10ft (2.4–3m).

THUYA A fine, dense, emerald green hedge. *T. occidentalis* 'Smaragd' makes a tight hedge to a great height – if you should need such a thing.
Plant: 18–24in (45–60cm) apart.
Clip: Late summer, and possibly late spring too.
Maximum height at maturity: 8–10ft (2.4–3m).

VIBURNUM *Viburnum tinus* 'Eve Price' makes a low, informal, evergreen winter flowering hedge with black berries to follow.
Plant: 18in (45cm) apart.
Clip: After flowering.
Maximum height at maturity: 4ft (1.2m).

6. BORDER PERENNIALS

First choices

YARROW (ACHILLEA) Three types.

The little white poms of *A. ptarmica* 'The Pearl' are very pretty on their dark green foliage, but this is a rampageous plant. It's good for new gardens, but even then should be treated with care.
Growing conditions: Most soils, in sun or partial shade.
Propagation: Division or seed.
Height: 2ft (60cm).

The *A. millefolium* hybrids are less rampant but are still vigorous, with dark feathery foliage and flat heads of flowers all summer. 'Salmon Beauty' is salmon pink, 'The Beacon' is red, 'Forncett Fletton' is a gingery marmalade shade, 'Burgundy' is deep purple. 'Summer Pastels' is an excellent new mixture in mostly soft shades.
Growing conditions: Most soils, in sunshine.
Propagation: Division. 'Summer Pastels' from seed.
Height: 2–3ft (60–90cm).
Problems: Can self-seed too prolifically.

'Moonshine' is a clump-former, with pale yellow flowers over silver-green foliage.
Growing conditions: Best in a sunny, fairly well-drained spot.
Propagation: Cuttings.
Height: 2ft (60cm).

MOTTLED ARUM (ARUM)   A version of lords and ladies, *A. italicum* 'Pictum' has arrowhead-shaped leaves right through winter, each leaf marbled in white. The greenish hoods follow in spring and then in summer stout stems carry dense heads of orange berries. Good for cutting and a fine winter feature.
Growing conditions: Good soil, partial shade.
Propagation: Division.
Height: 12–18in (30–45cm).

PERENNIAL ASTER (ASTER)   Most of the Michaelmas daisies are too tall and many too disease-prone for inclusion (but see page 205, 'Special selection'). However, *A.* × *frikartii* 'Monch' is long-lasting in flower from midsummer to late autumn, does not need staking, is disease-free, and has flowers of a beautiful lavender-blue colour with a yellow eye.
Growing conditions: Good soil, full sun.
Propagation: Division.
Height: 3ft (90cm).

ASTILBE   'Sprite' is a dwarf variety with dark, metallic green, prettily divided foliage overtopped in summer by dusty plumes of soft pink flowers.
Growing conditions: Best in moist soils and an open situation.
Propagation: Division.
Height: 15in (38cm).
Problems: Suffers in dry summers.

SEDGE (CAREX) Long narrow foliage is an important feature among both flowering and foliage plants, especially if it has a good colour. *C. comans* 'Bronze Form' has milky-chocolate-coloured, string-like leaves arching from a tight central clump. 18in (45cm). *C. oshimensis* 'Evergold' is smaller, stiffer, with narrow, arching foliage in green striped with yellow. 9in (23cm).
Growing conditions: Sun or part shade, most soils; 'Evergold' must not dry out.
Propagation: Division.

GARDEN PINKS (DIANTHUS) The combination of fairly neat growth, narrow grey-blue foliage and (usually) scented flowers over a long season makes pinks indispensable. The old-fashioned double white 'Mrs Sinkins' is lovely, but 'White Ladies' is even better. Many have been given Christian names like 'Doris', 'Joy', 'Thomas', etc.
Growing conditions: Sunshine, well-drained soil.
Propagation: Layer low shoots.
Height: 15in (38cm).

SPURGE (EUPHORBIA) The Mediterranean spurges are impressive evergreen structural plants all the year round, with many upright stems lined with narrow leaves. *E. characias* has dark-eyed greeny-yellow flowers. Its variety *wulfenii* has no dark eye, and 'Lambrook Gold' is yellow.
Growing conditions: Best in well-drained soil in sun, but tolerant of some shade.
Propagation: Cuttings.
Height: 4ft (1.2m).
Problems: Can be damaged in bad winters.

CRANESBILL (GERANIUM) Hardy geraniums come in great variety, but for small gardens, their modest size and a long flowering season are perhaps their most crucial qualities. They also have a knack of fitting in well with other plants.

'Buxton's Blue' flowers from early summer to autumn with pure blue flowers, each with a white centre. It spreads well.
Growing conditions: Good, well-drained soil, in sun or shade.
Propagation: Seed.
Height: 12in (30cm).

'Russell Prichard' has greyish leaves and soft pink flowers, a lovely combination. Shoots spread widely from a central rootstock, so it needs space.
Growing conditions: Sun, and any good soil that is not water-logged.
Propagation: Careful division in spring.
Height: 9in (23cm)

'Wargrave Pink' has salmony-pink flowers from early summer to autumn over fresh, daintily divided foliage. It's also a good weed suppressor.
Growing conditions: Any reasonable soil, sun or shade.
Propagation: Division.
Height: 2ft (60cm).

HAKENOCHLOA   No common name, I'm afraid, for the dainty but difficult to pronounce *Hakenochloa macra* 'Alboaurea', a small, yellow-striped ornamental grass with narrow foliage that arches up and over like a yellow waterfall from a slowly spreading rootstock. A fine frontal plant.
Growing conditions: Any good soil in sun.
Propagation: Division.
Height: 12in (30cm).

LENTEN ROSE (HELLEBORUS)   The easiest of the captivating hellebores is *H. orientalis*, which is as likely to be in flower at Christmas as the so-called Christmas rose, *H. niger*. The Lenten rose spreads but slowly, its large, deep green, fingered foliage smothers every weed. The flowers can be any colour from deepest inky purple to pure white and appear from December to April, depending on the season.
Growing conditions: Most soils that are not waterlogged, best in partial shade.
Propagation: Best left alone, as they take a year or two to settle, but divide them in August if you must.
Height: 18in (45cm).
Problems: Leaf spot and aphids.

HEUCHERA   One of the best-looking and best-behaved dark-leaved foliage plants, 'Palace Purple' has five-pointed bronze-purple

leaves overtopped with slender spikes of creamy flowers. It makes a good cover and spreads but slowly. There's also 'Scintillation', a good pink, and the green-flowered 'Greenfinch'.
Growing conditions: Any reasonable soil, in sun or part shade.
Propagation: Division. 'Palace Purple' also from seed, but throw out poorly coloured plants.
Height: 18in (45cm) when in flower.

HOSTA   Indispensable foliage plants, in sizes from 9in (23cm) to 4ft (1.2m) and in leaf sizes from a few inches to over a foot. Leaf colours may be any one of many greens and yellows, creams, white, various sea-blues and endless combinations of these. They spread slowly and are best left undisturbed, but make a dense weed-suppressing cover. 'Halcyon', 12in (30cm), is a neat blue-leaved variety, while 'Thomas Hogg', 18in (45cm), has fresh green leaves with white margins. 'Frances Williams', 3ft (90cm), has a blue centre to the leaf with the edge starting gold and fading to green.
Growing conditions: Any reasonable soil that does not dry out, in sun or shade.
Propagation: Divide in spring if necessary.
Pests: Slugs eat emerging shoots, which results in large holes in the leaves as they unfold.

GLADDON (IRIS)   Also known as gladwyn and stinking iris. The deep green, sword-like foliage of *I. foetidissima* is a feature in itself, but there are also the small, curiously coloured purple and ochre flowers which give way to fat, bursting pods of bright orange berries in winter. 'Variegata' has no pods, but cream stripes in the leaves. Both are 100 per cent evergreen, so are good in winter.
Growing conditions: Almost anywhere, including dry shade but best in damper conditions in sun.
Propagation: Seed, which usually self-sows; 'Variegata' by division.
Height: 2ft (60cm).

WINTER IRIS (IRIS)   The genuinely winter-flowering *I. unguicularis* is a real joy when its sweetly scented blue flowers appear among the stiff, upright leaves. They are good for cutting, indeed sometimes the flowers are best cut to protect the buds from slugs.

Growing conditions: Well-drained soil in a hot spot, such as the base of a sunny wall.
Propagation: Division.
Height: 18in (45cm).
Pests: Slugs eat young buds, ruining the flowers.

DEAD NETTLE (LAMIUM)   Low, spreading plant in a variety of leaf colours with flowers in magenta, pink or white. *L. maculatum*, with dark green, white-splashed leaves and magenta flowers, is rather vigorous and self-sows aggressively. Among the best of its varieties are 'White Nancy', with almost wholly white leaves and white flowers. 'Pink Pewter' is similar, with pink flowers, while 'Cannon's Gold' has pure yellow leaves and magenta flowers.
Growing conditions: Moist soil, in sun or shade.
Propagation: Layer by putting a stone on low shoots.
Height: 12in (30cm) in flower.

LUPIN (LUPINUS)   Among the most flamboyant of flowers, lupins are easy to raise in large numbers for a new garden but a mature small garden can cope only with one or two. 'Band of Nobles', 4ft (1.2m), is a tall, colourful mixture for quick space-filling, while 'Gallery', 2ft (60cm), is a dwarfer mix for longer-term planting.
Growing conditions: Any soil that is not waterlogged, in sunny conditions.
Propagation: Seed.
Problems: Big grey aphids.

OPHIOPOGON   A very small plant of restrained growth with stiff, arching leaves as near to black as you will ever see. The horribly named *Ophiopogon planiscapus* 'Nigrescens' makes open tuffets of leaves which look especially good planted in gravel.
Growing conditions: Sun or part shade, in any reasonable soil.
Propagation: Division.
Height: 6in (15cm).

LUNGWORT (PULMONARIA)   Staple plants for spring flowers and summer foliage. Low, slowly spreading plants with blue flowers, often opening pink. The rough green leaves are variously marked in silver. *P. saccharata* 'Argentea' has leaves almost entirely

silver. 'Lewis Palmer', is an especially sparkling rich blue, 'Cambridge' is soft blue.
Growing conditions: Any good soil, in sun or shade.
Propagation: Division.
Height: 12in (30cm).

BORDER SALVIA (SALVIA)   A compact, bushy plant with erect spikes of violet flowers in summer, the reddish bracts continuing the colour long after the flowers fall. *S. superba* 'Lubecca' is the neatest and best-coloured form.
Growing conditions: Any reasonable soil, in sun.
Propagation: Division.
Height: 18in (45cm).

Special selection

AGROPYRON   A startling, blue-leaved grass, *A. pubiflorum* (correctly *Elymus hispidus*) makes a tight clump of upright and eventually floppy foliage.
Growing conditions: Sun or part shade, in any reasonable soil.
Propagation: Seed or division.
Height: 18in (45cm).

LADY'S MANTLE (ALCHEMILLA)   A fashionable plant, *A. mollis* has slightly downy five-pointed leaves which make a pretty mound, topped with clouds of greeny-yellow flowers in early summer.
Growing conditions: Any fertile soil, in sun or shade.
Propagation: Seed; sometimes self-sows over-enthusiastically.
Height: 18in (45cm).

PEARL EVERLASTING (ANAPHALIS)   With its silvery foliage on upright stems, topped with flat heads of small white everlasting flowers, *A. yedoensis* is one of the most accommodating of grey foliage plants.
Growing conditions: Any reasonable soil, in sun or shade.
Propagation: Division.
Height: 2½ft (75cm).

JAPANESE ANEMONE (ANEMONE)   A very valuable late-flowering plant. 'Honorine Jobert' has pure white, yellow-centred

flowers wafting above dark foliage.
Growing conditions: Best in sun on a heavy soil.
Propagation: Division when necessary, but may take two or three years to settle down afterwards.
Height: 5ft (1.5m).

COLUMBINE (AQUILEGIA)   There are many lovely seed-raised columbines, including the 'McKana Hybrids' in an exciting range of colours and 'Nora Barlow', a fully double pink, green and white. They self-sow, but don't come true if grown together.
Growing conditions: Any good soil, but preferably with a little shade.
Propagation: Seed.
Height: Usually 3ft (90cm), but there are also dwarf forms.
Problems: Caterpillars.

YELLOW ASPHODEL (ASPHODELINE)   The stout, upright flower spikes of *A. lutea* spring out of a fountain of narrow, blue-grey leaves to carry bright yellow flowers in late spring.
Growing conditions: A sunny site which is not waterlogged.
Propagation: Seed or division.
Height: 3ft (90cm).

MICHAELMAS DAISY (ASTER)   Good, dwarf, self-supporting, mildew-free varieties are thin on the ground, but *Aster* 'Rose Bonnet', with its semi-double rose pink flowers, is good. Also try 'Lady in Blue', with semi-double blue flowers, and the double red 'Jenny'.
Growing conditions: Best in water-retentive soil, in sun or partial shade.
Propagation: Division.
Height: 12–15in (30–38cm). Much taller ones are also available.
Disease: Mildew.

LADY FERN (ATHYRIUM)   The soft and delicate lacy fronds of *A. felix-femina* rise from a central rootstock. An adaptable plant, delightful in its own right and a perfect foil for contrasting foliage.
Growing conditions: Thrives in shade and a moist soil, though adaptable to drier spots.

Propagation: Division. It may self-sow in ideal conditions.
Height: 2ft (60cm).

ELEPHANT'S EARS (BERGENIA)   With broad, rounded glossy
foliage from a slowly spreading rootstock, the flowers of 'Bressingham White' appear in early spring. *B. purpurascens* has beetroot-
coloured winter leaves, especially in an open spot, and pink flowers.
Growing conditions: Any reasonable soil, sun or shade.
Propagation: Division.
Height: 15in (38cm) in flower.

RED VALERIAN (CENTRANTHUS)   Easy to raise, easy to grow
and sometimes a nuisance, the rather succulent *C. ruber* has deep
pink flowers all summer. There is a darker variety and also a white.
Dead-head promptly if you don't want any self-sown seedlings.
Growing conditions: Dry walls and any sunny, well-drained spot.
Propagation: Self-sows far too enthusiastically for most gardens.
Height: 2ft (60cm).

CHRYSANTHEMUM   Hardy chrysanthemums are invaluable late-
flowering plants, and the dainty dark pink 'Mei-Kyo', 2ft (60cm),
flowers in November; the soft brown 'Bronze Elegance' is similar.
'Emperor of China', 4ft (1.2m), is taller, with larger, silver-rose,
slightly quilled petals.
Growing conditions: Any good soil, in sunshine.
Propagation: Division.
Problems: Aphids, earwigs, leaf miner.

LILY OF THE VALLEY (CONVALLARIA)   An unpredictable carpeter, *C. majalis* carries its sweetly scented string-of-pearls flowers in
late spring, with glossy foliage.
Growing conditions: Rich soil in semi-shade is probably best, but
it can thrive almost anywhere.
Propagation: Dig up foot-square clumps and transplant whole; do
not pull apart.
Height: 9in (23cm).

MONTBRETIA (CROCOSMIA)   The smaller crocosmias, with their
iris-like leaves and fiery summer flowers, are most valuable.

'Solfaterre' has peachy flowers and smoky leaves; 'Emily McKenzie' has larger, dark orange flowers with a mahogany central splash; 'Lucifer' is bright red but can spread too well and is also twice the height.
Growing conditions: Most soils that do not dry out, plus sunshine.
Propagation: Division.
Height: 2ft (60cm).

FOXGLOVE (DIGITALIS)   If you have space, *D. purpurea* 'Alba', the ghostly white variety of our native foxglove, is lovely, otherwise try the smaller 'Foxy' in a variety of shades.
Growing conditions: Moist soil, sun or shade.
Propagation: Seed. They will probably self-sow.
Height: 'Foxy', 2ft (60cm); *D. purpurea* 'Alba', 4–5ft (1.2–1.5m).

ECHINACEA   'White Swan' is a roughly-textured plant with stiff, upright stems carrying large, honey-scented, white-rayed flowers with orange, domed centres. Like a white rudbeckia.
Growing conditions: Sunshine, any reasonable soil.
Propagation: Seed or division.
Height: 2ft (60cm).

EPIMEDIUM   Dainty white, red or yellow flowers over long-lasting foliage, often prettily tinted when young, rusty when old. The red-flowered *E. rubrum* is especially pretty.
Growing conditions: Soil that does not dry out, in shade.
Propagation: Division.
Height: 15in (38cm).

SEA HOLLY (ERYNGIUM)   A spiny but delicate plant, *E.* × *tripartitum* is well branched, with small blue cone-like flowers at the tips of the shoots. Good for drying.
Growing conditions: Any reasonable soil, in full sun.
Propagation: Division.
Height: 2ft (60cm).

SPURGE (EUPHORBIA)   For interesting rather than flamboyant colour in shade, the upright stems of *E. robbiae*, with their long, dark foliage topped in spring with open heads of greenish-yellow flowers, is very effective.

Growing conditions: Reasonable soil, in sun or shade; succeeds even in dry shade.
Propagation: Division of slowly creeping roots.
Height: 2ft (60cm).

BRONZE FENNEL (FOENICULUM)   A pretty, upright plant with soft, wiry leaves which in *F. vulgare* 'Smokey' are a lovely shade of smoky bronze. In summer the stems are topped with flat heads of greeny-yellow flowers.
Growing conditions: Fairly well-drained soil, good or bad, in sun.
Propagation: Seed; self-sows readily.
Height: 5–6ft (1.5–1.8m).
Problem: Aphids.

HELENIUM   Valuable autumn-flowering members of the daisy family, with yellow, orange or rusty flowers in branching sprays. 'Moerheim Beauty', with its bronzy-red flowers, is an unusual shade.
Growing conditions: Sun and any reasonable soil.
Propagation: Division, every other year.
Height: 3ft (90cm).

GIANT HOGWEED (HERACLEUM)   Included only as a warning, *H. mantegazzianum* is a huge, 8ft (2.4m), unpleasant weed. It spreads rapidly by seed, its huge leaves overshadow precious plants for yards around it, and its sap can irritate the skin. Don't grow it.

SWEET ROCKET (HESPERIS)   A powerfully scented biennial or short-lived perennial, *H. matronalis* comes in deep lilac, pale lilac and white and is a pretty cottage garden favourite.
Growing conditions: Any reasonable soil that doesn't dry out, in sun or partial shade.
Propagation.   Seed.
Height: 4ft (1.2m).

FLAG IRIS (IRIS)   Bearded or flag iris are exotic and flamboyant, though fleeting, flowers of early summer in an enormous range of colours. There are many quite small and compact varieties especially suited to small beds. Choose them in flower or from a colourful catalogue.

Growing conditions: Sun and a well-drained fertile soil.
Propagation: Division of fat roots every three years after flowering.
Height: 9in–3ft (23–90cm), depending on variety.

TOADFLAX (LINARIA)   A purplish-grey-leaved plant with slender, very upright stems, *L. purpurea* 'Canon Went' has long spikes of tiny pale pink flowers topping the stems. Good for cutting.
Growing conditions: Well-drained soil in a sunny spot.
Propagation: Seed, including self-sown seedlings though they may revert to purple.
Height: 3–4ft (0.9–1.2m).

LIRIOPE   A neat, compact, autumn-flowering plant, *L. muscari* (avoid *L. spicata*) produces many short, dense spikes of purple flowers emerging from clumps of dark green, arching, rather grassy evergreen leaves late in the year.
Growing conditions: Sun or shade, in fertile soil.
Propagation: Division.
Height: 12in (30cm).

LYCHNIS   The grey, slightly woolly rosettes of foliage of *L. coronaria* are always pretty, and they produce branching stems in summer with flowers in various colours. The white 'Alba' is especially effective.
Growing conditions: Happy in poor soil, in sun or shade.
Propagation: Short-lived, but sometimes self-sows too readily.
Height: 3ft (90cm).

GOLDEN LEMON BALM (MELISSA)   The powerfully lemon-scented *M. officinalis* 'All Gold' is an erect plant with small nettle-like leaves in bright yellow, fading slightly as the season runs on. 'Aurea' is only speckled with yellow.
Growing conditions: Good soil, in partial shade.
Propagation: Division; self-sows but produces mainly green-leaved seedlings.
Height: 2ft (60cm).

BERGAMOT (MONARDA)   With fragrant foliage and mint-like leaves on upright stems topped with whorls of scarlet hooked

flowers, *M. didyma* 'Cambridge Scarlet' also spreads steadily and effectively.
Growing conditions: Moist soil, full sun.
Propagation: Division.
Height: 3ft (90cm).

YELLOW MARJORAM (ORIGANUM) Another yellow-leaved herb, *O. vulgare* 'Aureum', is lower in growth and rather floppy, with tiny yellow leaves fading to yellowish-green after midsummer. Clip back after flowering to create a dense leafy mound.
Growing conditions: Any soil that is not waterlogged, in partial shade.
Propagation: Division, or by detaching rooted stems.
Height: 18in (45cm).

RIBBON GRASS (PHALARIS) A beautiful but invasive grass, *P. arundinacea* 'Picta' has white striped leaves which should be cut back hard as the flowers appear to stimulate more growth low down. Very invasive, but a welcome sparkler in new gardens, probably to be discarded later.
Growing conditions: Any soil and aspect.
Propagation: Division.
Height: 4ft (1.2m).

OBEDIENT PLANT (PHYSOSTEGIA) An upright plant with neatly arranged leaves in rows along the stems, 'Vivid' is a dwarf variety that tops them with pink tubular flowers which can be twisted round the stems and stay in place. There is also a very pretty pure white form, 'Snow Crown'.
Growing conditions: In sun, in most soils that are not too dry.
Propagation: Division, every other year.
Height: 'Vivid', 15in (23cm); 'Snow Crown', 3ft (90cm).

SOLOMON'S SEAL (POLYGONATUM) Upright then arching stems, lined with pairs of leaves which in *P. × hybridum* 'Variegatum' are boldly margined in white and with small clusters of little greenish-white bells in late spring.
Growing conditions: Moist soil, in partial or full shade.
Propagation: Division.
Height: 2ft (60cm).

BISTORT (POLYGONUM) A vigorous plant for new gardens, *P. bistorta* 'Superbum' makes a dense cover of low foliage and creeps rapidly, shooting well away from the main plant. Dense but elegant pink flower spikes in early summer.
Growing conditions: Almost any soil that is not parched.
Propagation: Division.
Height: 3ft (90cm).

SOFT SHIELD FERN (POLYSTICHUM) The brownish-grey stems of *P. setiferum* carry soft and not shiny green fronds, creating a very elegant plant.
Growing conditions: Best in moist conditions, but also thrives in dry soil and indeed almost anywhere.
Propagation: Division.
Height: 3ft (90cm).

CANDELABRA PRIMULA (PRIMULA) Bright rosettes of green leaves produce elegant, absolutely vertical stems which in *P. pulverulenta* are covered in white dust and carry a series of whorls of rich crimson flowers in early summer.
Growing conditions: Damp soil, in sun or partial shade.
Propagation: Seed, will self-sow when happy.
Height: 2–3ft (60–90cm), depending on moisture.
Problems: Aphids, virus.

JAPANESE KNOTWEED (REYNOUTRIA) Another plant included here simply as a warning, *R. japonica* is an extremely invasive and rampageous weed 8ft (2.4m) tall which is almost impossible to get rid of. Never plant it.

ORNAMENTAL RHUBARB (RHEUM) 'Ace of Hearts' is a smaller than average rhubarb with dark green, heart-shaped foliage, each leaf with crimson veins and coloured crimson underneath. It also has pinky plumes in early summer.
Growing conditions: Sun or partial shade, in soil that doesn't dry out.
Propagation: Division, with care.
Height: 4ft (1.2m).

RODGERSIA An imposing foliage plant with bronze-purple, deeply-veined leaves in broad pairs, *R. pinnata* 'Superba' also has foamy flowers of brilliant pink.

Growing conditions: Water-retentive soil, in sun or partial shade.
Propagation: Division.
Height: 3ft (90cm).

RUDBECKIA   A very adaptable plant of stiff habit, the flowers of
'Goldsturm' have golden rays surrounding black centres.
Growing conditions: Most soils, wet or fairly dry, in sun or partial
shade.
Propagation: Division.
Height: 18in (45cm).

SCABIOUS (SCABIOSA)   A delicate plant with blue flowers on fine
stems, flowering all summer. 'Butterfly Blue' blooms for many
weeks and is appreciated by butterflies.
Growing conditions: Any reasonable soil, in sun.
Propagation: Division.
Height: 12–15in (30–38cm).

KAFFIR LILY (SCHIZOSTYLIS)   An invaluable late-flowering
plant with narrow, slightly floppy pale green leaves and, in 'Jennifer', spikes of soft pink flowers from late summer almost into winter.
Good for cutting.
Growing conditions: Sunshine and a little shelter, plus well-
drained soil.
Propagation: Division every other year, otherwise flowering
lessens.
Height: 2ft (60cm).

ICE PLANT (SEDUM)   Fleshy stems carry grey, fleshy leaves
topped in 'Autumn Joy' with flat heads of deep pink flowers which
bronze later. The dried heads are effective all winter.
Growing conditions: Any reasonable soil, in a sunny spot.
Propagation: Division.
Height: 2ft (60cm).

RED CAMPION (SILENE)   A rather floppy but nevertheless delightful wild flower, pretty enough for any border, *S. dioica* has
rosy red flowers for many weeks in early summer. There is a lovely
old-fashioned double form, 'Flore Pleno'.
Growing conditions: Any fertile soil, in sun.
Propagation: Division, preferably every other year.
Height: 2ft (60cm).

WAKE ROBIN (TRILLIUM)   An exquisite but very slowly spreading plant carrying three leaves at the top of each stem, which in *T. grandiflorum* back the three-petalled, pure white flowers, appearing in spring.
Growing conditions: Rich, moisture-retentive soil in partial shade.
Propagation: Division, but best left alone.
Height: 15in (38cm).

UVULARIA   A choice yellow-flowered version of Solomon's seal, *U. grandiflora* has larger flowers on much shorter stems in spring.
Growing conditions: Rich, moisture-retentive soil in partial shade.
Propagation: Division.
Height: 18in (45cm).

VARIEGATED PERIWINKLE (VINCA)   A boldly yellow-splashed evergreen with arching stems carrying the pairs of cheerful leaves, *V. major* 'Elegantissima' also produces five-petalled blue flowers in early spring.
Growing conditions: Most soils except waterlogged ones, in sun or shade.
Propagation: Shoots root where the tips touch the soil and can be detached.
Height: 15in (38cm).

7. ROCK AND DWARF PLANTS

First Choices

ACAENA   A low, creeping evergreen with tiny rose-like foliage and small, dense, rounded flower-heads. 'Copper Carpet' has coppery foliage and rusty flower-heads, while 'Blue Haze' has blueish-bronze leaves and reddish flower-heads. *A. anserinifolia* is pea-green but far too vigorous for most gardens.
Growing conditions: Most soils that are not waterlogged; sun or partial shade.
Propagation: Self-sown seedlings, and by digging up rooted shoots.
Height: 3in (7.5cm).

Formality suits front gardens. Here the main path to the door is laid in brick with the side paths in gravel and the whole layout softened by evergreen box hedges.

This effervescent mixture of bedding plants makes a good focal point in a small garden and will flower from June to September.

Window-box plantings need a mixture of upright, bushy and trailing plants; don't be afraid to mix perennials and annuals.

Hanging baskets filled with lobelia and trailing fuchsias can bring quick colour to new gardens and are invaluable around patios.

Overflowing flowers continue from the conservatory into the
garden and spill out over the paving; lawn would be ruined by such
exuberance.

This small narrow garden has quickly become a green haven on the estate. The interconnecting circles soften the straight lines of the boundaries.

Vegetables need not be grown in a plot of their own, their colours and shapes fit beautifully into flower borders.

No space should be wasted in a small garden and the soil under espalier fruit trees can be planted with flowers.

There's no garden too small . . . This tiny balcony features masses of flowers, space to sit and even a sand-pit.

A collection of alpines can be grown in a very small space if it's planned well and carefully constructed – there's even room for a pool and fountain.

BUGLE (AJUGA) One of the best carpeters for moist conditions, *A. reptans* comes in many forms. It makes an ever-expanding series of rosettes of foliage on questing runners, each throwing up short spikes of (usually) blue flowers in spring. The best are 'Atropurpurea', which has reddish-purple leaves and bright blue flowers, 'Rainbow', with green leaves variegated in cream and pink with pale flowers, and 'Variegata', with grey-green and white variegated foliage and sky-blue flowers.

Growing conditions: Moist soil in sun or, preferably, shade.
Propagation: Division.
Height: 6in (15cm).

AUBRIETA Familiar trailing perennial with single or double flowers in spring. Grows in dense mats of slightly greyish rosettes. There are many good named forms in various reds, pinks, purples and lilacs. Choose when in flower, but look out for 'Maurice Prichard' in pale pink, and 'Variegata' with more dense growth and golden-edged leaves. Seedlings are generally poor.

Growing conditions: Most reasonable soils, in a sunny spot.
Propagation: Cuttings.
Height: 4in (10cm).

CAMPANULA There are many good small campanulas that are easy to grow; all have blue, bell-shaped flowers. Beware of *C. poscharskyana*, which is a rampageous weed, difficult to kill. The dainty *C. cochlearifolia*, especially the pale 'Cambridge Blue' and the double 'Elizabeth Oliver', are delightful low carpeters. 'Dickson's Gold' is more tufted, with yellow foliage and blue flowers in summer.

Growing conditions: Well-drained conditions in full sun. 'Dickson's Gold' appreciates shade from midday scorch.
Propagation: Division.
Height: *C. cochlearifolia*, 3–4in (7.5–10cm); 'Dickson's Gold', 6–8in (15–20cm).

DWARF LAWSON'S CYPRESS (CHAMAECYPARIS) There are a huge number of genuinely dwarf varieties of *C. lawsoniana*, of which the following are especially good: 'Nana Gracilis', with deep green foliage in attractive sprays on a more or less conical plant, 15in (38cm) in ten years; 'Nana Lutea', golden-yellow all year, a basically conical plant, pleasingly irregular, 2ft (60cm) in ten years;

and 'Minima Aurea', bright yellow all year, a tall dome-shaped plant, 2ft (60cm) in ten years.
Growing conditions: Sunshine and any fertile soil, not water-logged.
Propagation: Cuttings, but difficult.

DIASCIA   Long-flowering plants with creeping roots, sometimes invasive in light soil. They may not be hardy in the coldest areas. The flowers come in various shades of pink and resemble those of nemesias. 'Ruby Field' is ruby pink with delicate stems, *D. rigescens* is stiffer and a paler pink.
Growing conditions: Full sun, in any soil that is not waterlogged.
Propagation: Division.
Height: 12in (30cm).

DOG'S TOOTH VIOLET (ERYTHRONIUM)   Given its common name from the shape of its roots, *E. revolutum* has yellow-centred, pink flowers with the petals thrown back like those of a cyclamen. They appear in spring on slender stems. The greyish-green leaves are prettily mottled in brown.
Growing conditions: In fertile soil among deciduous shrubs, or in part shade.
Propagation: Division.
Height: 8in (20cm).

CRANESBILL (GERANIUM)   Two dwarf cranesbills come to mind. *G. sanguineum* makes spreading mounds of fresh green, divided foliage overtopped with upturned flowers in various shades from purple to pale pink and white, usually from early summer into autumn. 'Lancastriense' is an especially good pale pink.
Growing conditions: Sunshine and any reasonable soil that is not too wet.
Propagation: Division.
Height: 8–10in (20–25cm).

'Ballerina' is an especially long-flowering plant, making mats of pretty, finely cut, silvery-green foliage with lilac flowers, eyed and veined in purple.
Growing conditions: Sun and well-drained soil.
Propagation: Root cuttings.
Height: 4in (10cm).

ROCK ROSES (HELIANTHEMUM)   Indispensable, low, spreading shrublets with evergreen foliage in deep green-grey. They flower first in early summer, but should be clipped back hard to flower again later. In most colours except blue, single and double. 'Wisley Pink' has soft pink flowers and grey foliage, 'Fireball' is double red, and 'Ben Nevis' is old gold.
Growing conditions: Sun and a well-drained soil.
Propagation: Cuttings.
Height: 12in (30cm).

CREEPING PHLOX (PHLOX)   Low, creeping, moss-like carpets sparkle with upturned flowers in late spring. Good as a ground-hugger or to trail over rocks and the edges of raised beds. Many colours: 'White Delight' has good green foliage to offset the pure white flowers, 'G. F. Wilson' is clear blue. 'Temiskaming' is rosy red.
Growing conditions: Sun and any reasonable soil, most compact when drainage is good.
Propagation: Cuttings, or by removing rooted shoots.
Height: 4–6in (10–15cm).

CREEPING POLYGONUM (POLYGONUM)   Two species are good small garden plants. *P. vaccinifolium* is the more delicate, with small, dark leaves on widely questing stems making a flat carpet or hanging over rocks. The slender upright spikes of soft pink appear in the autumn. *P. affine* is coarser, with rather earlier, stubbier spikes which darken as they age and with foliage that browns attractively in winter.
Growing conditions: Sun or partial shade, reasonable drainage at least.
Propagation: By detaching rooted shoots.
Height: 9in (23cm).

PRIMROSES (PRIMULA)   Primroses and cowslips come in many types.
Wild flowers   The familiar soft yellow wild primrose, *P. vulgaris*, is easy to grow and will self-sow when happy, though it will hybridise with other primroses and polyanthus.
Growing conditions: Any water-retentive soils, especially heavy ones in partial shade.

Propagation: Division.
Height: 4in (10cm).

The cowslip, *Primula veris*, is as easy, but is better grown in grass or in clumps in the border.
Growing conditions: Happy in better drained conditions and more sunshine than the primrose.
Propagation: Division.
Height: 4–6in (10–15cm).

Old-fashioned primroses   Double-flowered and other unusual primroses are delightful small garden plants but need more careful attention. Good doubles are 'Quaker's Bonnet' in lilac pink and the deep red 'Captain Blood', look out too for 'Gold Lace' with chocolate flowers edged in gold. They are all best divided and replanted every other year.
Growing conditions: Rich, water-retentive but not stagnant soil, in partial shade.
Propagation: Division.
Height: 4–6in (10–15cm).

Problems: Red spider mite, aphids, virus, vine weevil.

SAXIFRAGES (SAXIFRAGA)   Almost every saxifrage comes under the scope of this section, but many are difficult to grow and are suitable only for experienced growers. There are a number of groups, almost all neat and low-growing, but I will restrict myself to four slightly *ad hoc* groups: mossy saxifrages, rosette saxifrages, late-flowering saxifrages and London's pride.

Mossy saxifrages   Fresh green mossy hummocks and carpets, gradually increasing in height and spread. Open sprays of flowers in reds, pinks and white appear in spring. 'Gaiety' is deep pink, 'Pixie' is deep red and especially compact in growth.
Growing conditions: Well-drained soil but preferably in partial shade, rather than full sun.
Propagation: Cuttings and division.
Height: 4–8in (10–20cm).

Rosette saxifrages   Neat green rosettes making a low, steadily creeping carpet with compact heads of yellow or white flowers very

early in spring. *S.* × *apiculata* has yellow flowers; its white variety is
called 'Alba'.
Growing conditions: Gritty, well-drained soil in full sun or,
preferably, shaded around midday.
Propagation: Cuttings.
Height: 3in (7.5cm).

Late-flowering saxifrages   Looking more like a dwarf hardy peren-
nial than a traditional rock plant, *S. fortunei* is a valuable late-
flowering plant with glossy, lobed foliage which is red underneath.
In the autumn it produces open heads of unusual white flowers with
two very long lower petals and three shorter upper ones. 'Wada's
Form' has rich purple leaves.
Growing conditions: Moist soil, in full or partial shade. Tender in
the coldest areas.
Propagation: Division.
Height: 12in (30cm).

London's pride   A well-known cottage plant with large attractive
rosettes, *S.* × *urbium* produces slender stems with an airy cloud of
white, red-spotted petals.
Growing conditions: Sun or partial shade, with reasonable
drainage.
Propagation: Division.
Height: 12in (30cm).

TIARELLA   A neat tufted plant with lobed, darkly spotted foliage,
T. wherryi produces upright spikes of dusty white flowers in spring.
If plants are potted up and brought into a cold greenhouse, they will
flower from late winter.
Growing conditions: Partially shaded conditions, in any reason-
ably fertile soil.
Propagation: Division.
Height: 10in (25cm).

VIOLA   There are hundreds of violas and pansies to choose from,
most of them suitable for the small garden. They come in a wide
range of colours and colour combinations, and some flower for very
long periods. 'Maggie Mott' is a tall, long-flowering, slightly floppy

variety with large, cool, lavender blue flowers; 'Ardross Gem' has smaller, yellow-eyed blue flowers; the intriguing 'Molly Sanderson' is jet-black, while *V. cornuta* 'Alba' is a more sprawling type with pure white flowers from early summer into autumn.

Growing conditions: Sun or partial shade, in any reasonable soil that is not waterlogged.

Propagation: Division.

Height: 6–8in (15–20cm).

Problems: Aphids.

Special selection

ACORUS   A tiny, grass-like plant, *A. gramineus* 'Variegatus' makes neat fans of cream-striped green leaves.

Growing conditions: Moist soil, in sun or shade.

Propagation: Division.

Height: 6in (15cm).

ARABIS   Two varieties are good: the familiar double white-flowered spring companion to aubrieta, *A. caucasica* 'Plena', and the neater, white-variegated *A. ferdinandi-coburgii* 'Variegata'.

Growing conditions: Any reasonably well-drained soil in sun.

Propagation: Division.

Height: 4–6in (10–15cm).

SNOW IN SUMMER (CERASTIUM)   The silver-leaved, white-flowered, rampageous and ineradicable *C. tomentosum* should be avoided; choose instead the more compact *C. columnae*.

Growing conditions: Any reasonable soil in sun.

Propagation: Division.

Height: 4in (10cm).

SILVER HEBE (HEBE)   A flatly spreading silver-leaved shrub, *H.* 'Pagei' also has white flowers in summer.

Growing conditions: Sun and well-drained soil.

Propagation: Layering.

Height: 6in (15cm).

CREEPING JENNY (LYSIMACHIA)   The yellow-leaved form, *L. nummularia* 'Aurea', creeps flat on the ground with yellow

leaves all year and yellow flowers in summer.
Growing conditions: Any soil that doesn't dry out, sun or shade.
Propagation: Detaching rooted shoots.
Height: 3in (7.5cm).

MONKEY FLOWER (MIMULUS)   Short-lived, sticky-leaved perennials with tubular flowers all summer. 'Andean Nymph' is cream
flushed pink, 'Wisley Red' is crimson, 'A. T. Johnson' is yellow
splashed with red.
Growing conditions: Moist soil, sun or shade.
Propagation: Cuttings or division.
Height: 4–6in (10–15cm); 'A. T. Johnson' 15in (38cm).

OXALIS   The delightful grey foliage of O. *adenophylla* sets off the
shining pink flowers beautifully.
Growing conditions: Sunny site, in well-drained but not parched
soil.
Propagation: Seed, difficult.
Height: 2–3in (5–7.5cm).

PASQUE FLOWER (PULSATILLA)   A compact, tufted plant with
lacy leaves, *P. vulgaris* has dramatic, purple, bell-like flowers with
bold yellow centres in spring.
Growing conditions: Sunshine and a well-drained soil.
Propagation: Difficult – seed or root cuttings.
Height: 12in (30cm).

DWARF SPRUCE (PICEA)   The neat pyramidal habit of *P. glauca*
'Albertiana Conica' is enhanced by the brilliant green shoot tips.
Growing conditions: Sun and any reasonable soil.
Propagation: Cuttings, very difficult.
Height: 3ft (90cm) in ten years.

DWARF PINE (PINUS)   The grey-green needles of *P. mugo* 'Mops'
form a slow-growing, dense, rounded bush.
Growing conditions: Sun and any reasonable soil.
Propagation: Grafting, very difficult for the home gardener.
Height: 2ft (60cm) in ten years.

PRATIA   The spreading, ground-level mat of foliage of *P. tread-*

wellii carries small white spring flowers followed by purple berries in autumn.
Growing conditions: Moist soil, in sun or partial shade.
Propagation: Detach rooted shoots.
Height: 2–4in (5–10cm).

RAMONDA   A tough, African-violet-like plant, *R. myconi* has a crinkly rosette which throws up blue flowers on short stems in spring.
Growing conditions: Crevices in north-facing walls and raised beds; tolerates drought once established.
Propagation: From leaves, like African violets.
Height: 6in (15cm).

SILENE   A clump-forming plant with floppy stems, *S. schafta* carries deep pink flowers in summer and autumn. 'Robusta' is particularly long-flowering, 'Abbotswood' is especially floriferous.
Growing conditions: Sun and any reasonable soil.
Propagation: Division.
Height: 4–6in (10–15cm).

SISYRINCHIUM   Iris-like foliage and flared six-petalled flowers for many months. *S. bermudianum* is bright blue, *S. macrodenum* 'May Snow' is pure white.
Growing conditions: Sun and well-drained soil.
Propagation: Division.
Height: 4–6in (10–15cm).

DWARF GOLDEN ROD (SOLIDAGO)   'Golden Thumb' is a very tough, but dwarf and slowly spreading variety with yellow foliage and short but fat yellow flower spikes.
Growing conditions: Any reasonable soil, in sun or partial shade.
Propagation: Division.
Height: 9in (23cm).

DWARF THUYA (THUYA)   The upright dome of *T. orientalis* 'Aurea Nana' has yellow foliage in unusual flat, vertical fans.
Growing conditions: Sun and any reasonable soil.
Propagation: Cuttings, but not easy.
Height: 18in (45cm) in ten years.

THYME (THYMUS)   A small, lax shrublet, 'Silver Posie' has lemon-scented foliage, pink shoot tips, white-variegated leaves and lilac flowers.
Growing conditions: Sun and a well-drained soil.
Propagation: Cuttings.
Height: 8in (20cm).

8.   BULBS

First choices

ORNAMENTAL ONION (ALLIUM)   There are many delightful and easy-to-grow ornamental onions, often unjustly neglected because gardeners think they will smell oniony – they rarely do. *A. chris-tophii* has huge, 10in (25cm), silvery blue flower-heads in early summer. The daintier *A. cernuum* has many small rose-pink bells hanging down from upright stems in midsummer.
Growing conditions: A sunny, well-drained spot.
Planting depth: 3–4in (7.5–10cm).
Height: *A. christophii*, 2ft (60cm); *A. cernuum*, 1½–2ft (45–60cm).

SPRING ANEMONE (ANEMONE)   The pure white *A. blanda* 'White Splendour' is a creeping variety, with small, pretty, deeply cut leaves and pure white flowers in spring. Good among late starting perennials. There are others, such as the lovely soft blue 'Atrocaerulea' and the startling magenta 'Radar'. The more delicate British native windflower, *A. nemorosa*, is lovely under deciduous shrubs.
Growing conditions: Water-retentive soil, in sun or shade.
Planting depth: 3in (7.5cm).
Height: 6in (15cm).

CROCUS   Both spring- and autumn-flowering varieties are invaluable.

Spring varieties   The 'Dutch Hybrids' are big and blowzy and come in a restricted colour range, so choose instead the *C. chrysanthus* varieties which also flower early, in late winter and early spring. They are daintier, often prettily patterned, and are just right for a small garden. 'Blue Bird' is power blue, 'Lady Killer' has white inner petals and strongly feathered mauve outer petals, 'Zwanenberg Bronze' has golden inner petals and bronze patterned outer petals. For naturalising, try the earlier-flowering pale lavender *C. tomasinianus*, which will self-sow when happy.

Growing conditions: Sunny, in well-drained soil.
Planting depth: 3in (7.5cm).
Height: 4in (10cm).

Autumn varieties   Autumn-flowering varieties are not difficult to grow given the right conditions, but it pays to ensure that their space has not been invaded by larger plants during the previous summer. *C. ochroleucus* is pale cream, *C. speciosus* is deep purple.
Growing conditions: Happy in cooler conditions than spring varieties, good naturalised in grass or under deciduous shrubs.
Planting depth: 4in (10cm).
Height: 4–5in (10–12.5cm).

WINTER ACONITE (ERANTHIS)   The first spring-flowering bulb and especially welcome for that, *E. hyemalis* has big buttercup-yellow flowers on a neat green ruff in winter. Self-sows enthusiastically when happy.
Growing conditions: Under deciduous shrubs.
Planting depth: 4in (10cm). Dry bulbs may not establish well, so buy them in growth if possible. If happy, seedlings will soon appear.
Height: 5in (12.5cm).

SNOWDROPS (GALANTHUS)   Essential dwarf bulbs. Different varieties flower right through the spring. In a small garden, where relatively few bulbs will be needed, choose only the very best varieties. 'Atkinsii' is large, elegant and vigorous too, 'S. Arnott' is very large but a lovely shape and scented. Most double snowdrops have rather messy flowers, though they last very well. There's also the autumn-flowering *G. reginae-olgae*.
Growing conditions: Fertile soil, shady conditions.
Planting depth: 4in (10cm).
Height: 4–8in (10–20cm).

LILIES (LILIUM)   Opulent lilies are essential in the garden, with their powerful wafting perfume. Many modern hybrids are stiff and unattractive in habit, but some of the simpler wild species are more appealing. The Madonna lily, *L. candidum*, has pure white, scented flowers in short spikes, while *L. regale* has larger white trumpets in more clustered heads with a purple flush to the outside.

Growing conditions: Moisture-retentive but well-drained soil, in sun or partial shade.

Planting depth: *L. candidum* just below the surface; *L. regale* 6in (15cm).

Height: 4–5ft (1.2–1.5m).

Problems: Bulb rot, aphids, virus.

GRAPE HYACINTHS (MUSCARI) Dependable blue-flowering bulbs. The well-known 'Blue Spike' is large and vigorous but rather coarse, while *M. armeniacum*, with clusters of tiny white-rimmed blue bells, is prettier. There's also the sparkling *M. azureum*, which is smaller and neater, and others in various blues, plus white.

Growing conditions: Any reasonable soil, in sun or partial shade.

Planting depth: 3–4in (7.5–10cm).

Height: 4–8in (10–20cm), depending on variety.

DAFFODILS (NARCISSUS) The only question seems to be which to pick. Most of those on sale in garden centres are easy to grow, especially if you give them some liquid feeds after flowering. Plant them in clumps for the best effect. 'February Gold' is a yellow, early-flowering trumpet type, while the similar 'February Silver' has white petals and a yellow trumpet. 'Geranium' is the best and most prolific 'narcissus' type, white with a small orange trumpet.

Growing conditions: Fertile soil, in sun or partial shade. Do not tie the leaves in bunches after flowering.

Planting depth: 4–6in (10–15cm).

Height: 12–18in (30–45cm).

Dwarf varieties   Many dwarf types are now available. 'Tête à Tête' has two or three dainty flowers on a short stem but tends to fade away; 'Jumblie' is similar but tougher. 'Hawera' is more slender, with tiny yellow flowers in huge quantities, and 'Rip van Winkle' is a small, very full double in bright yellow.

Growing conditions: Fertile soil, not badly drained, in sun or partial shade.

Planting depth: 4in (10cm).

Height: 'Tête à Tête' and 'Jumblie' 4–6in (10–15cm); 'Hawera' and 'Rip van Winkle' 8–10in (20–25cm).

NERINE   One of the best late-flowering bulbs, *N. bowdenii* carries heads of narrow, flared, pink flowers in autumn before the leaves. Once happy, it increases well and needs little attention.
Growing conditions: A warm, sunny site, preferably at the foot of a wall.
Planting depth: Just below the soil surface.
Height: 2ft (60cm).

Special selection

ACIDANTHERA   A white, dark-eyed and more elegant version of a gladiolus, *A. mureliae* has arching flower spikes and a powerful fragrance.
Growing conditions: Containers, or any sunny, well-drained site. Tender; lift and store for winter.
Planting depth: 6in (15cm).
Height: 1½–2ft (45–60cm).

AGAPANTHUS   Imposing bulbs with a mass of white fleshy roots. With long, low arching foliage, the 'Headbourne Hybrids' have rounded flower-heads in a range of blue shades. The bright blue 'Lilliput' is much dwarfer and very neat.
Growing conditions: Containers, or any sunny site.
Planting depth: Just below the surface.
Height: 'Headbourne Hybrids' 3ft (90cm); 'Lilliput' 18in (45cm).

HARDY AMARYLLIS (AMARYLLIS)   Like a smaller, dark pink version of the indoor amaryllis, *A. belladonna* has heads of fragrant flowers in autumn before the leaves.
Growing conditions: Sunny, well-drained site, preferably at the base of a warm wall.
Planting depth: Just below the soil surface.
Height: 2ft (60cm).

CAMASSIA   With deep blue flowers on a short stem in early summer, *C. esculenta* is an easy bulb for borders, under trees or naturalised in grass.

Growing conditions: Moist soil, in sun or shade.
Planting depth: 4in (10cm).
Height: 12in (30cm).

GLORY OF THE SNOW (CHIONODOXA)   A pretty blue-flowered bulb with a white throat, *C. luciliae* is very hardy and flowers in early spring.
Growing conditions: Any reasonable soil, good under deciduous shrubs.
Planting depth: 3in (7.5cm).
Height: 4in (10cm).

AUTUMN CROCUS (COLCHICUM)   It may look like a crocus, but *C. speciosum*, with its rosy flowers on taller stems, also has long, broad, strap-like green leaves in spring and these need camouflaging. The double-flowered 'Water Lily' is a lovely lilac colour.
Growing conditions: Any deep fertile soil, in sun or partial shade.
Planting depth: 4in (10cm).
Height: 6–8in (15–20cm).

HARDY CYCLAMEN (CYCLAMEN)   Dainty *C. hederifolium* has pink or white flowers in early autumn and ivy-shaped silvery marked foliage which lasts till spring.
Growing conditions: Water-retentive but well-drained soil, good under deciduous shrubs and trees.
Planting depth: 1in (2.5cm).
Height: 4–6in (10–15cm).

BLUEBELL (HYACINTHOIDES)   A risky plant for the small garden, the familiar *H. non-scriptus* can seed itself too efficiently for comfort, but its blue spring flowers are lovely.
Growing conditions: Partial shade, reasonable soil.
Planting depth: 6in (15cm).
Height: 15in (38cm).

CROWN IMPERIAL (FRITILLARIA)   The stately *F. imperialis* makes fresh green early growth topped with heads of down-turned orange flowers in spring.
Growing conditions: Rich, limy soil in full sun.
Planting depth: 6in (15cm).
Height: 3ft (90cm).

SNAKESHEAD FRITILLARY (FRITILLARIA)   Chequered purple and white nodding flowers on slender stems. The pure white form of *F. meleagris* is also very pretty.
Growing conditions: Sunny, but not too dry.
Planting depth: 4in (10cm).
Height: 12in (30cm).

SUMMER HYACINTH (GALTONIA)   Like a huge white hyacinth, *G. candicans* makes a lovely group growing through low foliage.
Growing conditions: Sunny borders in any reasonable soil, self-sows when happy.
Planting depth: 6in (15cm).
Height: 3ft (90cm).

GLADIOLUS   A rather delicate and tender plant, *G. papilio* has creeping roots and forms a clump. In summer it has unusual white and greyish purple flowers in open heads.
Growing conditions: Sunny, sheltered site in well-drained soil.
Planting depth: 3in (7.5cm).
Height: 3ft (90cm).

SUMMER SNOWFLAKE (LEUCOJUM)   A dependable bulb with deep green leaves, *L. aestivum* has nodding heads of pure white bells in late spring.
Growing conditions: Moist soil, in sun or part shade.
Planting depth: 4in (10cm).
Height: 18in (45cm).

TUBEROUS NASTURTIUM (TROPAEOLUM)   A tender, tuberous-rooted climber with fiery orange and yellow flowers, *T. tuberosum* 'Ken Aslet' clings by its leaf tendrils but needs strong support. Lift the tubers in the autumn and store in a frost-free place.
Growing conditions: Water-retentive but not soggy soil, sun or partial shade.
Planting depth: 6in (15cm).
Height: 8ft (2.4m).

TULIP (TULIPA)   Few tulips thrive unless lifted every autumn and stored indoors, so they're ideal for containers and for temporary spring displays. 'Little Red Riding Hood' has darkly mottled foliage and bright scarlet flowers and is good for window-boxes. Lily-flowered varieties like the yellow 'West Point' and the white 'White Triumphator' are the most stylish.

Growing conditions: Sunshine and any fertile soil that's not waterlogged.

Planting depth: 6in (15cm).

Height: 'Little Red Riding Hood' 8in (20cm); lily-flowered varieties 2ft (60cm).

Problems: Tulip fire.

9. ORNAMENTAL FOOD PLANTS

Many of us with small gardens are reluctant to give over much space to vegetables – after all, they're not as colourful as flowers and in a small garden every inch must count. But there are now a number of smaller, neater-growing types which are also very attractive. Some are best in the greenhouse or conservatory, and all will do well outside in well-prepared beds, pots or growing bags, in a sunny sheltered spot.

Most herbs have ornamental varieties, and these are dealt with on page 308.

AUBERGINE   Aubergines are less suitable for growing out of doors than tomatoes, peppers and cucumbers, but the small fruited 'Little Fingers' is the toughest you can get. What's more, the fruits are the size of small sausages and are carried in clusters of three or four.

Propagation: Sow seed in warmth in spring.

Cultivation: Pot on eventually to 8in (20cm) pots or three to a growing bag and move outside after the last frost.

CHARD   A long-lasting, double-use version of spinach. 'Swiss Chard' has bright green foliage which is cooked like spinach, and broad, white midribs to sauté. 'Ruby Chard' has darker leaves and scarlet midribs. Both are very attractive.

Propagation: In spring, sow two seeds to a small pot and remove the weakest after germination.

Cultivation: Plant out 12in (30cm) apart in beds, singly in 8in

(20cm) pots or six to a growing bag. Never let them get short of water. Pick the outer leaves as you need them.

CHILI PEPPER   'Apache' is a small-fruited, bushy chili pepper reaching about 18in (45cm), covered in short, hot fruits. The lantern-shaped fruits of 'Red Cherry' come on a taller plant.
Propagation: Sow in warmth in spring and grow on in small pots.
Cultivation: Grow singly in 8in (20cm) pots or three to a growing bag, planting out after the last frost.

CUCUMBER   Neat, non-trailing, bush cucumbers are good on patios, and 'Bush Champion', with 8in (20cm) fruits all summer, is the best for this use.
Propagation: Sow seeds individually in 3in (7.5cm) pots indoors in late spring.
Cultivation: Plant out after the last frost, one per 8in (20cm) pot, three per growing bag.

LETTUCE   Non-hearting lettuce from which a few leaves can be removed whenever you need them are the best patio types. The oak-leaved 'Salad Bowl' and the very attractive 'Red Salad Bowl' are ideal, as are the red-tinted 'Carnival' and the frilly-leaved 'Lollo Red' and 'Lollo Green'.
Propagation: Sow outside or inside in spring. For container growing, move to 3in (7.5cm) pots.
Cultivation: Thin to 12in (30cm) apart for growing in beds, or plant six in a growing bag.

SWEET PEPPER   For pots, beds or growing bags choose the 15in (38cm) sweet pepper 'Redskin', with heavy crops of slightly pointed fruits, green first then ripening to red.
Propagation: Sow in warmth in spring and grow on in 3in (7.5cm) pots.
Cultivation: Grow in 8in (20cm) pots or three to a growing bag, planting out after the last frost.

MARROW   Most marrows are not very attractive or compact but 'Twickers' is a neat bush-growing type with large quantities of 10in (25cm) fruits shaped like rugby balls.
Propagation: Sow seeds individually in 3in (7.5cm) pots indoors in late spring.

Cultivation: Plant out in beds after the last frost, one per 10in (25cm) pot, or two per growing bag.

TOMATO   There are two types of tomato I would recommend. There are very short, compact varieties like 'Totem', which reach about 18in (45cm) and can be grown in an 8in (20cm) pot. There's also the very attractive and very tasty 'Gardener's Delight' which is a standard variety reaching 4–5ft (1.2–1.5m).
Propagation: Sow in warmth in spring and grow on in 3in (7.5cm) pots.
Cultivation: 'Totem' can be grown in 6in (15cm) or 8in (20cm) pots, four to a growing bag, or 15in (38cm) apart in beds. 'Gardener's Delight' should go in 10in (25cm) pots, three to a growing bag, or 2ft (60cm) apart in beds.

10. WATER AND WATERSIDE PLANTS

It would be unreasonable to expect a large number of plants in a large pond in a *small* garden, so my selection of aquatic plants for the open water and marginal plants for the boggy edges of the pond is but a modest one.

SWEET FLAG (ACORUS)   *A. calamus* 'Variegatus' has upright, iris-like foliage with bold, creamy lines along the length of the leaves. The flowers are unremarkable.
Growing conditions: A marginal plant, happiest in about 3in (7.5cm) of water.
Height: 2½ft (75cm).

MARSH MARIGOLD (CALTHA)   The shining, double yellow flowers of *C. palustris* 'Plena' appear in spring above deep glossy green foliage. Looks wonderful reflected in still water.
Growing conditions: A marginal plant for sodden soil above the waterline or in an inch or two of water.
Height: 12in (30cm).

WATER IRIS (IRIS)   The sumptuous flowers of *I. laevigata* appear all summer, just overtopping the fans of foliage. There are many varieties with purple, white and pink flowers plus 'Variegata', with

white-striped leaves. The familiar yellow flag, *I. pseudacorus*, is too vigorous for small ponds.
Growing conditions: Best in just an inch or two of water, but will usually thrive just above the waterline.
Height: 2ft (60cm).

SIBERIAN IRIS (IRIS)   Very upright, but elegant, *I. sibirica* is summer-flowering, with dark, narrow foliage. There are many varieties in the purple, blue, lilac and white colour range. Look out for 'Emperor' in blueish violet and the white 'Snow Queen'. A good cut flower.
Growing conditions: Around and just above the waterline and boggy soil anywhere. Also thrives in damp borders away from water.
Height: 4ft (1.2m).

CORKSCREW RUSH (JUNCUS)   *J. effusus* 'Spiralis' is a curious, dark-leaved rush with each stem twisted like a stretched corkscrew.
Growing conditions: Best in about 3–4in (7.5–10cm) of water.
Height: 18in (45cm).

MONKEY FLOWER (MIMULUS)   Most mimulus are too vigorous and self-seeding for small ponds, but 'Hose in Hose', with one rusty yellow flower sitting neatly inside another, is more modest and flowers on and off all summer. The seed-raised 'Malibu', 'Calypso' and 'Viva' (see page 241) are also worth trying.
Growing conditions: At around the waterline or just above.
Height: 9in (23cm).

WATER LILY (NYMPHAEA)   Dwarf varieties of water lily are ideal for the small pond – some will thrive in only 4in (10cm) of water and cover just 1 sq ft (0.1 sq m) of water. Consult a good catalogue for varieties in different sizes and colours.
Growing conditions: In still, open water with the roots from 4–36in (10–90cm) deep, depending on variety.
Height: Floating; spread varies from 1–25sq ft (0.1–2.25sq m).

WATER FRINGE (NYMPHOIDES)   *N. peltata* is a fast-growing floater with small, water-lily-like leaves, ideal for providing shade for fish quickly in new ponds. Small yellow flowers like frilly poppies.

Growing conditions: Happy in a 4–18in (10–45cm) depth of open water.
Height: Floating.

PRIMULA   Many species are suitable, including most of the candelabra types such as *P. pulverulenta*, as well as the much shorter, vivid pink *P. rosea* and the drumstick primrose, *P. denticulata*.
Growing conditions: Happy just above the waterline, where the soil is wet in summer as well as winter, and will then thrive in full sun.
Height: 12–24in (30–60cm).

ARUM LILY (ZANTEDESCHIA)   The bold, fragrant white-flowered arums, *Z. aethiopica*, with their fresh green foliage, make exotic waterside plants. Smaller varieties are becoming available.
Growing conditions: The roots need a covering of at least 6in (15cm) of water as a protection against frost.
Height: 2ft (60cm).

11.   TENDER PERENNIALS

Tender perennials are herbaceous plants or shrubs which grow well outside in Britain in the summer months but which are killed by frost. They are often very colourful and long-flowering, but as they don't last from year to year, fresh plants must be bought each season or your own plants must be kept over the winter. Some, like dahlias, have tuberous roots which must be dug up and stored, others need to be kept growing as plants in a frost-free greenhouse. All thrive in a fertile soil in a sunny place.

MARGUERITE (ARGYRANTHEMUM)   Also known as aggies, argies, marguerites and shrubby chrysanths, they are, basically, like chrysanthemums but grow as small rounded bushes from early summer until the first severe frosts. They have single, anemone-centred or double flowers. *A. foeniculaceum* has masses of single white daisies over grey foliage, 'Jamaica Primrose' is a single yellow, 'Vancouver' has anemone-centred pink flowers, 'Qinta White' is an anemone-centred white. A specimen plant will flower all winter in a conservatory.
Propagation: Cuttings at almost any time.

Overwintering: As rooted cuttings or young plants.
Height: 2ft (60cm).
Problems: Aphids.

DAHLIA   Very brightly coloured plants in an extremely wide range of colours, shapes and sizes of flowers and heights. Depending on variety, they flower from June to the frosts. Smaller types are good in containers and in the front of borders, larger ones make a bolder splash. Most are good for cutting. Many are so bright that relatively few plants are needed. I suggest you choose your own from the illustrated packs in the garden centre. When in doubt, err on the side of smaller flowers.
Propagation: Division of tubers in spring, cuttings from new spring shoots. Some good dwarf types can be raised from seed.
Overwintering: Store tubers in peat in a cool, but frost-free place.
Height: 1–5ft (30cm–1.5m), depending on variety.
Problems: Aphids, red spider mite, virus, earwigs.

TRAILING HELICHRYSUM (HELICHRYSUM)   The long trailing shoots of *H. petiolare* are covered in grey down and the heart-shaped leaves are grey too. This is an ideal plant to associate with pastel or strong colours in the border or in tubs. 'Limelight' has slightly greenish-yellow leaves, while *H. microphyllum* (correctly *Pleiostachys serpyllifolia*) has tiny grey leaves.
Propagation: Cuttings.
Overwintering: As rooted cuttings or young plants.
Height: 18in (45cm), but widely spreading.

GERANIUM (PELARGONIUM)   Geraniums, correctly called pelargoniums to distinguish them from the related but quite different hardy geraniums, come in many types. Those suitable for the small garden are the zonal, ivy-leaved and scented-leaved types. Height and spread varies with the individual varieties.

Ivy-leaved   Trailing varieties for baskets and tubs, with glossy green leaves and flowers all the way down the shoots, making a ball of colour. Look out for the 'Cascade' or 'Balcony' types.
Height: Trailing to 2ft (60cm).

Scented-leaved   This is a group of strongly scented varieties, many with attractive foliage but with small flowers. Some of them smell of

citrus or mint but there is quite a variety of other fragrances. 'Lady Plymouth' has white-edged deeply divided leaves and a lemon scent. 'Chocolate Peppermint' has softly hairy, chocolate-blotched leaves and a peppermint scent. Ideal for patio tubs.
Height: Up to 3ft (90cm).
Propagation: Cuttings.
Overwintering: As rooted cuttings or young plants.
Problems: Caterpillars.

Zonals   These are often now raised from seed, but can be rooted from cuttings. Bushy plants carry big heads of single, semi-double or double flowers in various reds, pinks, lilacs and white, and all but the whites may have darkly zoned foliage. Good in tubs, flowering till the frosts. There are hundreds of colourful varieties, plus variegated-leaved types like the white-edged 'Madame Shalleron'.
Height: Up to 2ft (60cm).

VERBENA   Many verbenas are now raised from seed, but the old-fashioned, mildew-free trailing types are raised from cuttings. They are low sprawling or trailing plants, flowering from early summer to the frosts. 'Silver Anne' is soft pink, 'Sissinghurst' is cerise, 'Lawrence Johnston' is scarlet.
Propagation: Cuttings.
Overwintering: As rooted cuttings or young plants.
Height: 9in (23cm), spreading or trailing.

12. HARDY ANNUALS

In a small garden hardy annuals can be used in three ways – they can be sown in clumps in the borders wherever there's a gap, they can be allowed to self-sow and so appear in both likely and unlikely places, and a few plants of appropriate varieties can also be grown in short rows specially for cutting.

First choices

QUAKING GRASS (BRIZA)   A dainty little grass with shimmering straw-coloured lockets of overlapping scales which rustle in the breeze. *B. maxima* needs a sunny spot and soil that is not too wet and will self-sow harmlessly, looking especially good in gravel.
Height: 12–18in (30–45cm).

CANDYTUFT (IBERIS)   An easy plant for most soils in a sunny or partially shaded spot, this is another that grows well along the edges of gravel drives. It flowers more quickly than most, but unless dead-headed by clipping over with shears after a downpour is liable to give up relatively early. 'Flash' is the best mixture, with a wider range of colours than the usual pinks and lilacs, including a few in rich red.
Height: 9–12in (23–30cm).

MALLOW (LAVATERA)   The annual mallows are among the most prolific of the taller annuals, and as they also bush out well very few plants are needed. The flowers are silky in texture, with the overlapping petals forming a flared trumpet. 'Silver Cup', in shining pink, is the best known, 'Pink Beauty' is much paler with dark veins, 'Mont Blanc' is pure white with very dark leaves, and 'Ruby Regis' is very deep pink.
Height: 2ft (60cm).
Problems: Plants sometimes die without warning.

ALYSSUM (LOBULARIA)   The flat, spreading growth of alyssum, *L. maritima*, is ideal for the edges of beds in small gardens and for gaps in paving. Its sweet scent is a bonus. 'Snow Crystals' is the best white, 'Creamery' is a rich creamy shade, and 'Wonderland Deep Purple' is the best dark shade. 'Easter Bonnet', in eight colours from deep purple to pure white, is the best mixture.
Height: 3in (7.5cm).
Problems: Mildew.

BABY BLUE EYES (NEMOPHILA)   Few hardy annuals do well in shade, but the sky-blue *N. menziesii* is one that does, as much because it dislikes drought as because it likes shade. The plants are sprawling, with slightly sticky foliage.
Height: 6in (15cm).

LOVE-IN-A-MIST (NIGELLA)   For cutting and for borders 'Persian Jewels' is a lovely mixture, with semi-double flowers in reds, purples, blues, pinks and white followed by ornamental seed-pods. The finely divided foliage is pretty too. 'Miss Jekyll' is a little taller and an exquisite blue. The dumpy 'Dwarf Moody Blue' is singularly inelegant.

Height: 'Persian Jewels' 15in (38cm); 'Miss Jekyll' 18in (45cm); 'Dwarf Moody Blue' 6in (15cm).

OMPHALODES   A pretty, upright, grey-leaved annual, *O. linifolia* has uncurling sprays of pure white, forget-me-not-like flowers for many weeks. It's scented, makes a good cut flower, and self-sows in any sunny, fairly well-drained situation.
Height: 15in (38cm).

CORN POPPY (PAPAVER)   Wild red corn poppies, *P. rhoeas*, are easy annuals with which to start a wild flower meadow, blooming well while perennials get established. 'Mother of Pearl' is a shorter variety in an exquisite range of unusual colours – grey, smoky lilac, dusty pink, soft apricot and no brash reds at all. Easy in any sunny spot, 'Mother of Pearl' self-sows well, but any bright-coloured plants should be removed promptly.
Height: Corn poppy 2ft (60cm); 'Mother of Pearl' 15in (38cm).

SWEET PEA (LATHYRUS)   Indispensable climbers for borders and for cutting. In borders grow them up stout shrubs, trellis or well-anchored tubes of netting; for cutting grow them up pea and bean netting stretched between two stakes. Any good soil in a sunny spot suits them. There are many varieties; pick those with the best scent, such as the cream and blue 'Old Times', the white 'Diamond Wedding' and the pink 'Charles Unwin'.
Height: 6ft (1.8m).

NASTURTIUM (TROPAEOLUM)   Climbing nasturtiums are rather difficult to cope with in the small garden, but the neater, bushy types like 'Alaska' are good in sunny sites where the soil is not too rich. 'Alaska' comes in many shades of red, orange, yellow and peach. But there's another attraction – the foliage is prettily flecked and speckled in white. The semi-double flowered 'Whirlybird' mixture is also excellent.
Height: 12in (30cm).

Special selection

CORN COCKLE (AGROSTEMMA)   A rare cornfield weed, the waving stems of *A. githago* carry plummy flowers in summer.
Height: 3ft (90cm).

LOVE LIES BLEEDING (AMARANTHUS)   With stunning, pendulous tassels in rich red or green, *A. caudatus* is easy to grow and even dries well.
Height: 2ft (60cm)

BORAGE (BORAGO)   *B. officinalis* has icy-blue flowers and hairy foliage. A good dry garden plant.
Height: 2ft (60cm).

ENGLISH MARIGOLD (CALENDULA)   Brilliant orange or yellow flowers for most soils in sunshine. *C. officinalis* 'Fiesta Gitana' is a dwarf mixture, 'Indian Prince' has mahogany petal backs and is good for cutting.
Height: 'Fiesta Gitana' 12in (30cm); 'Indian Prince' 24in (60cm).

ANNUAL CHRYSANTHEMUM (CHRYSANTHEMUM)   Flamboyant and easy annuals for most soils in sunshine. *C. segetum* is a bright yellow cornfield weed, 'Court Jesters' is a glorious mixture of fiery shades.
Height: 18in (45cm).

HELIPTERUM   Small, willowy, pale everlastings, helipterums have flowers in soft reds, pinks and white.
Height: 12in (30cm).

ANNUAL LUPIN (LUPINUS)   The bright yellow *L. luteus* is an upright plant for a sunny spot.
Height: 2ft (60cm).

NIGHT-SCENTED STOCK (MATTHIOLA)   An unprepossessing plant with lilac flowers, the chief quality of *M. bicornis* is its powerful evening scent.
Height: 12in (30cm).

OPIUM POPPY (PAPAVER)   Upright plants with blue-green foliage and big, blowzy, double paeony-like flowers, *P. somniferum* 'Paeony Flowered Mixed' comes in reds, pinks and whites.
Height: 3ft (90cm).

MIGNONETTE (RESEDA)   A sweetly scented but not showy plant, *R. odorata* has green flowers and is good in pots or borders.
Height: 12in (30cm).

13. HALF-HARDY ANNUALS AND BEDDING PLANTS

Half-hardy annuals and bedders are frost-tender and are planted out after the last frost in your area. Many are also sold as plants in garden centres, but the varieties recommended here may not be available as plants, in which case you will have to raise them yourself.

All are unusually colourful plants and as such may need careful integration into mixed borders. As they last only one season you have the opportunity to maintain a constantly changing display from year to year. Many of these varieties are also good in containers, and some are useful for cutting.

First choices

AGERATUM   Fluffy-flowered plants in various blues and irrelevant pinks and white. 'Southern Cross' is a beautiful blue and white bicolour, 'Blue Ribbon' is bright blue and the plants have a very rounded habit, 'Blue Horizon' is a tall one for cutting. Best in a rich soil and sunshine.
Propagation: Seed in spring, not difficult. Or buy plants, though these varieties may not be available.
Height: 'Southern Cross' 12in (30cm); 'Blue Ribbon' 8in (20cm); 'Blue Horizon' 2ft (60cm).

FIBROUS ROOTED BEGONIAS (BEGONIA)   Long-flowering and neat plants with green or bronzed foliage and red, pink or white flowers. *B. semperflorens* 'Lucia' is the best mixture, 'Party Fun' is bigger and bushier and will thrive in shade, while 'Pink Avalanche' is more trailing and good for window-boxes.
Propagation: Spring. Seed is very tiny and difficult to handle. Seedlings and young plants are available by mail order from seed companies.
Height: 'Lucia' 6in (15cm); 'Party Fun' 9in (23cm); 'Pink Avalanche' 12in (30cm).
Problems: Red spider mite. Seed very tiny.

TUBEROUS BEGONIA (BEGONIA)   Large, fully double flowers in sparkling colours with a bushy habit. Larger leaves than fibrous-rooted types and with a tuberous root. 'Non Stop' comes in twelve colours, flowers all summer and is especially good in containers. 'Illumination' has pink flowers and an arching habit suitable for window-boxes and baskets.

Propagation: Spring. Seed is very small and difficult to handle. Young plants are available by mail order from seed companies.

Height: 'Non Stop' 12in (30cm).

Problems: Fragile stems. Seed tiny.

WALLFLOWER (CHEIRANTHUS) Bushy, sweetly scented spring bedders in colours from blood-red, through orange, to pale lemon. The 'Bedder' varieties are the neatest. Best in a reasonably well-drained soil in full sun.

Propagation: Buy plants in autumn, sow seed outside in early summer.

Height: 'Bedder' series 12in (30cm); other varieties 18in (45cm).

Problems: Clubroot.

ANNUAL PINKS (DIANTHUS) There are many types of bedding pinks. *D. chinensis* are the most widely grown, making neat, bushy plants in a range of colours from deep red through pinks to white, some with bicolours. 'Telstar' and 'Princess' are good mixtures.

Propagation: Seed, in spring. Plants may be available in garden centres.

Height: 8–10in (20–30cm).

GERANIUM (PELARGONIUM) Correctly known as pelargoniums, there are two types, those raised from seed and those raised from cuttings (see page 234). Garden centres often sell both, not differentiating between the two. Seed companies sell young plants of both types.

Bushy plants, many with darkly zoned foliage. The best varieties flower all summer until the heavy frosts, in a wide range of reds, rose, salmon and blush pinks, plus white with a few eyed types. All are best in a rich soil with full sun. Good seed-raised mixtures include 'Gala', 'Century', 'Sensation', 'Multibloom', plus the dwarf 'Video'.

Propagation: Seed, sown early in spring; not easy, high temperatures needed and the seed is expensive.

Height: 'Video' 8in (20cm); others 12in (30cm).

BUSY LIZZIE (IMPATIENS) The best bedding plants for shade. Impatiens make low, spreading plants with succulent stems and foliage and a long succession of flowers from before planting until the first frost. They like a good soil and sun or shade, but must not dry out. The 'Super Elfin' series in sixteen colours with many attractive pastel shades is the best, with 'Accent' not far behind and 'Blitz' a good larger variety.

Propagation: Seed, in spring; not the easiest.

Height: 6in (15cm) plus, depending on variety.

MONKEY FLOWER (MIMULUS) Mimulus have flamboyant flowers and are quick-growing and quick to flower. They all hate to dry out and do well in partially shaded sites. 'Malibu' makes spreading plants in clear colours, 'Calypso' is larger and has many spotted flowers, 'Viva' is the biggest, with yellow flowers blotched in red.

Propagation: Seed, which is tiny but germinates easily; plant can flower in two months.

Height: 'Malibu' 4in (10cm); 'Calypso' 9in (23cm); 'Viva' 12in (30cm).

NEMESIA Very colourful, relatively early flowering bedders with flared flowers in the widest range of colours and bicolours. They need cooler, moist conditions to give their best, and perform poorly in hot, dry summers. 'Tapestry' has the widest range of shades, 'Carnival' has the largest flowers in hotter colours. 'Mello' is a small flowered red and white bicolour, 'Blue Gem' is a small flowered blue.

Propagation: Seed, in spring.

Height: 9–12in (23–30cm).

TOBACCO PLANT (NICOTIANA) Nicotianas come in two types. There are small, bushy, unscented bedding varieties, of which the best is 'Domino', and taller, scented, back-of-the-border or cutting varieties like 'Sensation'. All have sticky foliage and long tubed flowers with a flat face.

Propagation: Seed, in spring; easy. Or buy plants in late spring.

Height: 'Domino' 12in (30cm); 'Sensation' 3ft (90cm).

PANSY (VIOLA)   Pansies are now grown for summer, winter and spring, but I suggest leaving the summer to the many other summer plants. Winter and spring pansies are bushy in habit, with flowers in an astonishing variety of colours and patterns. 'Universal' flowers well in mild winter spells and in spring, as does 'Ultima', which has more colours. In small gardens the unusual colours are especially effective; look out for 'Joker' (prettily patterned in blue and white), 'Brunig' (mahogany with a gold edge), 'Imperial Silver Princess' (white with red blotch), 'Flame Princess' (yellow with red blotch) and many more.

Propagation: Seed, sown in late spring, or buy plants in autumn. Not all these varieties will be available in garden centres.

Height: 6–8in (15–20cm).

PETUNIA   Sun-loving plants with a spreading habit and flared, trumpet flowers in many colours. Give them a good soil and they will thrive in the hottest summers. Less good in wet seasons. The 'Carpet' series is superseding the 'Resisto' series as the best all-rounder; 'Mirage' has larger flowers and more sumptuous colours; the 'Picotee' series has dark flowers with white rims; the 'Daddy' series has veined flowers in many shades. 'Picotee' and 'Daddy' are less good in bad seasons.

Propagation: Seed, in spring. Seed companies sell seedlings, garden centres may have these or other varieties.

Height: 12in (30cm).

POLYANTHUS (PRIMULA)   These are, with pansies, the best spring-flowering plants, good in containers and in the open. 'Crescendo' is the toughest variety for all winter conditions and has large flowers in many colours. Some cheaper varieties, like 'Dobies Superb Mixed', have smaller flowers but more of them.

Propagation: Seed, in late spring. Seedlings are available from seed companies, plants from garden centres in autumn.

Height: 9in (23cm).

SALVIA   The scarlet salvias are going out of favour but the deep purple 'Phoenix Purple' is popular, with deep green leaves and dense spikes of rich purple flowers. *S. farinacea* 'Victoria' is different, with narrow grey-green foliage and tall, stiff spikes of small deep blue flowers. If you like a sparkling red go for 'Red Riches'. Give them sunshine and a fertile soil.

Propagation: Seed, in spring. Seedlings from seed companies, plants of red varieties from garden centres.
Height: 'Phoenix Purple' and 'Red Riches' 12in (30cm); 'Victoria' 18in (45cm).

SILVERDUST (SENECIO) Silver foliage is a fine foil to other colours, and the cut leaves of 'Silverdust' on the neat plants enhance the beds or tubs of any small garden. 'Cirrus' is a whiter, oak-leaved variety.
Propagation: Seed, sown in spring; easy.
Height: 9in (23cm).

Special selection

SNAPDRAGON (ANTIRRHINUM) Even the best antirrhinums flower in flushes, which is irritating when space is limited. 'Spring Giant' is a good cut flower or back of border plant, 'Royal Carpet' is a good dwarf, and 'Princess White with Purple Eye' a stunning single colour.
Propagation: Seed in spring; seed is small but not difficult.
Height: 'Royal Carpet' 8in (20cm); 'Princess' 12in (30cm); 'Spring Giant' 3ft (90cm).
Problems: Rust.

DOUBLE DAISY (BELLIS) Very useful dainty spring bedders. 'Pomponette' has neat buttons in red, pink and white, 'Goliath' is ragged and coarse.
Propagation: Seed, outside in late spring; easy.
Height: 4in (10cm).

CALCEOLARIA Clouds of small yellow slippers all summer. 'Midas' is also good for baskets.
Propagation: Seed in spring; very small seed, not easy.
Height: 12in (30cm).

ASTER (CALLISTEPHUS) Best as a cut flower, though dwarf varieties are useful late bedders. 'Compliment' has large, fully double, silvered flowers in pink, lilac and white.
Propagation: Seed in spring; easy.
Height: 3ft (90cm).
Problems: Wilt.

GAZANIA   Dwarf, sun-loving plants with big daisy flowers in fiery shades. 'Sundance' has the best colours and is a good cut flower, 'Mini-Star' is dwarfer.
Propagation: Seed, in spring; easy.
Height: 'Mini-Star' 8in (20cm); 'Sundance' 12in (30cm).

STRAWFLOWER (HELICHRYSUM)   Among the best everlastings, *H. bracteatum* is also good at the back of the border. 'Monstrosum Double Mixed' has a fine range of colours, 'Monstrosum Dwarf Art Shades' is similar but small garden size.
Propagation: Seed in spring, easy.
Height: 'Monstrosum Double Mixed' 4ft (1.2m); 'Monstrosum Dwarf Art Shades' 18in (45cm).

STATICE (LIMONIUM)   Favourite dried flowers that also look good in borders. 'Fortress Strain' has the clearest colours.
Propagation: Seed in spring, easy.
Height: 18in (45cm).

LOBELIA   Small, bushy varieties like the bronze-leaved, blue-flowered 'Crystal Palace Compacta' and the paler 'Cambridge Blue' are good for edging, while trailers like the 'Cascade' varieties are essential for baskets.
Propagation: Seed in spring; seed is tiny and not easy to deal with.
Height: Dwarf types 4in (10cm).

FORGET-ME-NOT (MYOSOTIS)   Clouds of blue flowers in spring. 'Blue Ball' is neat and bun-shaped, 'Blue Bouquet' is taller and airier.
Propagation: Seed, outside in late spring; easy.
Height: 'Blue Ball' 6in (15cm); 'Blue Bouquet' 12in (30cm).

POPPY (PAPAVER)   The bedding poppy 'Summer Breeze', in orange, yellow and white, is good in a sunny spot.
Propagation: Seed in spring; easy.
Height: 12in (30cm).

MARIGOLD (TAGETES)   Hundreds of varieties, many of ugly habit and with garish flowers. The single-flowered 'Mischief' series of varieties is more elegant than most, with some good dark colours.

The so called 'tagetes' have smaller flowers in larger quantities and aromatic leaves. 'Paprika', 'Lemon Gem' and 'Tangerine Gem' are self-explanatory. All best in sunshine and any reasonable soil.
Propagation: Seed, in spring; very easy.
Height: 10–12in (25–30cm).

VERBENA   Bushier version of those on page 235. Some are very blocky in shape. 'Romance' is the best all-rounder, with a good colour range.
Propagation: Seed in spring, can be tricky.
Height: 9in (23cm).

VIOLA   Pretty small-flowered plants with masses of flowers for many weeks in spring. 'Prince Henry' is purple, 'Prince John' is yellow. Best in a cooler spot.
Propagation: Seed, in late spring; easy.
Height: 6in (15cm).

Plants for Purposes

A guide to the best plants of different types, for solving particular problems and for different sites and situations. All the plants listed are described in the previous section.

Key to plant types

Trees for small gardens	T
Evergreen shrubs	ES
Deciduous shrubs	DS
Hedging shrubs	H
Border perennials	BP
Bulbs	B
Rock and small plants	RP
Hardy annuals	HA
Half-hardy annuals and bedding plants	HHA
Climbers and wall shrubs	CL WS
Hardy biennials	HB
Tender perennials	TP

1.   SOILS

Clay soil

Amaranthus caudatus   (HA)
Chaenomeles 'Rowallane'   (WS)
Choisya ternata   (ES)
Malus 'Golden Hornet'   (T)
Philadelphus 'Manteau d'Ermine'   (DS)
Rodgersia pinnata 'Superba'   (BP)
Rose varieties   (DS)
Tagetes varieties   (HHA)
Viburnum tinus   (H)
Vinca major 'Elegantissima'   (BP)

Sandy soil

Asphodeline lutea   (BP)
Berberis thunbergii 'Aurea'   (DS)
Betula pendula 'Youngii'   (T)
Borago officinalis   (HA)
Fagus sylvatica   (H)
Geranium sanguineum   (RP)
Juniperus sabina 'Tamariscifolia'   (ES)
Papaver 'Summer Breeze'   (HHA)
Pernettya mucronata   (ES)
Phlox, dwarf varieties   (RP)

Wet soil

Ajuga reptans   (RP)
Astilbe 'Sprite'   (BP)
Carpinus betulus   (H)
Mimulus 'Malibu'   (HHA)
Nemophila menziesii   (HA)
Physocarpus opulifolius 'Dart's Gold'   (DS)
Primula pulverulenta   (BP)
Salix caprea 'Pendula'   (T)
Salix hastata 'Wehrhanii'   (DS)
Sambucus nigra varieties   (DS)

Chalky soil

Antirrhinum varieties   (HHA)
Buxus sempervirens 'Suffruticosa'   (H)
Cheiranthus varieties   (HB)
Clematis 'Vyvyan Pennell'   (CL)
Daphne × *burkwoodii*   (ES)
Dianthus varieties   (RP)
Iris, bearded types   (BP)
Kolkwitzia amabilis   (DS)
Linaria 'Canon Went'   (BP)
Magnolia kobus   (T)

Acid soil

Begonia semperflorens varieties   (HHA)
Cornus kousa   (T)
Epimedium davidii   (BP)
Erica cinerea   (ES)
Erythronium revolutum   (RP)
Lupinus luteus   (HA)
Magnolia stellata   (DS)
Pieris japonica 'Debutante'   (ES)
Rhododendron yakushimanum hybrids   (ES)
Tropaeolum speciosum   (CL)

Exceptionally poor soil

Betula pendula   (T)
Cotoneaster 'Cornubia'   (ES)
Eucalyptus gunnii   (T)
Hesperis matronalis   (BP)
Hippophae rhamnoides   (DS)
Ligustrum ovalifolium   (H)
Phalaris arundinacea 'Picta'   (BP)
Ruscus aculeatus   (ES)
Sambucus nigra 'Albovariegata'   (DS)
Tagetes varieties   (HHA)

2. SPECIAL SITUATIONS

Dry shade

Alchemilla mollis   (BP)
Berberis wilsoniae   (DS)
Euonymus 'Silver Queen'   (ES)
Euphorbia robbiae   (BP)
Hedera helix 'Hibernica'   (CL)
Iris foetidissima   (BP)
Mahonia aquifolium   (ES)
Polystichum setiferum   (BP)
Symphoricarpus 'White Hedge'   (H)

Damp shade

Camellia varieties   (ES)
Fothergilla major   (DS)
Hosta varieties   (BP)
Impatiens varieties   (HHA)
Mimulus varieties   (HHA)
Ramonda myconi   (DP)
Rhododendron varieties   (ES)
Sarcococca confusa   (ES)
Taxus baccata   (H)
Uvularia grandiflora   (BP)

North walls

Azara microphylla   (WS)
Camellia varieties   (WS)
Chaenomeles 'Rowallane'   (WS)
Ercilla volubilis   (CL)
Hedera helix 'Glacier'   (CL)
Hydrangea petiolaris   (CL)
Itea ilicifolia   (WS)
Osmanthus delavayi   (WS)
Pyracantha 'Mojave'   (WS)
Rose 'Madame Alfred Carrière'   (CL)

East walls

Chaenomeles 'Rowallane'   (ws)
Cotoneaster horizontalis   (ws)
Forsythia 'Lynwood'   (DS)
Hedera helix 'Gold Heart'   (CL)
Jasminum nudiflorum   (ws)
Lathyrus latifolius 'White Pearl'   (CL)
Lathyrus – sweet pea   (CL)
Pyracantha 'Mojave'   (ws)
Tropaeolum peregrinum   (CL)

Cold gardens

Achillea millefolium varieties   (BP)
Bergenia 'Bressingham White'   (BP)
Calendula officinalis varieties   (HA)
Clematis viticella varieties   (CL)
Euonymus alatus   (DS)
Hesperis matrionalis   (BP)
Jasminum nudiflorum   (ws)
Rosa rugosa varieties   (DS)
Sorbus aria   (T)
Spiraea 'Pink Ice'   (DS)

Raised beds in shade

Astilbe 'Sprite'   (BP)
Epimedium davidii   (BP)
Galanthus varieties   (B)
Hosta 'Halcyon'   (BP)
Pieris 'Little Heath'   (ES)
Polygonatum × *hybridum* 'Variegatum'   (BP)
Primrose – doubles   (RP)
Ramonda myconi   (RP)
Rhododendron yakushimanum hybrids   (ES)
Trillium grandiflorum   (BP)

Raised beds in sun

Crocus chrysanthus varieties   (B)
Crocus speciosus   (B)

Cytisus × *kewensis*   (DS)
Dianthus 'Pike's Pink'   (RP)
Helianthemum varieties   (RP)
Lavandula 'Hidcote'   (ES)
Polygonum vaccinifolium   (RP)
Pulsatilla vulgaris   (RP)
Salvia officinalis varieties   (ES)
Thymus 'Silver Posie'   (RP)

3. HEDGING

Dense hedging plants

Buxus sempervirens 'Suffruticosa'
Cupressus lawsoniana 'Green Hedger'
Taxus baccata
Thuya occidentalis 'Smaragd'
Thuya plicata 'Atrovirens'

Spiny hedging plants

Berberis gagnepanii
Berberis × *stenophylla*
Ilex aquifolium
Pyracantha rogersiana
Rosa rugosa varieties

Flowering hedges

Berberis × *stenophylla*
Escallonia 'Donard Radiance'
Rose 'Iceberg'
Rosmarinus 'Miss Jessup's Upright'
Viburnum tinus

4. CONTAINERS

Spring tubs

Myosotis 'Blue Bouquet'   (HB)

Narcissus varieties (B)
Pansy 'Universal' (HB)
Polyanthus 'Crescendo' (HB)
Tulip varieties (B)
Wallflower varieties (HB)

Summer tubs

Begonia 'Non Stop' (HHA)
Geranium 'Gala' (HHA)
Helichrysum petiolare (TP)
Nicotiana 'Domino' (HHA)
Salvia farinacea 'Victoria' (HHA)

Permanent tub plants

Acer palmatum 'Dissectum Atropurpureum' (DS)
Fatsia japonica 'Variegata' (ES)
Laurus nobilis (ES)
Lavandula 'Hidcote' (ES)
Viola 'Maggie Mott' (RP)
Yucca filamentosa (ES)

Spring window-boxes

Bellis varieties (HB)
Muscari varieties (B)
Myosotis 'Blue Ball' (HB)
Narcissus 'Tête à Tête' (B)
Viola varieties (HB)

Summer window-boxes

Begonia 'Party Fun' (HHA)
Geranium 'Sensation' (HHA)
Helichrysum microphyllum (TP)
Lobelia 'Blue Cascade' (HHA)
Parsley 'Moss Curled' (HHA)
Petunia 'Carpet Series' (HHA)

Permanent window-box plants

Chives   (HP)
Crocus varieties   (B)
Hedera helix 'Glacier'   (CL)
Thyme   (ES)
Tiarella wherryi   (RP)

Spring baskets

Aubrieta varieties   (RP)
Cerastium tomentosum   (RP)
Hedera helix 'Glacier'   (CL)
Muscari 'Blue Spike'   (B)
Pansy 'Universal'   (HB)

Summer baskets

Begonia 'Illumination'   (HHA)
Calceolaria 'Midas'   (HHA)
Geranium 'Rouletta'   (TP)
Impatiens 'Super Elfin'   (HHA)
Lobelia 'Cascade'   (HHA)

Food plants for containers

Aubergine 'Little Fingers'
Chili pepper 'Apache'
Cucumber 'Bush Champion'
Sweet pepper 'Redskin'
Tomato 'Totem'

5.   SCENTED PLANTS

Fragrant shrubs

Buddleia varieties   (DS)
Daphne × *burkwoodii*   (ES)
Fothergilla major   (DS)
Hamamelis mollis   (DS)

Lonicera purpusii (DS)
Osmanthus delavayi (ES)
Philadelphus 'Manteau d'Hermine' (DS)
Sarcococca confusa (ES)
Syringa velutina (DS)
Viburnum carlesii 'Aurora' (DS)

Fragrant climbers

Clematis cirrhosa balearica
Jasminum officinale
Lathyrus – annual sweet pea
Lonicera periclymenum
Wisteria varieties

Fragrant roses

'Canary Bird'
'Fragrant Cloud'
'Margaret Merrill'
'Pretty Jessica'
'Royal William'
'Zéphirine Drouhin'

Fragrant perennials

Convallaria majalis
Dianthus 'Mrs Sinkins'
Hesperis matronalis
Iris unguicularis
Lilium regale
Phlox varieties

Fragrant annuals

Lobularia maritima
Matthiola bicornis
Nicotiana 'Sensation'
Reseda odorata
Sweet pea – selected varieties
Wallflower 'Bedder'

Plants with fragrant foliage

Foeniculum vulgare 'Smokey'   (BP)
Lavandula 'Hidcote'   (ES)
Melissa officinalis 'Aurea'   (BP)
Pelargonium 'Lady Plymouth'   (TP)
Rosmarinus 'Miss Jessup's Upright'   (ES)
Salvia officinalis 'Purpurascens'   (ES)

6.   FOLIAGE PLANTS

Grey foliage plants

Achillea 'Moonshine'   (BP)
Anaphalis yedoensis   (BP)
Artemisia 'Powis Castle'   (ES)
Caryopteris × *clandonensis*   (DS)
Convolvulus cneorum   (ES)
Hebe 'Pagei'   (RP)
Lamium 'White Nancy'   (BP)
Omphalodes linifolia   (HA)
Salix exigua   (T)
Senecio 'Silverdust'   (HHA)

Plants with gold and yellow leaves

Campanula 'Dickson's Gold'   (RP)
Choisya ternata 'Sundance'   (ES)
Hakenochloa macra 'Aureavariegata'   (BP)
Helichrysum petiolare 'Limelight'   (TP)
Ligustrum ovalifolium 'Aureum'   (ES)
Melissa officinalis 'Aurea'   (BP)
Philadelphus coronarius 'Aureus'   (DS)
Physocarpus opulifolius 'Dart's Gold'   (DS)
Robinia pseudacacia 'Frisia'   (T)
Thuya occidentalis 'Rheingold'   (ES)

Variegated foliage plants

Arabis ferdinandii-coburgii 'Variegata'   (RP)
Arum italicum 'Pictum'   (BP)

Cornus alba 'Elegantissima'   (DS)
Eleagnus pungens 'Maculata'   (ES)
Euonymus 'Emerald 'n' Gold'   (ES)
Fuchsia magellanica 'Variegata'   (DS)
Hedera helix 'Goldheart'   (CL)
Hosta 'Thomas Hogg'   (BP)
Pulmonaria saccharata 'Argentea'   (BP)
Tropaeolum 'Alaska'   (HA)

Dark and purple-leaved plants

Acer palmatum 'Dissectum Atropurpureum'   (DS)
Astilbe 'Sprite'   (BP)
Berberis 'Helmund Pillar'   (DS)
Heuchera 'Palace Purple'   (BP)
Malus 'Royalty'   (T)
Ophiopogon planiscapus 'Nigrescens'   (RP)
Rheum 'Ace of Hearts'   (BP)
Rosa glauca   (DS)
Salvia officinalis 'Purpurascens'   (ES)
Vitis vinifera 'Purpurea'   (CL)

Trees and shrubs for autumn colour

Acer griseum   (T)
Amelanchier lamarckii   (DS)
Berberis wilsonae   (DS)
Betula pendula 'Youngii'   (T)
Cercidiphyllum japonicum   (DS)
Cornus kousa chinensis   (T)
Euonymus alata   (DS)
Fothergilla major   (DS)
Sorbus vilmorinii   (T)
Vitis vinifera 'Purpurea'   (CL)

7. SEASONAL PLANTS

Winter-flowering plants

Eranthis hyemalis   (B)
Erica carnea 'Springwood White'   (RP)

Galanthus varieties   (B)
Hamamelis mollis   (DS)
Helleborus orientalis   (BP)
Iris unguicularis   (BP)
Lonicera fragrantissima   (ES)
Mahonia 'Charity'   (ES)
Sarcococca confusa   (ES)
Saxifraga × *apiculata*   (RP)

Spring bulbs

Anemone blanda 'White Splendour'
Chionodoxa luciliae
Crocus chrysanthus varieties
Crocus tomasinianus
Fritillaria imperialis
Leucojum aestivum
Muscari 'Blue Spike'
Narcissus 'February Gold'
Narcissus 'Geranium'
Tulip 'Little Red Riding Hood'

Summer bulbs

Acidanthera mureliae
Agapanthus 'Headbourne Hybrids'
Allium christophii
Camassia esculenta
Crocosmia 'Lucifer'
Dahlia varieties
Galtonia candicans
Gladiolus papilio
Lilium candidum
Lilium regale

Autumn bulbs

Amaryllis belladonna
Colchicum speciosum
Colchicum 'Water Lily'
Crocus ochroleucus
Crocus speciosus

Cyclamen hederifolium
Galanthus reginae-olgae
Nerine bowdenii
Tropaeolum tuberosum 'Ken Aslet'

Late autumn-flowering plants

Anemone 'Honorine Jobert'   (BP)
Aster 'Climax'   (BP)
Ceratostigma plumbaginoides   (DS)
Chrysanthemum 'Emperor of China'   (BP)
Clematis 'Bill McKenzie'   (CL)
Cosmos 'Yellow Garden'   (HHA)
Fuchsia magellanica 'Variegata'   (DS)
Liriope spicata   (BP)
Physostegia 'Vivid'   (BP)
Schizostylis 'Jennifer'   (BP)

Long-flowering plants

Argyranthemum 'Jamaica Primrose'   (TP)
Aster × frikartii 'Monch'   (BP)
Ceanothus 'Autumnal Blue'   (ES)
Cheiranthus 'Bowles Mauve'   (ES)
Choisya ternata   (ES)
Fuchsia magellanica 'Variegata'   (DS)
Geranium 'Wargrave'   (BP)
Rose 'Old Blush China'   (DS)
Rudbeckia 'Goldsturm'   (BP)
Solanum jasminoides 'Album'   (CL)

8.   FLOWER-ARRANGING

Flowers for arranging

Achillea varieties   (BP)
Alchemilla mollis   (BP)
Antirrhinum 'Spring Giant'   (HHA)
Argyranthemum 'Vancouver'   (TP)
Aster 'Compliment'   (HHA)
Crocosmia 'Lucifer'   (B)

Forsythia 'Lynwood'   (DS)
Rose varieties   (DS)
Schizostylis 'Jennifer'   (BP)

Foliage plants for arranging

Artemisia 'Powis Castle'   (ES)
Carex comans 'Bronze Form'   (BP)
Heuchera 'Palace Purple'   (BP)
Hosta 'Halcyon'   (BP)
Hosta 'Thomas Hogg'   (BP)
Ligustrum ovalifolium 'Aureum'   (ES)
Lonicera nitida 'Baggesons Gold'   (ES)
Ruta graveolens 'Jackmans Blue'   (ES)
Vinca major 'Elegantissima'   (BP)
Weigela florida 'Foliis Purpureis'   (DS)

Plants for drying

Achillea millifolium varieties   (BP)
Athyrium felix-femina   (BP)
Briza maxima   (HA)
Eryngium tripartitum   (BP)
Helichrysum monstrosum varieties   (HHA)
Helipterum roseum varieties   (HHA)
Limonium 'Fortress Strain'   (HHA)
Nigella 'Persian Jewels'   (HA)
Papaver somniferum   (HA)
Rose varieties   (DS)

9.   WATER GARDENS

Deep water plants

Nymphaea – dwarf varieties

Shallow water plants

Acorus calamus 'Variegatus'
Iris laevigata
Juncus effusus 'Spiralis'

Nymphoides pelata
Zantedeschia aethiopica

Marginal plants

Caltha palustris 'Plena'
Iris sibirica
Lobelia 'Bee's Flame'
Mimulus 'Hose in Hose'
Primula pulverulenta

10. WILDLIFE GARDENING

Wild flowers

Agrostemma githago (HA)
Anemone nemorosa (B)
Chrysanthemum segetum (HA)
Hyacinthoides non-scriptus (B)
Fritillaria meleagris (B)
Papaver rhoeas (HA)
Primula veris (RP)
Primula vulgaris (RP)
Silene dioica (BP)
Viburnum opulus 'Compactum' (DS)

Berrying shrubs

Cotoneaster microphyllus (ES)
Cotoneaster 'Cornubia' (ES)
Ilex aquifolium 'Pyramidalis' (ES)
Pyracantha 'Mojave' (ES)
Rosa moyesii (DS)
Sambucus nigra varieties (DS)
Skimmia japonica 'Foremanii' (ES)
Sorbus 'Sheerwater Seedling' (T)
Viburnum opulus 'Compactum' (DS)

Dense shrubs for cover

Berberis × *stenophylla* (ES)

Choisya ternata   (ES)
Ligustrum ovalifolium   (H)
Pyracantha 'Mojave'   (ES)
Taxus baccata   (H)
Thuya plicata 'Atrovirens'   (H)

Bee plants

Berberis × *stenophylla*   (ES)
Betula pendula 'Youngii'   (T)
Chaenomeles 'Nivalis'   (WS)
Dahlia, single-flowered varieties   (TP)
Daphne mezereum   (DS)
Malus 'John Downie'   (T)
Monarda didyma 'Cambridge Scarlet'   (BP)
Origanum vulgare 'Aureum'   (BP)
Salix alba   (DS)
Senecio 'Sunshine'   (ES)

Butterfly plants

Aubrieta, single-flowered varieties   (RP)
Buddleia varieties   (DS)
Caryopteris × *clandonensis*   (DS)
Centranthus ruber   (BP)
Echinacea 'White Swan'   (BP)
Helenium 'Moerheim Beauty'   (BP)
Lavandula 'Hidcote'   (ES)
Scabiosa 'Butterfly Blue'   (BP)
Sedum 'Autumn Joy'   (BP)
Solidago 'Golden Thumb'   (RP)

11.   SPECIAL SITUATIONS

Weed-suppressing plants

Bergenia 'Bressingham White'   (BP)
Cotoneaster horizontalis   (DS)
Geranium 'Russell Prichard'   (BP)
Helianthemum 'Wisley Pink'   (RP)
Hosta 'Thomas Hogg'   (BP)

Lamium 'White Nancy'   (RP)
Phlox, creeping types   (RP)
Polygonum vaccinifolium   (RP)
Pulmonaria saccharata 'Argentea'   (RP)
Rose, 'County' series   (DS)

Quick fillers for new gardens

Achillea millefolium varieties   (BP)
Achillea ptarmica 'The Pearl'   (BP)
Argyranthemum 'Vancouver'   (TP)
Buddleia varieties   (DS)
Chrysanthemum 'Court Jesters'   (HA)
Lavatera olbia 'Barnsley'   (DS)
Lupinus arboreus   (ES)
Lupinus 'Band of Nobles'   (BP)
Phalaris arundinacea 'Picta'   (BP)
Polygonum bistorta   (BP)
Sambucus nigra varieties   (DS)

Easy plants to raise from seed

Centranthus ruber   (BP)
Cheiranthus varieties   (HB)
Digitalis 'Foxy'   (HB)
Iberis 'Flash'   (HA)
Lilium regale   (B)
Lupinus arboreus   (ES)
Lupinus 'Band of Nobles'   (BP)
Lychnis coronaria 'Alba'   (BP)
Pansy 'Joker'   (HHA)
Tagetes varieties   (HHA)

Plants to avoid

Acer pseudoplatanus   (T)
Heracleum mantegazzianum   (BP)
Polygonum baldschuanicum   (CL)
Reynoutria japonica   (BP)
Salix chrysocoma   (T)
× *Cupressocyparis leylandii*   (T & H)

Plant Associations

There are plenty of people who know how to put in plants and care for them so that they grow well; they know how to prune them and how to deal with pests and diseases. But not all these people have attractive gardens. The secret is knowing how to put plants alongside and among each other so that they look good together, so that the whole display looks better than simply a collection of plants. In a small garden this is especially important, for every inch has to be encouraged to give its best and provide continuing interest and appeal.

There are two different aspects to plant associations, therefore. First, fitting in as many plants as possible next to each other so that there is always foliage, at least, and if possible flowers, to be seen. This is the practical element, if you like. And second, giving consideration to how all the shapes, colours and textures will look together.

1.   MAKING THE MOST OF THE SPACE

There are many ways in which more plants than you think can be grown effectively in a bed or border.

- Grow climbers and wall shrubs on fences and walls at the back.
- Sow annual climbers like sweet peas and canary creeper to grow up wall shrubs.
- Train clematis and other climbers to grow through mature shrubs, as they do naturally.
- Plant climbing roses to grow through trees.
- Plant bulbs among border perennials and ground cover plants.
- Plant dwarf bulbs and dwarf annuals in the edges of gravel paths and drives.
- Plant bulbs flowering at different seasons amongst each other.
- Plant tall, late-flowering plants behind earlier-flowering plants; they will tend to fall forward and fill the space.
- Allow selected annuals and biennials to self-sow into and among perennial plants.

2. CHOOSING PLANTS THAT LOOK GOOD TOGETHER

This is the real art. But it's not an art that you have to be born with – it can be learned, and it's not difficult. Some people equate it with planning the wallpaper and furnishings in the house; they think of it as decorating the room outside. But of course there is one unique factor you have to deal with in the garden, and that's time. Not only is every season different, with plants coming to their peak and then fading, but sometimes the flowers differ from one day to the next. And then there's the weather – which is not usually a problem in the house.

Flower colour and form

Flower colour is the feature that comes to mind first, and bringing colours together so that they look good is the main aspect, sometimes the only one, of plant association that many gardeners keep in mind. Of course, the added element of time means that you do have to make sure that plants whose flower colours you feel will go well together do actually flower at the same time. This can be a little more difficult than you'd expect, as plants vary in their response to changes in weather conditions. Your own experience will guide you, and you should never be afraid to move plants if schemes don't quite come off.

Bringing pastel colours together is one theme to follow. Soft rose-pinks and pale sky-blues look well together, perhaps with white or silver foliage. Lilac and pink is often good, pale blue and primrose too. Often success can depend on exactly what shade of a colour a particular variety is; shades of pink, for example, can vary so much and a salmony shade may work a great deal less well with sky-blue than a rose-pink one.

Another approach is to contrast colours. We all know the red, white and blue of old-fashioned parks bedding schemes, but these often fail because the plants used are so hackneyed. These same colours can seem unexpectedly stylish if presented by unfamiliar plants – white argyranthemums, red verbena and blue *Salvia patens*, perhaps. Other good contrasts include sparkling white looking wonderful against bronze, or pale primrose against rich purple and bright blue with butter yellow.

There's another alternative – using the same colour in different strengths. So white flowers and silver foliage go well, as do a combination of fiery red, orange and yellow, or Oxford blue with Cambridge blue.

Next, there's the question of the form of the flowers. Sometimes it's the individual flowers that make the impact, sometimes it's the heads, made up of small flowers. But they come in a great variety of shapes: large solitary daisy forms or masses of tiny daisies; large trumpets or spikes of small trumpets; rose-like flowers on their own, in loose clusters or lining a spike. Flowers may come in flat heads, foamy clouds, arching wands, stiff spikes, flat carpets – you name it. You can have fun with the shapes of the flowers or the heads of flowers. Putting daisy flowers of different varieties in different colours together is a bit subtle, but setting stiff spikes with flat heads or emerging from a foam of flower is much more striking.

Foliage colour and form

As well as the flowers, there is the foliage to consider. And you'll be looking at foliage for a long time before and after the flowers have come and gone. But that doesn't mean that you should pack your borders with variegated and yellow-leaved plants. Such a planting would not be a relaxing sight; it would be all highlights – you'd never want to step outside the back door. But there's so much variety in green foliage alone to make a border interesting that you need to use only a few variegated or silver-leaved plants as highlights.

It pays to select a variety of different variegations, and there's quite a range, in white, cream, yellow and gold. The colour may edge the leaves, or appear as a central splash or as mottling; there may be stripes in all these shades, spotting and speckling. The whole leaf may be yellow or gold. Silver and grey, when it appears, usually covers the whole leaf, though there are some plants where mottling or spotting occurs. All these colours, in whatever version they appear, can be matched with flower colours in the same way that flower colours can be matched with each other.

Fruits

Fruits and berries are a valuable and colourful feature of the autumn scene, and you can sometimes create a happy association within a single plant. Many mountain ashes, for example, have fiery autumn leaf colour at the same time that their berries are at their most colourful. Fruits on shrubs like pyracanthas and cotoneasters can be fronted by hardy chrysanthemums in appropriate shades, and many autumn fruits associate especially well with foliage that takes on autumn tints.

Stems

There are a few groups of plants which give an altogether unexpected bonus in terms of their colourful stems in the winter. To create the best stem colour – red, orange, yellow, green or purple – the plants are cut down hard in the spring to encourage plenty of new growth, which provides the best colour. This also has the effect of keeping the plant small, if it's cut back hard every spring it never gets out of hand.

The red stems of *Cornus alba* 'Elegantissima' associate well with white-variegated euonymus, and the leaves of the cornus are variegated in summer and turn red before falling in autumn. The greenish-yellow stems of *Cornus stolonifera* 'Flaviramea' are lovely with red-leaved bergenias.

Associating flowers and foliage

Coloured foliage planted with flowers can look stunning. Simple things, like planting white peas to climb up through a purple-leaved smoke bush, can be very effective. The peachy day lily 'Stella d'Oro' overtopping the reddish bronze leaves of *Heuchera* 'Palace Purple' also looks good.

Other tricks include allowing flowering plants with poor foliage to grow through foliage plants with poor flowers. Using silver and grey foliage to soften bright reds and purples and to blend in with pastel colours is a simple idea which is almost infallible – as long as you remember that most grey-leaved plants like a sunny spot that is not too wet. Foliage plants can also be used to follow on from bulbs, so that, for example, the tatty foliage of daffodils can be covered by new hosta foliage after the flowers are over.

Mini-themes

Themes for corners, beds or borders help concentrate the mind wonderfully if you're having difficulty planning your planting.

Seasonal themes are the easiest to plan and the most likely to be colourful; you can fine-tune the colour combinations later. Colour themes are very popular but it's difficult to make them successful. White, blue, yellow and gold, fiery shades, red flowers and foliage – all these work but it's perhaps easier for the newcomer to this sophisticated border planning to broaden it out a little. Yellow and blue, purple and white, grey and pink, grey and blue – any mistakes will be less destructive with a little more breadth to your theme.

3. SHORT CUTS TO GOOD PLANTING SCHEMES

- Pure white flowers will go with almost anything, although the effects they create will vary greatly according to their partners. But be careful – some 'white' flowers are actually cream, while pure white flowers may be pink in bud or develop pinkish shades as they fade.
- Grey and silver foliage is as versatile as white flowers and of course lasts longer. It also helps knit unlikely shades together happily.
- Creating a good background of foliage is always helpful to flowers. So a rich green hedge, a purple-leaved shrub or even a haze of tiny flowers can set off well those plants set in front.
- Picking up similar colours in flowers and foliage usually works well – bright red flowers with red-tinted foliage, for example.
- Put broad leaves with narrow or lacy leaves.
- Make sure that borders with coloured foliage themes also have some green leaves.

Buying, Making More and Raising Your Own

Plants have got to come from somewhere – they must be bought, received as gifts, swopped or you must raise your own.

1. BUYING SEED

Shops

A limited range of seed is available in garden centres, chain stores and DIY stores, and a much wider range can be had by mail order. Until recently only Mr Fothergill Seeds stated the number of seeds contained in their packets, but now other companies are doing the same and this makes it easier to ensure that you get good value.

The time to buy seeds in garden centres is in late winter and spring, when the racks have been newly stocked. I would not suggest buying in the autumn, not even varieties for autumn sowing, as they will have been exposed to the heat and possibly damp of the garden centre for many months by this time and the racks may not be well stocked. If the seeds are not sown within a few weeks of buying them, wrap them in a polythene bag and leave them in the bottom of the fridge until sowing time.

Mail order

Buying seeds by mail order gives you a much wider selection of varieties to choose from. The seed catalogues are all free and appear in the autumn. As well as listing and illustrating the varieties available, they also provide much useful information on the plants and how to grow them. Some of the mail order companies also produce leaflets or booklets giving guidance on how to grow their seeds successfully.

As well as seeds, catalogues (see page 419) usually list seedlings and young plants of some varieties, especially those which are difficult to germinate. These can be especially useful if you wish to grow seeds like begonias or geraniums that need starting off in warm conditions but you are without the appropriate facilities. If you order seedlings or young plants, you will receive them after the most difficult stage is over.

2. SOWING SEED OUTSIDE

Sowing seeds outside is the simplest method of raising them and is used for hardy annuals and biennials, some hardy perennials and most vegetables. Not all seeds are tough enough to withstand the rigours of the open garden, though.

Sowing technique

In a small garden there won't be much choice over where you sow your seeds. Most, except biennials and some vegetables, are sown where they are to grow, while the rest are raised in a seed-bed and then transplanted to their final sites.

Let's take as an example a group of hardy annuals for the border. You'll need scissors, a border fork, a rake, your measuring rod, some fertiliser and maybe some garden compost. Remove any weeds and then fork over the site to the depth of the fork; if the soil is poor add a bucketful, or perhaps a little more, of well-rotted compost per square yard and fork it in. Tread it, rake it level, and rake in a handful of Growmore to each square yard as well.

Check the instructions on the packet to see how far apart to sow the seed – they often suggest rows 9in (23cm) apart. Using your measuring rod as a straight edge, use a piece of stick to make a groove in the soil (a drill) about ½in (12mm) deep, or as directed on the packet. Then measure 9in (23cm) to the next drill and so on. You will end up with a series of parallel drills.

Cut the top off the packet with a pair of scissors and then, if there is a smaller pack inside, cut the top off that too. Make a crease half-way along one edge of the cut top and then hold the sides of the packet between thumb and middle finger. Holding the crease low over the end of the first drill, tilt the packet slightly and tap it with the index finger; this will encourage seeds to roll down the crease and drop off into the soil. You will be able to watch them as they fall and make sure that they are sown evenly as you move the packet along the length of the drill. Seeds which will germinate well and make large plants can usefully go in 1–2in (2.5–5cm) apart. Seeds of smaller plants should be sown more closely.

When the seeds have been sown, mark the ends of the rows with small pieces of twig or canes, then cover the seeds. This is done by standing upright and using the back of the rake to draw a little soil from alongside the drill over the seeds. Then use the flat of the rake to gently tamp them into place. Finally, put in a label naming the variety you have sown and the date.

Biennials and perennials are sown in just the same way, and vegetables too, although it's more common to sow vegetables in one long row rather than a number of short ones (but see page 285).

Timing

Hardy annuals are usually sown in March, April or May, and some of the tougher half-hardy annuals like marigolds and zinnias can also be sown outside, but not till May. Biennials and perennials are usually sown in May or June and transplanted later.

Thinning out

When the seeds come up, check the instructions on the packet to find the final spacing, as the seedlings will need thinning out (removing surplus seedlings). Thin them out in two stages: in the first you leave about three times as many as you will eventually need, and in the second you thin them to their final spacing. (Seedlings from this second stage of thinning can be transplanted elsewhere.)

The simplest way to thin seedlings is to place the first and second fingers of one hand closely on either side of the seedling you wish to retain, to prevent its disturbance; then pull out those seedlings that are surplus.

Transplanting

Biennials and perennials must be transplanted to a wider spacing to give them room to grow. Again, check the packet for precise instructions, as the spacing depends on the variety concerned. Transplanting is usually done after the seedlings have been thinned out once.

First water the row well and then, using a trowel, carefully lift the seedlings, keeping as much soil as you can on the roots of each one. Place them in a box and cover the roots with soil to prevent them drying out. Set out the garden line on the new site, and plant them at the required spacing, using the measuring rod as a guide. Water them in thoroughly.

Plants suited to this method

This method suits all hardy annuals, the tougher half-hardy annuals, biennials and perennials easily raised from seed. Most vegetables are also raised in this way.

Seed of some modern, highly-bred varieties is very expensive, so you may find only a few seeds in the packet. In such cases trusting them to the open ground is perhaps risky, and they may be better sown in trays which are protected from cats, big feet, slugs and so on, even if these trays are simply left in a sheltered place outside for the seeds to grow.

3. SOWING SEED INDOORS

Many of the more spectacular summer plants need warmth to get them going well.

House, greenhouse and conservatory

You can start seeds off in the house if you have nowhere else, but the truth is that it's not very satisfactory. On a window-sill the light comes from just one direction, and this encourages seedlings to lean that way and to produce rather lank growth. You can keep turning them but they always end up very spindly. If you want to use your window-sills, my advice is to buy a long narrow propagator specially designed to fit window-sills and to choose very dwarf and tough-stemmed varieties like French marigolds. But better still, start by buying seedlings or young plants. These are available from seed companies and may consist of anything from seedlings with just two or three leaves to young plants three months old. But at least they've had a good start in ideal conditions.

Of course, you may not fancy the idea of rows of pots lining your window-sills, and the same applies to a conservatory, which is often used more as a room than a greenhouse. But a shelf fitted along one side with a window-sill propagator need not look too out of place in an elegant setting, as long as all the paraphernalia – the bags of compost, stacks of pots and so on – are kept elsewhere.

A greenhouse will provide the best facilities – not only do seeds need warmth, they need light too, and a greenhouse, even one sited alongside a fence, will probably give them more light than a conservatory and far more than a window-sill. The problem with a greenhouse is that providing heat for a propagator can be difficult unless the greenhouse is sited near the house and electricity can be laid on simply. A practical compromise is to sow the seed indoors and move the pots out to the greenhouse as soon as they germinate. The only difficulty with that system is that the greenhouse may still be too cold.

Facilities and equipment

The warmth that many seeds need to germinate is best provided by a thermostatically controlled, heated propagator. These come in a wide range of sizes, from the narrow window-sill models already mentioned to much larger greenhouse models taking more than fifty pots. Choose the size that best suits your requirements, erring as usual on the large side, but make sure you get one that is thermostatically controlled – not to save on the modest electricity bills, but to ensure that the seeds don't get too hot in sunny weather.

When you consider that a standard seed tray can take 1,000 seedlings, you will realise the wisdom of sowing in 3in (7.5cm) pots. Using square plastic pots will enable you to get as many in the propagator as possible. When the seedlings get larger you can put them individually either into pots of the same size or into half-size or full-size seed-trays, depending how many plants you want. Seed-trays can be either stout, rigid and re-usable or flimsy and once-only. The former are easier to handle and less liable to accidental breakage, but cost a great deal more.

Never use garden soil for sowing seeds – choose one of the branded composts available in the garden centre. If you rely on a multipurpose, sowing-and-potting type, you can use the same compost for all stages of the plants' growth.

Sowing timing and technique

The seed packet is the best source of advice on when to sow, as varieties differ in their requirements. March and April, however, are the main months for sowing.

Fill the pots loosely with moist compost, push off any that is proud of the rim, then firm gently, using the base of another pot or a purpose-made plywood firmer cut to size. Now cut off the top of the seed packet with scissors, and do the same with the inner sachet if there is one, leaving a smooth edge. Make a crease half-way along one of the straight edges of the mouth of the packet. Holding the two edges of the packet between your thumb and middle finger, tap the packet gently with your first finger to encourage the seeds to roll down the new crease and off the edge on to the compost in the pot. As you can watch the seed falling, it is not difficult to ensure that even small, dark seed is distributed reasonably evenly.

Very fine seed will not need covering. Many seeds can be covered by gently stirring the top ⅛th of an inch (3mm) of compost with the point of a pencil. Larger seeds like lupins can be covered with a layer of compost straight from the bag and equal to the diameter of the seeds – but take out the lumps and twigs which often seem to turn up. It's often suggested that you sieve a little compost over the seeds, but finding the right sort of sieve can be a problem. I've come to the conclusion that an old kitchen sieve has too fine a mesh; a sieve made out of greenhouse shading tacked to a wooden framework is good, but buying a square foot of such netting is usually impractical.

After the seed is covered it must be watered. I favour watering from the top, using a very fine rose on the watering can, and I suggest adding some Murphy Traditional Copper Fungicide to the water to prevent damping-off disease. Alternatively, the pots can be stood in a tray of water until the water seeps up into the compost, but this sometimes causes the compost to pull away from the sides of the pot when the water drains off.

After watering, the pots need to go in the propagator; they will not need covering individually as long as the propagator itself is covered with newspaper or brown paper to prevent sun scorch. It's vital that the seeds be kept moist, and this is especially difficult with fine seed which is not covered. Soon the seedlings will come through and the paper can be removed.

It's important to label all pots with the name and date at the time of sowing. This not only prevents confusion but you can record on the back of the label when you prick out the seedlings and how many came up. Adding the name of the seed company may be useful when you come to do the following year's order. Using a garden marker pen on white plastic labels usually gives good results, at least for a couple of seasons, and they will remain clearly visible for longer if sprayed with aerosol varnish immediately after writing them.

Pricking out

The seeds must not stay in their seed pots for long, as they will become too crowded. When they are large enough to handle, the whole root ball should be removed from the pot into a spare seed tray and the seedlings pulled apart. Large seedlings which rapidly grow into good-sized plants, such as geraniums and dahlias, are best pricked out (transferred) into individual pots. Smaller plants like alyssum can go into seed trays.

Fill the pots in the same way as for seed sowing, and after firming make a hole in the middle of each one with a pencil or dibber. The roots of the seedling go into the hole, and the pencil or dibber is used to firm the seedling gently into place. The first pair of leaves, the seed leaves, should rest on the surface of the compost.

Seed trays should be filled in the same way, but the corners should be firmed with the fingers before the tray is filled to the top and the surplus struck off. The base of another seed tray or, better still, a purpose-made firmer can be used to firm the compost. A half-sized seed tray will usually take twenty seedlings – five rows across and four the other way. Put a row of seedlings along one long side and then down one short side, and this will give you a guide for the positioning of the others. Water them in using a fine rose on the can and some Murphy Traditional Copper Fungicide in the water.

Very small seedlings such as lobelia can more easily be pricked out in little patches of three or four. Alyssum and any mixtures can be pricked out in the same way to give a genuine mixture of colours.

Growing on seedlings

Ideally the seedlings should spend a week or so at the same temperature as that in which they were growing before pricking out, but this is rarely possible. So they will have to take their chance in a cooler regime, preferably a frost-free greenhouse at least. Water them regularly, using a fungicide in the water, and give them a liquid feed every week, starting about six weeks after pricking out. Watch out for aphids.

Hardening off

It's important to use the final two or three weeks before planting to acclimatise the seedlings to the open garden. This can be done by moving them to a cold frame, with the glass in place over the top for the first week and then left off a bit more each day. If you don't have a frame, the heat in the greenhouse can be turned off and more and more ventilation given until the young plants are moved to a warm, sheltered spot outside before planting.

In practice, many plants are remarkably tolerant as long as they are not actually frosted. Morning glory is probably the most fussy.

Planting out

When you are ready to plant them out, move all the plants to the site and water them well with a liquid feed such as Maxicrop. Stand the pots where you would like the plants to go, and place the trays in the middle of the area the plants will occupy. Move them around until you are satisfied with the arrangement.

Remove the young plants from their trays in one block and then pull them apart and stand them in their final positions. Plant these straight away and then plant those from pots. After planting, water them all in, adding some liquid feed to the water to give them a flying start, then use the border fork like a rake to remove footprints and leave the bed looking neat.

Plants suited to this method

The easiest plants to raise are marigolds, French and African (large seeds, strong germination), asters (large seeds), alyssum and anti-rrhinum (quick to germinate), lavatera (large seeds, vigorous seed-lings), and tomatoes (quick to germinate, large seedlings).

The most difficult plants to raise are geraniums (constant high temperatures needed), lobelia, begonia and petunia (very fine seed, tendency to damp off), verbena (reluctant to germinate even in good conditions), and impatiens (must not dry out at all).

4. COLLECTING AND STORING YOUR OWN SEED

Many plants in the garden produce their own seed. Some, like poppies and love-lies-bleeding, scatter prodigious quantities, so it seems obvious that this seed could be collected and sown. But it's not that simple. Many of the plants we grow, especially bedding plants, are complicated hybrids and when the seed they produce is sown, the resulting plants may be nothing like their parents.

Try it by all means. Plants grown from seed of some plants which are actually wild species, like poached egg plants and baby blue eyes, should be exactly the same as their parents, but be prepared for a few surprises among roses, chrysanthemums, dahlias and anything listed in a seed catalogue as an F1 hybrid.

5. CUTTINGS OUTDOORS

There are many ways of taking cuttings, but the method which requires the least equipment is the taking of hardwood cuttings of deciduous shrubs.

Hardwood cuttings

Hardwood cuttings are long cuttings, taken in the autumn, of shoots which have ripened during the summer and autumn to become hard and woody. After leaf fall in the autumn, shoots about 9in (23cm) long and the thickness of a pencil are cut from the shoots that have grown during the earlier part of the year. These are trimmed just below a bud at the base and just above a bud at the tip.

Choose a sheltered but not dark or shady spot outside, and improve the soil by forking in organic matter if necessary. Then make a slit about 6in (15cm) deep with your spade and put a layer of about 1in (2.5cm) of grit or sharp sand in the bottom. Dip the cuttings in hormone rooting powder, then stand them about 3in (7.5cm) apart in the slit with the base of each resting on the sand. Finally, close the slit by firming with your boot. Label the row and then simply leave them.

Most, if not all, should start to grow in the spring, and they are best left to grow on until the autumn, when they can be either planted in their permanent sites or replanted about 12–15in (30–38cm) apart in rows to grow on for another year.

If little material is available, shorter cuttings are quite satisfactory as long as there are about four buds. These shorter cuttings are best placed in pots of cuttings compost in a cold frame rather than in the open ground.

Plants suited to this method

Plants that root well using this method include roses (especially climbers and ramblers), willows and poplars, buddleias, blackcurrants, elder, cotoneaster, jasmine and philadelphus, plus a wide range of other deciduous shrubs and also some trees like laburnum.

Cuttings of many evergreen shrubs can be taken at the same time of year, but these should be of the shorter type and demand the protection of a cold frame or cold greenhouse.

6. CUTTINGS INDOORS

Cuttings of many plants can also be taken indoors. These are usually taken in spring and summer from soft, leafy shoot tips, and may be quite soft and new if taken in the early part of the season or from indoor plants. Alternatively they may be 'semi-ripe', that is, the tips may still be soft but an inch or two further down the shoot will have started to harden.

Soft and semi-ripe cuttings

Soft cuttings are taken from new spring shoots of shrubs and some herbaceous plants, and are more delicate and less easy to look after; semi-ripe cuttings of shrubs are taken in the second half of the summer and are slightly tougher but still need appropriate care.

A heated propagator is a very useful piece of equipment for rooting cuttings indoors, though an unheated propagator in a warm environment is also very useful. But most cuttings benefit from the heat at the bottom of the cuttings that a thermostatically controlled heated propagator provides. Ideally a temperature at the root of 70°F (21°C) should be provided. If the air temperature is cooler, which it usually is, this is an advantage.

You can buy a small unheated propagator at the garden centre fairly reasonably. A heated one will cost more. It can be stood on a window-sill (though not a hot south-facing one), but the same problem of low light levels applies as it does with seedlings. A greenhouse or conservatory is a better bet. In a greenhouse or conservatory which gets a lot of sun, shading may be needed to avoid the leaves being scorched and keep the temperatures in the propagator from rocketing.

One of the problems with these early season cuttings is that as they still have their leaves they need to be kept in a humid atmosphere. In a dry atmosphere they quickly wilt and die. For this reason a clear plastic top on the propagator is essential.

Cuttings about 4–5in (10–12.5cm) long are cut from the tips of healthy shoots on shrubs, using secateurs, and put straight into a polythene bag to prevent them drying out. A label should be written at once and put in the bag with the cuttings. Cuttings from perennials can be a little shorter, and the total length of the shoot on the plant should not be much longer. Pots are prepared using a branded cuttings compost or a 50:50 mixture of peat and grit. This should be moist and the pots should be prepared as for seed-sowing.

The cuttings are then trimmed to below a leaf joint, reducing the length to about 3in (7.5cm). This can be done using a new or very sharp and well-maintained pair of secateurs, a single-sided razor blade or an artist's scalpel. A clean cut with no ragged edges or torn tissue is essential to prevent disease.

The leaves on the lower half of the cuttings are removed carefully, and the bottom ¼in (6mm) of each cutting is dipped in a hormone rooting powder. Now use a pencil or dibber to make a hole in the compost that will allow the base of the cutting to sit on the bottom of the hole while the lowest leaves lie on the compost surface. A 3in (7.5cm) pot will take from three to eight cuttings, depending on the spread of their leaves. Each cutting is firmed in gently with the pencil or dibber, the pot watered and the label put in. As soon as possible the pots of cuttings are transferred to a propagator so that they have little chance to dry out.

Rooting of some plants can take as little as a few days, while others may take a few weeks. It's important that the cuttings never dry out in this time. You'll be able to tell when they have rooted, as they will start to grow; if a gentle pull on the cutting reveals resistance, you can be sure that rooting has begun. Roots will eventually appear at the drainage holes in the bottom of the pots.

Aftercare

When rooted, the cuttings can be potted up individually. Knock the cuttings out of their pot by upturning the pot and tapping the rim on the edge of a bench or worktop. Gently pull the rooted cuttings apart and pot them up carefully. They will need to be cosseted a little, perhaps kept in an unheated propagator, for a few days, until they start to grow again, when they can stand on the open greenhouse or conservatory bench.

Plants suited to this method

Plants suitable for this treatment include many shrubs (these are best rooted from semi-ripe cuttings), house plants (soft cuttings of tradescantia, for example, are produced all the year round), border perennials (choose new spring shoots from the base).

Window-sills

Some plants can also be rooted in water on a window-sill. Soft cuttings are prepared in the same way. Use a jam-jar, covered with a piece of kitchen foil which has had a series of small nicks made in it with the point of a kitchen knife. Remove the foil, fill the jar with water, then replace the foil and push the base of the cuttings through the holes into the water so that the foil holds them in place. Stand the jar on a warm window-sill and roots will soon form. The roots formed in this way are often rather brittle, so it pays to pot the rooted cuttings up while the roots are still short.

Plants to grow by this method include begonias, impatiens, ivies and African violets.

7. DIVISION

Division is one of the simpler and more basic methods of increasing your plant stock, and applies especially to a wide range of border perennial plants, along with some rock plants. Spring and autumn are the best times – choose spring if your soil is especially heavy and damp. You will need your digging fork and your border fork or, better still, borrow another fork the same size as one of yours from a neighbour.

Many border perennials grow sufficiently quickly to be divided every three years, indeed many suffer if not given this treatment. The technique is simple. First cut off any old stems, then dig up the plant and rest it on the soil. Now put one fork vertically right through the middle of the clump; you may need to put on some pressure if the roots are tough. Next put in your second fork in the same way, back to back with the first. To split the clump in two, simply pull the two handles together and the clump will start to split. A certain amount of wiggling usually follows but soon you have two clumps. You can repeat the process to get four, or sometimes the roots can be pulled apart by the hand after the first division.

Choose the most vigorous pieces from the outside of the clump to retain for planting. The woody pieces from the centre can be thrown away, though they will still make serviceable plants if you need a lot. The pieces you choose can be replanted, after improving the soil with organic matter and fertiliser, and the spares can be potted up to be sold at charity stalls, or given away to friends (especially the friend who lent the fork). You will be surprised how many young plants you can obtain from one clump.

Plants suited to this method

A very wide range of herbaceous perennials can be treated this way. Some, hostas, for example, have very tough roots which may need to be cut with a spade or even an old bread knife. These, hellebores and peonies are usually better left undivided for many years.

8. LAYERING

Layering is probably the simplest method of propagation and the one that requires least in the way of special facilities. At its simplest it is just a matter of keeping a branch in contact with the soil by weighing it down with a rock. Even at its most sophisticated it could hardly be said to be complicated. Many low-growing ground-covering plants will root themselves as their stems lie on the ground, and this can be encouraged by putting a stone on a leaf joint of any likely shoot. Autumn is the usual time of year to choose.

To achieve the best results, however, this is how to go about it. Select a healthy shoot which is near the ground and which has grown during the earlier part of the year. In the autumn, bend it down to the ground and excavate a depression at the point where it touches the soil. Fork in some well-rotted garden compost or used potting compost and, if the soil is heavy, some grit; use a hand fork. Firm it well. Bend the shoot down again, and at the point where the shoot touches the bottom of the hole, use a sharp knife to remove a sliver of bark.

Peg the shoot down into the hole with a piece of forked branch or a U-shaped piece of galvanised wire, and support the end of the shoot as it comes out from the hole by tying it as vertically as possible to a bamboo cane. Fill the hole with a 50 : 50 mixture of grit and garden soil, leaving a good mound. Then forget about it.

By late the following summer it will be worth investigating to see if roots have formed. Scrape away the soil on the shoot-tip side of the hole and you should find roots. If not, put back the soil, check the sturdiness of the cane, and look again a few months later. If you find more than just a few roots, cut the shoot on the main shrub side of the hole and leave the newly independent layer in place until the spring, when it can be transferred to its new home.

Although this is a simple method that requires almost no equipment, it takes longer than other methods to get an independent plant. But at least you end up with a good-sized shrub.

Plants suited to this method

Climbers like clematis, vines, Virginia creeper and wisteria, together with a wide variety of deciduous and evergreen shrubs, can be propagated this way. In fact it's worth trying with almost anything that produces branches sufficiently near the ground, and for magnolias it's about the only system you can rely on.

9.   OTHER METHODS

You may sometimes hear about plants being grafted or budded. These are techniques which are beyond the scope of the home gardener, though plants you buy from the garden centre may have been produced in this way. Both involve taking a piece of the variety you want to propagate and joining it with the roots of another (the rootstock). This is usually done with plants that are difficult to root from cuttings or that have weak roots. These are joined with the roots of a stronger growing plant. Fruit trees are also treated in this way, and in this case the rootstock has an influence over the eventual size of the tree.

Roses and fruit trees may be budded, that is, a single bud of the required variety may be joined to the rootstock. Conifers, rhododendrons and magnolias may be grafted, in which case a length of shoot is used.

The important thing about all this from the gardener's point of view is that if shoots grow up from the roots of plants which have been budded or grafted, they will turn out to be quite different from the rest of the plant and often very vigorous. They should be removed at once. This often happens with roses, especially after the roots have been damaged by hoeing.

10. BUYING PLANTS

The best places to buy plants are garden centres, specialist nurseries or gardens open to the public.

Choosing plants in the garden centre

Trees

Buy and plant both fruit and ornamental trees in the autumn, unless you are prepared to water diligently.

Trees are generally sold in large pots, though you may find fruit trees sold with their roots wrapped in hessian. Choose a tree with its branches spaced evenly around a stout, straight stem. Do not buy trees growing in what looks like fresh compost, and if there are no signs of roots coming through the drainage holes, give the trunk a good pull. It may only just have been put in the pot.

Check that the stem is not scraped or split and that ties which are too tight have not cut into it. Make sure that the branches are not broken or dead. Buy two tree ties and a stake to go with each tree.

Shrubs

Almost all shrubs are sold in polythene or stouter plastic pots, although you may still find some evergreens on sale with their roots wrapped in hessian or synthetic mesh. Shrubs grown in pots can be planted at any time of year when the soil is not waterlogged or frozen; hessian-wrapped plants should be planted in the autumn.

Roses sold in the autumn often have their roots wrapped in polythene, and these need planting as soon as possible. Do not buy roses with polythene-wrapped roots in spring; they will have been in the garden centre for months and may well be in poor condition. In spring, roses are usually sold in pots but are often newly potted, so before buying, check that they are firm in their compost and that roots are peeping from the drainage holes.

Do not buy shrubs that seem dry or have wilting leaves. Avoid those growing in what looks like fresh compost; make sure they are firm. Avoid shrubs with dead branches or shoots, and look out for pest or disease damage. In particular, look for plants of a good shape, with their branches spread evenly; these will make the most attractive specimens.

Border perennials

Perennials are usually sold in polythene or rigid plastic pots. Avoid those with a mass of roots growing out of the drainage holes. Spring is the best time to buy border perennials.

Avoid plants with many bare and leafless stems, but don't worry if a few leaves at the base are missing. Look for pots which are well filled, as you may be able to divide these plants into two or three pieces when planting. Avoid plants that are infected with greenfly or other pests and diseases.

Bedding plants

Don't buy summer bedding plants, most of which are frost-tender, until May at the earliest unless you have a greenhouse or conservatory in which to protect them from late frosts.

Pot-grown bedding plants are generally larger than plants grown in trays or strips, and will usually grow away more quickly after planting. They often come in better varieties, but are more expensive. Plants grown in strips or trays are on the whole cheaper but much smaller. They are ideal for planting in large areas, but if you just need a few for tubs, choose pot-grown plants.

Avoid pest-infested plants or any with wilted foliage or withered shoot tips; they may have been frosted. If there is a choice, buy plants without flowers as they will grow away more quickly.

Plants for spring flowering are sold in the autumn and are available in strips, trays and pots. Plant them as soon as the summer plants are over, usually in early October.

Wallflowers are not grown in pots but in the open ground, so they are sold in bunches which are kept in buckets of water. Choose plants with fresh-looking, dark green leaves.

Bulbs

Garden centres stock spring-flowering bulbs from late summer, and they are best planted as early as possible. Buying bulbs which are sold loose, for you to choose yourself, enables you to pick the largest and healthiest, leaving any soft or damaged bulbs behind.

Dry snowdrops, cyclamen and winter aconite bulbs do not usually grow well, so don't buy them. Buy these in growth from specialist bulb nurseries.

Buying from stalls and the roadside

Charity stalls can be unpredictable sources of plants. The first rule is not to buy sickly plants simply to support a charity; there's no reason why a good plant can't be sold in a good cause. Remember, if you give plants to a charity stall, don't use it as a way of getting rid of rubbish; they deserve better. WI stalls are usually very reliable.

Market stalls can be good sources of common plants at competitive prices – but look carefully at the quality of the plants and remember that the varieties on sale may be old-fashioned and not of the highest standard. Never buy house plants from markets, or any outdoor stall, especially in winter. They may already have been severely chilled when you buy them, though this may not become apparent until the next day. Be suspicious of roadside stalls.

Buying from gardens

When you visit a garden open to the public, either a private garden or one owned by the National Trust, you may well find plants on sale. This is a good way of obtaining the plants you have seen while visiting, and you may also find rare and unusual plants not on sale elsewhere.

Plant sales

Specialist societies are organising an increasing number of plant sales, not only at their regular meetings but as special events. These are good places to buy both unusual and more familiar varieties and support good causes. Some of the plants on sale will demand careful cultivation, but there is usually plenty of good advice to be had. Some plant sales also have stalls run by local nurseries.

Buying from ads in magazines and papers

This can be a good source of plants, but beware of advertisements making extravagant claims and offering mixed collections of un-named varieties – ten mixed heathers, that sort of thing.

Buying from mail order catalogues

Specialist mail order nurseries are good sources of the more unusual plants. And although you may be suspicious of buying plants by mail order, most nurseries offer good-quality plants.

- Write off for a catalogue, sending the right money.
- Read the terms of business in the catalogue carefully, and check whether they ask you to send your money with the order and if they advise sending a limit cheque.
- Fill in the order form correctly, listing any substitutes if necessary and not forgetting your name and address. Send off your order promptly, date it and keep a photocopy.
- Look in the catalogue to see if delivery dates are specified, and do not complain until this date has passed.
- Unpack your parcel the moment it arrives, and check that your plants are in good condition.
- If you need to complain, send the nursery a copy of your order with your complaint.

How and when to complain

If the plants you buy from a garden centre don't grow in spite of your planting them in a suitable spot and not letting them dry out, dig them up and take them back to the garden centre. They will usually offer a replacement if you do this in reasonable time.

When complaining about plants ordered by post, send a copy of your order form and describe the problems as clearly as you can; enclose a polaroid photograph of the damaged plants if you can. Some nurseries will refund your money or send replacement plants automatically.

If you receive no satisfaction from staff when complaining at a nursery or garden centre, complain to the manager. If the garden centre is part of a chain, ask for the address of the head office and write to the marketing manager, stating your complaint clearly. As a last resort your local trading standards office can help you resolve complaints, but most nurseries and garden centres are happy to replace plants that have been damaged in the post or died unaccountably, as long as you have looked after them properly.

Most newspapers and magazines belong to a scheme which protects customers when advertisers cease to trade. Details are published with the advertisements from time to time. They are also sometimes willing to help sort out problems between customers and advertisers when all else fails.

CHAPTER SIX

VEGETABLES

Growing Vegetables Outside

Finding space for vegetables in a small garden is often a problem, as most of us want the garden to look attractive for as much of the year as possible. But at the same time there really is nothing quite like eating food you've grown yourself just minutes after it's been picked. And some vegetables can look good too.

1. TRADITIONAL OR MODERN APPROACH?

The traditional way of growing vegetables is probably the least appropriate for a small garden. You need enough space to practise crop rotation and the whole system is altogether more wasteful of space than modern bed systems. In fact, to make the traditional system work well you need so much space that you probably wouldn't have any room left for flowers and a patio. And to utilise all the space properly you would need to fill this space with crops that are not really appropriate to the small garden.

So a bed system is more appropriate, especially when coupled with modern techniques. The deep bed system involves preparing a 4ft (1.2m) wide bed by double digging and growing the crops in short rows across the bed. The rich, deep, loose soil encourages plant roots to penetrate further than normal and so have access to greater reserves of moisture and plant foods. Combine this with tighter than usual spacing and you can get an astonishing yield from a small space.

Although it is unusual to organise a traditional crop rotation system for deep beds, it is also unusual for the pest and disease problems associated with a lack of rotation to cause problems. This is because walking on the beds is prohibited, so diseases like club root are less likely to be transferred from one bed to another – as long as you clean your tools properly.

A variation on this system is the potager, the ornamental food garden. A potager usually consists of a collection of beds edged with box, lavender, hyssop or some other useful, ornamental shrub. These beds may each hold just one crop or may be subdivided by rows of crop plants to create an attractive pattern.

Finally, perhaps I should mention that some of the more ornamental vegetable varieties – red cabbage, runner beans, the chards – can also be grown in flower borders.

2. THE DEEP BED SYSTEM

A deep bed consists of a bed about 4ft (1.2m) wide and as long as you care to make it. 15ft (4.5m) is usually about the maximum practical length, as longer beds encourage more walking. The precise width is determined by what is a comfortable reach for seed-sowing, weeding and so on.

Suitability for small gardens

The deep bed system is ideal for small gardens, as it can be adapted to fit whatever space is available. It also enables you to get the maximum yield from the minimum of space. As the rows are short, it's easy to grow small quantities for a small household, and by sowing a number of short rows over a period it's easier to avoid the glut of produce that so often results from sowing one long row. You will also enjoy the easy access from the paths, making harvesting in all weathers simple.

Deep beds are suitable for all crops except sprouts. These need wide spacing to encourage good-sized buttons, and spacing plants 18in (45cm) apart in a 4ft (1.2m) bed is very wasteful of space. In fact, growing sprouts in a small garden should not be a priority. The only way to manage runner beans in a deep bed system is to grow them on wigwams.

Siting

Deep beds should be sited in an open, sunny spot. If you can, run the beds from east to west so that taller crops shade lower-growing ones as little as possible. Shelter from wind is helpful, but if possible the beds should receive sunshine all day. The next best option is a site partially shaded by a fence or wall. Try to avoid making deep beds under trees; crops will be poor.

If you're making more than one deep bed, allow a path of about 2ft (60cm) between the beds.

Preparation of deep beds

Each bed should be double dug, incorporating organic matter. Rather than leaving the organic matter in a layer at the base of the trench as is sometimes recommended, I suggest forking it into both the lower and the upper layer to get a good mix and so spread the water-holding capacity and the nutrients evenly. Spread 2in (5cm) on the lower spit before forking that over, followed by 2in (5cm) on the surface, then fork that in. Do not tread on the soil at all after it has been dug.

The loosening of the soil and the addition of organic matter will raise the level of the bed considerably above the surrounding soil level. Apart from tidying the edges it should simply be left alone. It will sink, of course, but provided it has been dug evenly it will sink evenly. Extra fertiliser is raked in between crops, but beds are not dug for three years, after which they are completely remade with another generous application of organic matter.

General cultivation

Crops are grown in short rows running across the bed. Plants are thinned, or young plants set out closer than usual and in staggered rows, to make the most of the available space. The aim should be for the individual plants just to touch their neighbours when mature, leaving no visible soil. The space between crops which need wide spacing can be utilised by sowing quick-maturing crops like radishes in between.

Sowing and planting are carried out from the sides without treading on the bed and with the minimum of firming. Weeds can be removed by hand or hoed off easily. Early identification of pest and disease problems is possible, as all plants can be inspected closely from the path.

Early crops

Forcing a few early crops is easy in deep beds, as cloches are available which cover the whole bed to a length of 4ft (1.2m), and if a variety of crops are grown side by side under just one or two cloches they can all be forced together.

3. THE TRADITIONAL SYSTEM

The traditional system involves dividing the area on which vegetables are to be grown into three parts. Crops are segregated into
three groups of similar types which occupy the three areas. Each
area receives different pre-season treatment, with only one area dug
each year. The groups of crops rotate around the three plots year by
year, giving a three-year cycle of crop-growing and the preparation
that goes with it.

The problem in a small garden is that you may want to grow
more crops from one group than from another, so the system
becomes unbalanced. Crops need more space in this system, and are
usually grown in longer rows and more widely spaced apart so that
at maturity bare soil is visible between the rows. As the roots can
quest less deeply in the soil, the plants need more lateral space.

Siting

The traditional vegetable plot needs an open site as much as the deep
bed, and although it is not necessary for three plots to be alongside
each other, it can still be difficult to find the appropriate space.

Rotation of crops

Crops are rotated around the three plots on a three-year cycle and
so divided into three groups.

Group A: mainly root crops and the onion family – potatoes,
carrots, parsnips, beetroot, onions, leeks, shallots, garlic, celery,
celeriac, Florence fennel, Hamburg parsley, salsify, scorzonera,
tomatoes, courgettes, marrows, cucumbers.

Group B: legumes, that is all the peas and beans, plus some others
– peas of all types, broad beans, French beans, runner beans, lettuce,
chicory, endive, spinach, chards, sweet corn.

Group C: brassicas, all the plants in the cabbage family – all
cabbages and Savoys, Brussels sprouts, kale, broccoli, calabrese,
cauliflowers, Chinese cabbage, kohl rabi, swedes, turnips and
radish.

Each group is preceded by a different pre-season preparation:

Plot A: Double digging, incorporating organic matter in both
upper and lower levels. It has to be said that most people now

restrict themselves to single digging. At least try to double dig each plot once when you first start to grow vegetables, even if that's the last deep cultivation it gets. A general fertiliser is then added before sowing or planting. Some crops may need supplementary feeding.

Plot B: Forking over or single digging, followed by the application of a general fertiliser before sowing or planting. Some crops may need supplementary feeding.

Plot C: Forking over or single digging, followed by the application of lime to bring the pH level (see page 8) to 6.5–7.0. A general fertiliser is applied before sowing or planting. Some crops may need supplementary feeding.

The crop groups and their preparations always go together and move plots each year. So if in the first year the crops are on the three plots in the order A B C, in the following year they will be in the order B C A; the next year the order will be C A B and in the fourth year they will be back to the original A B C. So each plot is thoroughly dug once and limed once every three years.

In a small garden it is particularly difficult to keep strictly to this rotation, but it is especially important to ensure that potatoes, the onion family and brassicas are grown on the same spot only once every three years.

General cultivation and maintenance

Rows are usually longer and are spaced more widely than with the deep bed method. Most work will have to be done on the plot itself, so it's important not to walk on the soil if it's too wet. If necessary, use boards to avoid compaction.

Don't be tempted to sow or plant the whole of a long row in one go, otherwise you may have a glut of some crops. Although you'll have to hand-weed in the rows, regular hoeing will be necessary in between.

4.   THE POTAGER

A potager is an ornamental vegetable and herb garden, usually with a basis of permanent planting. As now practised in Britain it's a rather less formal version of that seen at Villandry in France. The beds are usually regular in shape and edged with low hedging in box, santolina, hyssop or lavender, or sometimes with a less permanent crop such as curled parsley or even cottage pinks.

The beds themselves may be planted up with just one crop or may be divided into sections by rows of neat plants, such as the bushy, variegated nasturtium 'Alaska' or chives. Each section is then planted with individual crops. If you like the idea of a potager and have the space, it's very practical to develop two, a winter one and a summer one, each planted with seasonally appropriate plants.

One particularly useful compromise is to grow most crops on the deep bed system and then grow the more unusual salads, herbs and garnishes in a potager. Suitable plants of this type, which can be used as divisions between blocks, as the blocks of planting themselves or as dot plants, might be: balm (yellow-leaved lemon balm), basil (green and purple leaved), calendulas, chervil, chives, fennel 'Smokey' (purple-leaved type), feverfew (yellow-leaved), hyssop, land cress, marjoram (yellow-leaved), mint (variegated ginger mint plus variegated apple mint), nasturtium 'Alaska', parsley (curled and French), par-cel, sage (coloured-leaved types), thyme (bushy types, ordinary and lemon), and violets.

The Crops

I have divided the vegetable crops into two groups: priority crops and secondary crops. As priority crops I've selected those which are especially suitable for small gardens. They may give a particularly good yield from a small space; good-quality produce of this vegetable may be difficult to find or be unreasonably expensive in the shops; they may be at their best when very fresh. But when space is limited the last thing you want to do is grow crops that take up a vast amount of room for a small yield of produce which is available in the shops anyway.

1. PRIORITY CROPS

In the following crop-by-crop examination of small-garden vegetables, I am assuming that they will be grown on the deep bed system unless I say otherwise.

New varieties of vegetables are constantly being introduced, so you may find that those I've suggested have been superseded. However, I have made a point of eschewing those that seem gimmicky, in favour of those with lasting value.

I've not mentioned under each specific entry the necessity of weeding. All the crops should be weeded by hand along the rows when at the seedling stage, and hoed between the rows until the leaves cover the soil.

DWARF OR FRENCH BEANS   Often expensive and of moderate quality in the shops, by growing your own you can pick at the optimum stage for maximum flavour. And they'll taste ten times better than frozen ones.

Sow: Cold frame or cold greenhouse in March and April, one seed per 3in (7.5cm) pot; harden off before planting. Outside from May to July, 2–3in (5–7.5cm) deep, in rows 6in (15cm) apart, with an extra seed or two at the end of each row as spares in case of failures. One sowing under glass, one outside in May and one in July will give a long cropping season.

Plant: Plant out pot-grown plants after hardening off in late May.

Final spacing: 6in (15cm) apart each way.

Cultivation: Mulch when growing well if possible; don't let the plants dry out when flowering or the beans may not set; support with twigs or sticks if necessary. After cropping, cut off at ground level, leaving nutrient-rich roots in the soil for future crops.

Harvest: Usually ready just over two months after sowing. Best at about 5–6in (12.5–15cm) long. Keep picking the beans, otherwise they will get stringy and stop cropping.

Varieties: Round- or pencil-podded types usually have the best flavour. 'The Prince' is early, with good flavour, freezes well, old favourite; 'Aramis' is very early, hardier than many, disease-resistant; 'Purple Teepee' is purple-podded (green after cooking), pods held above foliage for easy picking, flavour good.

CLIMBING FRENCH BEANS   These are more economical of space than dwarf beans, but the flavour is often less good. They usually set better in cold or dry weather than runner beans.

Sow: Cold frame or cold greenhouse in March or April, one seed per 3in (7.5cm) pot; harden off before planting. Outside from May to July, 2–3in (5–7.5cm) deep, two to each cane.

Plant: Plant out pot-grown plants in late May after hardening off carefully.

Supports: Make a wigwam of 8ft (2.4m) bamboo canes by pushing them into the ground 18in (45cm) deep and about 15in (38cm) apart, in a ring 3ft (90cm) across. Tie them together 6in (15cm) from the top.

Cultivation: Guide young shoots round canes. Mulch when growing well if possible; do not let the plants dry out when flowering or the beans may not set. Pinch out the tips when they reach the top of the wigwam. After cropping, cut off at ground level, leaving the nutrient-rich roots in the soil for future crops.

Harvest: Pick when no more than 6in (15cm) long, and keep picking regularly to ensure a continuous crop.

Varieties: 'Blue Lake' has tender pods with a fine flavour; 'Viola Cornetti' is a purple-podded bean with a fine flavour (most purple-podded beans are simply listed as 'Purple Podded'). 'Hunter' has flat, runner-bean-type pods that set well in bad seasons, flavour poor.

RUNNER BEANS   These are the familiar, prolific, easy-to-grow beans, grow only one wigwam, especially if you grow other beans too.

Sow: Cold frame or cold greenhouse in April, one seed per 3in (7.5cm) pot; harden off before planting. Outside in mid-May, 2–3in (5–7.5cm) deep, two to each cane.

Plant: Plant out pot-grown plants one or two per cane after hardening off carefully.

Supports: Make a wigwam of 8ft (2.4m) bamboo canes by pushing them into the ground 18in (45cm) deep and about 15in (38cm) apart, in a ring 3ft (90cm) across. Tie them together 6in (15cm) from the top.

Cultivation: Tie in young shoots so they grow up the canes; mulch when growing away well. Water generously in dry spells, especially once flowering starts, and pinch out the shoots when they reach the top of the canes.

Harvest: Usually ready from July onwards; pick regularly when the pods are about 8–10in (20–25cm) long for the tastiest beans and the longest cropping period.

Varieties: 'Polestar' is vigorous, reliably stringless, sets well in poor weather, good flavour; 'Royal Standard' is early cropping,

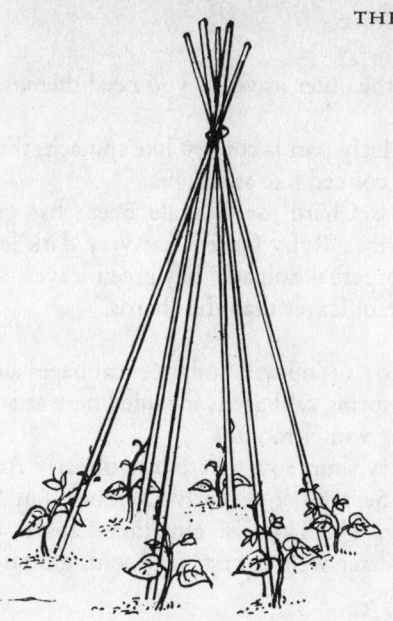

RUNNER BEAN WIGWAM
A wigwam of bamboo canes makes a compact support for runner beans and helps get a heavy crop from a small space.

crisp but stringless, has good flavour, sets well in bad weather; 'Painted Lady' gives a smaller crop, not stringless but very pretty with pink and white flowers. Dwarf runner beans such as 'Pickwick' and 'Gulliver' are earlier than the climbing types, and are grown like dwarf beans but at a slightly wider spacing.

CHARDS AND PERPETUAL SPINACH   There are various perpetual spinaches which can be cropped all season by pulling off the outer leaves and which overwinter to provide a crop in the spring too. White-stemmed 'Swiss Chard' and red-stemmed 'Ruby Chard' are pretty enough to be grown in the flower border.
Sow: Outside in March or April, in rows 9in (23cm) apart. Also sow in July for an overwintered spring crop.
Final spacing: Thin out leaving the plants 9in (23cm) apart in staggered rows; use the thinnings in the kitchen.
Cultivation: Ensure that the plants are well watered and remove the occasional one which may bolt.

Harvest: Pull the outer leaves as you need them, taking just a few from each plant.
Cooking: The leafy part is cooked like spinach; the midribs can be bundled up and cooked like asparagus.
Varieties: 'Swiss Chard' or 'Seakale Beet', has green leaves and pure white midribs; 'Ruby Chard' has very dark leaves and bright red midribs; 'Perpetual Spinach' has green leaves, slender midribs, more productive of leaves than the chards.

SPRING CABBAGE   You will find most cabbages among the secondary crops, but spring cabbage is included here as a crop to help fill the beds over the winter months.
Sow: Sow a very short row in late July or early August.
Plant: In late September or early October, 6in (15cm) apart in unstaggered rows which are also 6in (15cm) apart.
Cultivation: Water well at first, feed with a high-nitrogen fertiliser in early spring.
Harvest: Cut alternate plants for greens in spring, leaving plants in alternate rows to mature.
Pests and diseases: Club root, cabbage root fly, caterpillars, white fly and mildew.
Varieties: 'Pixie' is a pointed type, with small heads, good flavour, early to mature; 'Offenham Spring Bounty', pointed type, compact habit, very hardy, stands well once mature; 'Spring Hero', round type, stands well (sow late August, plant late October).

EARLY CARROTS   Quick-maturing, finger-sized carrots make an invaluable small garden crop which can mature all summer.
Sow: Thinly, in rows 6in (15cm) apart from March to July. Best sown in short rows every two or three weeks.
Thin: To 1in (2.5cm) apart. Remove the thinnings from the site to avoid attracting carrot fly.
Cultivation: Try not to let them dry out or they may split when watered. Can also be sown earlier and covered with a cloche for an extra early crop.
Harvest: Pull the largest first, leaving the remainder to grow on. Water the rows well first if the soil is dry.
Pests: Carrot fly.
Varieties: 'Early French Frame Rondo', a round carrot for quick early sowings, and can even be grown in window-boxes; 'Amster-

dam Forcing', excellent, quick to mature and very tasty; 'Early Nantes', early to mature, very sweet.

CHICORY   The fat heads of sugar loaf chicory are undeservedly neglected summer and autumn crops.
Sow: June or July, thinly in rows 10in (25cm) apart.
Final spacing: Thin to 10in (25cm), leaving the plants in staggered rows.
Cultivation: Keep well watered in dry weather.
Harvest: Late October onwards; cut heads like lettuce.
Varieties: 'Snowflake'/'Winter Fare', easy to grow, with 2–3lb (450–900g) heads, can be stored in the fridge for two months.

COURGETTES   Large, spreading plants producing small tasty fruits all summer.
Sow: Propagator in mid-April; cold greenhouse at end of April. Sow two seeds per 3in (7.5cm) pot and remove the weakest after germination. Outside in May, sow two or three seeds close together under a jam-jar and thin to one after germination.
Plant: Harden off early sowings and plant out at the end of May.
Final spacing: 2ft (60cm) each way in staggered rows, use space before plants mature for radishes.
Cultivation: Mulch after planting, water generously all summer, liquid feed once first fruits are ready.
Harvest: Mid-July onwards. The flavour and texture are best at about 4in (10cm); always cut before 6in. If left to mature into marrows, cropping will tail off.
Diseases: Virus.
Varieties: 'Ambassador', early, very heavy cropper, long season, good flavour; 'Supremo', early, crisp, dark green fruits, virus resistant; 'Gold Rush', bright yellow fruits, compact plants, good flavour.

CUCUMBER   Bush cucumbers can be very successful when grown outside and very tasty too.
Sow: Propagator in mid-April; cold greenhouse at end of April. Sow two seeds per 3in (7.5cm) pot and remove the weakest after germination. Outside in May, sow two or three seeds close together under a jam-jar and thin to one after germination.
Plant: Harden off early sowings and plant out at the end of May.

Final spacing: 2ft (60cm) apart in staggered rows; use the spare space for a quick crop of radishes.
Cultivation: Mulch when growing away well and keep well watered all season. Give a liquid feed every couple of weeks, from first picking onwards.
Harvest: Cut regularly, and don't leave mature cucumbers on the plants as cropping will decline.
Pests: Red spider mite.
Varieties: 'Bush Champion', early, heavy crop of 9in (23cm) fruits, good flavour; 'Bush Crop', smaller fruits, good flavour.

LETTUCE   There are four types of lettuce and all are worth growing: cabbage, butterhead or soft lettuce; crisp or Iceberg lettuce; cos lettuce; and loose leaf lettuce.

Cabbage lettuce   These have soft-leaved heads with dark green outer leaves and paler hearts. Some varieties can be overwintered for an early spring crop.
Sow: Inside in late February or early March; prick out into trays and harden off well. Outside from mid-March to late July. To avoid a glut grow in short rows, and sow the next batch when the previous one has germinated. Rows should be 9in (23cm) apart.
Plant: Plant those grown in trays 9in (23cm) apart in staggered rows.
Final spacing: Thin to 9in (23cm) apart in staggered rows.
Cultivation: Those sown in late spring should be in partial shade if possible to help prevent bolting. Keep watered in dry spells.
Harvest: Cut heads at their best, or before if necessary.
Varieties: 'Dolly', large, dense heads with good disease resistance; 'Avondefiance', soft heads, pest- and disease-resistant, good for later sowings; 'Tom Thumb', small hearts, very tasty, thin to only 6 × 6in (15 × 15cm).

Crisp lettuce   These have crisp hearts and crinkled foliage; some have a tendency to bolt in summer.
Sow: Outside from mid-March to late July. To avoid a glut grow in short rows, sowing the next batch when the previous one has germinated. Rows should be 9in (23cm) apart.
Final spacing: Thin out to 9in (23cm) apart.
Cultivation: Keep well watered in dry spells. Those sown in late spring should be in partial shade if possible, to help prevent bolting.

Harvest: Cut at their peak or before – do not leave them to stand, as although some will hold their heads for a while, others will bolt.
Varieties: 'Avoncrisp' has excellent pest- and disease-resistance, good for late sowings, good flavour; 'Saladin', a large dense Iceberg type, disease-resistant, slow to bolt; 'Pablo', attractive red outer leaves, good flavour.

Cos lettuce   An upright lettuce, with long narrow leaves and a distinctive flavour.
Sow: As crisp lettuce.
Final spacing: As crisp lettuce.
Cultivation: As crisp lettuce.
Harvest: As crisp lettuce.
Varieties: 'Lobjoits Green Cos' is an old favourite, with large dark green heads; 'Romance' is quick-growing, disease-resistant, good flavour; 'Little Gem', very small, superb flavour, stands well without bolting, space at 6×6in (15×15cm).

Loose leaf lettuce   These varieties do not produce a dense head to cut; instead, the outer leaves are pulled off regularly all through the season.
Sow: As crisp lettuce.
Plant: As crisp lettuce.
Final spacing: As crisp lettuce.
Cultivation: Keep well watered in dry spells; generally very resistant to bolting.
Harvest: Pull the outer leaves off regularly. If left too long the outer leaves may become tough, in which case pull them but put them on the compost heap.
Varieties: 'Salad Bowl' has flat rosettes of oak-shaped leaves, good flavour; 'Red Salad Bowl' is a red-leaved version of 'Salad Bowl', very attractive in flower borders; 'Lollo Green' has wide curled foliage with pretty frilly edges, sometimes forms a loose heart which can be cut whole; 'Lollo Red' is a very attractive red-leaved version of 'Lollo Green'.

Winter lettuce   Some varieties of cabbage lettuce can be sown late in the year to overwinter for early spring heads, but the flavour is less good than spring- and summer-sown types. Useful to fill beds in winter but not suitable for spring sowings.
Sow: Late August, in a sheltered spot.
Thin: To 2–3in (5–7.5cm) before winter.

Final spacing: Thin again to 9in (23cm) in spring, using spare seedlings to fill gaps.

Cultivation: Keep fallen leaves and other debris cleared from around the young plants. Use a hoe to loosen soil around them occasionally. Much more reliable if given cloche protection.

Harvest: Usually ready by late May.

Varieties: 'Valdor', tough, large deep green hearts, universally recommended; 'Arctic King', paler green colour, better flavour.

SPRING ONION The bulbous, rather-too-hot salad onions we sometimes see in the shops may be seedlings taken from rows of maincrop onions rather than genuine spring onions. For the best flavour it pays to grow the right thing.

Sow: Thinly, in short rows 3in (7.5cm) apart, every two or three weeks from March to June. Sow also in August for overwintering.

Final spacing: Do not thin out.

Cultivation: Given reasonably well-prepared soil, no special treatment is necessary.

Harvest: Pull as required; the first ones should be ready in 8–10 weeks.

Varieties: 'White Lisbon' is an old favourite, with slender stems and mild flavour; 'Ishikuro' has long, slender stems, stands exceptionally well without bulbing; 'Santa Claus' is similar to 'Ishikuro' but with a red-tinted base; 'White Lisbon Winter Hardy' is for late summer sowing to overwinter.

PEAS I can justify putting only certain types of peas in this section – mange-tout, tall purple-podded, and leafless. Mange-tout produce by far the best grop from a given area of ground, purple-podded peas (which also have purple flowers) are certainly the most decorative, and leafless peas are entirely self-supporting, which is very useful in deep beds.

Sow: March to June. Sow mange-tout in two rows, 4in (10cm) apart, in flat-bottomed drills; 2ft (60cm) between drills (intercrop with lettuce). Purple-podded, sow as above, 3ft (90cm) between drills. Leafless, sow 2in (5cm) apart in single rows, with 6in (15cm) between the rows.

Final spacing: No thinning required.

Cultivation: Protect from birds with netting after sowing. Water well in dry weather. Mange-tout and purple-podded will need support from pea-sticks or 4in (10cm) mesh plastic netting supported on stakes. Leafless peas, with their well-developed tendrils, will support themselves.

Harvest: Mange-tout when the pods are still flat and tender; purple-podded when fat and rich purple in colour, about 14 weeks after sowing; leafless about 12 weeks after sowing.

Varieties: Mange-tout: 'Oregon Sugar Pod', with pale fat pods, fine flavour, and 'Sugar Ann', which should be picked early when flat or later when the pods have fleshed out to a sugar pea. Purple-podded: only one variety, of that name. Leafless: 'Twiggy', a heavy crop, long pods, pods held at top of plants for easy picking, and 'Poppet', heavy crop, good flavour.

POTATOES Only early potatoes are worth growing in a small garden.

Chitting: Before planting, set the seed potatoes in an egg-tray for six weeks for the eyes to sprout. Choose a light, cool but frost-free place.

Plant: Late March or early April, 6in (15cm) deep, 12in (30cm) apart, in rows 2ft (60cm) apart.

Cultivation: When the shoots are 6in (15cm) high, give a fertiliser dressing at a handful per square yard then draw soil from between the rows up around the shoots, leaving an inch or two peeping out. Keep well watered in May and June.

Harvest: When the plants begin to flower, start to lift the tubers as you need them, using a fork from the side of the row.

Varieties: 'Maris Bard', good crop, fair flavour; 'Dunluce', earliest of all, floury, flavour fair; 'Concorde', very early, heavy crop, good in all soils, fine flavour.

PUMPKIN Included because sooner or later the kids will want to grow one.

Sow: Heaviest fruits are obtained from an early start indoors. Propagator in mid-April; cold greenhouse at end of April. Sow two seeds per 3in (7.5cm) pot and remove the weakest after germination. Outside in May, sow two or three seeds close together under a jam-jar and thin to one after germination.

Plant: You won't need more than two plants, and the second will only be an insurance against damage to the first. Allow masses of space.

Cultivation: Water and feed generously. To obtain the largest fruits, thin them to just two or three per plant. Set the fruits on bricks or slabs to keep them off the ground.

Harvest: During autumn, as required.

Varieties: 'Atlantic Giant' can reach nearly 500lb (225kg) in weight; 'Mammoth' is a good heavy fruiter, not difficult to grow to 100lb (45kg); 'Spirit' produces many 12in (30cm) fruits, the best genuine culinary type.

RADICCHIO   Green loose-leaved plants in summer, leaves redden in autumn and form hearts.

Sow: June or July, thinly in a short row.

Plant: Late August or early September, 9in (23cm) apart in staggered rows.

Cultivation: Protect over winter with straw or low cloches for reliable winter supply.

Harvest: Pull off leaves as required, or cut the whole head. Leave the root in the soil, as it will regrow usable leaves.

Varieties: 'Rossa di Verona', thin to only 6in (15cm), cut off all leaves in early October to encourage formation of tight red head, very hardy; 'Alouette', sow May, ready September till fierce frost, crops again in early spring.

RADISH   Ideal small garden crop, maturing so quickly that it can be easily fitted in among other crops.

Sow: March to September, thinly every two or three weeks, in short rows. June to August sowings are best in semi-shade to prevent bolting.

Final spacing: No need to thin if sown thinly; eventual spacing should be ¾–1in (20–25mm).

Cultivation: Keep watered in dry weather.

Harvest: Ready three to four weeks after sowing.

Varieties: 'Prinz Rotin' is a quick-growing, round, red-skinned variety, stands well without going pithy; 'French Breakfast' has long white-tipped roots, mild flavour; 'Cherry Belle' is an old favourite, with round red roots.

TOMATOES   Modern bush varieties are ideal for deep beds and produce a good crop in most parts of the country.

Sow: Late March in propagator, prick out into 3in (7.5cm) pots.

Harden off well before planting out.
Plant: Late May.
Final spacing: 18in (45cm) apart.
Cultivation: The fruits are best lifted off the soil by spreading straw or bark chips under and around the plants. Water well in dry spells, and don't let the soil become parched.
Harvest: The first fruits should be ready two months after planting.
Varieties: 'Red Alert', the first very early bush type, reliably early, good flavour; 'Tornado', slightly later than 'Red Alert', better flavour; 'Red Dawn', the first beefsteak bush type.

2.   SECONDARY CROPS

ASPARAGUS   A perennial vegetable that takes up a lot of space for the amount harvested and also takes three years before a full crop can be taken.
Preparation: Choose a well-drained site in full sun. Fork in plenty of organic matter.
Plant: 12in (30cm) apart each way, with roots well spread out.
Cultivation: Mulch every autumn with garden compost and rake in two handfuls of general fertiliser per square yard in early spring. Keep well weeded and well watered.
Harvest: Cut a few spears in the second year after planting, building up to full cropping in year four.
Varieties: 'Lucullus', with no useless female plants, heavy cropper; 'Franklim', all male, especially fat spears.

GLOBE ARTICHOKES   Decorative plants, good in the mixed border, but with a limited yield for the space they take up.
Sow: In February; raise like a half-hardy annual, pricking out into 3in (7.5cm) pots.
Plant: 18in (45cm) apart, in late spring.
Cultivation: Grow as annuals in deep beds and keep well watered. You get a far higher yield than when grown as perennials in permanent beds.
Harvest: Cut the heads when still well closed.
Varieties: 'Green Globe' is the tastiest and most productive.

JERUSALEM ARTICHOKES   Tall, leafy plants best used as a boundary or windbreak and not in beds.
Plant: Late winter, 6in (15cm) deep and 12in (30cm) apart.
Cultivation: Any good soil in a sunny spot suits them.
Harvest: Cut down the stems in autumn and lift the tubers as you need them. Keep enough back for the following season.
Varieties: 'Fuseau' has smooth tubers; 'Dwarf Sunray' is similar but shorter.

BROAD BEANS   Their yield is not usually good enough for the space they take up, but the flavour of fresh broad beans is wonderful.
Sow: In autumn or early spring, 6in (15cm) apart in staggered rows. Sow a few spares at the end of the rows, just in case.
Cultivation: Support the plants by stretching pea and bean netting horizontally across the crop 12in (30cm) above the soil and raising it as the beans grow to about half their eventual height as given on the packet. Protect against birds.
Harvest: Harvest the beans before the pods become too tough.
Varieties: The taller varieties give the best yield, though the dwarf ones are easier to manage. 'Aquadulce Claudia' is tall, best for autumn sowing; 'Jubilee Hysor' gives a heavy crop of well-filled pods, tall; 'The Sutton' is dwarf, good flavour.

SPROUTING BROCCOLI   A tall, winter-cropping plant, with small cauliflower-like heads for many weeks.
Sow: In May, in a seed bed.
Plant: In June, 2ft (60cm) apart, in staggered rows 12in (30cm) apart.
Cultivation: Water regularly. Protect against birds.
Harvest: Cut regularly, never letting the plants flower.
Varieties: 'Early Purple Sprouting' crops in January and February; 'Late Purple Sprouting' crops in March and April.

BRUSSELS SPROUTS   Large plants, giving a poor yield for the space they need and occupying the ground for most of the year.
Sow: In a seed bed in March.
Plant: May or June, 3ft (90cm) apart each way.
Cultivation: May need staking; use the space between the young plants for quick-maturing crops. Protect against birds.

Harvest: Start at the bottom of the stem, and never let the buttons become blown.
Varieties: 'Peer Gynt' is a long-standing early variety for September to Christmas; 'Rampart' for December to March.

SUMMER, AUTUMN AND WINTER CABBAGE Competition for space in summer is at its height, so these are relegated to the second division, though Savoys are a valuable winter crop.

Summer cabbage
Sow: March to May, in a seed bed.
Plant: May to July, 15–18in (38–45cm) apart each way; tighter spacing gives smaller heads.
Cultivation: Put a brassica collar round each plant when planting, to protect against cabbage root fly. Keep well watered. Protect against birds.
Harvest: Cut when the heads feel firm.
Varieties: 'Hispi', an early, pointed variety; 'Minicole', quick-maturing with a round head; 'Hawke', large round heads in late summer.

Autumn and winter cabbage
Sow: April and May, in a seed-bed.
Plant: July, 15–18in (38–45cm) apart. Put a brassica collar round each plant when planting, to protect against cabbage root fly.
Cultivation: Remove any yellowing leaves as necessary. Protect against birds.
Harvest: Start to cut when the heads are solid. Savoys especially stand hard frost well. Red cabbages are best cut in late autumn, cleaned of dead leaves and hung in nets in a cool shed.
Varieties: 'Celtic' has rock-hard heads standing until well after Christmas; 'Wivoy' is a Savoy which stands till April; 'Ruby Ball' is the best red cabbage.

MAINCROP CARROTS Good quality roots are often available from the shops, so don't bother to grow these unless vegetables are your particular enthusiasm.
Sow: In rows 6in (15cm) apart from April to early June.
Final spacing: Thin to 3in (7.5cm) apart, eating the larger thinnings. Remove all thinnings from the site to avoid attracting carrot fly.

Cultivation: Water in dry spells or the roots may split.

Harvest: Dig for immediate use from August to October. Lift the remainder and store undamaged roots in sand.

Varieties: 'St Valéry' has long, tapering roots, best for flavour; 'Autumn King' is good for storing.

CAULIFLOWER   This is the most difficult vegetable to grow well, and also one that takes up a lot of space. I suggest growing mini-cauliflowers which are easier and quicker to mature, forming one-person-sized, 3–4in (7.5–10cm) curds.

Sow: Every three weeks from late March to early July. Sow two seeds together 6in (15cm) apart, in staggered rows 6in (15cm) apart, and pull out the weakest of each pair after germination.

Cultivation: Weed carefully early on; water if absolutely necessary.

Harvest: Ready from late June to late October.

Varieties: Most varieties are unsuitable for this system. Use 'Snow Crown', 'Dominant' or 'Garant'.

CELERIAC   Fat round roots with a celery flavour, also known as turnip-rooted celery.

Sow: February in a heated propagator; prick out into boxes.

Plant: End of May or early June, after hardening off well.

Final spacing: 12in (30cm) apart each way.

Cultivation: Keep watered well all season; mulch well if the material is available.

Harvest: Lift as required from September to May. In the coldest areas, lift in November and store.

Varieties: Most are fairly similar; look out for 'Jose', 'Tellus', 'Iram' and 'Monarch'.

ENDIVE   An increasingly popular salad vegetable; the cut-leaved types are especially useful.

Sow: April to July, thinly in rows 9in (23cm) apart. Earlier sowings are best in partial shade. Do not transplant, as they may run to seed.

Final spacing: Thin to 9in (23cm) apart in staggered rows.

Cultivation: Keep well watered. Can be blanched to reduce bitter flavour by tying the leaves together and inverting a flower-pot (with the drainage holes blocked) over the top. Alternatively, lay a large dinner plate on each plant.

Harvest: From when leaves touch each other or three weeks after blanching; leave stumps in to re-grow.

Varieties: 'Ione' and 'Coquette' are modern selections, 'Moss Curled' is the most frequently seen.

FENNEL   An anise-flavoured vegetable, the leaf bases have swollen to form a bulb. Not easy to grow well.

Sow: May to early July, thinly, in rows 12in (30cm) apart.

Plant: Thin to 12in (30cm) apart, giving staggered rows. Do not transplant.

Cultivation: Keep well watered. Earth up when the bulb is about the size of a golf ball.

Harvest: Cut just above basic ground level (level of the surrounding soil), usually about three weeks after earthing up.

Varieties: 'Zifa Fino' – highly resistant to bolting; the variety is not always named.

KOHL RABI   A bizarre-looking vegetable, with the bulb above ground and the leaves growing out from it. Quick-growing.

Sow: March to September, thinly in a seed bed.

Plant: Plant out 9in (23cm) apart in 9in (23cm) staggered rows.

Cultivation: Tolerates poor conditions, especially heat and drought, but best when moist and growing quickly. Protect from birds.

Harvest: From May until winter when about tennis-ball size. For early season crops sow the white varieties from March to June, for later crops sow the purple ones from June to August.

Varieties: 'Lanro', white, high-yielding; 'Rowel', white, high-yielding, still edible at larger sizes; 'Purple Vienna', purple, best at smaller size.

LEEK   Valuable winter vegetable, only just missing out on inclusion among the first choices.

Sow: March, in a seed-bed outside.

Plant: May, 6in (15cm) apart, in staggered rows also 6in (15cm) apart. Make a deep furrow, then make the planting holes with a dibber and drop one seedling into each hole. Water in well, but do not refill the hole with soil.

Cultivation: Keep well watered. Fill in furrow later in the summer to aid blanching of stem.
Harvest: Lift as required right through the winter.
Varieties: 'Lyon Prizetaker', good flavour, one of the earliest; 'King Richard', long stems, high-quality, autumn and early winter; 'Autumn Mammoth Argentea', stands from late autumn to early spring; 'Cortina', long stems, very hardy, late winter and spring.

MARROW   Only bush marrows are suitable for small gardens, as trailing types take up too much space.
Sow: Sow, plant and grow as for courgettes (page 295).
Harvest: Do not leave the marrows to get too large, otherwise cropping will cease.
Varieties: 'Twickers' has small, rugby-football-sized fruits, cream-striped, a continuous crop; 'Early Gem' has dark green fruits, traditional marrow shape.

ONION   Ordinary bulb onions of good quality can easily be bought, but are still worth growing if you have the space. Sets are easiest in a small garden.
Plant: 2in (5cm) apart in staggered rows, 6in (15cm) apart.
Cultivation: Keep well watered and weed-free.
Harvest: Normally ready in late July when the tops start to collapse and the leaves go yellow. Do not bend the tops down.
Varieties: 'Turbo', round bulbs, very slow to bolt, stores well; 'Rocardo' flatter shape, good flavour, stores well; 'Showmaster', easy to grow 2lb (900gm) bulbs to surprise visitors!

PARSNIP   Long-season crop, good in deep beds.
Sow: April, three seeds to individual sites which should be 6in (15cm) apart in staggered rows 6in (15cm) apart. Thin to one strong seedling when all have come through.
Cultivation: Hoe carefully to keep the weeds down; do not damage the roots.
Harvest: First roots ready in early autumn; leave in the soil and dig as required.
Varieties: 'Avonresister', neat roots, canker-resistant; 'Gladiator', earlier than most, canker-resistant; 'Hollow Crown', long, tapering roots, best flavour.

SALSIFY AND SCORZONERA Uncommon root vegetables, both with long thin roots and a similar flavour. Salsify has a white root, while scorzonera is also white but with a black skin. They are grown in the same way. Neither takes up much space, but both need a long growing season.

Sow: April and May, thinly in rows 12in (30cm) apart.
Final spacing: Thin to 6in (15cm) apart.
Cultivation: Keep well watered in dry spells, mulch if possible.
Harvest: Ready from October through until spring.
Varieties: 'Mammoth' is about the only salsify; 'Habil' is the best scorzonera.

SPINACH A nutritious vegetable, but needs the right conditions to crop well.

Sow: Every four weeks from March to July, in rows 8in (20cm) apart, thinning to 8in (20cm) apart giving a staggered row. Sow also in September for cropping over winter.
Cultivation: Rich soil, plenty of moisture and shade from the hot sun are needed, so spinach is often grown between rows of tall peas and beans. May bolt in hot sun and dry conditions.
Harvest: Can be ready eight weeks from sowing, pick just a few leaves from each plant.
Varieties: 'Norvak' has large dark leaves, very slow to bolt, good flavour; 'Symphony' has erect habit, deep green leaves, slow to bolt.

SWEDE Winter roots with a distinctive flavour.

Sow: Late May, in rows 15in (38cm) apart.
Final spacing: Thin to 12in (30cm) apart in the rows.
Cultivation: A tolerant crop, but keep well watered in dry spells.
Harvest: Ready from late autumn onwards.
Varieties: 'Marion', good crop, disease-resistant, by far the best variety.

SWEET CORN This would be one of the best small garden vegetables if the plants took up less space, for the sugar starts to turn to starch as soon as they are picked, then the flavour deteriorates, so fresh cobs are best.

Sow: In a propagator in April, two seeds to each 3in (7.5cm) pot. Thin to one after germination. Alternatively, in early May sow three seeds together in the bed where they are to crop and cover with a jam-jar. In either case, remove the weakest leaving one strong seedling.

Plant: After the last frost, in staggered rows with 2ft (60cm) between plants and rows. This is also the spacing for outside sowings.

Cultivation: Protect the seedlings from slugs, keep weed-free, and water well when flowering starts.

Harvest: August onwards, depending on variety, season and district. Only one or two cobs per plant. When the tassels well withered, press the seed with your fingernail: watery juice means unripe, milky juice means ripe.

Varieties: 'Sundance', early-mid season, very reliable, good in poor summers; 'Sweet Nugget', early, bred to retain flavour well after cutting, must be grown in isolation from other varieties.

TURNIP   Grow as a quick summer crop, not for storage.

Sow: March and April, in rows 9in (23cm) apart.

Final spacing: Thin to 6in (18cm) apart.

Cultivation: Start thinning very early to avoid overcrowding, which leads to poor roots. Weed thoroughly and carefully.

Harvest: May onwards.

Varieties: 'Tokyo Cross', the fastest grower, ready in five weeks, can also be sown later, white flesh; 'Snowball' has white flesh, larger roots, still tender.

Herbs

BASIL (OCIMUM BASILICUM)   A half-hardy annual with a spicy flavour reaching 12–15in (30–38cm); broad glossy leaves and small purple flowers.

Uses: Much used on pizzas, with pasta and in Italian cooking. A favourite with tomatoes, fresh or cooked, and in sausages and stuffings.

Sow: Treat as a half-hardy bedding plant by sowing in March at 70°F (21°C) and pricking out directly into 3in (7.5cm) pots.

Plant: Harden off and plant out about 12in (30cm) apart after the last frosts.

Cultivation: Basil is a little delicate for many parts of Britain, so plant in a warm spot, sheltered from the wind, in a rich but well-drained soil. Can also be grown in a 5in (12.5cm) pot on a window-sill, in a conservatory or on a patio.

Harvest: Pick as necessary during the season, pinching out the tips in the process to encourage branching.

Drying: Cut in the morning after the dew has dried, choosing a dry day shortly before flowering. Handle the leaves carefully and dry in the dark in a relatively cool temperature, otherwise the leaves will turn black.

Varieties: Specialist catalogues list up to fifteen varieties, but 'Genovese' has the largest leaves and the strongest flavour, while 'Dark Opal' is similar except that the leaves come in a very attractive rich purple shade and so look delightful in containers with flowers like marigolds.

BAY (LAURUS NOBILIS)   An evergreen tree which can reach as much as 40ft (12m) tall in the open ground but is more often grown as a trained plant in a tub. The leaves have a pungent flavour which is strongest in the dried leaves.

Uses: An essential ingredient of *bouquet garni*, bay is also used in casseroles, in stock for fish dishes or poultry and gives a distinctive flavour to carrots and other vegetables when added to the water while boiling.

Buy: Rarely grown from seed, young or partially trained plants are usually bought. Do not buy a plant trained as a standard if you intend to plant it in the open.

Plant: In a sunny, well-drained site in the open garden, avoiding frost pockets. Alternatively grow in large pots of John Innes No. 3 compost.

Cultivation: Plants in the open may be damaged in bad winters, so need to have the dead wood pruned out as they start to shoot from low down in spring. Trained plants in tubs should be clipped over once or twice during the season to ensure that they keep their shape if picking for the pot does not do this naturally.

Harvest: Pick as needed.

Drying: Pick in midsummer and so avoid clipping. Dry slowly and store in a dark jar.

Varieties: There is a yellow-leaved variety, 'Aurea', which is less hardy than the green one usually grown.

BORAGE (BORAGO OFFICINALIS)   Once widely grown for 'the comfort of the hart, for the driving away of sorrowe', borage is a hardy annual reaching 2–3ft (60–90cm) in height with rough leaves and sparkling blue flowers.

Uses: Still an ingredient of Pimms No. 1, both leaves and flowers are used for their fresh cucumber flavour in cool summer drinks as well as for cider and claret cups.

Sow: Sow from March to May, outside where the plants are to flower, and thin to 18in (45cm) apart. Choose a well-drained soil and a sunny site.

Cultivation: Little attention is required, and if allowed to self-sow there will always be borage in the garden. But most plants should be dead-headed to encourage continuous flowering.

Harvest: Pick the young leaves, and especially the pretty flowers, as you need them.

Drying: This is hard to do effectively because the leaves are so succulent and rapidly lose their fragrance.

Varieties: Just the one.

CHIVES (ALLIUM SCHOENOPRASUM)   A grass-like plant 9–12in (23–30cm) high, with narrow cylindrical leaves, a light onion flavour and round heads of pink flowers.

Uses: Best in salads, soups or sandwiches or anywhere that a hint of onion is required; good as a garnish.

Sow: Can be raised from seed sown outside in spring, but clumps divide so easily at almost any time of year that a few bulbs can usually be obtained from friends.

Plant: Clumps are best lifted and pulled apart in spring or autumn and replanted 12in (30cm) apart.

Cultivation: Choose a rich, fertile soil that does not get too dry, preferably in sun or partial shade.

Harvest: Cut with scissors when the leaves are only 2–3in (5–7.5cm) tall, for at this stage they are at their most tender and tasty. Keep a number of clumps, cutting one at a time and allowing the others to grow. Eventually let each grow on and flower; the flower-heads can be picked for adding colour to salads. Lift a clump or two and move them into the greenhouse in autumn to provide a few snippings in winter.

Drying: Not usually worth drying, as the flavour tends to disappear.

Varieties: 'Forescate' flowers especially prolifically and is a fine border plant.

DILL (ANETHUM GRAVEOLENS) A feathery, slightly blueish-green annual reaching about 2ft (60cm), with flat heads of greenish flowers. The leaves are similar to fennel both in appearance and in flavour, with an overall aniseed aroma, but the seeds are also used.
Uses: The leaves have a more delicate flavour than the seeds and are best used with fish, while the seeds are used in pickles and curries.
Sow: From April to June, where the plants are to flower; thin the seedlings to 9in (23cm) apart.
Cultivation: Choose a sunny, well-drained site, sheltered from strong winds.
Harvest: For a seed crop, cut the whole plant as the flower-heads turn brown and hang it upside down over a sheet of newspaper. Leaves can be cut as they are needed.
Drying: Cut while still young and fresh and dry on newspaper in the airing cupboard.
Varieties: Seeds of different varieties for leaves, seeds for pickles and seeds for curries, are available from Suffolk Herbs.

FENNEL (FOENICULUM VULGARE) An attractive hardy perennial plant reaching 5ft (1.5m) in height, with clouds of thread-like leaves and flat heads of yellow flowers.
Uses: Especially good with grilled fish, it can also be used with potatoes instead of mint or parsley and in vegetable salads.
Sow: Plants can be bought or seed sown outside in April and thinned to 18in (45cm) apart.
Cultivation: Fennel likes a sunny, well-drained soil but one which is fertile and does not dry out. It is attractive enough to grow in the flower border.
Harvest: Cut the leaves as you need them. To produce a continuous supply of young leaves, tall stems should be cut to the ground occasionally to stimulate new growth.
Drying: Very difficult to dry well.
Varieties: There are a number of very pretty bronze-leaved varieties which are especially suitable for borders and they have names like 'Smokey' and 'Purpureum'.

GARLIC (ALLIUM SATIVUM)   A familiar pungent-smelling herb used in a wide variety of dishes. The bulb, which develops below ground, is made up of a cluster of cloves producing flat leaves up to 3ft (90cm) high. Easy to grow.

Uses: Valuable for its vitamin content as well as its distinctive flavour. Used in salads, roasts and casseroles, and there are even recipes for garlic soup.

Plant: Individual cloves are planted in October in the south or March in the north. Set them 2in (5cm) deep, 8in (20cm) apart in rows 12in (30cm) apart.

Cultivation: Apart from weeding, they need watering only in dry spells.

Harvest: When the leaves begin to yellow in August, lift the bulbs and leave to dry off – in the greenhouse or under a cloche if necessary.

Storage: Cut the foliage down to 2in (5cm) and tie in ropes like onions, then store in a warm dry place.

Varieties: Varieties adapted to growth in Britain are available from vegetable seed companies.

LEMON BALM (MELISSA OFFICINALIS)   A lemon-scented, herbaceous perennial reaching about 2ft (60cm), with wrinkly oval leaves, small white flowers and an over-enthusiastic tendency to self-sow.

Uses: Valuable whenever a less sharp lemon flavour is needed, especially with fish and in summer drinks.

Sow: Coloured-leaved varieties must be bought as plants and increased by division in spring or autumn. The green-leaved type can be raised from seed sown thinly outside in spring; the seedlings should be moved to their final site when large enough to handle.

Plant: 12in (30cm) apart.

Cultivation: A tolerant plant which will grow well in most soils and situations, but the yellow-leaved types are best in at least partial shade, or they may scorch.

Harvest: Pick leaves and shoots as required.

Drying: Cut just before the flowers open and dry quickly but not in a very high temperature. Store in the dark.

Varieties: The very attractive 'Allgold', whose leaves are entirely golden, is a fine border plant, while 'Aurea' is speckled with yellow. Self-sown seedlings from these varieties will have green leaves.

MARJORAM (ORIGANUM VULGARE) A slightly floppy perennial reaching about 2ft (60cm) in height, with small, softly hairy leaves and pretty purple flowers in summer. Distinctive and powerful flavour.
Uses: Best used in small quantities as the flavour is so strong. Vital for pizzas and also used in stuffings and salads.
Plant: In spring, 12in (30cm) apart.
Cultivation: Best in a sunny place and a well-drained soil, although the yellow-leaved types benefit from shade from the hottest sun. Cut back flower-heads after flowering to encourage more shoots from low down.
Harvest: Cut shoots whenever they are needed.
Drying: Cut shoots shortly before the flower-buds open and spread on newspaper for drying in an airing cupboard. The flavour becomes more pungent in dried marjoram.
Varieties: 'Aureum' has yellow leaves, while 'Gold Tip' has the leaves tipped in yellow. Both are good border plants.

MINT (MENTHA SPECIES) A familiar but variable plant, usually invasive, in a variety of flavours.
Uses: A favourite with roast lamb and with potatoes and peas, the various flavours have many uses.
Plant: In spring or autumn, 9–15in (23–38cm) apart depending on type.
Cultivation: Most mints like a moist soil, in full sun or partial shade, but many need containing to prevent their roots running and smothering other plants. An old galvanised bucket or bath is suitable, although the lip must be raised 2–3in (5–7.5cm) above the soil or the runners will simply go over the top.
Harvest: Cut the shoots and pick the leaves as you need them. Peppermint and spearmint should be cut back regularly to produce fresh young shoots, though this encourages their spread.
Drying: Remove flower-buds, then cut the stems but do not remove the leaves. Spread out on a net frame and dry slowly.
Varieties: Spearmint (*M. spicata*), vigorously spreading but reaching only 18in (45cm), with powerfully flavoured bright green leaves; peppermint (*M. × piperita*), a vigorously spreading plant reaching 2–3ft (60–90cm) in height, with purple stems and lilac flowers; variegated ginger mint (*M. × gentilis* 'Variegata'), a small, less vigorous plant reaching 15in (38cm), with very pretty yellow-

veined leaves; pineapple mint (*M. suaveolens* 'Variegata'), a relatively slow-growing, rather floppy plant with pale green leaves
irregularly marked in white.

PARSLEY (PETROSELINUM CRISPUM)   A biennial plant producing rounded hummocks of bright green, curly leaves.
Uses: Garnishes, sauces, soups, salads; the strongly flavoured
stems are included in *bouquet garni*.
Sow: In spring and again in summer for the following spring. Sow
in a propagator at 70°F (21°C) and prick out into boxes, then plant
out 9in (23cm) apart. Seed can be very slow to germinate.
Cultivation: Plant in fertile soil in full sun or partial shade, good
in flower borders and tubs.
Harvest: Cut stems as needed.
Winter: Plants can be lifted in autumn and potted for the greenhouse for a winter supply.
Varieties: 'Bravour' is the prettiest curly variety, while the less
ornamental 'Plain Leaved' has a stronger flavour. 'Par-cel' is a
celery-flavoured version of the plain-leaved parsley.

ROSEMARY (ROSMARINUS OFFICINALIS)   An upright-growing
evergreen shrub sometimes reaching 5ft (1.5m), with narrow leaves
and attractive blue flowers in spring.
Uses: Use sparingly in soups and with fish, also with lamb and
poultry. Increasingly being used on barbecues.
Plant: In spring, as a specimen shrub or 2ft (60cm) apart for an
informal hedge.
Cultivation: Choose a sunny site in well-drained soil. In cold
areas or on badly drained soil, plants may die in winter. Brush snow
off branches to prevent damage. A very attractive shrub, ideal for
sunny borders.
Harvest: Cut sprigs as you need them, trying to keep the shape of
the plant well balanced.
Drying: No need, as shoots can be picked from the plant in
winter.
Varieties: 'Miss Jessup's Upright' is an elegant shape and a good
specimen plant; it's also the best for hedges. 'Severn Sea' is a dwarf
variety with especially bright blue flowers.

SAGE (SALVIA OFFICINALIS)   A low, spreading, evergreen shrub with velvety foliage and spikes of blue flowers.

Uses: Widely used in stuffings and sausages, also good with veal or pork but should be used sparingly as the flavour is strong.

Plant: In spring, 2ft (60cm) apart.

Cultivation: Choose a well-drained, sunny spot towards the front of a border. Often damaged in winter, so pruning may be necessary in spring; be prepared to replant every three or four years as the plants get bare and leggy. Shoots root where they lie on the soil.

Harvest: Remove leaves and shoots as necessary.

Drying: Although evergreen, leafage may be sparse in winter. Sage is not easy to dry, as it is very fleshy and discolours if given too high a temperature.

Varieties: 'Purpurascens' has purple leaves and 'Icterina' is green and yellow. Both are valuable ornamentals.

SUMMER SAVORY (SATUREJA HORTENSIS)   A slim annual about 12in (30cm) high, with narrow leaves and small pinkish flowers.

Uses: Strong flavour, not unlike marjoram, so use sparingly, especially with vegetables.

Sow: In April, outside where it is to grow. Thin to 6in (15cm).

Cultivation: Choose a sunny, fertile and well-drained spot. Will usually self-sow, and seedlings can be transplanted when young if necessary.

Harvest: Snip off shoots when necessary.

Drying: Cut just before flowering, spread on netting and dry cool.

Varieties: Just the one.

TARRAGON (ARTEMISIA DRACUNCULUS 'SATIVA')   A hardy herbaceous perennial, spreading by underground runners. The shoots are upright, the leaves long and narrow and the flowers small.

Uses: Very distinctive flavour, ideal for salads, vegetables and chicken.

Plant: In spring, 2ft (60cm) apart.

Cultivation: Best in a rich but well-drained soil that does not dry out, in a sunny spot. Lift and divide every three or four years in spring, or plants will deteriorate.

Harvest: Pinch off leaves whenever they are needed.

Drying: Cut shoots off at ground level as the flowers start to open and dry cool, in the dark. Avoid bruising the leaves. Once established, plants can be cut two or three times a year.

Varieties: French tarragon ('Sativa') has the finest flavour and is less vigorous than the acrid Russian type ('Inodora'), which should be avoided.

THYME (THYMUS)   Lemon thyme and garden thyme both make small, twiggy, evergreen bushes about 12in (30cm) high, with lilac or pinkish flowers.

Uses: Garden thyme has a strong aroma and should be used thoughtfully, in stuffings with pork and in *bouquet garni*. Lemon thyme is altogether more versatile, being less pungent and with a slightly citrus tang.

Plant: In spring, 6–9in (15–23cm) apart. Buy plants raised from cuttings, as those raised from seed can be variable.

Cultivation: A sunny, well-drained spot is ideal for all thymes.

Harvest: Nip off shoots whenever they're needed.

Drying: Flowering shoots about 6in (15cm) long should be laid on a tray and dried in a temperature which is not too high.

Varieties: Both these thymes have a number of variegated varieties, which are very pretty little plants but may be less sturdy.

CHAPTER SEVEN

FRUIT

The Fruit Garden

A few years ago growing fruit in a small garden would have been a problem – everything available was so big. But as techniques and varieties have been improved for the commercial fruit-grower, there have been invaluable spin-offs for anyone wanting to grow fruit in a small space.

Dwarf trees and new ways of training them have enabled apples to be grown in small spaces and even in pots; disease-resistant varieties have reduced the need for spraying; the removal of virus diseases from planting stock has greatly increased productivity, so you need far fewer plants to get a good crop. Completely new, heavy-cropping fruits like the tayberry have been invented; new pruning techniques have been developed to enable gardeners to get large crops from small trees; varieties have been developed that extend the cropping season at the beginning or the end of the season. All these innovations have made it possible to grow more and more luscious fruit from smaller and smaller spaces.

1. THE BASICS

Siting

In larger gardens fruit is usually grown in a separate area of its own; this is very practical, as it enables you to clothe the whole lot in a large, birdproof cage and so do away with endless odd bits of netting. This can be sensible in a small garden too, especially if you make the most of the protected space by moving salad crops or cut flowers into the fruit cage. But some crops, such as small-scale apples and cherries, cordon and fan-shaped trees and alpine strawberries, can be happily integrated into the rest of the garden. And most smaller fruit can be easily grown with vegetables.

Generally speaking, fruit needs an open sunny situation with shelter from the wind. Shelter is especially important in spring, when biting winds can deter vital pollinating insects. Frost is another problem that needs considering, and planting fruit in a frost pocket will increase the likelihood of damage to blossoms, ruining the crops.

Soil improvement

The soil for fruit needs to be fairly rich and well drained. The ideal requirements of different fruits vary, but in most gardens it's perfectly possible to grow a wide range of types, although sometimes careful selection of varieties will be necessary. Suitable soil can usually be created from almost any basic material except waterlogged soil, which will not grow good fruit without improvements to the drainage.

You can improve the fertility by adding liberal quantities of organic matter to dry, sandy soil and to heavy clay and then by mulching regularly.

The fruit cage

If at all possible, it pays to gather as much of your fruit as you can together in one spot and protect it from marauding birds with netting. The fruit cage is simply a netting structure supported on steel poles which keeps the birds off the crop. Fruit cages come in easy-to-build kit form and can be supplied in a size to fit your plot exactly.

Planting

Most fruit except strawberries is planted in the autumn, and details are given under the various crops.

Feeding

For most fruits, feeding consists of a dressing of fertiliser in spring immediately followed by a mulch with organic matter to keep down weeds, improve long-term fertility and provide a long, steady supply of plant foods.

General pruning advice

Pruning techniques vary considerably from crop to crop, but the one thing you must remember is that pruning is vital in a small garden. Not only will pruning restrict the size of your trees and bushes to manageable proportions, it will ensure that you pick the heaviest possible crop from your plants.

2. TECHNIQUES

Much of the traditional wisdom that is liable to be passed down to you from relations and neighbours is probably out of date or more suited to cultivation on a larger scale than this book is dealing with. Things have changed a lot in the last twenty years, and techniques which were accepted as the norm in the 1960s have been completely superseded.

Tree Fruit

A big old apple tree that fruits badly is a depressing but all too common feature of the small garden attached to an older property. But fruit trees in small gardens need not end up so large and unproductive, for there are now new techniques and new varieties that enable almost all fruits to be grown on small trees that fit a small space.

1. APPLES

The way to manage apples successfully in small gardens is by careful choice of variety and rootstock and by thoughtful pruning.

An apple tree is made up of two parts, the join usually being just above ground. The rootstock governs the eventual size of the tree, how quickly it will start to fruit and the sort of soil it will grow on. Different rootstocks are identified by a mixture of letters and numbers. Almost all of the above-ground part of the tree is the variety by which it is usually known – 'Cox's Orange Pippin', 'James Grieve', etc.

Rootstocks

There are four rootstocks suitable for apple trees grown in small gardens.

M27 produces a very dwarf tree and is the best choice for trees to be grown in pots. In the garden, a bush tree will have reached only about 6ft (1.8m) in height after fifteen years. It is unsuitable for weak-growing varieties but is good for vigorous varieties grown as cordons. This rootstock needs good soil and regular watering and feeding; trees also need a permanent stake. The first fruits will appear when the tree is two or three years old, and when five years old it will be cropping well.

M9 is a slightly less dwarfing rootstock, and is the best all-round choice in a small garden where the soil is good. It is suitable for both small bush trees, which eventually reach 7–8ft (2.1–2.4m) in height, and for cordons. Again, feeding, watering and staking will always be necessary. The first fruits will appear when the tree is three or four years old, and there should be heavy crops a couple of years later.

M26 is the best choice in a small garden with poor soil. It is similar to M9 but a little more vigorous, so will produce an altogether taller bush on good soil. The first fruits will appear when the tree is three or four years old and the crop will be heavy a couple of years later.

MM106 is an altogether less dwarfing rootstock and is not suitable for the smallest gardens or for cordons. Most trees are grown on this stock, and it is the one most widely available in garden centres. The first fruits will appear when the tree is four or five years old, and trees will be cropping well three years later.

MM111 and M2 produce large trees unsuitable for small gardens.

Training and support

In a small garden there are five forms of apple tree that are suitable – cordon, espalier, step-over, bush and column. They can also be grown in pots.

Cordon

This is a tree grown on a single stem planted at an angle of about 45° and supported on wires or a fence. You can grow a number of cordons in a relatively small space and they make a good boundary to a vegetable plot. M9 is usually the rootstock to choose, and regular pruning keeps growth limited to a single stem. Support is by a system of posts and wires; the 4 × 4in (10 × 10cm) timber posts should be 8–10ft (2.4–3m) apart, and the horizontal galvanised wires 18in apart to a height of 6ft (1.8m).

Espalier

This is a tree grown as a series of parallel tiers, supported by wires or a fence. Each tier is treated like a cordon, but although a mature espalier is very elegant, pruning and training are more difficult than for a cordon. M9 is again the right rootstock. Buy them ready trained. Their support system should be the same as for cordons.

Step-over

This is like a very low single-tier espalier trained horizontally just 12in (30cm) above the ground. Step-over trees are used as an edging to formal vegetable beds, but need M27 rootstock on all but the hungriest soils to keep them dwarf. Buy them ready trained. For support, a single wire 12in (30cm) above ground is strained between 3 × 3in (7.5 × 7.5cm) posts set 5ft (1.5m) apart.

Bush

These are easy to maintain, and popular with gardeners daunted by the supposed but non-existent difficulties of pruning cordons. Grown on M27 or M9, bush trees stay at about 6–8ft (1.8–2.4m) in height on a short trunk. Support them using a short stake, renewing whenever necessary for trees on M27.

Column

These are a recent innovation. Certain specific varieties retain a very narrow, columnar shape, reaching about 8ft (2.4m) after five years but continuing to grow. Although they take up little space, they eventually become very tall and the fruit is difficult to harvest. Usually grown on MM106. Staking is not usually necessary except on windy sites, but a short stake is a sensible precaution.

Soil and situation

Apples will grow on most soils and in most situations, although the rootstock you choose will be affected to some extent by the fertility of your soil. There are some conditions that apples do not like, although there are also remedies, as follows.

- Shallow soil over solid chalk – make a raised bed and use plenty of organic matter.
- Salt winds – set up a windbreak.
- Very heavy rainfall – no answer.
- Waterlogged soil – drain garden before planting.
- Shade – no answer.
- Very high altitudes – no answer.

This may look like a long list but these problems are specialised ones and some have solutions; in fact the vast majority of gardens will grow apples well, especially if you choose your variety and rootstock carefully.

You should expect to harvest your apple trees for many years, so it's important to prepare the planting site well in the first place. Ideally the area should be double dug (see page 61), and plenty of organic matter should be mixed into the soil so that a fertile soil is available to the roots for a good depth. If you're planting cordon trees, there's no need to dig the whole plot, simply prepare a strip 2ft (60cm) across. For bush trees planted singly, prepare an area 3ft (90cm) square. If your soil is especially heavy, add grit as well as organic matter to improve the drainage.

Planting

Trees bought or received by mail order with bare roots should first be soaked for four hours to ensure that the roots are thoroughly saturated with water. Cut back any especially long shoots or any damaged ones. Container-grown plants should be watered thoroughly.

Prepare your soil, and if planting a number of trees, mark where they are to go and decide which variety is to go where.

For free-standing bush trees, dig a hole that is both wider and deeper than the root spread or root ball of the tree. Make up a planting mix of two handfuls of bonemeal to a bucket of composted bark, or use a proprietary planting mix. Mix this into the soil in the bottom of the hole and into the soil that will go back in.

Bare-rooted trees

Bare-rooted trees should be planted only when the branches too are bare – usually from November to March. Set the tree in the hole and add or remove soil until the old soil level (visible at the top of a wet mark on the stem) is the same as the new level. Lay a board or cane across the hole to make this easy to judge. Look for a space in the roots 2–3in (5–7.5cm) from the trunk through which the stake can pass, and rotate the tree to bring this space to the windward side.

Remove the tree from the hole. Knock in a stake so that at least 12in (30cm) is below the base of the planting hole and the top of the stake is 8in above the graft (the kink in the tree stem a little way above ground level). Replace the tree and refill the hole, ensuring that your planting mixture filters in between the roots well. Jiggle the stem occasionally to help the soil filter through. Firm with the toe of your boot to ensure that there are no air spaces; do not use your heel, it's too easy to firm too hard.

Leave a ridge of soil around the edge to help retain moisture, and mulch with 2–3in (5–7.5cm) of planting mixture. Tie the tree to its stake about 6in above the graft.

Container-grown trees

Dig a hole 3–4in (7.5–10cm) deeper and at least 6in (15cm) wider than the rootball of the tree. The top of the compost in the container should be just below the existing soil level. Fork about 3in (7.5cm) of planting mixture into the base of the hole, firm it, then cut away the polythene container (or remove the rigid pot) and stand the plant in the hole. Tease out any roots which seem especially tight and tangled. Fill the gap around the root ball with a mixture of soil and planting mixture, firming with the fists as you go, leaving a slight depression to collect water. If planting when the tree is in leaf, water thoroughly and then mulch with 2–3in (5–7.5cm) of planting mixture.

Container-grown trees are best supported using two stakes, on either side of the root ball, with a tree tie fixed to both and supporting the tree 6in (15cm) above the graft. Cordon and espalier trees do not need individual staking but should be tied in securely but not tightly to their supporting wires.

Planting distances

- Cordon – 2½ft (75cm) apart.
- Espalier – 12ft (30cm) apart.
- Step-over – 5ft (1.5m) apart.
- Bush – 8ft (2.4m) apart on M9, 6ft (1.8m) apart on M27.
- Column – 3ft (90cm) apart minimum.

Initial pruning

Cordon

Cut the main shoot back, removing about one third of the brownish, unbranched growth made the previous year. Also cut back side shoots to about 3in (7.5cm). In July or August of their first year, cut back side shoots growing from the main stem to about 3in (7.5cm), and cut back growth from existing side shoots to about 1in (2.5cm).

Espalier

Buy trained trees, although these are more expensive than trees needing training. Three tiers are usually sufficient. If your tree has only two, prune the vertical shoot about 15–18in (37–45cm) above its top tier. Train one of the resulting shoots along the wire on each side, and cut out any other shoots. Prune each arm as if it was a cordon.

Step-over

Step-overs come with two shoots tied to a horizontal cane, so need little training. Treat each arm like a cordon, treating the tip of the main shoots like side shoots once they meet the shoots of the neighbouring plant.

Bush

In winter, cut back main branches by half above an outward-facing bud. Cut back weak branches by two-thirds and remove spindly branches and snags altogether. In the following year or two, cut back the five main branches by about half, and other new growth to about 3in (7.5cm). Remove any crossing or rubbing shoots and those growing across the middle of the tree.

Column

No initial pruning is usually required.

Regular pruning

Cordon

Continue to prune the main shoot back by one-third each winter until the maximum height is reached, then treat as a side shoot and prune in summer. Prune every July or August by cutting new side shoots back to 3in (7.5cm), and by cutting growth from existing side shoots to 1in (2.5cm).

Espalier

Prune each tier as for cordons.

Step-over

Prune each arm as for cordons.

Bush

Once established, prune in winter by cutting out all dead, diseased, damaged, rubbing and crossing branches and any growing across the centre of the tree. Then you must make a distinction between tip-bearing varieties like 'Worcester Pearmain' and the spur-bearing types which make up the majority.

Tip-bearing varieties produce fruit at the tips of the shoots. Cut about a third of the main shoots to good side shoots. Do not prune any shoots with fat fruit buds at their tips.

For spur-bearing varieties, you must treat the outer shoots differently from the inner ones. Outer shoots need no pruning, but inner side shoots must be cut back to about 4in (10cm) to avoid the centre becoming too crowded.

There are also some intermediate, partial tip-bearing varieties, which produce long spurs with fruit buds at the base and at the tips. Shoots longer than about 9in (23cm) should be cut back to five or six buds. Shorter laterals usually have fruit buds at their tips and are best left.

Column

No pruning necessary. If the main shoot is cut, a number of side shoots will grow up vertically, completely spoiling the shape of the tree.

Feeding

Many complicated feeding regimes have been recommended in the past, but there is a simple and effective programme which, while not giving the supreme results that a more detailed plan will produce, will still produce good grops every year.

In early spring, give 2oz (60g) of general fertiliser to the square yard (m). Growmore or fish, blood and bone are suitable. On larger trees the area close to the trunk can be left untreated, as there are no feeding roots in this area. When it has washed into the soil, mulch the whole area under the tree and out to a little beyond its spread with 2in (5cm) of well-rotted garden compost, farmyard manure or other organic matter – which should be weed-free.

Feeding larger trees growing in grass is obviously more difficult. Apply 3oz (90g) of general fertiliser and of course do not mulch. You may need to water trees growing in grass more often in summer, as the grass will take moisture which would otherwise reach the tree roots, and the lack of annual dressings of organic matter will also prevent the organic (moisture-holding) content of the soil increasing each year.

Pests

Aphids, woolly aphids, red spider mite, capsids, leaf-eating caterpillars, codling moth. (See page 380.)

Diseases

Scab, mildew, canker, brown rot, bitter pit. (See page 390.)

Pollination

The flowers of almost every apple tree must receive pollen from an apple tree of a different variety to ensure a good crop of fruits. Different varieties flower at different periods in the spring, so to enable the bees to take pollen from one tree to another, trees intended to pollinate each other must flower at the same time.

Apples can be arranged into three groups, based on their flowering times. Ideally at least two of your trees should come from the same group, but because the flowering times of consecutive groups can overlap, you will often get reasonable crops from pollination by a variety in the preceding or succeeding group.

There is one additional factor. A few varieties, known as triploids, are genetically incapable of producing pollen and so cannot pollinate other apple trees. These varieties need a pollinator, but because they produce no pollen themselves, you need a third tree to pollinate the pollinator.

Bees can fly a long way and you will often find that trees in neighbours' gardens or crab apples planted in the street will pollinate your trees. But it is unwise to rely on them, as they may be cut down or die without warning. If you find that you have one tree which is not being pollinated, a short-term solution is to cut a flowering branch from a friend's tree (a different variety, of course) and stand it in water by your tree. If you can secure it among the branches of a larger tree, so much the better. This will provide all the pollen that is required to pollinate your tree.

Eating apple varieties

COX'S ORANGE PIPPIN   This is the apple everyone names as their favourite, for its superb colour, texture and flavour. It does poorly in cold and wet areas and is susceptible to disease, so is not recommended for organic gardeners.
Pollinating group: Mid-season.
Ready to eat: Mid-September.

DISCOVERY   White, crisp, juicy fruits on a tree of upright habit. The blossom has some tolerance of frost.
Pollinating group: Mid-season.
Ready to eat: Late August.

ELLISON'S ORANGE   An easy-to-grow tree for all gardens, with frost- and disease-resistance but a distinctive flavour not enjoyed by everyone. Upright growth.
Pollinating group: Late season.
Ready to eat: Mid-September.

EGREMONT RUSSET The best russet apple, with its brown skin, yellowish flesh and nutty flavour. Growth is upright and the blossom is frost-tolerant.
Pollinating group: Early.
Ready to eat: Late September.

FIESTA A new British-bred variety, essentially a heavy cropping and grow-anywhere version of Cox, with a fine flavour and crisp, juicy fruits. Easy to grow in all areas and heavy-cropping.
Pollinating group: Mid-season.
Ready to eat: Early October.

GOLDILOCKS A new, genetically dwarf variety reaching only 4–5ft (1.2–1.5m) at maturity, so ideal for tiny gardens, narrow borders and large pots. Yellow-skinned and very juicy.
Pollinating group: Mid-season.
Ready to eat: Late September.

GREENSLEEVES A new British variety that will produce a reasonable crop without another pollinating tree. Pale yellow fruits, crisp and juicy with a good flavour. Fruits well when young. The trees are compact, the blossom is resistant to frost and it will grow in the north.
Pollinating group: Mid-season.
Ready to eat: Late September.

JAMES GRIEVE A tough and adaptable old favourite, good in the north, on poor soil and in difficult conditions. Thin skin, very juicy with a fine flavour. Also stews or bakes well. Will produce a moderate crop without a pollinator.
Pollinating group: Mid-season.
Ready to eat: Mid-September.

JESTER Easy-to-grow variety on a compact tree with crisp, juicy and tasty fruits. Compact growth, frost-tolerant blossoms, grows anywhere.
Pollinating group: Mid-season.
Ready to eat: Early September.

JONAGOLD Unusually large fruits with a rich flavour, producing

heavy crops. Rather too spreading for the smallest gardens.
Pollinating group: Late season. Triploid.
Ready to eat: Mid-October.

JUPITER   Another new British variety, similar to Cox but with
larger fruits and at least twice the crop. Rather vigorous, so a
dwarfing stock is essential.
Pollinating group: Mid-season. Triploid.
Ready to eat: Early October.

LORD LAMBOURNE   Valuable, as it thrives and crops well anywhere and in the most adverse conditions, making a small, compact
tree. Juicy and well-flavoured.
Pollinating group: Early season.
Ready to eat: Mid-September.

REDSLEEVES   A new British variety, bright red in colour and with
sweet, juicy flesh. Resistant to scab and mildew. Heavy and reliable
crops, with good harvests from young trees. Compact growth.
Produces a moderate crop without a pollinator.
Pollinating group: Mid-season.
Ready to eat: Late August.

SPARTAN   Deep, almost plum-red skin with juicy well-flavoured
flesh. A regular cropper of upright growth. Prone to canker.
Pollinating group: Late season.
Ready to eat: Early October.

SUNSET   Perhaps the best of the Cox-like varieties, a tougher
variety with better disease-resistance and a heavy and regular yield.
The flavour is wonderful.
Pollinating group: Mid-season.
Ready to eat: Late September.

WORCESTER PEARMAIN   An old favourite but becoming out-
dated. Sweet and juicy when fully ripe, and best left on the tree as
long as possible. Resistant to mildew but prone to scab and canker.
Tip-bearing.
Pollinating group: Mid-season.
Ready to eat: Early September.

Cooking apple varieties

ARTHUR TURNER   Large yellowish fruits, ideal for baking. A good cropper with upright growth, the pink flowers are also outstanding in spring. Good in the north, and produces a fair crop with no other trees to pollinate.
Pollinating group: Mid-season.
Ready to cook: August.

BOUNTIFUL   The first new cooker for many years, it has a good flavour and needs little sugar. It makes a smaller, more upright tree than 'Bramley', fruits earlier in life and is resistant to mildew.
Pollinating group: Mid-season.
Ready to cook: October.

BRAMLEY'S SEEDLING   The all-time favourite cooker, but difficult in small gardens as it makes a large, widely spreading tree.
Pollinating group: Mid-season. Triploid.
Ready to cook: November.

GRENADIER   A pale-coloured but tasty cooker which crops well, it is hardy, scab-resistant and compact in growth.
Pollinating group: Mid-season.
Ready to cook: Mid-August.

LORD DERBY   Very large fruits with white flesh that turns slightly pink when cooked. Does well in poor conditions and is disease-resistant.
Pollinating group: Late season.
Ready to cook: Late September.

Summary of pollination groups

Early season: 'Egremont Russet', 'Lord Lambourne'.
Mid-season: 'Cox's Orange Pippin', 'Discovery', 'Fiesta', 'Goldilocks', 'Greensleeves', 'James Grieve', 'Jester', 'Jupiter', 'Redsleeves', 'Worcester Pearmain', 'Arthur Turner', 'Bountiful', 'Bramley Seedling', 'Grenadier'.
Late season: 'Ellison's Orange', 'Jonagold', 'Spartan', 'Lord Derby'.

Tip bearers

'Worcester Pearmain'.

Partial tip bearers

'Bramley', 'Discovery', 'Lord Lambourne'.

Apples to avoid in small gardens

'Ashmead's Kernel', 'Early Victoria'/'Emneth Early', 'Elstar', 'Gala', 'Golden Delicious', 'Granny Smith', 'Idared', 'Newton Wonder'.

Crab apples

For crab apple jelly, the variety 'John Downie' is generally reckoned to be the best. It makes an erect tree with large orange fruits and it will also pollinate eating and culinary apples. But the best crab apple for use as a pollinator is 'Golden Hornet', with its long season of flowering followed by large golden fruit. Other varieties which are good pollinators are: 'Aldenhamensis', 'Hillieri' and 'Wintergold'.

Many of the more popular crabs are available on M27 dwarfing rootstocks, to make small trees suitable for tubs, patios or very small gardens. The best pollinators are also available as upright cordons, which can be planted by the post at the end of a row of cordon eaters and cookers to pollinate them all. This allows you to choose the culinary varieties you prefer without worrying about pollination.

2. PEARS

Pears are altogether less easy to deal with in small gardens than apples. Although looked after in much the same way, they are less reliable.

- Trees can easily become too large for small gardens.
- They flower early, so are more liable to frost damage.
- Pears dislike cold exposed sites and need more sun and shelter than apples; most will not thrive in the open in the north.

- Yields are usually lower than for apples.
- Pears are unhappy on dry, sandy soils, on chalk and by the sea.
- Drought is more of a problem than with apples.
- There are fewer varieties to choose from.

The story is not entirely gloomy, however:

- Pear trees usually live at least twice as long as apples.
- Pears thrive on heavy soil.
- Pests and diseases (except birds) are usually much less trouble-some.

Rootstocks

There are only two rootstocks available for pears and only one that should be chosen for pears in a small garden, Quince C. This is by no means as dwarfing as apple rootstocks like M27, and a bush tree will eventually grow to 8–16ft (2.4–4.8m), depending on variety and location. But it's the best there is. The other rootstock, Quince A, can produce a tree 20ft (6m) high, but should be used if you wish to attempt to grow good pears on very poor, gravelly soils. (Don't ask me what happened to Quince B!)

Training

Pears can be trained using some of the same methods as those suggested for apples – cordon, espalier or bush. However, because pears are susceptible to cold and like to be cosseted a little more than apples, it is especially sensible to grow them as cordons or espaliers.

In southerly areas, planting cordons in a sheltered spot gives them all the protection they need and the regular pruning will prevent growth getting out of hand. In the north, espalier trees are more suitable and should be trained on a sunny fence or wall where the extra protection will be much appreciated.

Soil and situation

Pears need a soil that does not dry out, so sandy, gravelly and chalky soils are unsuitable, especially if there are likely to be water shortages in your area. Most other soils can be improved with organic matter, although waterlogged soils are also unsuitable. They need protection from cold winds and early frosts, as the blossoms and also the young leaves are susceptible to damage. In the north they are best grown against fences and walls; in the south a warm sunny site, together with shelter from the north and east by evergreens, is ideal.

Planting

Planting pear trees is just the same as planting apples (page 322).

Initial pruning

As for spur-fruiting apples (page 324).

Regular pruning

As for spur-fruiting apples (page 325).

Feeding

As for apples (page 326).

Pests

Aphids, winter moth, woolly aphids, codling moth, wasps.

Diseases

Mildew, fireblight, canker, bitter pit, brown rot, scab.

Pollination

Pears cannot be pollinated by apples; they need pollinators of their own. Just like apples, you must choose two varieties that flower together so that they can pollinate each other, although some will produce quite a good crop without a pollinator. One of the tastiest is a triploid so, like triploid apples (page 327), two pollinators are needed.

Pear varieties

There are specific pears for cooking, but slightly unripe dessert pears cook perfectly well and this eliminates the need for extra varieties. Some varieties do not develop their full flavour until they have been stored for some time. These are generally unsuitable for small gardens, where there may not be enough trees to provide fruits for storage as well as eating soon after picking; and there may not be facilities for good storage.

BETH   A regular and heavy-cropping new variety, with excellent texture and delicious flavour.
Pollination group: Late season.
Ready to eat: Early September.

CONCORDE   Another new and very heavy-cropping variety, with almost double the crop of other varieties. The fruits are large, sweet and juicy. Crops well on young trees.
Pollination group: Late season.
Ready to eat: Late October.

CONFERENCE   Easy to grow in less than ideal conditions, the long, narrow fruits are very distinctive. Flavour is good but not superb. 'Conference' is good in the north and produces a fair crop without a pollinator.
Pollination group: Mid-season.
Ready to eat: Late September.

DOYENNE DU COMICE   One of the two tastiest pears, but unreliable in poor conditions, rather vigorous and can crop irregularly.
Pollination group: Late season.
Ready to eat: Late October.

DURONDEAU   One of the best small garden pears, with compact growth and the ability to crop quite well without a pollinator, especially in warm areas. Flavour is very good, and there's the bonus of flaming red autumn leaf colour.
Pollination group: Mid-season.
Ready to eat: Early October.

IMPROVED FERTILITY .   Another good small garden variety, but the flavour is less good than many. Very hardy and easy to grow, a heavy cropper, good disease resistance, and crops well without a pollinator.

Pollination group: Mid-season.
Ready to eat: Early October.

MERTON PRIDE   Wonderful flavour, with crisp flesh, but has a tendency to biennial bearing (cropping only every other year).
Pollination group: Mid-season. Triploid.
Ready to eat: Mid-September.

ONWARD   Tasty fruits, heavy crops and an upright habit are the features of this relatively new variety.
Pollination group: Late season.
Ready to eat: Mid-September.

WILLIAMS' BON CHRÉTIEN   A tasty old favourite, hardy enough for the north and a regular cropper, but susceptible to disease and rather spreading in habit.
Pollination group: Mid-season.
Ready to eat: Early September.

Summary of pollination groups

Mid-season: 'Conference', 'Durondeau', 'Improved Fertility', 'Merton Pride', 'Williams' Bon Chrétien'.
Late season: 'Beth', 'Concorde', 'Doyenne du Comice', 'Onward'.

Pears to avoid in small gardens

'Beurre Hardy', 'Seckle', 'Thompsons'.

3.   PLUMS

Plums, damsons and greengages can all be dealt with together. Damsons are smaller than plums and usually have a rather astringent flavour; greengages are especially sweet and scented but need good growing conditions to thrive.

Rootstocks

Until recently it has been hard to recommend plums for small gardens. The rootstocks available, such as St Julien A, produce trees as tall as 20ft (6m) unless pruned carefully. St Julien A should still be used on especially hungry soils in a difficult site, but in most small gardens Pixy is the rootstock to choose. It will give trees about 10ft (3m) in height and encourages the tree to fruit early.

Training

Fruits in this group are usually grown either as a bush or in colder areas as a fan on a wall.

Soil and situation

Plums and their relatives flower early and the blossom can be damaged by frost, ruining the crop. So do not plant in a frost pocket, in a site exposed to cold winds or where the early morning sun can thaw the frozen flowers quickly.

Plums prefer a rich soil, although reasonable drainage is essential. It's difficult to grow good plums on a dry, hungry soil unless it has been improved with plenty of organic matter.

Planting

Bush trees on Pixy rootstocks should be planted 8–10ft (2.4–3m) apart in November. They will need a stout stake for support. Fan-trained trees should be planted at the same time.

Initial pruning

In the first year or two, the system of building up a branch structure to form a bush tree is the same as for apples (page 324). Fans are built up in the same way as for peaches (page 343).

Regular pruning

Once established, pruning of bush trees is a simple matter, as little is needed. In June or the first half of July, remove all dead, diseased, crossing and rubbing branches and any others that need taking out to keep the tree open and prevent the branches becoming crowded. If you wish to restrict the size of the tree, cut back the current season's growth to five or six leaves.

Plums, damsons and greengages should be pruned only at this time of year, as sliver leaf, a very serious disease, infects the tree through pruning cuts at other times.

Fan-trained trees are pruned by rubbing off buds growing directly towards the wall or straight out from the wall as they start to grow in spring. In July, all the side shoots are cut back to about six leaves; after picking, all the side shoots are cut back to about half their length. Once the area to be covered is almost filled, the tips of the shoots should be dealt with in the same way.

Feeding

Give 2oz of Growmore per square yard (60g per sq m) in early spring, and mulch with well-rotted compost or other organic matter in spring when the soil is wet.

Birds

If possible, net the trees to protect the buds against bullfinches in winter and spring and the fruits against blackbirds and thrushes in summer. Wall-trained trees are the easiest to net.

Pests

Aphids, sawfly, red spider mite, wasps. Plus birds.

Diseases

Silver leaf, bacterial canker, plum pox.

Pollination

Many varieties of plums are self-fertile and so produce a good crop without a pollinator. In a small garden, where there may be room only for one tree, these are the varieties to consider first.

Plum varieties

CZAR   Most people's favourite plum for cooking, but can also be eaten fresh when fully ripe. Dark skin, yellow flesh. Very reliable in poor conditions; upright growth, good frost resistance.
Pollination: Self-fertile, no pollinator needed.
Ready to pick: August.

EDWARDS   A new variety, recommended for its heavy crop of large, sweet, juicy fruits. Blue skin with creamy flesh. Can be eaten

from the tree when fully ripe, or cooked.
Pollination: Needs a pollinator such as 'Czar', 'Victoria' or 'Merryweather' (damson).
Ready to pick: Mid-September.

MARJORIE'S SEEDLING   Good for cooking or for eating from the tree, the skin is pale blue-black and the flesh yellow. Produces a very heavy crop but the trees are rather vigorous. Flowers late, so usually misses frosts.
Pollination: Self-fertile, no pollinator needed.
Ready to pick: Late September.

OPAL   An early fruiting variety with a very heavy crop of reddish-purple fruits and yellow flesh. The flavour is outstanding.
Pollination: Self-fertile, no pollinator needed.
Ready to pick: Late July.

SANCTUS HUBERTUS   A new variety, replacing the old favourite 'Early Rivers'. Dark purple fruits with gold flesh and a very heavy crop. A culinary or straight-from-the-tree variety.
Pollination: Produces only a moderate crop without a pollinator. Best pollinated by 'Victoria', 'Czar', 'Opal', 'Edwards' or 'Merryweather'.
Ready to pick: Early August.

VICTORIA   The cherished old favourite, with pale red, yellow-fleshed fruits. Good flavour and a heavy crop, but tends to biennial cropping. Disease-resistance lower than many.
Pollination: Self-fertile, no pollinator needed.
Ready to pick: Late August.

Damson varieties

MERRYWEATHER   Blue-black skin with yellow, juicy flesh and an acidic flavour. Hardy and good in all areas.
Pollination: Self-fertile, no pollinator needed.
Ready to pick: Late September.

SHROPSHIRE DAMSON   Its compact growth makes this ideal for the small garden. Blue-black skin and a slightly greeny-yellow flesh with a very good flavour.

Pollination: Self-fertile, no pollinator needed.
Ready to pick: Late September.

Greengage varieties

DENNISTON'S SUPERB   Upright in growth, tough, reliable, hardy but rather vigorous. Delicious flavour and good in the north.
Pollination: Self-fertile, no pollinator needed.
Ready to pick: Late August.

EARLY TRANSPARENT GAGE   The best-flavoured of all the plums and gages. The fruits are yellow with red dots and the flesh pale yellow. The fruits are not large, the crop is only moderate but growth is neat and upright.
Pollination: Self-fertile, no pollinator needed.
Ready to pick: Mid-August.

Plums to avoid in small gardens

'Bullace', 'Cherry Plum', 'Pershore Yellow', 'Purple Pershore'.

4.   CHERRIES

Cherries come in two types: sweet cherries for eating straight off the tree and 'Morello' cherries for cooking. Until recently it would have been difficult to recommend any cherries for small gardens, but the arrival of the self-fertile varieties which do not need a second variety as pollinator, together with dwarfing rootstocks and special pruning techniques, have made it possible to grow cherries in a relatively confined space.

Rootstocks

There is only one rootstock suitable for cherries to be grown in small gardens, Colt. This keeps trees to about a third of the height of those grown on the previous rootstock, F12/1, that is about 12ft (3.6m) without special pruning or even 7ft (2.1m) if the branches are bent down (see page 340).

Training

Sweet cherries are grown either as bushes or, in colder areas where they do not always thrive in the open, as fans on a wall. Until the arrival of the dwarfing Colt rootstock, 'Morello' cherries were the only ones chosen for small gardens because of their less vigorous growth. They are tough enough to be grown as fans on north- or east-facing walls.

Soil and situation

All cherries prefer a good, fertile and well-drained soil and grow poorly in dry, hungry conditions. A sheltered sunny site suits them best, and they will not thrive in the shade or in a frost pocket.

Planting

Most gardens will have room for just one cherry, but if you like them so much that you want to grow two, plant them 15ft (4.5m) apart unless you intend to train them by bending.

Initial pruning

For bushes, initial pruning is the same as for plums. For fan-trained trees, follow the training regime described for peaches (page 343).

Regular pruning

Sweet cherries grown as bushes should then be treated in the same way as plums, but 'Morello' cherries are treated differently once the initial training is done. They should have all the dead, diseased, crossing and rubbing shoots removed, together with some of the branches carrying poor crops. This will stimulate the new growth which carries the fruit.

Sweet cherries grown as fans should be treated in the same way as fan-trained plums (page 336), but fan-trained 'Morellos' are pruned like peaches (page 344).

Bending

Bending is a training technique used on bush cherries to keep them to a manageable size. This makes picking easy without a ladder and enables the tree to be netted against birds.

A stout stake is knocked into the ground a short distance from the base of the young tree. In early spring, twine is tied to all the side branches and they are pulled down to just below horizontal and tied to the stake. The main shoot is tied down at a sharper angle. Each spring any branches you wish to retain are tied down in this way; others that would crowd the tree are cut out. After one year the twine can be removed and the branches will stay in their new positions.

Feeding

2oz of Growmore per square yard each spring, followed by a mulch of organic matter, is the best treatment.

Pests

Blackfly, winter moth, birds.

Diseases

Bacterial canker, silver leaf.

Pollination

'Morello' cherries are self-fertile, so need no pollinator. Older varieties of sweet cherries need a pollinating tree, but many modern varieties are self-fertile.

Cherry varieties

LAPINS   New, heavy-cropping variety with large dark red fruits which are resistant to splitting.
Pollination: Self-fertile, no pollinating tree required.
Ready to pick: August.

MERCHANT   A new British variety with heavy crops of large black fruits. The flavour is especially good and it has some resistance to bacterial canker. One of the best for pollinating other varieties.
Pollination: Not self-fertile, but can be pollinated by 'Stella'.
Ready to pick: Early July.

MORELLO   The only easy-to-find cooking cherry, the deep red fruits have a bitter-sweet flavour when ripe. 'Morello' crops well and regularly.
Pollination: Self-fertile, no pollinating tree required.
Ready to pick: August.

NAPOLEON BIGGAREAU An old favourite with very sweet red and yellow fruits which produces a heavy crop.
Pollination: Not self-fertile, pollinated by 'Stella', 'Merchant' or 'Morello'.
Ready to pick: Early August.

STELLA The first of the new generation of 100 per cent self-fertile sweet cherries. The red fruits have a good flavour and the trees are upright in growth for many years.
Pollination: Self-fertile, no pollinating tree required.
Ready to pick: Late July.

COMPACT STELLA As you might guess, a naturally compact version of 'Stella' with a very heavy crop for the size of tree.
Pollination: Self-fertile.
Ready to pick: Late July.

SUNBURST The first self-fertile black cherry, otherwise similar to 'Stella'. The flavour is excellent and the crop good.
Pollination: Self-fertile, no pollinating tree required.
Ready to pick: Early July.

5. PEACHES AND NECTARINES

Picking a peach or nectarine fresh from your own garden may be something to boast to the neighbours about, but producing a good crop is not easy. If you live in the south or in East Anglia your changes are much higher than if you live in the Midlands or the north, and wherever your garden you need a warm, sunny wall – facing south or south-west.

The problems are these. First, the flowers open very early in the spring and are easily ruined by frost. Second, even if the frost doesn't kill the flowers there may be few bees around to pollinate the flowers for you. Finally, peach leaf curl is such a menace that it may greatly reduce the crop and weaken the plant – even if it doesn't kill it.

If you still want to have a go after me doing my best to warn you off, read on. (A nectarine, by the way, is no more than a smooth peach.)

Rootstocks

Almost all peaches and nectarines are grafted on to St Julien A rootstock, which will produce a fan-trained tree about 15ft (4.5m) across. You may occasionally find plants grafted on to Pixy rootstock, and these trees will reach only about half the size of those on St Julien A.

Training

The best way to train a peach or nectarine is as a wall-trained fan on a south- or south-west-facing wall. The extra warmth and protection of the wall is necessary to help prevent the flowers being frosted. Bush trees in the open are a waste of time in most areas.

Soil

Both peaches and nectarines prefer a slightly acid soil. It should not be too well drained, and a rich, medium to heavy soil is ideal. Light soils can be improved by the addition of well-rotted compost, but gravelly soils and shallow soils over solid chalk are unlikely to be successful.

Planting

Beds at the foot of a south-facing wall can become very dry, so dig deep and mix plenty of organic matter into both lower and upper levels. Plant when the tree is dormant, usually between November and March, although container-grown trees can be planted at any time. If planting a container-grown tree in summer, be sure to keep it well watered.

The wall should be strung with wires to support the tree. Ideally these should run at 6in (15cm) intervals, starting at about 15in (38cm) above the ground. Plant about 9in (23cm) away from the foot of the wall, with the stem sloping backwards towards it. Mulch with 3in (7.5cm) of weed-free compost or well-rotted manure after planting.

Initial pruning and training

It's possible to buy partly-trained fan trees but these can be 50 per cent more expensive than young trees ready for training.

If you're starting with a young bush tree, first select two branches, one to the left and one to the right, which are growing close together low down on the plant. In early spring, just as the tree is starting to grow, cut the main stem just above the upper of the two.

Tie two 2ft (60cm) canes, one on each side, and at an angle of 45° or lower, to which the two branches should be tied. The two branches will produce shoots during the season, and it is at this stage that they are sold as partly-trained fans. As the season progresses, the best of these shoots should be selected – one to continue the growth of this main branch, one below to cover the lower area, and two above to start to fill the central area. These can be tied to canes in the same way or simply tied to wires.

In winter, cut back each shoot to an upward-facing bud, leaving about 2ft (60cm) of ripened wood. The following season train in more branches, keeping the centre open as vertically growing shoots have a tendency to become too dominant. You should aim for the branches to be spaced about 6–9in (15–23cm) apart. Some fruits may be produced in this season.

Regular pruning

Peaches produce their flowers and fruit on shoots that have grown during the previous season. So the aim must be to ensure a fresh supply of such growth each year, with older shoots that have carried fruit being removed. So every year, each old shoot must be replaced by a new shoot in approximately the same spot.

In spring look at the base of each shoot and you should find some bursting buds. Select one to produce the replacement shoot. Select another a little further along as a reserve in case the first fails.

In late spring, pinch back all other shoots to just one leaf. Allow the shoot at the tip of the fruiting branch to grow on if there is room, otherwise pinch back to four leaves. Replacement shoots can be allowed to grow to about 18in (45cm) if there is space. Any new shoots resulting from all this pinching back should themselves be pinched back to one leaf. Remove any shoots growing towards the wall or directly away from the wall. Tie in all shoots loosely to keep them stable.

After fruiting, cut back all the shoots that have produced fruit to the replacement shoot at the base and tie this in firmly. At the same time remove any weak, diseased or rubbing growth and generally tidy things up. Ensure that these new shoots are evenly spread over the wall.

Feeding

Peaches and nectarines need feeding regularly. Give 3oz of Growmore per square yard (60g per sq m) in spring, followed by a mulch of organic matter. To help with fruit development you could also give a gallon of tomato feed once a fortnight until the fruits start to ripen.

Trees planted against south walls can dry out quickly, and you may need to drench regularly in dry spells.

Fruit thinning

Well-grown fans often produce more peaches than the tree can ripen comfortably, and the result may be a large number of small fruits. To ensure that the fruits are of a good size, thin them out in early June, removing any growing next to the wall and in other congested spots, together with any others needed to leave them about 4in (10cm) apart.

Around the end of June, thin again to about 8in (20cm) apart. Nectarines need rather less thinning and can be left 6in (15cm) apart.

Pests

Aphids, red spider mite, scale.

Diseases

Peach leaf curl, bacterial canker.

Pollination

Because both peaches and nectarines flower so early in the year, when few bees will be working, they may need help from artificial pollination. They are self-fertile, so you need only one tree, but every day while the flowers are open, preferably in good weather, pollen should be transferred from one flower to another, using a cotton-wool bud.

Even on a south-facing wall it may be necessary to protect the buds and flowers against frost. This can be done by fixing netting to the wall or fence above the plant and rolling it down to ground level in the evening. It can be held away from the branches by pushing 8ft (2.4m) canes into the bed about 18in (45cm) away from the wall and securing them to the wall at the top.

Peach varieties

DUKE OF YORK   The variety with perhaps the best flavour. A vigorous, heavy cropper.
Ready to pick: Mid-July.

HAYLES EARLY   A very heavy cropper with a good flavour. Reliable in all areas. Needs thinning.
Ready to pick: Late July.

PEREGRINE   The choice of most gardeners. A heavy crop of large tasty fruit; a very reliable variety.
Ready to pick: Early August.

ROCHESTER   A late-flowering variety, so valuable when frosted blossom is a problem. Not the best for flavour, but very juicy.
Ready to pick: Mid-August.

Nectarine varieties

Nectarines are often less vigorous and more delicate than peaches and the yield lower, though some insist that the flavour is better.

EARLY RIVERS   Well-flavoured, juicy fruits and a heavy, early crop.
Ready to pick: Late July.

LORD NAPIER   Superbly flavoured aromatic fruits, regularly produced in heavy crops.
Ready to pick: Early August.

Varieties to avoid

'Bellegarde', 'Elruge', and 'Pineapple' ripen late, and are unsuitable for growing outside except in the warmest parts of the country.

6. APRICOTS

In many ways apricots are treated in much the same way as peaches, so it can be assumed that they need the same cultivation, with the following exceptions. For there are some important differences, especially in the soil required and the pruning.

Apricots have a definite preference for a well-drained, limy soil, and like nothing better than a good loam over limestone – though any well-drained limy soil will do. They especially appreciate the addition of plenty of organic matter.

Pruning of established plants is very different. Apricots fruit from spurs in the same way as apples, so there is no need to cut out shoots and train replacements every year as there is with peaches. When the framework has been built up, spurs can be encouraged by pinching out the tips of side shoots in May, when they are about 3in (7.5cm) long, then pinching back any shoots that grow later in the season to one leaf. Thinning can be less dramatic, reducing the fruits in two stages to about 3in (7.5cm) apart.

Apricots suffer from the same pests and diseases as peaches, but are also susceptible to die-back.

Apricot varieties

ALFRED   Early-ripening and juicy variety, but prone to die-back and flowers early.
Ready to pick: Early August.

MOORPARK   The most widely available variety, reliable and tasty but prone to die-back.
Ready to pick: Late August.

7. GRAPES

As our climate improves and as experience shows exactly which varieties thrive best in our climate, growing grapes in Britain is becoming increasingly popular. In colder areas, however, they are still rather a gamble, especially north of a line from Worcester to Lincoln.

Grapes can be grown in a warm, sheltered, preferably south-west-facing spot in the open, or can be trained on a south or south-west-facing wall or fence.

Training

On a fence or wall, grape vines should be trained to wires on a cordon system – though they are more often left to ramble, in which case they fruit poorly. When grown in the open they are trained on wires and a system of renewal pruning known as the Guyot system is adopted.

Soil and situation

Grapes thrive in many soils, including poor ones, as long as the soil is well drained and has plenty of added organic matter. Heavy clay soils and shallow soils over chalk are the least successful. Vines crop most reliably when trained on a sunny wall, but in the south of the country they can be grown successfully in the open as long as the site is sheltered from cold winds, faces south or south-west, gets the evening sun and is not in a frost pocket.

Supports

For growing on a wall or fence, erect wire supports 12in (30cm) apart to a height of 6ft (1.8m). Tie an 8ft (2.4m) cane pushed in by 2ft (60cm) to the wires at the site of each plant. For growing in the open, use posts and wires with 6ft (1.8m) posts knocked in to leave them 4ft (1.2m) high and positioned 5ft (1.5m) apart; a wire should be strung 18in (45cm) from the ground with two more 15in (38cm) apart.

Planting

Plant in autumn or early winter with 5ft (1.5m) between the plants, positioning a plant alongside each cane or post. Dig a good-sized hole, up to 2 × 2ft (60 × 60cm), and fork in plenty of organic matter. Mulch well after planting.

Cordon system for walls and fences

Initial pruning

Cut back the vine to 2ft (60cm) immediately after planting and tie it to the bottom wire. The following year, train the top shoot vertically up the cane and choose strong side shoots to train to left and right on alternate wires. Cut them back to five leaves and remove the flowers.

In the early winter of the second year, cut back the side shoots to about 1in (2.5cm) from the main shoot. Shorten the main vertical shoot by half.

When growth commences, choose just one shoot to train along each wire and rub off all others. Cut back this shoot two leaves beyond the flower buds and trim back any secondary shoots to just one leaf.

Regular pruning

Continue in the same way, cutting back the shoots that have carried fruit to about 1in (2.5cm) each year in early winter. After a few years fruiting, allow each fruiting lateral to grow longer and carry two or three bunches.

Continue to cut back the main shoot by half each winter until it has reached the top wire, then prune it back to 1in (2.5cm) from the old growth, treating it in the same way as side shoots.

Guyot system for posts and wire

Initial pruning

Immediately after planting, cut back the main stem to around the level of the bottom wire, ensuring that there are three strong buds at about this level.

During the following season, train the three shoots from these buds vertically and tie them in loosely to the post. Rub out any other shoots that grow from lower down.

In late winter, untie the three vertical shoots, train two of them horizontally and tie them in well to the bottom wire. Trim them at about 2ft (60cm). Cut back the middle shoot to three buds.

Regular pruning

Each season the shortened central shoot will produce three shoots, which are tied in vertically as they grow and then treated as above. But as these are growing, vertical shoots will also grow from the two shoots tied in horizontally, and it is these shoots that will carry the fruit. Tie these shoots in as they reach each wire and pinch out the tips when they pass the top wire.

Allow a total of only four bunches of grapes to develop in the first year. One bunch per shoot can be allowed to mature in subsequent years. After fruiting, cut out completely the horizontal shoots and the subsidiary vertical shoots that have carried fruits.

Continue this system indefinitely, so that the shoots to be trained horizontally for the following year's crop are retained in a vertical position while the current season's crop develops.

Feeding

Feed with a handful of Growmore around the base of each vine in early spring, then mulch generously with well-rotted manure or weed-free compost. For the best quality, give a liquid feed of tomato fertiliser every two weeks as the fruits develop.

Pests

Birds and wasps.

Diseases

Mildew and botrytis.

Pollination

All grapes are self-fertile, so pose no pollination problems.

Harvesting

When the stems turn brown the grapes are ready to pick. Cut them off carefully using secateurs and keeping a couple of inches of branch attached. Handle them gently, especially if they are for table use.

Grape varieties

Not all varieties are suitable for growing outside in Britain – many are for greenhouse cultivation only.

BRANDT Tough, black-fruited variety with many small bunches of tiny but very sweet grapes. Very good autumn foliage colour. *Ready to pick*:   Mid-October.

MÜLLER-THURGAU   A golden grape, very popular for wine-making, producing a hock-like wine. Not the best for eating fresh. Best on a wall.
Ready to pick: Late September.

SEYVAL BLANC   An easy and reliable green-skinned grape, good on chalky soils and in cold gardens. Makes a light and fruity wine and has some resistance to mildew.
Ready to pick: Late September.

FRAGOLA   Small bunches of very large grapes with a wonderful musky flavour with a hint of strawberry, hence known as the 'strawberry grape'. Good autumn colour. Best on a wall.
Ready to pick: September.

MADELAINE SILVANER   A very pale grape, happier than most in cool conditions. Very good for wine, less good to eat fresh.
Ready to pick: September.

Varieties to avoid in small gardens

Well-known varieties like 'Muscat of Alexandria' and 'Black Hamburg' are for greenhouses only.

Cane Fruit

Cane fruit includes raspberries, loganberries, blackberries and a number of lesser-known but sometimes very tasty hybrid berries. All are characterised by their long, generally spiny shoots, which usually grow during one season and carry their fruit in the next. They are among the tastiest of all fruits and also some of the easiest to grow.

1.   RASPBERRIES

One of the most popular of cane fruits, raspberries need a fair amount of space and are not the ideal crop for a small garden.

However, many gardeners will want to try a short row if they like soft fruits, even if almost the whole crop is eaten at one summer party.

Soil and situation

Raspberries are at their best in a rich, well-cultivated soil that is neither heavy and sticky, nor gravelly and dry; wet, sticky soils are especially disliked. Most soils can be improved by digging in organic matter, but raspberries will not be at their best in drier parts of the country unless they can be well watered. They are especially successful in the damper west and north, especially in Scotland.

Planting

Planting is best carried out in November. Raspberries are supplied as canes, which are short lengths of stems with a length of creeping root attached, usually in bundles of five, ten, or fifteen. They are planted so that the top roots are about 2in (5cm) below the surface, with any new buds at about soil level. Keep them well watered during their first summer.

It is essential to plant only certified virus-free stock. Raspberries suffer from a number of debilitating virus diseases which can ruin the crop and infect the soil. The Ministry of Agriculture runs a scheme by which stock is inspected on the nursery and if free of virus diseases is given a certificate. Only by buying certified stock can you be sure of buying virus-free canes which will give good crops and prevent your soil becoming infected. Nurseries will always state in their catalogue or in their advertisements if their stock is certified virus-free.

There are a number of systems of planting and training, but the simplest is to plant the canes in rows 2ft (60cm) apart with 5ft (1.5m) between the rows.

Supports

During the winter after planting or after the first season's growth, posts and wires must be erected to support the canes. I've seen raspberries trained on trellis but this is an expensive option, though more decorative in winter. Use 8ft (2.4m) pressure-treated, 3 × 3in (7.5 × 7.5cm) fence posts, driven 2ft (60cm) into the soil or fixed with metal fence spikes. The posts should be 10ft (3m) apart.

Use 6in (15cm) straining bolts to tension the wire, drilling just below the top of each post and also at 2ft (60cm) and 4ft (1.2m) from the ground. Soak the holes in plenty of timber preservative after drilling to prevent rotting. Use 13 gauge galvanised wire between the posts.

Tie the canes in to the wires either individually or by looping soft twine around both the wire and the canes, leaving the canes about 3–4in (7.5–9cm) apart.

Initial pruning

Prune the canes back to 12in (30cm) immediately after planting if this has not already been done by the nursery.

Regular pruning and training

Fruit is carried on short side shoots growing from canes which developed during the previous season. So the new shoots are tied in as they grow and are nipped off 6in (15cm) above the topmost wire or, better still, looped over and the tip tied in to the wire. This will increase the crop but may necessitate the use of steps for tying in and picking. As these canes are carrying fruit, new canes will be growing up from below and these need tying in loosely to prevent them waving about and damaging themselves or you.

As soon as the fruit has been picked, the canes which have carried the fruit are cut off at ground level and removed. There is now space for the new shoots to be tied in securely. Retain up to nine in each position, pulling out the weakest. Remove also any canes growing away from the main cluster.

Single post system

In very small gardens, where there is not room for a row of raspberries but where a few canes would be appreciated, two canes can be grown up a single post which can be sited at the end of a vegetable bed or even in a border. Use an 8ft (2.4m), 3 × 3in (7.5 × 7.5cm) post knocked in by 2ft (60cm). Two canes can be planted alongside the post and all growth secured to the post with two or three loops of soft string. This is a fiddly way of growing raspberries but useful if space is very short.

Feeding

Apply Growmore at 2oz per square yard (60g per sq m) along the row in March, then mulch with well-rotted garden compost, manure or other peat-free organic matter. Water generously in dry spells in summer.

Autumn-fruiting varieties

All the above advice applies to summer-fruiting varieties, but there are also a small number of autumn-fruiting types. These are grown in the same way, although they are best at 15in (38cm) apart; they grow to only about 5ft (1.5m), so need shorter posts and fewer wires. They are also pruned differently: all the canes are cut down completely every winter.

Pests

Aphids, raspberry beetle, birds, raspberry moth.

Diseases

Virus, cane blight, spur blight, grey mould.

Raspberry varieties

AUTUMN BLISS   The best autumn-fruiting raspberry, very heavy-cropping, with large tasty berries. Short growth, so may not need support at all. Supersedes the more familiar 'Zeva'.
Ready to pick: August and September.

DELIGHT   Very heavy crop of large fruits, though the flavour could be better. Not good in the wettest areas.
Ready to pick: July.

GLEN CLOVA   Probably the best for small gardens, as it ripens early but crops for many weeks. Excellent flavour and a good yield. Makes tall canes.
Ready to pick: July and August.

GLEN MOY   Large tasty fruits on thorn-free canes, and you may get a small autumn crop as well as the main pick. Virus-resistant.
Ready to pick: Early July, plus possibly September.

MALLING JOY   Very heavy-cropping, so ideal when there's space for only a short row. Dark tasty fruits on very spiny canes, with a long season.
Ready to pick: Late July and August.

MALLING PROMISE   Early-fruiting and heavy-cropping but poorly-flavoured variety that thrives on poor soil.
Ready to pick: Early July.

SCEPTRE   Self-supporting canes carry a very heavy autumn crop of exceptionally large and tasty berries.
Ready to pick: Early September.

Not for small gardens

The tangy 'Leo', the tasty but tall and floppy 'Malling Admiral', the old favourite 'Malling Jewel' and the superseded 'Zeva' all produce yields which are low compared with other varieties – which is important if you have space for only a short row.

2.   BLACKBERRIES

Blackberries take up much more room than raspberries. Even the most compact variety needs 6ft (1.8m) per plant, while the largest needs 15ft (4.5m) – which might be the full length of your garden! But if you're especially fond of blackberries there are worse things to do with a north- or east-facing fence than train a blackberry on it.

They are difficult to manage in a small space, though, as the canes of even the shortest varieties are too long to train vertically. With blackberries growing so luxuriantly in the hedgerow people sometimes wonder why they are grown in gardens, but by choosing the right varieties you can grow a very heavy crop of large juicy berries with a superb flavour – and there are thornless varieties too.

Soil and situation

Blackberries are tough; they will thrive in most soils and situations, although soggy soils and thin, dry soils over chalk are not usually satisfactory. They are ideal for training against a fence or trellis, but thornless varieties should be chosen if they are planted near a path.

Although they will thrive in most situations, blackberries are best grown in the open in full sun. They will produce a fair crop against a north-facing fence or even an east-facing one, as they flower after the last frosts. They will not do well if shaded from overhead.

Planting

Planting is best done in November, using certified virus-free stock as for raspberries. They will be available as individual bare-root or container-grown plants, and while the latter can be planted at any time, planting in the autumn removes the necessity for regular watering while they become established.

Fortunately it's not necessary to dig the whole area which the top growth of the blackberry will cover, but it pays to take out a hole 2ft (60cm) square, fork some organic matter into the bottom, return some of the soil, then fork some into the top too. Plant in the same way as raspberries, but leave a shallow depression around each plant to help collect water; then rake in 2oz (60g) or so of Growmore. Mulch around the roots with well-rotted compost or manure if you have it.

Supports

If you intend growing blackberries in an open situation, you can erect square-patterned trellis or post and wire supports as suggested for raspberries. But you will need more wires. 8ft (2.4m) posts should be set 2ft (60cm) into the ground, with wires strung at heights of 3ft (90cm), 4ft (1.2m), 5ft (1.5m) and just below 6ft (1.8m). Wires at the same heights can be strung on a fence or wall.

Initial pruning

When planting in November, cut back all shoots to 12in (30cm), but if planting container-grown plants in spring or summer, leave unpruned.

Regular pruning and training

There are a number of systems for training blackberries. Like raspberries, they produce fruit on shoots which grew the previous year, and the idea behind most training systems is to keep the new shoots separate from the fruiting shoots. This prevents the spread of disease and makes the fruits easier to pick.

Some methods, while effective, produce plants which are not particularly attractive to look at – an important factor in a small garden. Some of the simpler and less time-consuming methods also produce relatively low yields, and when you may be growing only one plant, you should aim for the heaviest possible crop. So although the method I'm going to suggest is probably the most time-consuming, it's also the most elegant and will produce the heaviest crop.

As the new shoots grow in the spring, they are tied in together loosely in a vertical position. When they reach the top wire they are divided into the two groups and tied in – half along the wire to the left, half to the right. During the winter the canes are untied from their temporary vertical position and retied in a fan shape, spacing the canes out evenly with the lowest canes at an angle of about 45° to the ground or slightly lower. Tie each cane to each wire as it crosses it. When the new canes start to grow the following year, these are again tied in vertically and then along the top wire. Any time after fruiting, but usually during the winter, all the old fruiting canes are cut out at ground level and the new growth is spaced out and tied in to create a new fan.

Feeding

Generous feeding will produce a generous crop. Apply Growmore at 2oz (60g) per plant in March, perhaps increasing this amount by half as the plants get older or on very light soils. Follow up with a mulch of 2–3in (5–7.5cm) of well-rotted compost, manure or a proprietary mulch.

Pests

Raspberry beetle.

Diseases

Botrytis, cane spot, spur blight, virus.

Blackberry varieties

I would suggest that whether you have 8ft (2.4m) or 16ft (4.8m) of space, you still put in only a single plant, as one is so much easier to manage than two. So here I will list both the compact varieties and the large vigorous ones, but specify the space they occupy.

Some varieties are rather late to mature, so can be spoiled by frost in northern areas before the crop is all picked. So the colder your garden, the more you should concentrate on earlier varieties, especially if you grow them in the open rather than against a fence or wall.

ASHTON CROSS   Genuine wild blackberry flavour but with a very heavy crop. Good for eating straight from the plant, for pies and for freezing – if there are any left over.
Prickliness: Average.
Space needed per plant: 12ft (3.6m).
Ready to pick: Early August to late September.

BEDFORD GIANT   A very vigorous variety, very early and especially tolerant of poor conditions, but the flavour and yield are only average.
Prickliness: Above average.
Space needed per plant: 15ft (4.6m).
Ready to pick: Late July to late August.

BLACK SATIN   Heavier-cropping and earlier than other thornless varieties, but needs sun to thrive and flavour is only average.
Prickliness: No prickles.
Space needed per plant: 12ft (3.6m).
Ready to pick: Late July to late August.

FANTASIA   Heavy crop of exceptionally large fruits the size of a 10p piece. Flavour and yield quite good.
Prickliness: Below average.
Space needed per plant: 15ft (4.6m).
Ready to pick: Late July to late August.

HIMALAYAN GIANT   Rather acid flavour, so better for cooking than for eating fresh. This is the least suitable variety for small gardens, due to its vigour and thorns.
Prickliness: Vicious.
Space needed per plant: 15ft (4.6m).
Ready to pick: Late August to late September.

LOCH NESS   A new variety with short upright stems that can be grown more like a summer-fruiting raspberry. Flavour and yield are quite good.
Prickliness: Average.
Space needed per plant: 4–6ft (1.2–1.8ft).
Ready to pick: Late August to late September.

MERTON THORNLESS   An ideal small garden variety with compact growth, good flavour and yield and no thorns.
Prickliness: No prickles.
Space needed per plant: 8ft (2.4m).
Ready to pick: Mid-August to mid-September.

OREGON THORNLESS   Another excellent thornless variety, and the best for a small garden if you have the space, as it is blessed with attractive dissected foliage which colours well in autumn. Large, tasty fruits in generous quantities but rather late.
Prickliness: No prickles.
Space needed per plant: 10ft (3.9m).
Ready to pick: Late August to late September.

3.   HYBRID BERRIES

There are a number of berried fruits derived from crossing blackberries, raspberries and various similar wild fruits, some of which are well worth growing. They are grown like blackberries. The following are those which you are most likely to come across.

BOYSENBERRY   Looks like a big, dark, slightly stretched raspberry but with a blackberry flavour. Especially good on sandy soils and in dry areas.
Prickliness: Above average, but there is a thornless version.
Space needed per plant: 8ft (2.4m).
Ready to pick: July and August.

HILDABERRY   Big, red, tasty fruits which are ideal for eating fresh and especially for jam. Very early, with a good yield and with unusually large and attractive flowers – up to 2in (5cm).

Prickliness: Average.
Space needed per plant: 8ft (2.4m).
Ready to pick: Late June to late July.

LOGANBERRY   The most familiar hybrid, with distinctive, long, dark red fruits with a sharp flavour. Best for cooking rather than for eating fresh.
Prickliness: The usual variety, known as LY59, is quite thorny, but L654 is thornless and less vigorous.
Space needed per plant: 8ft (2.4m).
Ready to pick: Early July to the end of August.

SUNBERRY   Large conical fruits in rich dark purple and with a good acid flavour. Vigorous.
Prickliness: Above average.
Space needed per plant: 15ft (4.6m).
Ready to pick: Mid-July to late August.

TAYBERRY   Probably the best of the hybrid berries, the fruits resemble large, dark purple loganberries but the flavour is sweeter. A heavy cropper, but less successful in cold areas.
Prickliness: Few prickles.
Space needed per plant: 8ft (2.4m).
Ready to pick: Early July to mid-August.

TUMMELBERRY   Similar to the tayberry, but bred for toughness and losing a little sweetness in the process. Large red fruits.
Prickliness: Stiffly hairy rather than prickly.
Space needed per plant: 8ft (2.4m).
Ready to pick: Mid-July to late August.

VEITCHBERRY   A good crop of very large, dark red fruits with an excellent flavour, but the fruit is a little difficult to pull off the plugs.
Prickliness: Average.
Space needed per plant: 8ft (2.4m).
Ready to pick: August and September.

Bush Fruit

It's doubtful whether most small gardens can justify giving space to bush fruits, but if you especially like currants or gooseberries, then it is possible to fit them in. Dessert gooseberries are perhaps the best value, as it's not easy to buy good ones in the shops. Good quality blackcurrants are easier to buy, but it is worth considering growing red and white currants if you like them, as again they are not always easy to track down, even on pick-your-own farms.

1.   BLACKCURRANTS

In some ways blackcurrants are similar to raspberries, in that the fruits are carried on the previous year's shoots at the same time that new shoots are growing for the following year. So correct pruning is crucial. New varieties have made blackcurrants a far easier crop for the less experienced or busy gardener, superseding most of the old favourites.

Soil and situation

Blackcurrants are tolerant plants and should thrive in most soils, while doing better in damp conditions than most other fruits. But they appreciate a rich soil that has been improved with plenty of organic matter. They prefer an open, sunny situation but will tolerate a little shade.

   Frost can ruin the crop by damaging the flowers, so do not plant them in a frost pocket or in a position exposed to east winds.

Planting

It is normally suggested that blackcurrants are planted in rows 5ft (1.5m) apart with 6ft (1.8m) between the rows. If you follow this traditional approach, you should prepare for planting by digging out a hole 2ft (60cm) square and 1ft (30cm) deep. Fork plenty of organic matter into the bottom of the hole, then partially refill, forking more organic matter into the top layer.

   To maximise your limited space in a small garden, however, you can plant the individual bushes at half the normal spacing within the row, although this will of course cost you twice as much. The result of this close planting is to produce about twice as much fruit for a given length of row for the first few years, although after a while yields will drop back to normal.

Plant the bushes in November if possible, and certainly before Christmas, as blackcurrants start into growth unusually early in the year. Plant 3–4in (7.5–10cm) deeper than you would normally, to encourage the production of new shoots from below ground level.

Initial pruning

Cut back all shoots 1in (2.5cm) above the ground immediately after planting; no fruit will be produced in the first year. At the end of the first year, remove any spindly shoots and cut off one of the main shoots at the base to encourage fresh shoots during the first cropping season.

Regular pruning

The shoots that grow during the first season carry fruits the following year. After fruiting, these shoots can be cut back to a new side shoot or to the base of the plant to stimulate fresh growth for fruiting the following year. As the bush builds up in size you will need to be more brutal, and you should aim to cut out at least a quarter and probably a third of the old shoots each autumn. Mature bushes should have no wood at all that is more than four years old.

There is another way of going about things which is simpler and a little less refined. Instead of picking the fruit and then pruning later, the branches carrying the fruit are cut off when it's ripe – the whole branch is harvested. You then sit in a deckchair and pull the fruit off their stalks with a dinner fork. In effect you are harvesting and pruning in one go, and the amount of back-breaking work is reduced. This is rather a rough and ready approach, but one which generally works quite well.

Feeding

Blackcurrants like rich feeding. Give each bush 4oz (110g) of Growmore every March and follow up with a mulch of 3in (7.5cm) of well-rotted compost or manure, covering the complete area under the branches.

Pests

Big bud mite/reversion virus, aphids.

Diseases

Leaf spot, American gooseberry mildew.

Blackcurrant varieties

Recent developments in blackcurrants have seen the introduction of late-flowering and frost-resistant varieties which avoid the problem of late frosts ruining the crop. These have more or less superseded older but more familiar names. More compact but heavy-cropping varieties are also now appearing, and these are ideal for the small garden.

BEN LOMOND   Exceptionally large berries of good flavour, dark colour and high vitamin C content but with tough skins. Good frost resistance but susceptible to mildew. Upright habit.
Ready to pick: Late July.

BEN MORE   Easy-to-manage variety and the most frost-resistant of all, with a sharp flavour but low on vitamin C. The yield is only moderate.
Ready to pick: Early August.

BEN NEVIS   A taller, more vigorous version of 'Ben Lomond', ripening a little earlier and doing well on poor soil. Good mildew and frost resistance.
Ready to pick: Late July.

BEN SAREK   Probably the best variety for a small garden, as the bush is very compact yet the crop very heavy. Good flavour plus frost and mildew resistance, but the floppy branches may need supporting and the fruit needs picking promptly or it drops off. Plant 3ft (90cm) or 1½ft (45cm) apart.
Ready to pick: Mid-July.

WELLINGTON XXX   This old variety is still recommended if a superb flavour is your main criterion. But the growth is vigorous

and spreading and the crop is often damaged by frost.
Ready to pick: Mid-July.

Varieties to avoid

'Boskoop Giant', 'Laxton Giant' and 'Malling Jet' are too vigorous
for most small gardens, 'Black Reward' and 'Tsema' suffer badly
from mildew, while 'Baldwin' has a very moderate crop compared
to the 'Ben' varieties and suffers from frost.

2.   GOOSEBERRIES

Although gooseberries will continue to produce fruits even when
completely neglected, as you can see on abandoned allotments, they
need care and attention in order to crop heavily. They can be grown
as bushes or cordons, and you should make sure you specify your
preferred type when ordering.

Soil, situation and planting

Gooseberries are best on a well-drained but rich soil, though they
will produce a good crop in a wide variety of conditions. Prepare
the soil and plant, preferably in the autumn, as for blackberries and
blackcurrants, with the bushes planted 5ft (1.5m) apart.

Gooseberries can also be grown as cordons, and this is a very
good way of treating them in small gardens. It also makes it easier to
pick the fruits without getting scratched by the vicious thorns. They
can be trained on a fence or on a system of posts and wires.

Supports for cordons

A post and wire structure similar to that used for raspberries should
be erected, with the wires strung at 12in (30cm).

Pruning

Different varieties of gooseberries vary in their growth habit and
this dictates exactly where the pruning cuts are made. Varieties with
an upright growth habit are pruned to a bud facing outwards, while
those with a spreading habit are pruned back to buds facing

inwards. This prevents the over-development of the growth habits
of the individual varieties.

Initial pruning

Bushes

Cut all low branches off flush with the stem, to produce a leg about
6in (15cm) high. The long-term aim is to create a bowl- or
vase-shaped bush with an open centre, so any branches which will
grow across the centre can also be cut off flush with the stem at this
stage. Cut back all other branches by half unless this has already
been done by the supplier.

Initial pruning

Cordons

Single and double cordons are available, the former with a single
stem and the latter with a pair of stems which are trained in parallel.
If growing a double cordon, prune each stem as if it were a single
cordon. Cut back the one main shoot to about half its length if this
has not already been done by the supplier, and trim all side shoots
to a bud, leaving short shoots about 1in (2.5cm) long.

Regular pruning

Bushes

Gooseberries are pruned twice a year, in winter and in late June.
Unlike blackcurrants, the idea is to build up a permanent
framework of branches into a bowl- or vase-shaped plant on which
fruit will be carried year after year.

In late June all the new side shoots are pinched back to four or
five leaves from the base of the shoots. In winter any diseased or
spindly shoots are cut out completely, and any growing into the
centre of the bush are also removed. This is necessary to maintain
the necessary open shape. All the new growth made on the main
shoots during the previous season is then cut back by about half.
Side shoots are pruned too, reducing them to a length of about 2in
(5cm).

Regular pruning

Cordons

In late June cut back all the side shoots to four or five leaves. In winter prune back the main shoot on each cordon to leave about 6in (15cm) of the previous season's growth, and at the same time cut back all the side shoots to about 1in (2.5cm). When the main shoot reaches the top of its supports, treat it as a lateral and cut it back to 1in (2.5cm).

Feeding

Apply about 3oz (75g) of Growmore to each bush in March, or 1oz to every yard run (30g per metre) of cordons. Follow up with a 3in (7.5cm) mulch of well-rotted compost, manure or proprietary mulch.

Pests

Birds, gooseberry sawfly.

Diseases

American gooseberry mildew, leaf spot, grey mould.

Gooseberry varieties

Some varieties are best for cooking, other for eating fresh, while some are dual-purpose – the unripe fruits can be cooked, the ripe ones eaten fresh. In a small garden, dual-purpose varieties with an upright habit seem to offer the best value.

INVICTA Superb gooseberry for cooking, mildew-resistant and smooth-skinned. It's a very heavy cropper with a very good flavour for cooking, but is less good for eating fresh.
Growth habit: Spreading.
Ready to pick: Late July.

JUBILEE A fine dual-purpose variety with a good flavour both ripe and for cooking.
Growth habit: Upright.
Ready to pick: Mid-July.

KEEPSAKE The earliest to pick for cooking, with a fine flavour, but also excellent when left to ripen. Susceptible to mildew.
Growth habit: Spreading.
Ready to pick: Early July.

LEVELLER One of the tastiest for eating fresh, but at its best only on good soil, where it produces heavy crops of very large fruits. 'Whinham's Industry' is often a better bet.
Growth habit: Spreading.
Ready to pick: Late July.

WHINHAM'S INDUSTRY Excellent flavour, on an upright plant which thrives on most soils and ripens to a rich dark red. Also good in partial shade.
Growth habit: Upright.
Ready to pick: Late July.

Avoid 'Howards Lancer', which is very vigorous and spreading in its habit and also throws a lot of suckers.

3. RED AND WHITE CURRANTS

In their cultivation, red and white currants are more akin to gooseberries than to blackcurrants, and the advice given above for gooseberries can be confidently followed. Red currants are used exclusively in sauces and preserves, while white currants are sweet enough to eat fresh.

Pests

Birds, aphids.

Diseases

Coral spot, leaf spot.

Red currant varieties

JOHKHEER VAN TEETS The earliest and one of the tastiest varieties, but with its vigorous and untidy growth it is best grown as a cordon.
Ready to pick: Early July.

REDSTART Impressive late-cropping variety with very heavy crops of rather acid fruits ideal for jelly.
Ready to pick: Early August.

RED LAKE Reliable old favourite, with a good crop and a good flavour.
Ready to pick: Late July.

ROVADA A new late variety, and potentially the heaviest cropping of all. Flavour good.
Ready to pick: Early August.

STANZA A compact variety, but producing a heavy crop of unusually dark fruits with a good flavour.
Ready to pick: Late July.

White currant varieties

WHITE VERSAILLES Reliable, heavy-yielding, easy-to-grow variety with a pleasant sweet flavour.
Ready to pick: Early July.

WHITE GRAPE Superb flavour, better than 'White Versailles', but a lighter crop.
Ready to pick: Mid-July.

Ground Fruit

1. STRAWBERRIES

Perhaps the most popular of soft fruits, the strawberry is not the easiest to grow well. However, modern varieties can give a very large crop from a relatively small space if cultivated carefully. Always order certified virus-free stock, as these are the most productive plants.

Soil and situation

Strawberries grow best in an open site sheltered from strong winds. They will grow in most soils, although heavy soils and sandy, free-draining soils need to be improved by digging in plenty of organic matter. Rake in Growmore at 2oz per square yard (60g per sq m) before planting.

To maintain productive disease-free plants, strawberries are usually grown on a rotation system, so that after every four years completely new stock is introduced. This is best planted in a new part of the garden to help prevent the carry-over of disease. Other fruits or vegetables can follow or precede strawberries.

Alpine strawberries are best in partial shade and can be planted between cordon fruits or in flower borders. They are raised from seed every two years.

Planting

Strawberries are best planted in July or August, and pot-grown plants are available for planting at that time. Grow them on a bed system; they can be sited at the ends of vegetable deep beds. Plant in a staggered double row along the length of the bed, with 2ft (60cm) between the rows and 18in (45cm) between plants in the rows. They should be planted with the surface of the compost on the roots at ground level.

Maintenance

The most productive method of growing strawberries is to allow some of the runners to root into the soil around the plants, creating more new plants which will also carry fruit. The first seven to ten runners are pegged down in a ring about 9in (23cm) all around each plant, and any subsequent runners from the new plants or the main plants are cut off. This system should give an increase in yield of about 40 per cent compared with the normal system of removing all runners, but the plants need regular attention to ensure that only a limited number of runners are allowed to root and develop. In a small garden, where you'll probably not have a large strawberry bed, this is at least possible.

As the fruit develops it should be protected from slugs and splashes by placing small mats or straw under the trusses of fruit as they start to develop. After fruiting the straw is removed and composted, weeds are removed, and all the old foliage is cut off. If conditions are dry at this stage, more water will be required to help build up productive plants for the following year.

Feeding and watering

Spread Growmore at 2oz per square yard (60g per sq m) over the bed in March and sulphate of potash at 1oz per sq yd (30g per sq m) after fruiting.

Watering is essential to ensure a heavy crop of succulent fruits, and if drought is a problem a heavy soak with a sprinkler after flowering will be necessary.

Containers

Strawberries can also be grown in containers – half barrels, large pots, growing bags or purpose-made tower pots. This is an interesting rather than a productive method of growing strawberries, but is a useful way of producing a small crop if there's no room for plants in the garden.

Pests

Capsids, aphids, leatherjackets, red spider mite, tortrix moths.

Diseases

Botrytis, mildew.

Strawberry varieties

There are four types of strawberry grown. Apart from the familiar summer strawberries there are also autumn or perpetual fruiting types which carry fruit in flushes in late summer and early autumn. You may also come across day neutral strawberries, which behave like autumn types outside but crop until Christmas if grown in a greenhouse. Finally there are the small-fruited but tasty alpine or wild types.

Summer strawberry varieties

HAPIL   A tasty, heavy-cropping variety which does especially well on light and sandy soils.
Ready to pick: Mid-June to mid-July.

HEDLEY   By far the best for jam, this variety has an upright growth habit and a wonderful flavour.
Ready to pick: Early to late June.

HONEOYE   A new, very heavy-cropping early variety, with a better flavour than 'Pantagruella' but a few days later.
Ready to pick: Early to late June.

PANTAGRUELLA   The earliest of all varieties, and a neater grower than most so can be spaced closer. Flavour and yield are good but not stunning. Usually needs watering.
Ready to pick: Late May to mid-June.

ROYAL SOVEREIGN   A classic from the past, rejuvenated since it has been freed from virus. Wonderful flavour, moderate crop.
Ready to pick: Early to late June.

TENIRA   My favourite for flavour, and more vigorous and heavier-cropping than 'Royal Sovereign'. Also holds its fruit off the ground.
Ready to pick: Early to late July.

Autumn strawberry varieties

AROMEL   Another berry with fantastic flavour, best prevented from cropping early to boost the later, otherwise moderate, crop.
Ready to pick: August to October, in flushes.

RAPELLA   Heavier-cropping than 'Aromel', though the flavour is less good.
Ready to pick: August and September.

Alpine strawberry varieties

BARON SOLEMACHER   Very tasty, small fruits produced in huge numbers for many weeks. Upright plants with no runners.
Ready to pick: July onwards.

Day neutral strawberry varieties

SELVA   Poor flavour, but the best of this type if you fancy keeping a few in the conservatory for Christmas.
Ready to pick: August onwards outdoors, up to Christmas if protected.

2.   RHUBARB

Is it a fruit or a vegetable? I reckon that as we eat it for pud it's a fruit. Like so many other fruits, the arrival of virus-free stock has greatly improved productivity.

Soil and situation

Rhubarb is happy in most soils that are not too wet. But it likes rich conditions so dig in plenty – and I mean plenty – of well-rotted manure or compost before planting. Finish off with 8oz (225g) of bonemeal for each planting site. Choose an open or partially shaded spot for the best results.

Planting

Pot-grown plants can go in at any time, mature roots are planted in winter. If you put in more than one, which is unlikely as they are very productive when mature, put them 2½ft (75cm) apart. After ten or twelve years the plants are best replaced, as they tend to decline.

Feeding

Feed each plant with 4oz (120g) of bonemeal per plant in the autumn and then mulch with 3in (7.5cm) of well-rotted compost or manure in the autumn.

Forcing

Leave the plants to get established in their first year without cutting any stems. In the next year you can pull stems, finishing in June, and don't force them until their third year. You can use antique earthenware forcing pots, but although these are the most elegant, an upturned black plastic dustbin with a paving slab on the top is simpler to manage. Put the bin in position in December after the plants have been well frosted, and remove in March to allow them to grow on normally.

Pests

Aphids.

Diseases

Virus.

Rhubarb varieties

CAWOOD DELIGHT   Produces sticks early without forcing, and although the yield is low they are a wonderful deep red.

GLASKIN'S PERPETUAL   Raised from seed and without the bitterness of other varieties late in the season, so can be pulled until November if given a year to recover. So you need at least two plants.

STOCKBRIDGE ARROW   The best for forcing, with long, fat, deep red sticks and an excellent flavour.

TIMPERLEY EARLY   Naturally the earliest of all, and good for forcing too, but with only a moderate flavour and yield of rather narrow sticks.

The orange and yellow of achillea and heleniums are beautifully set off by the purple smoke bush behind.

The fiery autumn colour of the stag's horn sumach, *Rhus cotinus*, really lights up the garden at the end of the season.

The long catkins of *Garrya elliptica* 'James Roof' are especially welcome in winter.

Brooms like 'C. E. Pearson' are good plants for new gardens as they grow quickly and thrive in poor soil.

Fremontodendron 'California Glory' is a quick-growing shrub for a sunny wall and flowers all summer.

Cistus make a brilliant show in a hot sunny spot and are set off well by paving.

Lupins raised from seed quickly make good-sized plants so are ideal for new gardens.

Kniphofia 'Little Maid' is a dwarf, prettily coloured form of the red hot poker.

This close planting of heliopsis, achillea and helenium not only looks good but will also smother the weeds.

Weigela 'Bristol Ruby' is well matched with the long flowering *Geranium* 'Wargrave Pink'.

This foliage combination of hosta, euonymus and rodgersia will provide a colourful edging for many months.

Two coloured-leaved forms of culinary sage show that herbs are pretty enough for the flower border.

Set pots of dainty crocuses like this 'Princess Beatrix' wherever you need a little extra spring colour.

Tough lilies like this elegant *Lilium pyrenaicum* will spread well once established.

Cosmos 'Sea Shells' sown outside in spring will give you elegant colour all summer long.

With its variegated foliage and fiery flowers *Nasturtium* 'Alaska' gives double value.

Pink and silver always look good in summer, this is *Argyranthemum* 'Vancouver' with grey-leaved *Helichrysum petiolatum*.

Choosing the right plants to go together makes all the difference. This is *Dicentra* 'Stuart Boothman' and Bowles' golden grass in the evening sun.

PART THREE

Solving the

Problems

CHAPTER EIGHT

PREVENTION AND CONTROL

Most plants are attacked by pests and diseases at some time or other, but please don't infer from the long list that follows that gardening is nothing more than a continuous war against nature's predators. And don't believe that because the chemical companies advertise their products widely you will necessarily need them all.

Prevention

As usual, prevention is the best policy, and there are quite a few things you can do to prevent pests and diseases ever getting established in your garden. These are discussed on pages 80–1. But however diligent you are in your preventative measures, problems will arise sooner or later. Vigilance and prompt treatment are the two things that together will ensure that your pest problems never get out of hand.

Cultural methods

Using the so-called cultural methods of pest and disease control really boils down to growing the plants well. This means giving the plants the conditions that they like and that the pests and diseases dislike – not planting a rambler rose on a south wall, for example, as it encourages mildew.

The routine cultural techniques fit in here too – hoeing to prevent weed growth, correct pruning to prevent die-back and so on.

Chemical methods

The first thing to reiterate is the importance of following the instructions on the pack you intend to use. (It is now illegal to use a pesticide in a way which is not recommended.) In response to increasing concern from gardeners, the chemical companies are now producing more information, and leaflets are often available at garden centres or free from the chemical companies.

There are four methods of applying chemicals – spraying, dusting, soil treatment and fumigation. Spraying is the most common, and for a discussion of method and safety precautions see page 69. Using dusts is rather a hit-and-miss affair. Applying them accurately and achieving an even coverage is difficult, so this is not a method I would generally recommend.

Soil is treated in different ways for different problems. Dusts or small granules may be mixed into the soil to deal with soil-living pests which attack roots. Small pins or pellets impregnated with insecticide are available to push into the compost of pots and containers, and these release the chemical over a few weeks, avoiding the need to spray. These are especially useful for house plants and containers near the house, where you may not wish to spray.

Fumigation is used exclusively in greenhouses and conservatories. It consists of using a purpose-made fumigant cone which, when lit, produces billowing clouds of insecticidal smoke which carry the chemical to every corner of the greenhouse and right into the shoot tips of the plants. This is a very effective method if the vents on your greenhouse are a tight fit but ineffective and antisocial if they are not. I would also be very wary of using it in a conservatory connected to the house, as fumes may seep in round the door.

Biological control

In recent years, methods of pest control using predatory and parasitic organisms have been developed, primarily for use in the greenhouse. The creatures are introduced to the greenhouse as the pests start to build up and then, depending on the problem, either eat the pests or parasitise the eggs.

This is a very effective method, though there are restrictions. In some cases the greenhouse has to be maintained at a high enough temperature to suit the parasite or predator, and if it drops too low they may die out. And although certain specific pests may be dealt with effectively, it will be impossible to use chemical controls against others as these may kill the beneficial insects. The development of biological control for use outside in the garden is still in the early stages.

Organic control

In this book I am using the term 'organic control' to mean any control method except those involving chemicals which are not of natural origin. So it covers the use of chemicals of natural origin, together with manual and cultural techniques.

The simple manual methods are often overlooked. Some pests, caterpillars for example, can simply be picked off by hand and you can squash the caterpillar eggs that are sometimes found underneath foliage – especially of cabbages and other brassicas. Pinching off a badly infested shoot and putting it on the fire or in a sealed bag in the bin can often stop pests spreading.

Encouraging birds into the garden will help with a number of pest problems but don't forget that some crops, especially fruit, may need protection from birds.

CHAPTER NINE

THE PROBLEMS AND THEIR SOLUTIONS

Pests

1. UNIVERSAL PEST PROBLEMS

There are a few pests which are very common and which attack a wide variety of plants.

Aphids

Greenfly, blackfly and flies in a variety of colours are the commonest pests, attacking a wide range of flowers and vegetables, indoors and out. There are many different types; some tend to attack specific plants, while others are more omnivorous.
The damage: Weak growth, deformed shoots, groups of insects under leaves and along shoots.
The pest: Small, sap-sucking insects in a wide variety of colours. Greenfly and blackfly are the most familiar. Many colonies have no winged individuals.
Prevention: Little hope of prevention, and indiscriminate spraying should be avoided as this kills insects which feed on them.
Organic control: Encourage predators, rub off small infestations with fingers, spray with insecticidal soap such as Savona. Pay special attention to the undersides of the leaves.
Chemical control: Spray with ICI Rapid.

Ants

Ants undermine the roots of plants and 'farm' aphids by moving them from one plant to another.
The damage: Drying out, through the removal of soil from roots plus increasing aphid infestation. Anthills can disfigure the lawn.
The pest: Needs little description.
Prevention: Little can be done.

Organic control: Boiling water poured into the nest is sometimes successful.

Chemical control: Powders and baits such as Nippon Ant Killer are carried back to the nest, but it's important to continue baiting until all signs of activity have ceased.

Birds

The damage: Pigeons can strip cabbages and sprouts, finches eat fruit and flower buds, sparrows peck off the flowers of crocus and polyanthus as well as shrubs like mahonias and forsythias. Many birds eat fruits. Their dust bathing can make holes in newly sown lawns.

The pest: Two legs, two wings, feathery, very appealing – but infuriating.

Prevention: Plant susceptible shrubs in front gardens, where birds are often frightened by passers-by. Crocus and polyanthus can be protected using black cotton tied to sticks and stretched between the plants, but avoid nylon thread, which can tangle in birds' feet. Net food crops. Lay net or twigs on new lawns.

Capsids

The damage: Small, ragged, often yellow-edged holes in tips of shoots, the holes enlarging as the leaves expand. A wide variety of plants are attacked, especially in spring and early summer.

The pest: Small pale green larvae and bright green adults pierce tender tissue and suck sap.

Prevention: Clear away plant debris and dry leaves, especially from underneath hedges.

Organic control: Pinch out shoot tips.

Chemical control: Spray with a systemic insecticide such as ICI Sybol.

Leaf caterpillars

Caterpillars of a wide variety of moths and butterflies attack a huge range of garden plants. Some are not fussy about which plants they eat, others are more specific in their tastes and are given separate entries.

The damage: Leaves are eaten, usually from the edge and often giving a characteristic scalloped appearance.

The pest: Comes in many sizes and colours; small green ones are the most difficult to spot.
Prevention: Squash eggs on the undersides of leaves, encourage insect-eating birds.
Organic control: Pick off caterpillars by hand, spray with Bactospeine (a parasitic bacterium) or pbi Liquid Derris.
Chemical control: Murphy Tumblebug or pbi Crop Saver.

Cats

We love them, but they cause havoc in the garden.
The damage: Scratching up and fouling seed-beds, sometimes fouling individual plants.
The pest: Four legs, fur, purrs – and scratches.
Prevention: Four cats from the neighbours are far worse than one cat of your own. Get one, and get a tough one. Or a lively dog, a Jack Russell perhaps. Special plots can be netted. Pellets, liquids, pepper dust and other repellants are, in my experience, quite useless.
Organic control: A squirt from a hosepipe or a drench from a bucket of water is very effective. But unless you are at home all day and can keep up the attack, training the neighbours' cats is not easy.
Chemical control: Desperate gardeners invent ever more horrible solutions. But rarely put them into practice . . .

Slugs and snails

Slugs tend to be more of a problem on acid soils, while snails are more common on limy soils. But many gardens boast damaging populations of both!
The damage: Seedlings are eaten off at ground level, new shoots are eaten as they peep through the soil, softer foliage can be eaten all through the season; root vegetables are also highly susceptible, as are fruits, especially when they come into contact with the soil.
The pest: Slugs come in browns, greys and black and range in size from big black monsters which can be 6in (15cm) long to half-inch (12mm) eating machines.
Prevention: Both like to rest up in cool damp spots, so clear away long grass and weeds and consign all debris to the compost heap. Individual plants can be protected by surrounding them with a line of grit or lime, which slugs dislike.

Organic control: Various traps can be used, ranging from the old favourite, the saucer of beer, to upturned half-orange skins which will also trap them. Some organic gardeners resort to night-time expeditions with a torch and a tin. Preparations include Fertosan, which works by causing shrinkage of the slime glands and is simply watered onto the soil, while Nobble disrupts their reproduction and although it takes its time to affect the population, works very well. Neither affects wildlife or other organisms.

Chemical control: Pellets containing methaldehyde and methiocarb are still popular, and mini-pellets are coloured blue to be unappealing to animals. They also contain a repellant. It's worth remembering that you need very few to do an effective job. You will find that placing single pellets 4–6in (10–15cm) apart is usually just as safe as putting fifty in a trap – it's more effective and cheaper too. Pellets containing methiocarb, such as pbi Slug Gard, are the most effective, especially in wet weather, and will also deal with some other soil pests.

2. COMMON PEST PROBLEMS

There are many other pests which attack a wide variety of different plants.

Chafer grubs

The damage: Damage to roots, bulbs, tubers, stems and a wide range of food and ornamental plants, including lawns. Potatoes, carrots and other root crops are ruined, and other plants wilt and die as their roots are severed.

The pest: Soft, white, C-shaped grub with prominent brown head. Eventually hatches into a chafer beetle, for example a maybug.

Organic control: Usually most troublesome in newly cultivated areas, and regular cultivation soon reduces numbers.

Chemical control: Use a soil insecticide such as pbi Bromophos to protect special plants or plants in newly cultivated soil.

Cuckoo spit (froghopper)

The damage: Unsightly frothy liquid on shoots, sometimes leading to distortion and wilting on a range of shrubs and herbaceous plants.

The pest: Small green larvae which secrete froth as a protection. They hatch into green, frog-like insects.

Organic control: Wash off with garden hose.

Chemical control: Many insecticides meant for more severe problems will also deal with cuckoo spit. Use Murphy Liquid Malathion if specifically necessary.

Cutworms

The damage: Stems, especially of young plants and seedlings, are eaten at ground level and collapse.

The pest: Fat, soft, grey or brown grubs up to 2in (5cm) long which eventually hatch into moths.

Organic control: Cultivate in winter, to allow birds to find them.

Chemical control: Protect rows of seedlings with pbi Bromophos.

Dogs

The damage: Fouling of beds and borders, dead patches in lawns.

The pest: Four-legged and barks. Bitches cause brown patches on lawns by urinating.

Prevention: Regular walks; fencing off some areas of the garden such as the vegetable plot. Think carefully before buying a dog if your garden is very small.

Organic control: Remove fouling, water grass immediately after fouling to dilute urine.

Earwigs

The damage: Flowers chewed and eaten, especially in summer and autumn. And especially dahlias and chrysanthemums, but other plants too.

The pest: Lively, small brown insect with 'pincers' on the front.

Prevention: Tidy up rubbish and maintain good garden cleanliness.

Organic control: Trap earwigs in rolls of corrugated cardboard or pieces of orange peel laid on the soil. Or use the traditional flower-pots stuffed with straw on the tops of dahlia stakes.

Chemical control: Spray with Murphy Liquid Malathion at dusk.

Leaf miner

The damage: Silvery tunnels in the surface of leaves of a number of plants, such as hollies, chrysanthemums, laburnums, lilacs, etc.
The pest: Tiny moth caterpillar which can sometimes be seen at the end of one of the tunnels.
Organic control: Pick off affected leaves.
Chemical control: Difficult, but check susceptible plants regularly and spray at the first sign of the tiny dots which mark egg-laying sites. Use Murphy Systemic Insecticide.

Leatherjackets

The damage: Roots and stems of many different plants eaten, including grass. Vegetable seedlings are especially susceptible. Affected plants collapse and die, and yellow patches appear in lawns in dry weather. Starlings and other birds sometimes make a mess of lawns trying to winkle them out.
The pest: Greyish-brown grub up to 2in (5cm) long, the larvae of the daddy-long-legs or crane fly.
Prevention: Usually troublesome only when grass is dug up for beds.
Organic control: Cultivation, followed by a fallow period, allows birds to eat many.
Chemical control: Slug-killers, for example, pbi Slug Gard, also control leatherjackets, as does pbi Bromophos.

Mice and voles

Seeds (especially peas and beans) dug up and eaten as well as tubers and bulbs.
The pest: Mice have pointed snouts, voles are more rounded.
Organic control: Keep an effective cat, set traps.
Chemical control: Use baits. ICI Mouser houses the bait in a plastic box to prevent access by pets and other animals.

Millipedes

The damage: Pea and bean seedlings and other succulent plants are eaten, sometimes by increasing a wound started by another creature.
The pest: Slow-moving, tightly coiled segmented creatures,

usually black. By contrast, centipedes are useful, quick-moving, usually reddish and carnivorous.

Prevention: Good garden hygiene is important.

Organic control: Check in likely hiding places – under pots and trays, for example – and remove any you find.

Chemical control: Murphy Gamma-BHC Dust can be worked into the soil to protect seedlings or special plants.

Red spider mite

The damage: Fine yellow mottling of foliage, followed by fine grey webbing on the plants indoors and out.

The pest: Tiny reddish sap-sucking insect, hardly visible.

Prevention: Most prevalent in hot dry conditions, so keep the atmosphere damp in the greenhouse by spraying foliage and dousing paths.

Organic control: Predatory mites can be used in greenhouses. Spray with pbi Liquid Derris, which has some effectiveness.

Chemical control: This is one of the most difficult pests to control, especially in hot dry summers. No insecticides seem completely effective, partly because the mites develop resistance. Try pbi Longlast and ICI Sybol.

Root aphid

The damage: Weak growth and death in stressed conditions.

The pest: Groups of pale aphids, often covered in white wax, infect the roots of lettuces and some greenhouse plants.

Prevention: Inspect newly bought plants.

Organic control: Difficult. Roots can be washed completely of soil and doused in pbi Liquid Derris.

Chemical control: Drench with Murphy Liquid Malathion.

Thrips (thunderflies)

The damage: Fine flecking, speckling and sometimes silvering of foliage or flowers, which can eventually become distorted.

The pest: Short (4mm), very thin, sap-sucking insects in many colours.

Prevention: On house and greenhouse plants the worst damage occurs in hot dry conditions, so keep the atmosphere cool and moist.

Organic control: Spray with pbi Liquid Derris.
Chemical control: In the greenhouse use a fumigant such as ICI Fumite General Purpose Insect Smoke Cones, out of doors use Murphy Liquid Malathion.

Vine weevil

The damage: Bulbs, crowns of plants, fleshy roots and sometimes juicy stems are chewed; plants wilt and die. Mostly occurs on pot-grown plants but increasingly common outside.
The pest: A white grub with a ginger head hatches into a small black weevil which eats holes in foliage.
Prevention: Difficult. Usually comes in on an infected plant but is hard to detect. Dress the tops of pots with sharp grit.
Organic control: Remove grubs when repotting. Use Nemasys, a parasitic eelworm, which also kills mushroom fly larvae; it's expensive but very effective.
Chemical control: Mixing ICI Sybol dust into compost and dusting it over the surface can be effective.

Whitefly

The damage: Sap-sucking insects reduce the vigour of plants and drop honeydew on to foliage; this is then infected with sooty mould. Mainly occurring on greenhouse plants and brassicas.
The pest: Small white insects shaped like Lightning fighter/ bombers.
Prevention: Inspect newly bought plants carefully.
Organic control: Biological control with a parasite is very effective in a warm greenhouse.
Chemical control: pbi Longlast and insecticidal fumigants are effective.

Wireworms

The damage: Bulbs, tubers and roots are eaten, especially in spring. Potatoes are particularly susceptible, as the wireworms burrow inside. Common in grass and in new beds made in lawns.
The pest: A thin, 1in (2.5cm) long, creamy-coloured grub which eventually turns into a click beetle.
Organic control: Regular cultivation and weed control on new beds should soon banish wireworms.

Chemical control: pbi Bromophos is effective when chemical treatment is necessary.

Woolly aphid

The damage: Colonies disfigure the bark of apples, pyracanthas, cotoneasters, sorbus and other shrubs and trees in the rose family (though not roses), and cause cracks and fissures through which diseases can infect.
The pest: A small brown aphid which covers itself in white woolly wax.
Organic control: Limited infestations can often be dealt with by painting colonies with methylated spirits.
Chemical control: Murphy Systemic Insecticide can be sprayed over the plant, and will deal with most infestations.

3. SPECIFIC PESTS

Some pests are specific to one plant or to a small group of related plants.

Apple sawfly

The damage: Small creamy grubs tunnel into apples and eat out holes.
Organic control: Spray with pbi Liquid Derris one week after blossom fall.
Chemical control: Spray with Murphy Liquid Malathion.

Big bud mite

The damage: Fat buds on blackcurrants show the presence of big bud mite, which transmits reversion virus, the main problem it causes.
Organic control: Pick off any fat buds and burn them. Renew bushes every five or six years.
Chemical control: None.

Box sucker

The damage: Shoot tips curl up like tiny cabbages; growth slowed.

Organic control: Trim in April and burn clippings.
Chemical control: Spray with Murphy Systemic Insecticide.

Cabbage root fly

The damage: Roots of cabbages, sprouts and other brassicas eaten by white grubs.
Organic control: Place brassica collars around stems to prevent egg-laying.
Chemical control: pbi Bromophos.

Carrot fly

The damage: Grubs tunnel into roots, and any but a light infection renders them useless in the kitchen. Foliage turns orange.
Organic control: Surround plot with a vertical polythene barrier 15in (38cm) high to divert flying adults.
Chemical control: pbi Bromophos.

Codling moth

The damage: Caterpillars eat into maturing apples and tunnel through the flesh.
Organic control: The Trappit Codling Moth Trap can be hung in the trees – this catches the male moths so that the females remain unfertilised and lay eggs which do not hatch.
Chemical control: Difficult, but Bio Longlast is as effective as any.

Narcissus fly

The damage: Grey-brown grubs eat into bulbs, especially daffodils, which produce weak, distorted foliage and then die.
Organic control: Plant in shade and rake soil into the holes left when the foliage dies.
Chemical control: Murphy Gamma BHC Dust can be raked into the soil where bulbs are planted.

Pear leaf blister mite

The damage: Leaves on pears become puckered and blistered and sometimes tinted yellow or pink. Leaves are often killed and growth of shoots much reduced.

Organic control: Pick off and destroy infected leaves.
Chemical control: A systemic insecticide, such as Murphy Systemic Insecticide, is sometimes effective.

Onion fly

The damage: Grubs eat into the stems and bulbs of onions, shallots and leeks. Seedlings die, bulbs rot.
Organic control: Cultivate well in winter to expose pupae to birds. Adults are attracted by onion scent, so grow onions from sets to avoid thinning (which releases scent).
Chemical control: Treat soil with pbi Bromophos.

Pea moth

The damage: Small maggots eat into the growing peas inside their pods.
Organic control: Spray with pbi Liquid Derris. Sow early or late to avoid the main infection period.
Chemical control: Spray with pbi Fenitrothion a week after flowering and a fortnight later.

Raspberry beetle

The damage: Yellowish grubs eat into developing fruits.
Organic control: Cultivate the soil lightly to expose pupae to the birds. Spray with pbi Liquid Derris when the fruits turn pink.
Chemical control: Use pbi Fenitrothion rather than derris.

Diseases

Creating the right growing conditions is even more helpful in preventing disease attack than it is in relation to pests.

Cultural methods

In the greenhouse and conservatory in particular, sustaining the appropriate growing conditions for the plants is half the battle in preventing disease problems. In particular, avoiding a damp and stagnant atmosphere in the winter months is crucial.

Regular dead-heading in the greenhouse is important, as is the regular removal of dead and dying foliage and the collection of fallen leaves and other debris. Splashes of water should be kept off foliage and flowers. This should help prevent rots getting a hold. Overwatering can cause rots too. Aphids should be well controlled, as they can carry virus. Slugs and other insects should also be controlled, as rots can infect following their damage.

Outside, it's more a question of putting the right plant in the right place. Plants put in soil conditions which don't suit them or in the wrong aspect are simply more susceptible. Again, pest damage can let rots in, and sources of infection such as weeds and rotten fruit should be removed.

Chemical control

If growing conditions are constantly encouraging disease, it will be difficult to keep the problems under control even with regular treatment. Spraying is the commonest method of disease control, though dusts are sometimes used against rots of tubers in storage.

A relatively limited number of broad spectrum fungicides are available in garden centres, but diseases can develop resistance if plants are sprayed with the same material over a long period. This greatly reduces the effectiveness of the chemical. So don't buy the same product each time.

Organic and biological control

There are few organic fungicides, and I've found that the most common, sulphur, gives unpredictable results. So far, there are no methods of controlling diseases biologically.

1.   UNIVERSAL DISEASE PROBLEMS

Grey mould

Grey mould, or botrytis, is a disease of damp conditions and is especially common in the autumn and winter. Foliage, flowers or fruits turn grey-brown and soft and a long, white, furry mould develops. It attacks foliage, especially when it has been damaged, also flowers – dead flowers in particular – together with the stems left after flowers have fallen; it then spreads into healthy tissue quickly. Fruits such as raspberries, cucumbers and tomatoes can also be affected.

Grey mould can be prevented to some extent by watering sparingly, avoiding splashing water on foliage and on the greenhouse floor, and installing automatic ventilators set to open whenever conditions are warm enough and so guarantee a brisk flow of air.

If the greenhouse or conservatory is heated, a dry heat such as electricity or a radiator will reduce the chances of botrytis becoming a problem, while a damp heat from paraffin or gas will exacerbate the problem.

Grey mould can be controlled effectively by pbi Supercarb, ICI Benlate or M&B Systemic Fungicide.

Damping-off

Damping-off is a disease of seedlings. A fungus in the compost attacks the young seedlings either as they germinate or at soil level soon afterwards, causing them to collapse. The infection usually starts in one part of a pot or tray, and spreads as the fungus moves through the compost.

The fungus is usually introduced on dirty pots or trays, a dirty dibber, through compost which has been stacked on a dirty floor or bench, by re-using old compost, and often through water which is taken from a rainwater tank. It develops and spreads quickly in badly drained compost, which has been firmed too hard, or compost which is overwatered.

You will realise, from discovering how the problem is caused, that there are several ways of preventing it. Use clean equipment and fresh compost straight from the bag. Don't overfirm compost, especially peat-based types, and don't overwater.

Another tip: if you're raising a lot of seedlings of one variety, sow in two smaller pots rather than one large one. Then if one pot is infected you still have the other. The disease will also spread less quickly if seed is sown thinly, so that the seedlings are not too crowded when they emerge.

As an extra precaution and especially once the first signs are seen, it helps to add a copper fungicide to the water when watering.

pbi Cheshunt Compound and Murphy Traditional Copper Fungicide are suitable.

Mildew

There are two types of mildew and quite a number of variants of each, attacking different groups of plants.

Rose mildew and others like it are known as powdery mildews and show as a white powdery coating over leaves and flower buds. Powdery mildew is encouraged by hot, dry conditions and is especially destructive in long hot summers. Contrary to popular belief, all mildews are not dependent on damp conditions, though some other fungus diseases are.

As well as roses, apples, Brassicas (especially swedes, turnips and sprouts) cucumbers, gooseberries, peas, strawberries and vines all have their own particular strains of mildew which will not infect other plants.

Resistant varieties can play a part in preventing infection, and in particular there are resistant roses and gooseberries. Mildew-resistant roses include 'Alec's Red', 'Allgold', 'Peace', 'Queen Elizabeth', 'Silver Jubilee' and 'Southampton', while mildew-resistant gooseberries are 'Black Velvet' and 'Invicta'.

Careful siting of susceptible plants is helpful. Climbing roses growing on south-facing walls are especially susceptible, so roses should be planted on walls and fences facing west or east. You can pick off the first mildew-affected shoots, but if the conditions are right for it, it will soon turn up again. Spraying regularly with ICI Benlate usually solves the problem.

There is also a group of rather less important and less obvious mildews, the downy mildews, which are more like soft brown rots with much less in the way of white dust. The brown rot that sometimes affects the midribs of lettuce is a good example, and there are others which attack cabbages, spinach, vines, beetroots, onions and peas. This group of mildews is encouraged by damp conditions. Avoiding overwatering and not splashing water is important here, and the disease can also be controlled by spraying regularly with pbi Dithane 945 or Murphy Traditional Copper Fungicide. Systemic fungicides like ICI Benlate are not effective against downy mildews.

Virus

Virus diseases of plants are becoming increasingly common, and there is no cure. Viruses are carried from plant to plant by aphids, and a few are carried by soil-borne organisms. They cause a wide variety of symptoms, some quite difficult to detect. These include: generally weak growth, poor fruit set, twisted shoots, mottled or streaked foliage, poor yields, difficulties in rooting cuttings, coloured streaks in flowers – etc.

Controlling the aphids which spread the virus is a big help, but otherwise the only way of dealing with this insidious problem is to dig up and burn infected plants.

2. SPECIFIC DISEASES

Some diseases are specific to one plant or a small group of related plants.

Apple scab

The problem: Leaves develop dark-centred brown blotches, while spots and woody-edged cracks appear on fruits.
The control: Rake up and burn leaves from infected trees. Spray with ICI Benlate or pbi Supercarb every two weeks from bud burst to the end of flowering, or up to the end of the season if infection is severe.

Bacterial canker

The problem: Depression or long slits in the bark of cherries and plums which often ooze yellow gum. Leaves may develop neat circular spots or holes. Whole branches die back.
The control: Do not prune in winter as this encourages infection. Treat all cuts with pbi Arbrex. Cut out all infected wood, and spray with Murphy Traditional Copper Fungicide three times at monthly intervals, in midsummer and autumn.

Black spot

The problem: Rose leaves develop black spots. The leaves turn yellow and then drop off.

The control: Collect and burn all foliage in autumn, prune hard in spring, spray with ICI Roseclear every fortnight.

Brown rot

The problem: Soft brown spots appear on apples, pears, plums and other tree fruits either on the tree or in store. Blossom may wilt.
The control: Remove 'mummified' fruits, which stay on the tree through the winter to spread new infections. Spray with pbi Supercarb or ICI Benlate when the flowers are open, one week later to control blossom wilt, and in mid August and a fortnight later to protect fruits.

Club root

The problem: Roots of brassicas (and also wallflowers) swell up and become distorted; growth is very weak.
The control: Do not buy in or accept presents of seedlings, as this is how infection arrives. Raise cabbage plants in 4–5in (10–12.5cm) pots and plant out large plants, to get a crop from infected soil. Dip garden-raised plants in M&B Liquid Club Root Control before planting.

Coral spot

The problem: Coral-coloured speckles appear on dead branches of shrubs and fruit trees, then move into and kill healthy wood.
The control: Cut out infected wood as soon as it is seen.

Fireblight

The problem: Flowering shoots and sometimes foliage of shrubs and trees in the rose family look as if they have been scorched by fire.
The control: Dig up and burn badly infected plants, otherwise cut out infected shoots to below the red stained wood.

Honey fungus

The problem: Trees, shrubs or parts of hedges die suddenly, often when in flower or in dry spells. Honey-coloured toadstools are seen around nearby tree stumps, black 'bootlaces' found in soil, white 'fungus-scented' growth under the bark, especially near the ground. *The control*: Cut down and remove dead trees, including the stump through which infection starts. It then travels through the soil and attacks roots of healthy plants.

Leaf spot

The problem: Dark spots and blotches occur on a wide range of garden plants, especially in warm, wet weather. Different plants are susceptible at different times.
The control: Pick off and burn infected foliage, keep the air in greenhouses dry, spray with ICI Benlate at fortnightly intervals.

Peach leaf curl

The problem: Curling and red-tinted puckering of leaves on peaches, almonds and nectarines.
The control: Collect and burn affected leaves. Spray the twigs and branches with Murphy Traditional Copper Fungicide after leaf fall, and again just as the buds are swelling in late winter.

Potato blight

The problem: Dark blotches appear on leaves of potatoes, and white mould grows under the leaves. This mould is washed into the soil and infects the tubers. It also affects tomatoes. Especially bad in wet summers.
The control: Spray pbi Dithane 945 every two weeks from early July until harvest, more frequently if wet.

Potato scab

The problem: Scabby areas of rather woody tissue on the tubers, sometimes almost completely covering them. Yield is not reduced, but the tubers are unsightly and must be peeled. Worst on light soil.
The control: Less common on the earlies recommended on page 299. Add plenty of organic matter on light soils.

Silverleaf

The problem: A silvery sheen develops on plum leaves, with twigs discoloured brown within. Small bracket fungi appear on branches.

The control: Cut back the branches to beyond the brown stain in wood. Dig up and burn badly affected trees, especially if suckers produce silvered leaves.

Tulip fire

The problem: Grey mould, eventually turning reddish, on tulip leaves. Flower buds are distorted and fail to open.
The control: Pull up and burn infected bulbs, and spray others with ICI Benlate or pbi Supercarb. Soak bulbs in the same fungicides as a precaution before planting.

Wilt

The problem: Aster plants collapse, turn brown and often die before flowering.
The control: The fungus infects the soil and lasts for many years, so grow other plants in infected beds. If you must grow asters, raise them in 5in (12.5cm) pots and plant them out in summer.

Weeds

Weeds may be always with us, but that doesn't mean they must constantly be causing us trouble.

1. NEW BEDS AND BORDERS

The first principle is never to let weeds get a hold in the first place – attack is the best form of defence, if you like.

Weeds should never be left to shed their seeds, as seedlings will appear for many years afterwards, causing continual problems. The ground should always be cleared thoroughly before planting, even if it means waiting longer before you can get the plants in. It's almost impossible to remove perennial weeds once the plants are in place.

For the sort of blanket clearances required of new ground or when whole beds or borders are being prepared, you have a number of options. First, you can dig the plot over and remove the weeds by hand. This will enable you to reduce the weed population greatly, but it's important to leave it all for a few weeks afterwards for the remainder of the weeds to come through so that you can remove them. A third session is no bad thing.

Alternatively, you can do the same job with a weed-killer. One spray of a total weed-killer such as Murphy Tumbleweed will kill almost everything. Again, leave it for a couple of weeks and give another application. This product is expensive, and it can seem as if you're laying out quite a sum on a relatively small area. But this should not tempt you to skimp on the application, as the weeds will not be killed effectively. Follow the directions on the pack. This product breaks down quickly on contact with the soil and will not affect the plants you put in afterwards.

Another method, especially if you have plenty of time and prefer not to use chemicals, is to use an old carpet. Carpet? By cutting down all top growth, with a mower perhaps, and then simply laying a carpet over the whole area, the weeds will eventually die out through lack of light. It will take many months, but it does work.

Another approach which is sometimes recommended is the repeated use of a rotovator. The theory is that the first pass cuts up all the perennial weed roots into little bits. They then start to grow, using up the food reserves in the small pieces of root; then when they've begun to emerge you go over the whole area again. This chops up the even smaller roots and many will then have insufficient food reserves to get the shoots to the surface. You keep doing this until there are hardly any weeds left, and you dig these last few up by hand.

This method has two big problems. You need access to a rotovator and you need to have the time and inclination to do the job regularly and at the right time. Few of us can meet these conditions, so I would not recommend this system. Flame throwers are also sometimes suggested and these too should be avoided. They make a show of doing a wonderful job but in fact the heat from the flame penetrates only about half an inch and weeds promptly regrow from below this level.

2. EMPTY AREAS

Dealing with weeds on areas like gravel drives, where plants are never going to be grown, is simpler. You can use a persistent weed-killer such as ICI Pathclear, which not only kills the existing weeds, and does not creep sideways into borders, but also prevents weeds growing for a whole season. If you prefer not to use chemicals, regular raking of the gravel will prevent weed seedlings taking root. And keep the irrigation water off the area when watering borders.

3. WEEDS AMONG GARDEN PLANTS

Weeds among garden plants are more of a problem. The conventional solution is to use a hoe, and this is very effective with vegetables, cut flowers and other plants grown in rows. It is also very quick, though it's important to hoe regularly even when there are few weed seedlings to be seen.

But in a crowded border hoeing can easily damage plants, and in any case borders should be planted densely so that few weeds can penetrate to the light. In such congested conditions, hoeing is almost impossible.

In a small garden, when beds and borders are unlikely to be huge, hand-weeding can be both practical and very enjoyable. All you need is a hand fork, a bucket, and maybe a kneeling pad. You simply work through the border, forking out weeds from among the plants. If you come across some young plants that look as if they may be seedlings from your garden plants, leave them in place and see how they turn out. If, in the end, you realise they're weeds after all, you can pull them out individually.

Mulching is a very practical and aesthetically pleasing way of keeping down weeds, as well as feeding the soil and the plants. It relies on a relatively weed-free soil to start with, but the looseness of the material makes the removal of any weeds that blow in very easy.

But perhaps the most sensible way of dealing with weeds is by planting. Most gardeners know about ground cover plants which spread out and smother weeds, but the fact is that most plants, if planted in groups without bare patches in between, will make a weed-free cover. And if you think about it, the best borders show no soil at all for most of the season. So rather than put in one plant of one variety and then one plant of another, put them in groups of three or five without big blank spaces in between – it doesn't matter if they grow together, in fact they will probably look better. And there won't be much chance for the weeds to penetrate.

Individual weeds growing among established plants can be a problem, as it's not always possible to dig out the entire root system. Repeated removal of the top growth will work in the end, but new shoots from below only tend to come through in even more inaccessible places.

One answer is weed-killer, but applied only to the weed concerned. Murphy Tumbleweed is available in a gel formulation, with a small brush in the cap of the bottle. This is used to paint the weed-killer onto the foliage of the weed. Two applications are often used, and this is usually effective. Alternatively the shoots of the weed can be dipped in a bowl of normal strength diluted weed-killer.

Weed-killer can also be applied in borders using a sprayer, if it is fitted with a hood which prevents the spray from reaching your plants. This is the big problem of using weed-killer in borders – it must be kept off the plants which you are trying to protect, otherwise it will kill them too.

There is, however, one product which can be sprayed over almost the whole border to kill couch grass, May and Baker Weed Out. Because it kills only couch grass and one or two related members of the grass family while leaving other plants completely unscathed, it is not necessary to keep it off other plants.

4. PREVENTING WEED GROWTH

Planting thoughtfully and using mulches are very good ways of preventing weeds getting hold. It also pays to look at plants you buy, to make sure you're not bringing weeds into the garden. Small annual weeds are sometimes to be found growing in the pots along with the plant you actually intended to buy.

There are also weed-preventing chemicals available, such as Murphy Weedex, which do not kill existing weeds but prevent weed seeds germinating. These are very useful, not only for established borders but also on drives and paths. A number of products are available for use on both fruit and ornamental plants, but most are suitable only for use around plants which are well established.

5. COMMON WEEDS

Annual meadow grass

This is a very common grass weed, appearing in beds and borders while also being present in most lawns. It flowers and fruits while still small, especially in dry conditions, and re-roots quickly if hoed off and left on the surface. In lawns it can be the dominant grass and browns quickly in dry summers. It also seeds prolifically, as you will find if you spread the grass cuttings on the borders – your reward will be a forest of weeds.

Annual meadow grass can be hoed off in borders while still small, and mulching deals with it effectively, as does ICI Weedol. In a well-maintained lawn, proper lawn grasses will usually smother it.

Annual weeds

Many annual weeds, such as groundsel and shepherd's purse, also seed when small and have the ability to re-root into the soil if left on the surface. They can all be killed by a thorough treatment with ICI Weedol, which kills all green tissue. This is enough to finish off annual weeds as they have no below ground reserves; perennials with food storage roots simply shoot again.

Hoeing is also effective in hot or very windy weather, when the disturbed weeds soon shrivel. But in damp conditions they are likely to re-root and go on to produce seeds.

Bindweed

More difficult to remove from borders, in uncultivated situations a couple of treatments with Murphy Tumbleweed or Vitax New Formula SBK Brushwood Killer will do the trick. Where there are established plants to consider, repeated applications of Murphy Tumbleweed Gel before growth is too advanced will work, as will untwining the shoots from their hosts and dipping them in Vitax New Formula SBK Brushwood Killer.

This is one weed which seems to have such reserves that it will creep along under carpet for some feet and then emerge at the edges.

Celandine

Lesser celandine is a pretty but infuriating weed which starts to grow in the autumn and flowers in early spring. It has roots like tiny dahlia tubers, which break up when disturbed and are easily spread around, emerging in the middle of treasured plants. Some gardeners simply tolerate them, others want to have them out.

New gardens rarely suffer from them unless the garden is on the site of an old wood or hedgerow. Celandines usually arrive with a plant given as a present by a friend or neighbour. They are best removed carefully by hand early in spring, when the tubers hold together well. Weed-killing, except perhaps with Murphy Tumbleweed Gel, is difficult because of the danger to other plants.

Chickweed

A vigorous annual weed, growing strongly, and flowering and seeding in early spring as well as in mild spells in the winter. Easily pulled out by grasping the slender stem where it enters the ground, but difficult to remove by simply pulling at top growth. ICI Weedol is very effective.

Cleavers

A vigorous climbing weed with clinging hooked hairs and fruits which scrambles up into shrubs. Seems resistant to some weed-killers, and the seeds are easily spread. Should be pulled out when young before it shades out shoots of shrubs.

Clover

Clover can seem difficult to banish from lawns, but good lawn cultivation is generally the answer. Regular fairly close mowing, regular raking, feeding together with watering in dry spells, will often reduce the problem greatly. If you wish to use a lawn weed-killer, check on the pack to ensure that clovers are killed, as not all weed-killers kill clover.

Couch grass

One of the most persistent and persistently unpopular weeds, couch grass can be controlled chemically by using Murphy Tumbleweed in uncultivated areas, or May and Baker Weed Out in established borders. Both do a very effective job. The carpet treatment works in uncultivated areas, and couch is also possible to remove by careful work with a border fork in light soils.

Dock

These are deep-rooted perennials, often needing two or more treatments of Murphy Tumbleweed or Boots Nettle and Bramble Weedkiller before being killed. Can be forked out if not surrounded by other plants, but the roots go deep. Don't waste time cutting or pulling off the top, as it will reshoot strongly from the root.

Ground elder

Another big problem in borders, this is perhaps the most difficult weed to remove from among other plants. Murphy Tumbleweed and Vitax New Formula SBK will kill it, but the problem is getting the weed-killer on to the ground elder and on no other foliage.

Unfortunately, the answer is often to dig up the plant concerned and tease out all the ground elder roots before dividing and replanting your original plant. Or better still, putting it somewhere else and leaving a space in the border in case more ground elder comes through which needs treatment.

Hairy bittercress

This is a small but infuriating little weed which often arrives in the garden in the top of container-grown plants. It has the irritating habit of flinging seeds in your eye when you try and remove it. One reason why it is such a problem is that it can produce seed, sometimes just three or four seeds, when only 1in (2.5cm) tall. So it has multiplied almost before you knew it was there.

Hoeing is often ineffective, as when the plants are left to lie they often manage to produce seed before they finally expire. Apart from inspecting all newly bought plants carefully and pulling out even seedlings, regular removal by hand is the only answer; check especially around newly planted plants.

Horsetail

This is impossible to deal with when growing with other plants. In an uncultivated area, knock the plants about a bit, perhaps by rolling them to bruise the stems and leaves, as this enables weedkillers to penetrate the otherwise resistant skin; then spray with Vitax New Formula SBK. You will probably need to do it many times. Turning the area into a lawn, and regular close mowing, can also work, but may only force this depressing weed into neighbouring borders.

Moss

Moss in lawns can be cured, but you need a double-barrelled approach. The first thing to do is to remove the conditions which encourage moss and at the same time lead to poor growth of the grass. Primarily, this involves improving the drainage.

You can do this by going over the mossy area with the digging fork and pushing it into the grass to about half its depth. Make each set of holes about 6in (15cm) apart. This is a tedious and tiring business but works, especially if you then scatter some sharp sand over the area and brush it into the holes. Better still, use a hollow tining tool, with tubular tines that remove a core of soil which is deposited on the grass for you to sweep up. This is an expensive tool considering how rarely you're likely to use it, so borrow one if you can.

Moss is also common in shady spots, so removing some low branches from trees can help. In old gardens moss is encouraged when lawns are not cut for long periods.

Having improved the drainage, use the lawnraker to remove most of the moss and allow air in around the grass roots. Finally apply a combined moss-killer and grass feed, such as ICI Lawnsman Mosskiller, which will stimulate the grass to make a dense sward as the moss dies out.

Nettles

Nettles come in two types, annual and perennial; the presence of either is a sign of good fertility – actual or potential. Annual nettles can be dealt with in the same way as other annual weeds, although in spite of various suggestions it's not possible to pull them out without them stinging unless you wear gloves.

Perennial nettles make a tight mass of yellow shoots near the surface, and when forked out tend to come up in a dense mat from which the soil should be shaken. Regular mowing will weaken and then kill them, and they can also be killed by using two applications of Boots Nettle and Bramble Weedkiller or Vitax New Formula SBK Brushwood Killer.

Rosette weeds

Rosette weeds such as daisies, dandelions and plantains can be difficult to extract, but are easy to kill with a weed-killer. The natural habit of these plants is to smother others, so that they present plenty of foliage on which to paint the weed-killer without getting it on neighbouring plants.

Thistles

Thistles come in a variety of types, some with very glossy foliage from which weed-killer is quickly shed. These milk thistles are also very easily broken when being removed, leaving the root behind. Some also have white, fleshy, creeping roots which can reshoot after treatment. Murphy Tumbleweed and Vitax New Formula SBK Brushwood Killer are effective, but two applications may be necessary.

Willowherbs

The bright pink flowers of rosebay willowherb are a familiar sight on railway embankments, and their windblown seeds often bring them into gardens. There are a number of smaller species. Most can be forked out with a little care, but the fleshy, running roots are easily broken. They should also be prevented from seeding. Murphy Tumbleweed is effective.

PART FOUR

Inspiration and

Information

CHAPTER TEN

GARDENS TO VISIT

1. LARGE GARDENS

Just because a garden is large, don't think it can provide no inspiration for a small plot. Although it's true that landscaped parks are less relevant than gardens divided into smaller sections, even parks can provide design ideas which can be adapted.

With large gardens, however, it is true that it is those that are divided into smaller sections or have some small, self-contained areas that will provide more inspiration.

I would especially recommend a visit to the following gardens:

Beechgrove Garden, Aberdeen.
Capel Manor, Hertfordshire.
County Demonstration Garden, Probus, Cornwall.
Crathes Castle Garden, Banchory, Grampian.
East Lambrook Manor, Somerset.
Great Dixter, East Sussex.
Harlow Carr, Yorkshire.
Hatfield House, Hertfordshire.
Hexham Herbs, Northumberland.
Hidcote Manor, Gloucestershire.
Newby Hall, Yorkshire.
Royal Horticultural Society, Rosemoor, Devon.
Royal Horticultural Society, Wisley, Surrey.
Sissinghurst Castle, Kent.
Threave School of Gardening, Castle Douglas, Dumfries.

There are a number of books which list gardens such as these, with their opening times, and perhaps the most useful is *Historic Houses and Gardens Open to the Public*, a large-format paperback published each year by British Leisure Publications.

2. SMALL GARDENS

Recommending small gardens worthy of a visit is a dangerous business, as most of those that open do so on only a few days a year; and they may not even be open every year.

The best advice I can give is to look in the 'Yellow Book', whose full title is *Gardens of England and Wales*. This paperback, published by the National Gardens Scheme, which raises money for nursing charities, lists the opening times of over 2,500 gardens, many of which are small private ones which are open on only a few days in the year. You will find that the standard of gardens varies enormously, but there is something useful to be learned from most. Similar schemes operate in Scotland and Ireland.

CHAPTER ELEVEN

BOOKS, MAGAZINES AND VIDEOS

1. BOOKS

One look at the gardening shelves in the bookshop will tell you that there are too many books on gardening published (so says the author of six!). With so many on sale, it can be difficult to decide which are the most suitable for your own circumstances and which are the best value. They can be grouped in a number of categories.

Beginners' books

The *'Expert'* books by Dr David Hessayon, published by the garden chemicals company pbi, are basic, easy to follow, not expensive, and have provided good advice for hundreds of thousands of newcomers to gardening. The subjects they cover are general gardening, trees and shrubs, roses, bedding plants, vegetables, fruit and house plants.

As this book itself assumes very little basic knowledge, I can hardly recommend any others at this level!

General and reference

Three books published by Readers' Digest make a good, basic yet comprehensive library. *The Gardening Year* provides a month-by-month guide to what to do in the garden, and information on the plants which are at their best at each season. *The Readers' Digest Encyclopaedia of Garden Plants and Flowers* is a comprehensive A–Z of plants, and although a little dated it is still excellent value. *The Readers' Digest Guide to Creative Gardening* is full of inspiring ideas.

The RHS Gardeners' Encyclopedia of Plants and Flowers (Dorling Kindersley) is more up to date and more colourful, but is organised according to plant type, size and colour, which not everyone finds helpful. *Notcutts Book of Plants* (Notcutts) covers only plants which are likely to appear in garden centres, and is also very useful for the figures it gives on eventual heights and spreads.

The Plant Finder (Headmain) is an invaluable paperback, revised annually, which lists about 45,000 garden plants and the nurseries that stock them. It also serves as a checklist of correct plant names.

The Well-Tempered Garden by Christopher Lloyd (Viking) is not exactly a reference book, but is a witty yet practical book covering most aspects of hardy plants. *Organic Gardening* by Geoff Hamilton (Dorling Kindersley) is an exceptionally well-illustrated book packed with good ideas for those who wish to garden without pesticides and fertilisers.

Practical

The RHS Concise Encyclopaedia of Gardening Techniques (Mitchell Beazley) is full of good, practical advice and very helpful line drawings. It is a condensed version of eight large format paperbacks on *Growing Techniques*, *Pests and Diseases*, *Pruning*, *Propagation*, etc. which are also available separately.

Creative Propagation by Peter Thompson (Christopher Helm) covers both the basics and the more advanced techniques of making more plants.

Planning and design

John Brookes's *The New Small Garden Book* (Dorling Kindersley) is a very useful book whose pictures will give you plenty of ideas for the layout of your garden. His earlier book on the subject, *The Small Garden* (New Orchard Editions) is still good value.

I would also suggest *The Small Garden Planner* by Graham Rose (Mitchell Beazley) and *The Garden Border Book* by Mary Keen (Viking). *Colour in Your Garden* by Penelope Hobhouse (Frances Lincoln), and *Good Planting* by Rosemary Verey (Frances Lincoln), are full of inspired ideas on plant associations. There are also two books entitled *Plans for Small Gardens* by Geoffrey Coombs in the Wisley Handbook Series (RHS/Cassell).

Leisurely Gardening by Nigel Colborn (Christopher Helm) is an imaginative, practical, and also entertaining book for those who wish to grow lots of plants but do not have much time. The title of my own *Plants for Problem Places* (Christopher Helm) is self-explanatory.

Trees

There are no substantial books I can recommend specifically on trees for small gardens, but there is a short paperback in the Wisley Handbook series called *Trees for Small Gardens* by Keith Rushforth (RHS/Cassell), which is as much as many gardeners will need. *Designing with Trees* by Yvonne Rees and Anthony Paul (Windward), although more useful for owners of larger gardens, illustrates plenty of good planting ideas.

Shrubs

Another useful booklet in the Wisley Handbook series, also by Keith Rushforth, is *Shrubs for Small Gardens*. On a larger scale, *Shrubs* by Martin Rix and Roger Phillips (Pan) is a very attractive, largely pictorial guide, while *The Gardeners' Illustrated Encyclopaedia of Trees and Shrubs* by Brian Davis (Viking) describes more plants but is less elegant. There is a companion volume on *Climbers and Wall Shrubs*.

There are a number of other relevant titles in the Wisley Handbook series: *Camellias*, *Clematis*, *Evergreens*, *Heaths and Heathers*, *Pruning Ornamental Shrubs*, *Rhododendrons* and *Roses*.

Hardy perennials

Perennial Garden Plants by Graham Thomas (Dent) is the standard reference book, and a fine work it is. *The Green Tapestry* by Beth Chatto (Collins) concentrates on foliage plants, and is packed with good ideas on how to use them in the garden. *Hardy Plants and Alpines* by Alan Bloom (Floraprint) is very colourful and authoritative. There is also my own *Hardy Herbaceous Perennials* (RHS/Cassell), in the Wisley Handbook series.

Rock and dwarf plants

A Guide to Rock Gardening by Richard Bird (Christopher Helm) is a very practical introduction to the subject, while *Alpines in the Open Garden* by Jack Elliot (Christopher Helm) is a most readable book packed with personal experience.

Annuals and bedding plants

Seed catalogues, especially the one from Thompson & Morgan, are the best value for information on annuals and bedding plants, as they are all free of charge. But if you prefer a more comprehensive book with planting ideas and practical advice on how to raise the plants, I cannot but suggest my own *Handbook of Annuals and Bedding Plants* (Christopher Helm).

Bulbs

Bulbs by Martin Rix and Roger Phillips (Pan) is very colourful and inspiring, while *The Year-Round Bulb Garden* by Brian Mathew (Souvenir Press) is a very useful book by the country's leading bulb expert. *Growing Dwarf Bulbs* by Jack Elliot (RHS/Cassell) is an excellent short, basic introduction.

Containers

The Container Garden by Nigel Colborn (Unwin Hyman) is a well-written and well-illustrated guide to gardening in pots of all kinds, while *The Terracotta Gardener* by Jim Keeling (Headline) concentrates on terracotta pots, with plenty of planting plans. *Gardening in Ornamental Containers* by Ray Waite (RHS/Cassell) is a very useful introduction in the Wisley Handbook series.

Vegetables and herbs

Vegetables from Small Gardens by Joy Larkcom (Faber) is an essential buy for any vegetable grower, and is crammed with concisely expressed information. The same author's *The Vegetable Garden Displayed* (RHS/Cassell) is the best basic book on vegetable growing, and her *The Salad Garden* (Windward) is a good companion volume. *Vegetable Varieties for the Gardener* (RHS/Cassell) describes the best varieties as recommended by the National Institute for Agricultural Botany. Although not colourfully illustrated, *Herb Gardening* by Clare Lowenfield (Faber) remains the most useful and best value book on herbs.

Fruit

The Fruit Garden Displayed by Harry Baker (RHS/Cassell) is an excellent general book. *The Handbook of Soft Fruit Growing* by

Ken Muir and David Taylor (Christopher Helm) will tell you all you need to know about soft fruit, while *Growing Tree Fruits* by Bonham Bazeley (Collins) is a well-illustrated guide to the subject.

2. MAGAZINES

There is quite a variety of good gardening magazines, which are never static but always changing and improving.

AMATEUR GARDENING   A rather conservative, long-established weekly magazine which covers all aspects of the subject, though it is less strong on garden design. There are columns by gardening personalities and a comprehensive jobs-for-the-week section.

BBC GARDENERS' WORLD   A monthly magazine from the BBC which covers the whole spectrum of gardening in a lively and colourful style. Most of the TV and radio gardeners make regular appearances.

GARDEN NEWS   A weekly tabloid newspaper with plenty of show news and features on specialist subjects. It is strong on vegetables and the practical aspects of gardening.

GARDEN ANSWERS   The question and answer format, in which readers' queries are answered, is supplemented by features on special subjects. Very practical.

GARDENING FROM WHICH?   Published by the Consumers' Association, this subscription-only magazine surveys different groups of plants and tests tools and equipment.

HORTUS   A rather literary, small-format quarterly journal illustrated with engravings rather than colour pictures. Strong on historical subjects and the literature of gardening.

ORGANIC GARDENING   A small-format bi-monthly magazine on all aspects of gardening without chemicals and pesticides.

PRACTICAL GARDENING   A stylish and colourful monthly magazine, full of design and planting ideas for gardeners who like to relax in the garden as well as enjoy looking after it. Not strong on vegetables and fruit.

THE GARDENER   A good-looking, colourful and comprehensive monthly magazine with design ideas and features on plants, plus surveys on garden equipment.

THE GARDEN   The *Journal* of the Royal Horticultural Society and available only to RHS members. A colourful, magazine with an unpredictable blend of features on plants, gardens, nurseries and historical subjects.

3. VIDEOS

Almost without exception, purpose-made gardening videos are of poor quality and are not good value for money. Some are also designed to promote particular products. Better to record the best of the TV gardening programmes.

CHAPTER TWELVE

SUPPLIERS

Although many gardeners accumulate plants as gifts, most plants are bought from garden centres, nurseries, by mail order or as seeds.

1. GARDEN CENTRES

The range of plants on sale in garden centres is increasing slowly, but except in those which specialise in plants it is still relatively limited. Those on sale will usually be the most popular and easy-to-grow varieties, which is a recommendation in itself, but many other easy and good plants will not be available.

Garden centres vary enormously in the range of varieties they stock and the prices they charge. Most of the major chains, such as Country Gardens, Notcutts, Cramphorns, Wyevale, Hilliers and the like, may be a little pricey but the quality is usually good. Most of these chains have developed from older nursery businesses, and they tend to have a good range of plants compared with DIY chains and groups such as Gardenstore.

You may not always be able to get advice at a garden centre, and when you do, it may not be that of an expert. But helpful leaflets are often available, and many of the larger garden centres have a selection of reference books for customers to consult.

As well as plants, you can find a wide variety of equipment and tools, together with composts, pots, chemicals and so on, not to mention sweets and Christmas novelties. Many of these items are better value at the DIY chains, but the range of tools at garden centres is sometimes of higher quality.

2. DIY CHAINS

Chains like B&Q, Gardenstore, Payless and Homebase are strongest on bulky goods like paving and fencing, together with tools and equipment. There is often a good choice of these items and they are usually good value, whereas the range of plants on offer can be poor and the quality likewise.

3. NURSERIES

Nurseries concentrate on plants and do not usually sell tools and equipment. Most of the plants are grown on the nursery rather than bought in, and many are small businesses which specialise in certain groups of plants – alpines perhaps, climbers or dwarf shrubs.

In small nurseries you may not find the most popular and easy-to-grow plants, indeed many may be unusual and need specific growing conditions. But you will usually get expert advice, often from the people who have propagated the plants and grown them on. Sometimes they will even refuse to sell you a plant if they feel that it is not suitable for your garden!

Not all small nurseries are this good, of course; some are disorganised and weedy, with poor plants and staffed by grumpy owners. But these are the exception. *The Plant Finder* (Headmain) lists a large number of nurseries and gives their opening times and the cost of their catalogues.

Nurseries and plant centres which stock a good range of plants and which I can recommend you visit include:

Bressingham Plant Centre, Bressingham, Norfolk.
Bridgemere Nurseries, Bridgemere, Nantwich, Cheshire.
Highfield Nurseries, Whitminster, Gloucestershire.
Hopleys Plants, Much Hadham, Hertfordshire.
Kelways Nurseries, Langport, Somerset.
Langthorn's Plantery, Great Dunmow, Essex.
Margery Fish Plant Nursery, East Lambrook, Somerset.
Plants from the Past, Belhaven, Dunbar.
Scotts Nurseries, Merriott, Somerset.
Unusual Plants, Elmstead Market, Essex.
Wisley Plant Centre, RHS Garden, Wisley, Surrey.

Some of these nurseries also offer a mail order catalogue. Full addresses and details of opening times are revised annually for *The Plant Finder* (see page 411).

4. MAIL ORDER PLANTS AND BULBS

Many less common plants and bulbs are available only from specialist nurseries, and if there is not a suitable one in your area you can use their mail order service. Most nurseries which offer a mail order service sell good plants and pack them well. It pays to read those tedious terms of business in the catalogue before ordering, and if you have any complaints, make them quickly after receiving your plants.

Nurseries producing the most colourful catalogue do not necessarily sell the best varieties or grow the highest quality plants. Those with unprepossessing lists may sell plants which are as good, if not better. The use of a limit cheque reduces the clerical work and the chances of confusion over refunds if plants you order happen to be sold out.

I have bought plants from all the following nurseries and can recommend them. All sell plants suitable for small gardens. Those marked with an asterisk (*) are also open to visitors.

Avon Bulbs Burnt House Farm, Mid Lambrook, South Petherton, Somerset, TA13 5HE.
Specialises in dwarf bulbs for spring, summer and autumn flowering, with a small range of alpines and woodland plants.

Peter Beales Roses London Road, Attleborough, NR17 1AY*
Specialist rose grower, with an unrivalled selection of old-fashioned and species roses and the best of the modern varieties. The descriptive catalogue is useful as reference.

Bressingham Gardens Bressingham, Diss, Norfolk, IP22 2AB*
Strongest on perennials, heathers and dwarf conifers, with a good range of alpines and less common shrubs, especially smaller varieties and climbers. Very colourful catalogue, two editions a year.

Broadleigh Gardens Bishops Hull, Taunton, Somerset, TA4 1AE
Specialists in dwarf bulbs, with a wide variety listed. Also a good range of woodland plants and some choice perennials. Two catalogues a year.

Buckingham Nurseries 4 Tingewick Road, Buckingham, MK14 4AE*
Specialises in hedging plants, with a wide range of formal and informal, tall and dwarf plants for hedges.

David Austin Roses Bowling Green Lane, Albrighton, Wolverhampton, WV7 3HB*
Old-fashioned shrub roses, modern hybrid teas and floribundas and

'English roses', their own range of modern, long-flowering roses in the old style. Colourful catalogue.

Fibrex Nurseries Honeybourne Road, Pebworth, Stratford-upon-Avon, CV37 8XT*
Three contrasting specialities – geraniums (pelargoniums), hardy ferns and ivies, with a catalogue for each.

Four Seasons Nursery Forncett St Mary, Norwich, NR16 1JT
A large selection of cottage garden plants and hardy perennials, including some raised on the nursery, plus a few shrubs and alpines.

Highfield Nurseries Whitminster, Gloucester, GL2 7PL*
A general nursery with a very good range of tree fruit, including many dwarf types, soft fruit, trees and shrubs and an increasing range of hardy perennials.

Hillier Nurseries Ampfield House, Ampfield, Romsey, SO51 9PA
Old-established nursery, specialising in trees and shrubs with an exceptional range of both familiar and unusual varieties. Garden centres in southern England.

Holden Clough Nursery Holden, Bolton-by-Bowland, Clitheroe, BB7 4PF*
Small nursery with an exceptionally wide range of alpines as well as dwarf shrubs, conifers and hardy perennials.

Hollington Nurseries Woolton Hill, Newbury, RG15 9XT*
Specialist herb nursery with as wide a range of herbs as you could wish for.

Hopleys Plants High Street, Much Hadham, SG10 6BU*
A choice selection of smaller shrubs and perennials, together with conservatory plants.

W. E. Ingwersen and Son Birch Farm Nursery, Gravetye, East Grinstead, RH19 4LE*
Old-established alpine nursery with a wide range of traditionally grown varieties.

Notcutts Nurseries Woodbridge, Suffolk, IP12 4AF
General nursery with an especially good range of trees and shrubs, including rhododendrons and roses. Garden centres in southern and eastern England. Catalogue is useful for reference.

Reads Nursery Hales Hall, Loddon, Norfolk, NR14 6QW*
Specialities are grape vines, citrus and unusual fruits. Also a wide range of conservatory plants.

Stapeley Water Gardens London Road, Stapeley, Nantwich, CW5 7LH*
Water garden specialists, with a full range of pools, liners, pumps and other equipment, together with a comprehensive range of water plants.

Treasures of Tenbury Burford House Gardens, Tenbury Wells, WR15 8HQ*
Clematis specialist with a very wide range of familiar and unusual varieties.

van Tubergens Bressingham, Diss, IP22 3AA
British subsidiary of famous long-established Dutch bulb specialist, with good range of tulips, daffodils and hyacinths as well as dwarf bulbs. Colourful catalogue.

Unusual Plants Beth Chatto Gardens, Elmstead Market, Colchester, CO7 7DB*
Inspired choice of mainly hardy perennials, many chosen for their foliage effect. Catalogue is very useful for reference.

Most of these nurseries charge for their catalogue. Please check in the current edition of *The Plant Finder* to find the up-to-date cost. It is also possible to visit many, but not all, of these mail order suppliers, see mature plants on display and choose your own plants. Full details are given in their catalogues.

5. SEED COMPANIES

The following seed companies sell seed by mail order and publish catalogues annually in the autumn. Some of these brands, together with others, are also on sale in garden centres and other outlets.

All except Chiltern Seeds produce very colourful catalogues, but Chiltern's has more plants and more information in it than any.

Chiltern Seeds Bortree Stile, Ulverston, Cumbria, LA12 7PB
Specialist company with more different varieties than any other and

with many very unusual items. Fewer bedding plants than most, but more trees, shrubs and perennials.

Dobies Seeds Broomhill Way, Torquay, TQ2 7QW
Known for its progresssive but not rash approach to new varieties and techniques, and with a good range of seedlings and young plants. Very accessible catalogue presentation.

Marshalls Seeds Regal Road, Wisbech, PE13 2RF
Vegetable specialists, with particular emphasis on the best new introductions and a good range of seed potatoes and onion sets. Limited range of flowers too.

Mr Fothergill's Seeds Gazeley Road, Kentford, Newmarket, CB8 7QB
Comprehensive range of flowers and vegetables, with the best of the traditional varieties augmented by the best of the new. A seed count on every packet. Also available in garden centres.

Suffolk Herbs Sawyers Farm, Little Cornard, Sudbury, Suffolk, CO10 0NY
Herb and wildflower seed specialists with extensive ranges of both as well as dried flowers and vegetables including Oriental types.

Suttons Seeds Hele Road, Torquay, TQ2 7QJ
Long-established company, with a traditional air and with a special emphasis on well-tried varieties and a cautious approach to novelties. Also available in garden centres.

Thompson & Morgan Seeds London Road, Ipswich, IP2 0BA
A very large range, with many unusual varieties and an extensive selection of new flower and vegetable introductions each year. Seed count for every packet. Colourful catalogue, useful as reference. Also available in garden centres.

Unwins Seeds Histon, Cambridge, CB4 4LE
Carefully chosen varieties of the most popular flowers and vegetables, with selected less common plants plus seedlings and young plants. Very large range of sweet peas. Also available in garden centres.

Appendices

GLOSSARY

Acid (of soil) With a pH level below 7, opposite of limy. Good for rhododendrons and blue hydrangeas.

Alkaline (of soil) Limy, with a pH level above 7. Rhododendrons hate it, hydrangeas go pink.

Alpine Small plant from the mountains, usually needing free-draining soil and sometimes protection from rain in winter.

Annual Plant such as alyssum which lives for only one season.

Bedding plant Plant raised in pots or trays and planted out for spring or summer before being replaced.

Biennial Plant such as Canterbury bell which lasts for two seasons, growing during the first and flowering in the second. Some perennial plants, wallflowers, for example, are treated as if they were biennials.

Biennial bearing The tendency of fruit trees, usually apples, to crop well one year but badly or not at all in the next.

Bolt To produce flowers or seed prematurely, thereby not fulfilling requirements, especially lettuce and spinach.

Cloche Glass or polythene tent used to cover plants and protect them from severe weather or encourage early growth.

Cold frame Low brick or timber structure with removable glass roof, used to protect plants in pots from severe weather.

Compost Two senses. 1: Special soil mix for raising seeds or potting plants (seed or potting compost). 2: Well-rotted vegetable matter (garden compost).

Cordon Plant, usually fruit tree, trained as a single unbranched stem.

Corm Bulb-like structure formed from a swollen stem base, as in crocus and gladiolus.

Crown Two senses. 1: The part of the plant at or just below soil level from which shoots develop. 2: The branched growth of a tree.

Dibber Device for making a planting hole for seedlings in potting compost or the garden. Usually wood or plastic.

Die-back Death of shoot tips due to disease or frost.

Drainage The seeping away of water through the soil. Good or free-drained soils lose water quickly, badly drained or waterlogged soils stay wet for a long time.

Drawn Stretched, due to lack of light.

Drill Long, shallow depression in which seeds are sown.

Earthing up Drawing soil up around shoots of plants, especially potatoes, to exclude light.

Espalier Trained tree with horizontal branches arranged in tiers.

Etiolated Stretched, due to lack of light.

F1 hybrid Usually a bedding plant or vegetable created by crossing two specially selected and highly bred parents.

Floribunda Type of rose with many-flowered heads of relatively small flowers. Also known as Cluster-flowered.

Forcing Encouraging early flowers or crops by the use of extra heat or protection from severe weather.

Ground cover plants Plants which spread to create an effective weed-suppressing cover.

Half-hardy Used of plants which will grow happily outside in British summers but will not survive our winters.

Hardening off The acclimatising of plants raised in a greenhouse to the harsher conditions in the open garden.

Herbaceous Having stems and leaves which die down each year, usually in winter, though not necessarily all at once.

Humus The final result of vegetable matter rotting down.

Hybrid Tea (HT) Type of rose with relatively few, large, shapely flowers. Also known as Large-flowered.

Lateral Stem branching off from a larger one.

Leaching The tendency of plant foods to drain out of the soil dissolved in the soil water.

Leader Main shoot of a tree or shrub.

Leggy Stretched, due to lack of light.

Marginal Two senses. 1: Of plants which like to grow in wet conditions, such as at the edges of ponds. 2: At the edges of leaves.

Mulch Layer of organic matter spread among plants to prevent weed growth and improve the soil.

Naturalise Allow plants to grow naturally and with the minimum of attention, bulbs in grass, for example.

Neutral (of soil) Neither acid nor alkaline, with a pH of 7.

Offset A young plant which develops at the base of a larger plant.

Perennial Plant with a life span of more than two years.

pH Measure of soil acidity and alkalinity. pH7 is neutral, below 7 is acid, above 7 is alkaline.

Pinching out Removal of a shoot tip, usually to encourage branching.

Pricking out Transferring seedlings from the seed-pot to a pot or seed-tray where they will have more space to develop.

Rhizome Creeping underground stem, as seen in flag irises and couch grass.

Runner Stem which creeps across the soil growing roots from the leaf joints, as in strawberries.

Self-fertile Producing fruits or seeds without pollination by another plant.

Self-sterile Not producing fruits or seeds unless pollinated by another plant.

Series Group of very similar plants (usually bedding plants) differing in just one or two details, usually flower colour.

Sterile Not able to produce fruit or seeds.

Stolon Shoot which arches over or spreads across the ground and roots at its tip.

Stopping Removal of a shoot tip, usually to encourage branching.

Succulent (of leaves or a plant) Fleshy, adapted to storing water.

Sucker Shoot arising from the roots of a plant, sometimes away from the main stem or crown.

Tender Susceptible to frost damage.

Truss Closely grouped cluster of flowers or fruits.

Tuber Swollen underground storage organ developed from a root or stem.

Variegated (of leaves) With stripes, spots, speckles, edging or streaks of another colour, usually white, cream or yellow.

Weed Any plant which is a nuisance.

SOCIETIES

Both the general and the more specialist societies provide journals and newsletters, local groups and events, advice and other privileges.

Alpine Garden Society
Coverage: Alpines, rock plants and dwarf bulbs. Many local groups.
Address: The Pettit Centre, Pershore College of Horticulture, Pershore, Worcestershire, WR10 3JP.

Arboricultural Association
Coverage: Will supply a list of members qualified to undertake tree surgery and removal.

Cottage Garden Society
Coverage: Cottage gardens and their plants. Increasing network of local groups.
Address: 5 Nixon Close, Thornhill, Dewsbury, West Yorkshire, WF12 0JA.

Hardy Plant Society
Coverage: Hardy herbaceous perennials. Many local and specialist groups.
Address: 214 Ruxley Lane, West Ewell, Surrey, KT19 9EZ.

Henry Doubleday Research Association
Coverage: Organic gardening; runs the National Centre for Organic Gardening.
Address: Ryton-on-Dunsmore, Coventry, CV8 3LG.

Herb Society
Coverage: Herbs, herb growing and herbal medicine.
Address: PO Box 415, London SW1P 2HE.

National Council for the Conservation of Plants and Gardens
Coverage: Conservation of gardens and garden plants. Many local groups.
Address: The Pines, RHS Garden, Wisley, Surrey, GU23 6QB.

National Trust
Coverage: Owns and maintains gardens of historic interest.
Address: 36 Queen Anne's Gate, London SW1H 9AS.

Northern Horticultural Society
Coverage: All aspects of gardens, but from a northern point of view.
Address: Harlow Carr Botanical Gardens, Crag Lane, Harrogate, HG3 1QB.

Royal Horticultural Society
Coverage: All aspects of plants and gardens.
Address: 80 Vincent Square, London SW1P 2PE.

Scottish Rock Garden Club
Coverage: Alpines, rock plants and dwarf bulbs from a Scottish point of view.
Address: The Linns, Sherriffmuir, Dunblane, Perth, FK15 0LP.

Society of Garden Designers
Coverage: Will supply a list of members qualified to design private gardens.
Address: 23 Reigate Road, Ewell, Surrey, KT17 1PS.

WEIGHTS, MEASURES AND CONVERSIONS

In gardening there is no need for absolute accuracy when converting between metric and imperial measures unless you're building something. You don't need to plant out 30.5cm apart, 30cm will do. So all these conversions are rounded off conveniently.

Length

1 inch = 2.5 centimetres
2 inches = 5 centimetres
3 inches = 7.5 centimetres
4 inches = 10 centimetres
6 inches = 15 centimetres
9 inches = 23 centimetres
1 foot = 30 centimetres
1 yard = 0.9 metre (90 centimetres)
10 yards = 9 metres

1 rod, pole or perch = 5½ yards
1 centimetre = 0.4 inch
10 centimetres = 4 inches
25 centimetres = 10 inches
50 centimetres = 20 inches
1 metre = 39 inches
10 metres = 8 yards

Area

1 square foot = 0.1 square metres
1 square yard = 0.8 square metres
1 (square) rod, pole or perch = 30¼ square yards (25.5 square metres). This measurement is still used for allotments.

Volume

2 tablespoons = 1 fluid ounce = 28 millilitres
20 fluid ounces = 1 pint = 0.6 litres
1 gallon = 4.5 litres

1 litre = 1.8 pints = 35 fluid ounces
10 litres = 2.5 gallons

1 bushel = 36 litres = 8 gallons

Weight

1 ounce = 28 grams
4 ounces = 114 grams = 0.1 kilograms
1 pound = 454 grams = 0.4 kilograms

100 grams = 3 ounces
250 grams = 9 ounces
500 grams = 1.1 pounds
1 kilogram = 2.2 pounds

Temperatures

°Celsius	°Fahrenheit
0	32
5	41
7	45
10	50
13	55
15	59
20	68
21	70
25	77
30	86
35	95

Index